The Bright Face of Danger

The Bright Face of Danger

Margery Fisher

THE HORN BOOK, INC.
BOSTON

Printed in Great Britain
ISBN 0-87675-288-1

To my sister, Cicely Swift,
for our childhood with books

Contents

Introduction

It is customary to begin a long critical work with a statement of intent, as a guideline for readers and a control on the writer. I propose, then, to make some investigation of a particular genre of fiction, the adventure story. Anthony Burgess once wrote that, 'However we split up the contemporary novel, we shall have to admit merely to freezing its living stream and then hacking it into arbitrary lumps of ice.' The lump of ice (or, perhaps better, the fiery lump of lava) which we call the adventure story, with the longest ancestry of any fictional form, is easily recognised but hard to define exactly. I can say that *King Solomon's Mines* belongs in my book but not *Adam Bede*: I hope that my reasons for making this distinction will be apparent in the course of my argument.

Certain points of overlap may be conveniently noted here. I include some historical adventure stories but not true historical fiction – that is, I include tales of action in which fictional individuals are projected in past periods but not stories focused on the march of recorded history or the exploits of real historical personages. I exclude fantasy as a genre but have used one or two examples (notably, the space-novels of André Norton) for my own purposes. Where it could be stated as a general principle that any fiction is by its very nature 'adventure', the magical epic and space-story come close enough to the genre I have chosen to write about to need an arbitrary decision to exclude them.

The purpose of my book is to explore the likenesses and differences between adventure stories written and published for adult readers and those written and published for children. In this I have to assume that there *is* a difference between adult and junior fiction although, like most critics, I am haunted by the mischievous but insistent question, 'Do children's books exist?' The division, in so far as we have to accept it, seems less noticeable in my chosen genre than in any other. On one hand, there is a special exhilaration in the adventure story which could be termed youthful: on the other, the particular challenge of dangerous action and mystification seems to beckon the young forward to maturity.

The adult domain of the adventure story has always been open to young readers, though they have visited it less in the past half-century because of the increasing number of books provided especially for them. Things were otherwise in my childhood. Apart from the fact that fewer children's books were published in the twenties, I was probably less well provided with 'children's stories' than most English children of my age and class. The books I was able to take with me as a nine-year-old emigrant to New Zealand were relatively few and the library provision (before the influence of Dorothy Neal White was felt) was meagre. As a result (and, as I believe, fortunately) I spent the reading years between nine and thirteen or so with Weyman and Sabatini, Rider Haggard and Conan Doyle, Dumas and Jeffery Farnol, and was unaware that anyone had suggested any difference between, let us say, *Treasure Island* and *Captain Blood*.

After working in the sphere of junior fiction for thirty-five years I have come to think that there *are* formal differences between adventure stories for adults and for children but that these differences – of tone, of approach, of subject matter – are less important than the *way* stories are read by adults and by children. More than any other type of fiction, the adventure story should be read with the openly imaginative, susceptible, unprejudiced response which belongs to youth but which *can* be summoned up in later years, and not only by books we read in childhood. It seems appropriate to give an example, from my own experience, of the kind of whole-hearted reading I have in mind.

An emigrating child leaves many things behind. For sixty years I was haunted by the memory of a story followed in successive numbers of *Chatterbox* but never finished. As far as plot was concerned memory held on to little more than the fact that two children, a boy and a girl, presumably with an attendant adult or two, were searching for a secret room in a ruinous stone building somewhere in the Egyptian desert. Two things had remained firmly fixed in my mind. First, I had retained something of the extraordinary mixture of fear and excitement, almost a smell in the nostrils and a clutch at the heart, as the small room, long built into a wall, was at last rediscovered: and then, the strong image of an illustration showing the boy and girl looking out from a square, high window over a stretch of sand. While researching on adventure stories I identified the story as *Abdulla. The Mystery of an Ancient Papyrus*, by William Rainey, published in book form in 1928 but serialised twelve years earlier. When I read the book as a continuous whole I realised that I must have been completely unaware of the date of the adventure, 1894, and the circumstances of the Mahdi rising which activated most of the plot.

I could remember nothing about the papyrus sent to the inevitable Omniscient Uncle in the story or of its record of a scribe of Amenhotep's reign, walled up in the secret room as a punishment, who had contrived to drop the papyrus out of the window before it was blocked in. Most significantly, I had evidently so thoroughly immersed myself in the story that I had placed myself in it. The drawing which had stayed so long in my mind showed, in fact, the two boy cousins who were central to the story, leaning out in front of their uncle's faithful Egyptian servant. I doubt whether this switch of memory meant that I was identifying precisely with one of the boys, though the fact that I would always have liked to have a brother may have had something to do with it: but it appears that the story, a competent but not outstanding piece of fiction, had exercised my imagination with unusual power so that I had been impelled to join myself to it. Certainly the feeling of awe, terror and excitement is something I can still, distantly, recall.

Looking back at my childhood reading, I can see that almost always it was the atmosphere of a scene which captured me rather than the people concerned in it. Some characters became part of my life – Allan Quatermain was one, D'Artagnan another – but it is places and auras that have stayed in my mind and I suspect, from reading the reminiscences of Graham Greene and others, that it is the interpenetrating light of strong emotion thrown on imagined settings which constitutes the true spell of adventure stories for the young. At any rate, it is partly to try to recapture this particular pleasure in reading that I have set out to examine the literary conventions and elements of the genre as it exists in its adult and junior forms.

The title I have taken for my book comes from Violet Needham's *The Betrayer*, a tale of youth inspired and sustained by a sense of honour operating in a particular social sphere. Danger has a 'bright face' in the traditional adventure story in the sense that whatever hazards and hardships are included in the action, the basic tone will be optimistic: the good characters will triumph over great odds. But in the classic stories which have outlasted the changes in social attitudes and literary taste, this triumph comes from a serious and responsible motive as much as from those operations of good fortune or coincidence which are among the structural conventions of the genre.

The adventure story, overlapping as it does with the domestic novel of character on one hand and the quasi-poetic exploration of fantasy on the other, is sometimes distinguished by the term 'story of action'. This may be justified by the peculiar urgency and sharpness of the events which have been chosen to keep the vital question 'What happens next?' in the forefront of the reader's mind. A proper evaluation of the genre, though, must rest on its totality – not on plot or character, not on motive or setting, but on a specially intense, compelling combination of these elements offering a unique aesthetic experience. In this book I have tried to explore and isolate the quality of this experience and to make some attempt at a definition of the adventure story as a literary form.

I have found the British Library, the London Library and the National Book League invaluable in my work on this book. I am especially grateful to Mrs Brown, until her retirement in 1984 Head of the School Library Service of the Northamptonshire Leisure and Libraries Service, and her colleagues, for their patient help in finding so many of the books I needed.

I am also grateful for special help from Michael Harrison in the matter of versions of *Treasure Island*; from Virginia Haviland and Margaret Coughlan in the matter of the authorship of the Hardy Boys stories; from Walter McVitty for advice on the Australian bushranger known as Captain Starlight; and from Hilary Wright, who has generously allowed me to quote from her work on Violet Needham's novels which shed new light on them for me.

Most of all I am indebted to my friend and editor Jane Osborn for her continued support and her acute and timely comments; without her I very much doubt whether I could have stayed the course.

Definitions and Themes

1. Escape or Enlargement?

Every type of fiction depends for its defining and acceptance on certain conventions which are, in effect, agreements between author and reader. The basic convention underlying all fiction marks its difference from fact. The form of story depends on rearrangement. The disparate elements of human experience are selected and ordered in a structure which includes its own version of time, place and personality. Tidiness takes the place of disorder, compactness of meandering, outline of formlessness. We are invited by the story-teller to believe that the part-random, part-intended day-to-day course of life would lend itself to discipline, with a beginning, a middle and an end. In spite of attempts, from time to time, to re-establish the formlessness of 'real life', in fiction, story exists almost always by courtesy of a '*shape*'.

While the adventure depends like any other fictional form on this agreed rearrangement of reality, it also works on conventions of its own which have often seemed to take it still further away from that reality. Dictionary phrases defining adventure as 'a hazardous enterprise or performance' or 'a novel or exciting incident' make it clear that this is a kind of fiction offering surprise rather than confirmation, strangeness rather than familiarity. The reader's expectation is to be satisfied by the unexpected: he is to be taken away from normal concerns by events of an exaggerated, heightened nature, often taking place in exotic, distant surroundings.

Another hyperbole must be added to this. To quote the dictionary again, the word 'adventure' contains in it an element of the unexpected, of chance and Fate, which means that the protagonist must be able to call on more than normal attributes to meet the challenge set for him. We may expect, to some degree, a hero (or, more rarely, a heroine) of more than ordinary stature. Any novel invites one to enjoy a vicarious experience outside one's own life. The size and force of the experience offered in an adventure story means that it has attracted to itself, more than any other fictional form, the pejorative label of 'escape'. Is it fear of fictional artificiality or a puritanical distrust of pure pleasure which has led to an increasing relegation to the status of 'popular' and, by implication, 'inferior' literature of a genre which has myth and legend as its ancestors? As Paul Zweig commented:

15

The modern world's dismissal of adventure as an entertaining but minor experience is unprecedented. Few cultures have been so willing to tempt the gods. That we should do so says a great deal about the arrogance of our cultural values.[1]

The compulsion to arrange books and authors in hierarchies is no new thing. Almost ninety years ago Stevenson's romantic adventures were put in their place by a reviewer in the London *Daily Chronicle* who remarked that 'great literature cannot be composed from narratives of perilous adventures'.[2] In the increasing number of critical surveys of the English novel published during the present century Conrad is the sole writer ever to be included in the safe, accepted procession from Fielding to Henry James and beyond who could, to some degree, be considered to write of adventure in the traditional sense; and it is always made perfectly clear that Conrad's moral and philosophical probings constitute his true value, his story-telling expertise being, by implication, no more than a means to an end.

The assumption behind this critical selectiveness is confirmed by the one exception I have been able to find, in a brief, perverse and witty account of the English novel composed by Ford Madox Ford for American students. His unusual preferences culminate in the following declaration:

> Marryat – as a writer read by boys, men being already too dulled in the sense at twenty to appreciate him – has probably, through the boys, exercised the greatest influence on the English character that any writer ever did exercise. His magnificent gifts of drawing – not exaggerating – character and of getting an atmosphere have so worked that few of us have not been to sea in frigates before the age of eighteen and come in some way in contact with non-comfortable men and women. I have seldom been so impressed as when, the other day, I reread *Peter Simple* for my pleasure. It was to come into contact with a man who could write and see and feel. For me, nothing in *War and Peace* is as valuable as the boat-cutting-out expeditions of Marryat and for me he remains the greatest of English novelists. His name is not even mentioned in the manual of literary dates with which I have just been refreshing my memory.[3]

Happy the students who were inspired to independent judgements by this shrewd praise of a master of his particular genre.

Such dissenting voices are rare. Colin Watson ruefully accepted, twelve years ago, the 'attitude of good-natured, if slightly supercilious tolerance'[4] with which reviewers treated the latest batch of detective stories. The forthright tones of Quentin Oates were heard more recently in *The Bookseller* suggesting that 'a sensible, enthusiastic feature'[5] about adventure stories would do a power

16

of good to readership and publishers' advertising alike. The accepted view holds its own. A panel of former Booker Prize judges questioned on a television programme in 1983 were agreed that the prize was for 'serious' novels and was unlikely to be awarded to a thriller, however skilful or original it might be.

The junior adventure story has not suffered the same extremes of literary discrimination. This may be because of the built-in didactic nature of any story written specifically for the young. The adventure story offers the writer as many chances as the more staid domestic chronicle does for the exploration of the progress of a young person towards adulthood. At the same time, many critics show notable preference for stories with a moral conclusion over those which seem to offer simple entertainment; and any critic who looks at a book from the angle of the potential reader rather than of the book itself is in danger of being tempted by false hierarchies.

But from a general view the status of the junior adventure story is unassailable. Paradoxically, it is because the adventure story *is* essentially youthful as well as mature that it is a valuable part of adult literature. Yet this, too, is often seen not as a value but as an additional reason for not taking the genre seriously. The accusation that the adventure story offers an escape for adult readers implies that the escape is into a kind of second childhood or, at the least, suggests a limited expectation of a novel's purpose. Michael Innes's analysis of one of his characters, a creator of best-selling crime novels, expressed this view by implication:

> His imagination was of the refrigerating sort from which the fantasies of boyhood can step with convincing freshness; and it was this quality, no doubt, that made the stories the instant and almost embarrassing success that they were.[6]

The literary judgement contained in the phrase 'almost embarrassing success' is offered in another way when the author, writing this time under his real name of J. I. M. Stewart, led his readers to an understanding of a super-hero, spy and adventurer whose exploits were made possible because he had retained the boyhood characteristics nourished by a certain area of reading. The famous explorer Mogridge is seen by his university friend Duncan Patullo as, in fact, an overgrown schoolboy:

> A single glance at the actual contents of Mogridge's cupboard embarrassed me. I don't think I'd have been more so had the door opened on, say, a Teddy Bear, redolent of the fabulous Oxford of Evelyn Waugh. The first thing I saw was a batch of Biggles books, stacked beside several of their Kaiser's War equivalents, written by

a man called Percy F. Westerman. Then I saw – rapidly – *The Scarlet Pimpernel*, *The Riddle of the Sands*, *King Solomon's Mines*, *The Four Adventures of Richard Hannay*, *Revolt in the Desert*. There were dozens of books of that sort. The majority, which I didn't have time to scan, appeared designed for juvenile rather than adult readers.[7]

The attitude of Patullo, a conventional, observant, middle-class intellectual, is a familiar one, and so is his ambiguous attitude to this kind of reading, expressed in a later comment on the unexpected heroism of the man he had regarded with a certain scorn:

> The Mogridge of *Mochica* wasn't much more than a boy. But he took charge of men; organized them; persuaded or inspired or commanded them to endure incredible things. It was a thoroughly down-to-earth job in a way. But what enabled him to put it through was a high romantic imagination.[8]

The door to childhood which the adventure story is supposed to open to the adult may also involve the childlike activity of role-playing. Kornei Chukovsky, in his account of his boyhood in Odessa in the 1890s, described how he and his friend Timosha used to climb into deep rubbish boxes:

> . . . to tell each other stories about cannibals and cowboys, pathfinders, volcanoes and African mirages. It was a very peculiar thing. The minute we got settled down in the bottom of our Kalamachka, rocking as if we were inside a boat and 'talking about Baghdad', we felt transported to another country. And we ourselves became different people from those we had been a minute ago, when we were teasing Filimon the goat or getting into a fight with Pechonkin's street gang.[9]

The same kind of escape (or enlargement, if you look at the process in a favourable light) is allowed for in a discussion of half a century ago in which the thesis that all novels contributed to a sense of escape from the artificial complexities of civilisation was turned to a commercial purpose. The adventure story was particularly favoured as a genre to be attempted by the aspiring writer:

> Romance and vicarious excitement are what the average reader wants; he has enough of what is drab, prosaic, and everyday. People like even their sunsets to be a little embellished. Their imaginations are eager to go rather more than half-way to meet the audacious writer.
>
> The pallid, underpaid, underfed city clerk does not want to read about cheap boarding houses, suburban back gardens, and dingy offices. In his dreams he is wild, untamed, primitive man, and with Jack London sails strange seas, or with Tarzan fights lions single-handed.[10]

To today's citizen this method of escaping from the monotony of everyday life may seem naïve and even ludicrous. The modern world is more likely to forget its apprehensions in what Brian Aldiss has called 'cosy catastrophe'. The formula of the bookstall blockbuster is only too persuasive, offering an optimistic view of social dangers and confusions. John Sutherland includes disaster-tales among the types of best-sellers which he discusses, for this reason:

> . . . within the disaster area there are discovered close-knit groups – little communities, families, husbands and wives – all brought into even closer intimacy by the catastrophic events that overtake them. And in a larger sense community is affirmed, and the complexities of social life dissolved. Officers of law and practical, simple, good men take command. Public servants (nurses, firemen, pilots etc.) are glorified in their competence to handle emergency, and a new social solidarity between previously antagonistic groups is forged.[11]

We may well feel cynical about the type of best-selling adventure which assumes heroism without accounting for it. Yet for ten novels of adventure using this formulaic, superficial method there will be one, if we can find it, which by stretching the convention of improbable excitement by an acceptance of human nature both as it is and as it can be, offers not an escape but an enlargement of life through imagination. We may consider it a virtue rather than a vice that we possess and exert the power to live, as it were, outside ourselves. John Carwelti argues that certain types of formula-stories, 'Adventure, Mystery and Romance', must be judged by their own standards and conventions and he deplores the literary assumption that this type of writing is 'subliterature'. 'The trouble with this sort of approach', he suggests:

> . . . is that it tends to make us perceive and evaluate formula literature simply as an inferior or perverted form of something better, instead of seeing the 'escapist' characteristics as aspects of an artistic type with its own purposes and justification. After all, while most of us would condemn escapism as a total way of life, our capacity to use our imaginations to construct alternative worlds into which we can temporarily retreat is certainly a central human characteristic and seems, on the whole, a valuable one.[12]

This temporary retreat may bring the immediate refreshment of change or it may widen our horizons either by romantic hyperbole or by an unexpected psychological authenticity close to the reality of life as we know it. Anthony Burgess drew a distinction between Graham Greene's serious novels which 'probe into the world as it really is' and the 'entertainments' which, he claimed,

19

'falsify the world, manipulate it'.[13] Yet he made the distinction invalid by admitting that 'in the work of the writer who has serious pretensions we often gain a new image of the world, an insight into human character'.[13] Whatever Graham Greene intended by the use of the label 'entertainment' for certain of his novels, some of us have found a greater intuition and emotional force in *The Man Within* than in the more elaborate analysis of personality in *The Heart of the Matter* or *A Burnt-Out Case*. It is, perhaps, a matter of balancing *intention* against the total literary tone and integrity of each book. Literature works by the sum of its elements, not by any one of them.

The balance of reality and hyperbole in the adventure story can be its downfall or its glory. Nowadays we may respond more readily to the sharpness of actuality than to the romantic atmosphere more natural to the adventure story in the past. Harvey Darton's definition of the nature of *King Solomon's Mines* and *Treasure Island* touches present-day taste very closely, with its prescription of 'surprise upon surprise, each one sudden, but each one also natural, capable of rational and brave explanation when you knew all the facts.'[14] Yet, for adults and children alike, the enlarging ideal is as necessary as the acknowledgement of the actual. Graham Greene regarded Rider Haggard's greatest achievement that he 'fixed pictures in our minds that thirty years have been unable to wear away'[15] and he defined the sphere of imagination when he wrote of his memories of the characters in the Quatermain novels:

> Quatermain and Curtis – weren't they, even when I was only ten years old, a little too good to be true? They were men of such unyielding integrity (they would only admit to a fault in order to show how it might be overcome) that the wavering personality of a child could not rest for long against those monumental shoulders. A child, after all, knows most of the game . . . it is only an attitude to it that he lacks. He is quite well aware of cowardice, shame, deception, disappointment. Sir Henry Curtis perched upon a rock bleeding from a dozen wounds but fighting on with the remnant of the Greys against the hordes of Twala was too heroic. These men were like Platonic ideas: they were not life as one had already begun to know it.[16]

Even so it was a life, an approach, a horizon as necessary to the nourishment of young and old as the most penetrating picture of what we like to call reality.

2. The Romanticising of Fact

The predominant conventions of the adventure story, the victory of good over evil and the happy ending, have led to a subtle demotion of the genre from the highest ranks of literature on the grounds that its main aim is a contrived entertainment; for experience suggests, often though not invariably, that the challenge of adventure is more likely to meet with disaster and defeat than survival and triumph. The particular colour which fiction casts over action in this type of story, in rearranging its components, is usually termed 'romantic' – a word, as I shall try to show, that can be used with many meanings. How far is it inevitable that the manipulation of fact for the purposes of fiction leads to romanticising? One branch of adventure may serve as example, the sea story, in two kinds in particular – the story of endurance in the face of natural disaster and the historical adventure with its most popular subject, the British Navy in the Napoleonic period.

Artistically, Conrad must be allowed pre-eminence, yet he insisted, against the determined assumptions of his readers, that he was not a writer of 'sea-stories', while in his novels he both used and contradicted the conventions of the adventure story. In fact, to discuss the reason why his work is the exception rather than the rule in the category of traditional adventure is to find one way to define that category.

Conrad was well aware of the many facets of the word 'romance' – idealism towards women and events, the hero's victory over extreme hazard, exotic details of place and circumstance. The retired seaman Peyrol offers almost a catalogue of such familiar elements as he recalls:

> . . . a multitude of impressions of endless oceans, of the Mozambique Channel, of Arabs and negroes, of Madagascar, of the coast of India, of islands and channels and reefs; of fights at sea, rows on shore, desperate slaughter and desperate thirst, of all sorts of ships one after another: merchant ships and frigates and privateers; of reckless men and enormous sprees.[1]

Yet Conrad uses these elements, which we may term romantic, in a way that sets him far from stories, seemingly similar, by (say) Rider Haggard or Buchan.

Occasionally he will offer a character in the true romantic style, but it will be a minor character. The young Russian trader with his brown holland suit almost obscured by coloured patches, a youth whose courage in venturing into the dark interior of Africa is viewed with astonished admiration by Conrad's foremost narrator, Marlow, belongs to the familiar heroic convention:

> He surely wanted nothing from the wilderness but space to breathe in and to push through. His need was to exist, and to move onwards at the greatest possible risk, and with a maximum of privation. If the absolutely pure, uncalculating, impractical spirit of adventure had ever ruled a human being, it ruled this bespectacled youth.[2]

Youth was, for Conrad, a period all too brief when romance prevailed over practical considerations, when it flourished because of inexperience and for want of maturity. It was a time which Conrad allowed himself to regret, through his characters, but not to exalt above other periods and other philosophies of life. At the end of the story significantly called *Youth*, a story in which Conrad calls on his own memory of the testing of ardent feelings in critical conditions in describing the last fatal, curtailed voyage of the old *Judea*, Marlow as narrator, sitting in comfortable middle age among men who, like him, had served an apprenticeship at sea, challenges them to deny that this was the best time of their lives:

> And we all nodded at him: the man of finance, the man of accounts, the man of law, we all nodded at him over the polished table that like a still sheet of brown water reflected our faces, lined, wrinkled; our faces marked by toil, by deceptions, by success, by love; our weary eyes looking still, looking always, looking anxiously for something out of life, that while it is expected is already gone – has passed unseen, in a sigh, in a flash – together with the youth, with the strength, with the romance of illusions.[3]

Of *The Shadow-Line*, a story still more autobiographical in its essence, Conrad said that he was aiming at 'the presentation of certain facts, which certainly were associated with the change from youth, care-free and fervent, to the more self-conscious and more poignant period of maturer life'.[4]

Against critics who had accused him of choosing to write of the sea and lonely islands in order to have greater freedom for his imagination, he protested that his own youth had worn 'the sober hue of hard work and exacting calls of duty, things which in themselves are not much charged with a feeling of romance' and that if he had any 'romantic feeling of reality' it was disciplined by 'a recognition of the hard facts of existence shared with the rest of mankind', a recognition which, he believed, tried to make the best of the hard truth and to discover in it 'a certain aspect of beauty'.[5] The beauty he saw was, for him, in the fallible yet indestructible spirit of man. It was a beauty more apparent to him in man's defeat than in his triumph. His overriding literary aim was to make his readers realise through their senses, through the power of words, his own uniquely ironic vision of life, his own unusual conception of the heroic.

Romance, in his novels, is set against the inconvenient intervention of reality taking the form of chance. Not, for him, chance as the hero's luck but as the effect of random events on the particular weakness or strength of an individual. His most successful hero (and neither word is really suitable, in any case) is Captain McWhirr of the *Nan-Shan*, a middle-aged man whose prosaic letters to parents and then to wife, full of comments like 'On Christmas Day at 4 p.m. we fell in with some icebergs',[6] bore them into coma. The sheer stolid, unimaginative common sense of the man (stupidity, to his lively young mate Jukes) brought the ship through appalling seas and produced the only possible solution to the confusion into which the typhoon had thrown the precious dollars of his Chinese passengers.

The irony in the kind of unconscious, unsung heroism described in *Typhoon* is significantly reversed in *Lord Jim*, where in similar circumstances (an old ship threatened by tempest, a challenge to ship's officers, a crowd of helpless passengers) it is imagination that is the cause of the failure of a 'hero'. Here is a young man of twenty-three, second mate of the *Patna*, who secretly hopes that his life of efficiency will become romantic:

> On the lower deck in the babel of two hundred voices he would forget himself, and beforehand live in his mind the sea-life of light literature. He saw himself saving people from sinking ships, cutting away masts in a hurricane, swimming through a surf with a line; or as a lonely castaway, barefooted and half naked, walking on uncovered reefs in search of shellfish to stave off starvation. He confronted savages on tropical shores, quelled mutinies on the high seas, and in a small boat upon the ocean kept up the hearts of despairing men. Always an example of devotion to duty, and as unflinching as a hero in a book.[7]

It is Jim's book-nourished imagination, in fact, that betrays him into unheroic behaviour. Instead of 'saving people from sinking ships', when the *Patna*, carrying hundreds of Malayan pilgrims on the way to Mecca, strikes a hidden wreck and appears to be sinking, Jim at first dissociates himself from the deplorable trio of captain and officers, when they lower the only boat for their escape; and then, on an impulse he can never explain, jumps

23

overboard to join them, leaving the passengers, as he believes, to certain death.

The irony of his failure to act as a hero is as severe as anything in Conrad. The ship remains afloat and is towed by a French gunboat to the port where the four in the small boat, picked up by a passing ship, are duly landed and detained for a court-martial. Jim had not in 'a small boat upon the ocean kept up the hearts of despairing men'. On the contrary, he had spent the hours of peril trying to establish in his mind his superiority to the abject cowardice of his companions, seeming more concerned with his own soul than with the fate of the helpless pilgrims on the *Patna*.

As Conrad, through the narrator Marlow, follows the wanderings which Jim undertakes to escape the imputation of cowardice, he contrasts the romantic and the realistic view of the case as he assembles opinions of Jim, elicited or overheard by Marlow. Marlow himself, listening to Jim's confused, hesitant version of the affair as the court-martial proceeds, realises that 'with every instant he was penetrating deeper into the impossible world of romantic achievements'[8] and cuts across the young man's evident yearning to make some heroic restitution by the blunt reminder, 'If you had stuck to the ship, you mean!'[8] The wise old merchant Stein defends imagination as man's most valuable driving-force:

> 'A man that is born falls into a dream like a man who falls into the sea. If he tries to climb out into the air as inexperienced people endeavour to do, he drowns . . . The way is to the destructive element submit yourself, and with the exertions of your hands and feet in the water make the deep, deep sea keep you up. . . .'[9]

but the French officer who had controlled the dangerous tow from the bridge of the battered *Patna* looks at courage and cowardice in another way:

> . . . one may get on knowing very well that one's courage does not come of itself . . . There's nothing much in that to get upset about. One truth the more ought not to make life impossible . . . But the honour – the honour, monsieur! . . . The honour . . . that is real – that is! And what life may be worth when . . . the honour is gone . . . I can offer no opinion.[10]

Nor does Conrad offer an opinion. Jim never escapes the torment of self-doubt, even when in the remote kingdom of Patusan he has given all his energy and his intelligence, as well as his physical courage, to settling internal feuds and establishing prosperity – when, in fact, he has become to his people 'Lord

Jim'. The disreputable, starving pirate Brown, invading the peaceful settlement which Jim has recreated by his own efforts, excuses his attack on the village with unconscious force, enquiring:

> . . . whether he himself – straight now – didn't understand that when it came to saving one's life in the dark, one didn't care who else went – three, thirty, three hundred people.[11]

Jim feels 'as if a demon had been whispering in his ear' and goes to his death with the whisper still sounding, killed by the people he had tried, in one final, tragic mistake, to save for the future.

Was it heroism or was it, as Marlow suggests, 'his exalted egoism' that brought about the death of Lord Jim? In a traditional adventure story the pursuit of personal honour is drawn to an absolute conclusion. The hero is vindicated as a character completely realised, uncontradictory even when (as so often in Stanley Weyman, for instance) he steps aside from the path of correct behaviour. Action in the majority of adventure stories is seen both to affect and to be affected by character but in the end it is action that has the final word, in the romantic happy ending in which the heroism of man is affirmed. In *Lord Jim* there is no final word. Jim remains an enigma, penetrated through action only to a certain point. Action has been a means, not an end.

Actively employed at sea for nearly twenty years, for the most part in Far Eastern seas which can legitimately be called romantic, Conrad had no need to add extra colour to his raw material, nor did he have to go beyond fact to find episodes, incidents and nuggets of action to transfer to fiction. He did not in the simplest sense romanticise fact but used it as a way of making his readers see a complex and various world. The sea and ships, his raw material, were not altered but were enlarged by his vision of life, for which vision they served as examples of larger issues. Each ship he described is a microcosm, an enclosed community where individuals will be challenged by nature and by the crowded pressures of their comrades in service: each is, besides, a microcosm standing, in an archetypal metaphor, for the whole world.

Nobody except Masefield has ever matched the precision, the pictorial strength and intensity of Conrad's descriptions of storm and calm, of men working or at ease, contending or submitting. But in all these descriptions, as in his characters and his story lines, we are taken from the particular to the general; we are led to see that it is not what happens that is important nor what effect action has on the people concerned, but what meaning we can extract, or guess at, from the impact on our senses and our intellect of the whole. To take one example, in *The Nigger of the*

Narcissus we are shown the paddle-steamer as she draws out of harbour in a composite picture of image and actuality:

> She resembled an enormous aquatic black beetle, surprised by the light, overwhelmed by the sunshine, trying to escape with ineffectual effort into the distant gloom of the land. She left a lingering smudge of smoke on the sky, and two vanishing trails of foam on the water. On the place where she had stopped a round black patch of soot remained, undulating on the swell – an unclean mark of the creature's rest. . . .[12]

but from this precise description we are drawn into a larger concept:

> The passage had begun, and the ship, a fragment detached from the earth, went on lonely and swift like a small planet. Round her the abysses of sky and sea met in an unattainable frontier. A great circular solitude moved with her, ever changing and ever the same, always monotonous and always imposing.[13]

Conrad used the adventure story for purposes which stretched it perhaps beyond its technical bounds. Another writer with a far briefer experience of life under sail, John Masefield, stands by contrast right in the centre of the convention of action and narrative in which the glory of adventure-story lies; for at least one period of his life Masefield would have agreed, as Conrad would not, that he was a 'writer of sea-stories'.

Masefield's years in training on the *Conway* and his scant year at sea were among many experiences in his early life in which he pursued a quest for beauty, in nature and in man, a quest whose romantic zest was combined with a strong interest in technical matters, in the structure and working of everyday. The raw material of his experience was transmuted into story – for whether he was working in the poetic or prose medium, Masefield was above all a story-teller. His novels, and in particular two novels of the sea which in many ways closely resembled certain of Conrad's extended stories, assert the pre-eminence of story, of what happens next: in the balance he holds between character and event, in the way he directs his narrative, he provides almost a blueprint of the classic adventure genre.

In his buoyant narrative style, his particularly exact, observant eye for detail, his confident concentration on a particular event coloured by emotion but not by an intensity of analysis, he offers a significant contrast to Conrad's dense, probing accounts of similar events. Where Conrad was essentially dramatic in his use of a background of storm and danger to show off his characters, Masefield in *Victorious Troy* and *The Bird of Dawning* gives character and background equal rights. In these two magnificent novels, sea and sky and ships become, as it were, characters themselves, acting as stabilisers in a way for the romantic, poetic colour implied in the titles of the books and constantly correcting what might otherwise be a predictable good-luck formula of a hero's triumph over great odds.

A poet's imagery throughout the descriptions of storm and weather is strengthened by a visual exactness and a sense almost of an external agency inimical to man: it is no accident that at many points the movement of waves is compared to the malice of active devils. Masefield's extreme selectiveness in the choice of words turns description into its own form of narrative, reflecting the responses of the characters to immediate circumstances but also giving individual life to those circumstances. Here is a moment when the danger to the dismasted *Hurrying Angel* becomes apparent to the exhausted crew as the light grows and they can view the sea they had been fighting in the dark:

> All the dirty surface was made filthier by scufflings and smearings of tattered foam, cruddled like old wool. All the rags of newspapers, that a mob will scatter, seemed to have been scattered on the sea and then danced and trodden on till mess was everywhere. In such a mess in a town the lighter fragments blow about: the main squalor is on the ground. Here the whole filthy floor was alive and lifting with menace. It was raggedness linked with raving and ruin, such as none there had looked at nor dreamed of.[14]

The scene is observed but it also has its own life and its own place in the narrative.

Masefield's descriptions of storms, of a typhoon in the South Pacific and a sinking wreck in the Atlantic, are notably technical, and his account of the efforts of his two heroes to avert disaster is professional in its detail. In learning exactly what they do, as well as what they think and feel, we get to know the two young men who affirm, for him, the indestructible spirit of man (which, to Masefield, was above all symbolised by Troy as he saw it).

The challenge which they have to face is summed up almost casually as Cruiser Trewsbury talks to a seaman in a pause from effort. He answers Chedglow's question 'What do you call real, sir?':

> 'When you've got nothing except just your bare life and you're up against destiny or death. When you're up against your Fortune, whether it goes for or against you.'[15]

It is a moment when despair could have defeated the men, enduring hardship in a small boat after the sinking of their clipper ship. It is also a moment of generalisation for the twenty-one-year-old second mate who on this voyage from Australia, carrying grain and bent on winning the famous grain-race, had had to contend with an arrogant and hostile captain and who had cast off his boat, after a collision in the dark had given a mortal blow to the *Blackgauntlet* and he had waited in vain for orders.

This strong, confident youth takes command as an almost prosaic hero. It is through common sense, fair dealing and strength of will that he dominates the men he now has to command, first for days in an open boat with scant food and water and then in the *Bird of Dawning*, a rival grain-clipper found deserted and drifting and brought once more into the final and victorious stages of the race. Masefield declines to overstress Cruiser's success. He offers us a practical young man who, unprepared for such a challenge, faces it boldly, controlling moments of doubt simply because there is so much to be done that there is no time for introspection. Yet there is more than a simple, professional solution to an unusual but possible problem at sea. Cruiser's words about Fortune echo through the book by virtue of Masefield's narrative method.

The Bird of Dawning, like *Victorious Troy*, is a novel without chapters and without formal pauses of any kind in its sequence of events. Instead, the narrative is shaped by internal rhythms, by a dynamic of mood and tone and by an unseen control of pace in which tension is slackened, sometimes by a particularly close attention to detail, sometimes by the interpolation of dialogue into the account of the movements and actions of certain individuals, sometimes by one of those exuberant lists of objects which Masefield clearly enjoyed compiling and which bring a peculiarly droll, unexpected quirkiness to relieve the enumeration of dangers from wind and water.

Humour is one of the most typical ingredients in Masefield's adventure stories as a whole. In the two sea-stories it is an important clue to character as well as a way of releasing tension. More especially it is a means of showing the changing moods and capacities of the hero of *Victorious Troy*, a younger hero than the capable Cruiser Trewsbury. Dick Pomfret, senior apprentice on the *Hurrying Angel*, is seventeen and still dependent on his elders for advice and leadership. He is in his third year at sea when the misjudgement of Captain 'Battler' Cobb, reckless with drink and determined to win the grain race, runs the ship into a typhoon in the South Pacific, where she is dismasted and the Captain is seriously injured. With the experienced old mate Duckwich killed and the second mate overboard, Dick finds himself in command of a ship whose survival seems doubtful indeed. Moments of self-doubt, fear, determination and rapid planning come over as pauses in an extremely close, tense account of the measures taken by Dick and his crew to cut wreckage clear and get the ship under control. His thoughts are random and rambling, not intense but swift and changeable, often involuntary (as he remembers incidents at home) and often compelling (as he regrets the passing of Duckwich, a strong influence on him). At one moment of inaction he checks over what he has done and what still remains to be done, in an unspoken conversation when he imagines he is being examined for his second mate's ticket, his present goal in life and the strong motivation of his apprenticeship.

In this dialogue Masefield offers a brief recapitulation to steady his headlong narrative and offers also a facet of the lad's character, linking the ebullience of youth to the enforced maturity of the adventure. Dick fancies that the Examiner has asked him why he has not thought of rigging a drogue (a thought which has in fact harassed Dick for some time). His reply is terse and informative:

> 'Because our decks are full of wreck and awash. Because the officers are gone and the Boatswain drunk. Because it's black as pitch and blowing like blazes, and any man moving on deck will be washed from Hull to Hackney before he can cast a rope from a pin. If you and your kind had made it obligatory for a ship to carry a drogue, all ready bent, for letting go, I would have let one go. You haven't, and I haven't got one, and the time's long past for rigging one. If you believe in a drogue, or sea-anchor, up-hook, scratch-in, and rig one, then ride it out and ride with it and tell me when you sight London Bridge.' . . .[16]

and he supplies an equally appropriate riposte from the Examiner:

> 'I will make note of these expressions, Mr Pomfret, which seem to me to be a part of that insolence which accompanies intolerance to veil incompetence.'[16]

The literal reader might suggest that an articulate and stylistic expression of doubt in this vein is unlikely on a dismasted ship wallowing in stormy seas – might, that is, if Masefield's storytelling did not preclude such comment. By his technique, by the force of words and theme, by the disciplined speed of his narrative, he draws us into a fiction which takes off from a foundation of known fact and recognisable truth. There is his Author's Note to *Victorious Troy* to assure us that he has spoken with a boy whose experience had been similar to that of Dick Pomfret and that cases where dismasted sailing ships without officers had been brought to port by boys were not unknown, but we hardly need this assurance in order to believe that Dick, not unaided but with a responsibility beyond his years, did in fact bring the *Hurrying Angel* home in the end. If the word romance suggests improbability more often than not, then Masefield's sea-stories are basically realistic rather than romantic, in tone as well as in material.

During the 1960s these two sea-adventures were republished for young readers in Penguin's Puffin division; there was more confidence then than there seems to be in the eighties that the accessibility of Masefield's story lines and his energetic prose would justify offering to capable readers in the early and mid-teens novels written for adults. In the same period a man with seventeen years of experience as apprentice and officer in tankers, passenger- and tramp steamers all over the world was at the height of a career as a popular author of tales which bore the legend 'a story for boys' on title-pages as well as on dust-jackets. Richard Armstrong's books divide naturally into two sections. One group of stories follows a fashionable course in involving lads in the mid-teens (the almost obligatory age for junior-adventure heroes for many decades) with criminals of one kind or another. In *The Lost Ship*, for instance, a couple of merchant navy apprentices, overboard by accident from a tanker, are picked-ed up by a sinister couple planning to snatch gold from a wreck on a Caribbean island, and in *Horseshoe Reef* a similar young couple is rescued from shipwreck by a strange, isolated family with criminal intentions. The sea served Armstrong as a background to adventures with a more mature approach to character and circumstance, in books like *Island Odyssey*, a tale set in Crete in 1941, *The Mutineers*, in which a setting resembling Easter Island backs up a narrative strongly resembling *Lord of the Flies*, and *The Albatross*, a striking version of Chaucer's *Pardoner's Tale* which I shall return to. But his personal experience of sea and ships is more directly reflected in a group of documentary adventure stories written with that special educational purpose that characterises most fiction for the young.

The first of these, *Sea Change*, was awarded the Carnegie Medal in 1948 and in an interview the author explained the way in which he was using the adventure-story genre:

> I wanted as far as possible to forearm the boy at the beginning of adolescence – not ramming a weapon into his hand willy-nilly, but showing him the size and shape of it and where it lies in such a way

that he would take it up without realizing he was doing so and find himself using it when he needed to.[17]

To this end he set out to give a 'factual picture of life as it comes at a boy in the Merchant Service', offering details of the kind of people he would meet and 'some of the problems and emotional conflicts he would have to face . . .' The first prerequisite of this plan was, of course, completely authentic details; the second, an ultimate moral message:

> I try . . . to make him aware . . . of his own power, his value as a human being; to give him confidence in himself, in the richness of life in the real world and his capacity for living it.[17]

The lesson was offered in the particular terms of the four years, from sixteen to twenty-one, which a youth would expect to spend as an apprentice working towards officer status; it was to be interpreted by each of the readers according to his own aim in life. *Sea Change* and its successors have something in them of the career novel, a popular genre in the first decades after the Second World War, as well as the more general intention of inspiring youth to purposeful activity and ambitions. The result of this is very evident in the style and approach of the six books of which *Sea Change* is the prototype.

When Cam Renton, central character of that book, joins the *Langdale* as junior apprentice at the age of sixteen he has already served a year of his training and is disillusioned about the whole process. He explains to his fellow-apprentice Rusty Roberts, a less ambitious lad:

> 'I started with a whole lot of ideas and a plan. I wanted to learn. I wanted a second mate's ticket; I wanted to get on to the bridge and do things. And what's happened? I've spent a year . . . polishing brass, chipping rust, and slapping paint on bulkheads, and so far as being a deck officer goes, I'm just where I started.'[18]

Cam endures in a hostile frame of mind a voyage carrying cargo to the Caribbean, resenting the work given to him by the mate, indulging in futile practical jokes against him which are coldly ignored and doing his work with sullen reluctance. Gradually his attitude changes, partly for the almost absurdly simple reason that the weather changes from uncomfortable cold to pleasant warmth and partly because he is too intelligent to be totally unaware that he is learning, whether he wants to or not. He realises that certain members of the crew, the hated mate Andy among them, have a quality which he begins to define:

31

action as examples of young people learning by experience – and, for the most part, experience of an unexpected and dangerous kind. Anything more probing than Richard Armstrong's treatment of his apprentices would have disqualified the books from the definition suggested in a dust-jacket comment on a sea-story three decades older about 'a wholesome tale with plenty of sea-water in it, and a fine run of breezy adventure'. Yet if Richard Armstrong was writing according to a tried formula, concrete detail and well-conceived plots and the firm line of his character-drawing helped him to achieve a special, moderate, even low-keyed reality in his books.

Stories about merchant navy apprentices (or, equally, naval midshipmen) are able to avoid false romanticisation because this is an area where youth under training has in reality to respond to emotional and practical challenge rapidly and thoroughly. Courageous behaviour and dogged endurance are more believable here than in many other types of adventure-story. Besides, Richard Armstrong was careful to allow his young heroes the support of older men whose experience could be called upon at need. So, in *Danger Rock*, the practical knowledge of small ships and heavy seas belonging to the sailor known as Shelty is available to the apprentice of eighteen, Jim Naylor, who for his part rises to the challenge of danger (when he and his fellow apprentices land on an uninhabited island off the Newfoundland coast after their ship has been holed by ice) because he has been trained with command in mind.

These are stories written well within calculated limits and those limits include a certain simplistic idea of heroism, unaffected either by irony or by a variation of mood, an idea very different from the intensely human variables in the adult novels by Conrad and Masefield which I have already discussed. This is very obviously the approach of someone writing exclusively and specifically for the young. The final paragraphs of *The Lame Duck*, a vigorous tale of a convoy attacked by submarines in the North Atlantic during the Second World War (a story partly based on the true fortunes of the *San Demetrio*), may serve to illustrate this point:

> Only then, with their perilous passage ended, did her crew agree to transfer themselves to the destroyer. And there these twelve men and two boys, who, with nothing much but bare hands, the sailor-man's gift for improvisation, and their indomitable guts, had fought sea and fire for their ship and won, were cared for and each of them given his heart's desire. Gib Sparling had his ham and eggs, and Scruffy the pleasure of watching somebody else peel spuds; Dutch

his pea soup thick enough to skate on, and Tex his coffee and bed
with clean white sheets; and so on through the list.

But Bull Barlow wanted nothing. He watched them eat and,
listening to their carefree laughter, was content. He had kept faith
with the Old Man and brought them home.[22]

It was not until a decade or so later, when the junior adventure
story was beginning to examine the nature of heroism more
searchingly, that Richard Armstrong ranged beyond the frontiers
of his documentary adventures into a world of greater hazards, a
more exacting world for the writer to describe. Free from the
constraints of didacticism, allowing his particular example to
make a point without feeling he had to underline it, he showed in
The Albatross four sharply realised apprentices learning too late
the lessons of experience which greed and folly had brought to
them. In introducing his characters he follows his usual method of
direct statement in thumbnail sketches of red-haired Judd, the
slow-witted giant Brett, ruthless, brilliant Wick and the plodding
conformer Stringy. Initially these are single-point characters,
each designed to make a particular contribution to the course of
the story, but during the narrative the lads, all around seventeen
or eighteen, act with a degree of independence which lends a new
depth to the book. For they have the capacity to change – for
example, Judd's enthusiasm for their treasure-hunting plan turns
to disillusion as he watches greed enhance Brett's obstinacy and
rouse passive Stringy to obstructive malice. These are far less
formal, contrived changes than those in the documentary novels.

A simple plot gives room for a rapid but intense picture of
disintegration. The *Yaruba* is sent from Texas to San Fernando
with a supply of drinking water for the port, devastated by earthquake. While the slow process of discharging cargo goes on the
four apprentices, firm friends in spite of temperamental differences, are fired by legends of hidden treasure to explore the hills
behind the town in their free time. With a reasonable amount of
intelligent deduction and a good deal of luck they find the loot of
churches on the Spanish Main hidden by the priest-turned-pirate
Domingo Mugnoz. Casting scorn on Stringy's suggestion that
they ask the mate's advice on what to do with their almost
embarrassingly rich discovery, the other three youths make fever-
ish plans. They steal a schooner and embark on a voyage through
the Caribbean and along the Central American coast, terrified of
retribution but indulging in the comfort of increasingly fantastic
plans for a luxurious future. The distasteful physical proximity on
a small craft, the slow effect of fear and the inevitable hostility
born of greed breaks a unity of purpose precarious from the

outset. Quarrels, arguments, in Brett even the beginning of mania, lead to inevitable tragedy. The story ends as it began, with a boy of seventeen rescued from an inflatable life-raft in a confused, incoherent state. Through Judd, sole survivor of the enterprise, the treasure gone and his companions dead, the sorry tale is pieced together.

The use of flashback alone, teasing the reader's attention with its enigmatic promise of a strange tale, suggests how far removed this book is in technique and emotional depth from the simple formula of Richard Armstrong's documentary adventures. The tightness and speed of the narrative, too, has its effect on the direct, concrete prose style which, too often in the earlier books, had become prosy and had lost shape in informative interpolations. Told retrospectively as though from Judd's disjointed, unhappy remembering, the book achieves a sad, distant, emotional intensity which gives it a special unity of tone. Above all, the reader is led into the inevitable decline from triumph to despair not by authorial direction but obliquely through Judd's halting attempt to understand what has happened. The combination of suggestion and statement is especially striking when the youth recalls the way the four had divided the treasure, on Brett's insistence:

> Judd saw his own hand, held hovering uncertainly over the heap of treasure, quiver as Stringy's had done and wondered if that meant he looked as mad as the rest of them did; and he wanted to say they could have it, that he was opting out and they could divide his share among the three of them and stuff it.
>
> 'It wasn't being noble or any of that sort of saliva,' he said afterwards. 'I was just dead scared without knowing why . . .'[23]

We are never told exactly why. As much because of what is left unsaid as because of what is directly described, *The Albatross* is one of those exceptions which suggest that the junior adventure story has always suffered under unnecessary limitations: the names that stand out in the genre are those who in various ways have ignored or overridden these limitations.

Two limitations in particular have driven young readers for many decades to prefer adult adventure stories to those written specifically for them or at least to find more satisfaction in junior tales with adult heroes. They can then be spared the basic unreality of young people triumphing in circumstances too much for their capacities as well as the inevitable thinness of emotional experience which is bound to restrict the scope of an author wanting

36

to draw characters in the round rather than stereotypes. The sea-story, as I have suggested, demands less falsifying of youth's capacities since, in both navy and merchant navy ships, boys in their middle and even early teens have been called upon to act beyond their years often and as a matter of course, from the period, so fruitful for novelists, of the Napoleonic Wars to the present day as Richard Armstrong described it. From this point of view at least the actions of the young do not need to be romanticised.

As for reality in character-drawing, the ancestor of the English sea-story, Marryat, had his own way of dealing with the difficulty. His novels, whether for young or adult readers, are centred on boys in the process of growing to manhood: he does not probe in depth into the feelings of his young heroes, but he does develop them in relation to events in which they may play convincingly passive or active roles in the fortunes of war.

This method is especially valuable in adding depth to the story of the Beverley children unfolded gradually and thoroughly in *The Children of the New Forest*. It is obscured to some extent by the heavily didactic purpose of *Masterman Ready* and this may partly account for the fact that young readers have always claimed the adult novel, *Mr Midshipman Easy*, as their own, even though it must always have made considerable demands on their reading skills and their understanding. This is not to claim that Marryat ever intended his sea-stories to be read primarily as studies in character. His approach to personality, by way of descriptive set-pieces, robust dialogue and direct explanation, may seem to be less subtle and complex than the post-Freudian attitude of C. S. Forester and Patrick O'Brian. Yet for psychological insight and acute comment it is not easy to match the way Marryat, in *Percival Keene*, states and develops the situation of an illegitimate boy steadily and tenaciously working out how to persuade his noble father, under whom he serves as midshipman and later as lieutenant, to acknowledge him openly and alter his reserved, cold but unmistakably responsible behaviour towards his son.

The emotional warmth of this novel never exceeds the space allotted to it in a strongly active story but it does benefit by one physical fact of great importance to any sea-story – the constriction in terms of space on a ship, intensified in time of war, the effect of protocol and strict discipline and a lack of privacy on normal human feelings. The social and cultural conditions under which Marryat and his successors have written, even up to the present, have led them to explore individual personality mainly in terms of officers and warrant officers rather than members of the lower deck. Dana claimed that he expanded his diary into the narrative *Two Years Before the Mast* (the significant subtitle is 'An authentic narrative of a sailor's Life at Sea') in order to represent the seaman's view ignored in other sea-stories, but as a young undergraduate, sent to sea for his health, he presented a life of hardship and monotony from an educated point of view and seems in any case to have been more concerned with exact recording of weather, cargoes and seaman's techniques than with personal behaviour and attitudes. In the matter of social balance one could say that most sea-stories, from the time of Marryat onwards, romanticised fact at least by omission. Those who demand strict realism in fiction of this kind might take the same extreme view as Patrick O'Brian's sardonic Dr Maturin who, in discussing the Spithead Mutiny with his more conventional friend Captain Aubrey, pronounces himself in favour of the rebellion:

> 'You take men from their homes or their chosen occupations, you confine them in insalubrious conditions upon a wholly inadequate diet, you subject them to the tyranny of bosun's mates, you expose them to unimagined perils; what is more, you defraud them of their meagre food, pay and allowances – everything but this sacred rum of yours. Had I been at Spithead, I should certainly have joined the mutineers. Indeed, I am astounded at their moderation.'[24]

Maturin counters the captain's protestation that happy ships did exist by asserting that harmony on a ship depends 'upon the whim, the digestion and the virtue of one or two men, and that is iniquitous'. Authority – 'that egg of misery and oppression' as the doctor has it – is the norm in the long line of historical adventures drawing for material on the extensively recorded history of the navy in the Napoleonic Wars; but the outstanding writers in the genre look round widely from this stance. It is not necessarily romantic – that is, restrictive, unreal, exaggerated – to draw on the upper deck for the individual characters whose attitudes and decisions are to be the driving force of a story.

If Marryat made this choice, it was because he wrote from within the experience of many years serving in the navy from 1806, not continuously but when employment was available: more than one of his novels was written in the cabin of a ship under his command. In a prefatory note to his first novel he told his readers, 'Except the hero and heroine, and those points of the work which supply the slight plot of it, as a novel the work itself is materially true, especially in the narrative of sea-adventure, most of which did (to the best of our recollection) occur to the author'.[25]

Many of his lower-deck characters were comic figures – Chucks the boatswain in *Peter Simple*, for example, whose passionate desire to be a gentleman is satisfied when in return for his help with the newly constituted Danish Navy he is awarded the title of Count Schucksen, or Muddle the carpenter in the same book, who believes the world works in a repeating cycle of 27,672 years. But the roles assigned to the various characters, and the preponderance of officers over seamen, was a matter of literary choice and not of social prejudice. Marryat's common-sense attitude to life was certainly not insensitive. When the seaman Peters, a thief and later a mutineer, protests against the commuting of the death sentence to the disgrace of being flogged round the fleet, Marryat as author finds it a matter for critical comment that the members of the court-martial are clearly surprised that a mere seaman should act from a sense of honour:

> . . . they meant well – they felt kindly towards him, and acknowledged his provocations; but they fell into the too common error of supposing that the finer feelings, which induce a man to prefer death to dishonour, are only to be recognised among the higher classes; and that, because circumstances may have placed a man before the mast, he will undergo punishment, however severe, however degrading . . . in preference to death.[26]

This is only one of many instances of the breadth of Marryat's view, the sturdy wholeness of his reconstructions of life on men-of-war and escort vessels at a crucial period of British naval history. Although each of his books has a compact plot and a central, young hero, he was always ready to shift the point of vision from this hero. We cannot as readers see this as a fault, since it made for such richness of scene and mood, though Marryat seems to have felt it so. Reflecting on the author's problems, he confessed that 'On turning over the different chapters' of *The King's Own*, he felt that the designated hero, Willy Seymour, was not sufficiently 'the hero of my tale':

> As soon as he is shipped on board of a man-of-war he becomes as insignificant as a midshipman must unavoidably be from his humble situation. I see the error – yet I cannot correct it without overthrowing all 'rules and regulations', which I cannot persuade myself to do, even in a work of fiction. Trammelled as I am by 'the service', I can only plead guilty to what it is impossible to amend without commencing *de novo* – for everything and everybody must find their level on board of a king's ship.[27]

Yet it is in the management of his various heroes that Marryat's reliable treatment of fact is most apparent. These young men – sanguine, bold, resourceful and opportunist as they are – do seem to be cut from the same cloth. Yet as individuals they are believable, not only for themselves but by virtue of their involvement with other people and the opinions of their behaviour that come to us from their shipmates and their superiors. This does not mean to say that Marryat was writing documentary fiction. If his novels are in any way romantic, it is because of the melodramatic plots, whether (as in *Poor Jack* or *Jacob Faithful*) they have a rags-to-riches theme or whether they turn on the discovery that the humble hero (like Percival Keene or Willy Seymour) is really of noble birth. The sequence of accidents through which the hero has to steer his suffering way to achieve fame and fortune (even to the extent, in *Peter Simple*, of years incarcerated in Bedlam by a wicked uncle) must be viewed in the context of society nearly two centuries ago; even so, these are organised, contrived and deliberately sensational plots which serve to contain the sprawling, spanking reality of Marryat's detail.

Michael Sadleir suggested that it was partly from professional jealousy of his enormous popularity that Marryat's contemporaries 'treated him with patronising tolerance as a jolly tarpaulin who told a rattling good story'.[28] Certainly Marryat encouraged comments of this kind by the breezy attitude to his work with which he saw fit to hide a sincere purpose. He told his readers:

> . . . if I calculated stages before I ordered my horses, I should abandon the attempt, and remain quietly at home. Mine is not a journey of that methodical description; on the contrary it is a ramble hand-in-hand with Fancy, with a light heart and lighter baggage; for my whole wallet, when I set off, contains but one single idea – but ideas are hermaphrodite, and these creatures of the brain are most prolific. To speak more intelligibly, I never have made any arrangement of plot when I commenced a work of fiction, and often finish a chapter without having the slightest idea of what materials the ensuing one is to be constructed. At times I feel so tired that I throw down the pen in despair; but it is soon taken up again, and, like a pygmy Antaeus, it seems to have imbibed fresh vigour from its prostration.[29]

He summed up the disseminated structure of his novels (often in his case a necessary result of serial publication, but also probably a matter of personal preference), in the same work, when he compared the chapters of a novel to a convoy of vessels and himself, the inventor, as a man-of-war turning attention now to one ship, now to another, in order to bring them all safely to port.

The deeper purpose of his novels was no more than one must expect from any responsible man who draws on his experience and knowledge of the world for readers who will rightly expect both the general and the particular in the fiction. Marryat was no 'jolly tarpaulin' but he chose to please his readers in the way that best suited his circumstances. He believed that the true art of novel-writing was to draw characters who became 'beacons' pointing to moral truths as well as vehicles of 'amusement', and that:

> . . . crime and folly and error can be as severely lashed, as virtue and morality can be upheld, by a series of amusing causes and effects, that entice the reader to take a medicine, which, although rendered agreeable to the palate, still produces the same internal benefit as if it had been presented to him in its crude state, in which it would either be refused or nauseated.[30]

The broad-minded opinions and solid common sense of this robust story-teller are expressed sometimes in dialogue in which officers (and, interestingly, sometimes officers and men) exchange views on slave-trading, naval punishments, privateering, or discuss the attributes of a good or a bad captain. Occasionally the author, with the privilege of his time, directs a disquisition straight to the reader, but such interpolations, and even the wild doodling with which, now and then, he seemed to be whipping up his flagging invention in order to fill a prescribed number of pages, contribute to a unique, first-hand view of the navy in Nelson's day, delivered through narratives whose combination of tight, lateral movement and meandering subincidents has never been surpassed. Virginia Woolf defined it inimitably when she wrote that 'for pages at a time he writes that terse springy prose which is the natural speech of a school of writers trained to the business of moving a large company briskly from one incident to another over the solid earth'.[31]

The satisfied reader, rejoicing in Marryat's broad humour, his acceptance of and delight in the vagaries of mankind, his shrewdness and his talent for controlling the varied pace of his stories, may well decide that his greatest virtue could be the sheer confidence of the man, his assurance that the hierarchies and authority in which he has been trained and which form the basis of his novels are essential to the well-being of his country and its navy. Far less obvious and less easy to rebut than the imperialism of Henty and Ballantyne, Marryat's good-humoured, unself-conscious, professional patriotism is the ultimate strength of his work. Today we may find his attitude most approachable when it is oblique, as it is in *Mr Midshipman Easy*, when the sense and reason behind naval rules and regulations are stated through the absurd mistakes, misconceptions and malfeasances of a youth who has been brought up to believe in the ideal of total equality.

Writing of what he knew at first-hand, Marryat could be allusive in a way which later writers could not emulate. Virginia Woolf stressed the difference between contemporary and historical detail when she wrote:

> . . . no living writer, try though he may, can bring the past back again, because no living writer can bring back the ordinary day. He sees it through a glass, sentimentally, romantically; it is either too pretty or too brutal; it lacks ordinariness. But the world of 1806 was to Captain Marryat what the world of 1935 is to us, at this moment, a middling sort of place, where there is nothing out of the way in a sailor with a pigtail or in a bumboat woman volleying hoarse English. Therefore the world of 1806 is real to us and ordinary, yet sharp-edged and peculiar.[32]

One writer of our time might have induced Mrs Woolf to modify her words. Patrick O'Brian, surely the most closely related of Marryat's successors, understands very well that rare concomitant of the adventure story, the effective partnership of mind and body in action, and displays this in a continuing group of adult novels which give a notable unlaboured picture of the Nelson era.

It is true that the carefully authentic material has to be explained more fully than it had to be for readers of Marryat's day, who could be supposed to possess a modicum of previous knowledge of naval affairs. This may be shown by comparing two passages concerning one particular concept of honour held by the navy in the period concerned. Marryat's Percival Keene, writing a report to the Admiralty of an action in which he has acquitted himself well, sees his success realistically, while he is happy to acquire the reputation of a hero:

> Although the despatch was written modestly, still the circumstances in themselves – my having recaptured an Indiaman, and carried, by boarding, a vessel of equal force to my own, and superior in men – had a very good appearance, and I certainly obtained greater credit than I really deserved. It was not at all necessary to say that I hoisted French colours, and therefore took the schooner unawares, or that at the time most of her men were on board of the Indiaman; the great art in this world is, to know where to leave off, and in nothing more than when people take the pen in their hands.[33]

Marryat's readers would bring at least some associations and some understanding to this piece of special pleading. Patrick O'Brian's sardonic Dr Maturin, in conversation with a philosopher deeply interested in the ways of naval life, and perplexed by certain tactics in an engagement just ended, is more obviously *explaining*, and to O'Brian's readers as well as to Professor Graham, when he enlarges on the customs of war:

'To the nautical mind some false signals are falser than other false signals. At sea there are clearly-understood degrees of iniquity. An otherwise perfectly honourable sea-officer may state by symbol that he is a Frenchman, but he must not state that his ship has struck upon a rock, nor must he lower his colours and then start to fight again, upon pain of universal reprehension. He would have the hiss of the world against him – of the maritime world.'[34]

This example of peculiarly nautical logic, coloured by Stephen Maturin's ironic view of men and affairs, cannot escape the air of an exposition.

All the same, Patrick O'Brian's skill in stitching what is, to him, historical fact into a unified fabric helps us to forget the often tiresome contrivances of historical fiction. In the ten books so far published about the fortunes of Jack Aubrey there is a remarkable absence of hindsight. One particular test at hand for critics is the way Nelson is approached: references to him in the conversation of Aubrey and his fellow officers are natural and appropriate to men who were pursuing the same career at the same date. The minutiae of naval, political and social life are introduced with the utmost literary tact so that the reader can enjoy the piquancy of surprise and can sense the author's secret enjoyment of allusions which give the books their total authenticity. The eccentricities of Dr Maturin are endured with fortitude by his landlady; her opinions are indicated, in a direct account of his situation at a particular period in his life, with perfect naturalness:

Some of his little ways had indeed been quite surprising in the past, seeing that they ranged from the quartering of badgers, rescued from a baiting, in her coal-shed to the introduction of separate limbs and even of whole orphans for dissection when they were in good supply towards the end of winter; but she had grown used to them little by little.[35]

Patrick O'Brian surmounts a more difficult problem in a scene where Aubrey and Maturin exercise their passion for music in the captain's cabin. Jack describes how 'London Bach' had written pieces for his uncle and how he had searched the papers of the copyist for the originals. The ensuing exchange between the two close friends is a fair example of the way a fiction-writer can combine, in the neatest and most intriguing manner, supportive material with the implied interplay of personality. Stephen Maturin, in the dry tone with which he recognises unobtrusively the exuberance and naïveté of Lucky Jack Aubrey, receives the news that 'Bach had a father' with:

> 'Heavens, Jack, what things you tell me. Yet upon recollection I seem to have known other men in much the same case.'
> 'And this father, this old Bach, you understand me, had written piles and piles of musical scores in the pantry.'
> 'A whimsical place to compose in, perhaps; but then birds sing in trees, do they not? Why not antediluvian Germans in a pantry?'
> 'I mean the piles were kept in the pantry. Mice and black-beetles and cook-maids had played Old Harry with some cantatas and a vast great passion according to St Mark, in High Dutch; but lower down all was well, and I brought away several pieces, 'cello for you, fiddle for me, and some for both together. It is strange stuff, fugues and suites of the last age, crabbed and knotted sometimes and not at all in the modern taste, but I do assure you, Stephen, there is meat in it.'[36]

Later, Stephen being absent, Jack looks to music to calm certain professional anxieties but in exploring the great Chaconne of the Partita in C he is almost unnerved by the force of the work compared with the Scarlatti and Hummel pieces with which he and Stephen had so often relaxed. The author seizes on the chance, as he often does, to suggest a sensibility in his hero, the impetuous, extrovert Aubrey, but such moments are never allowed to become sentimental, any more than the frequent musical excursions of captain and doctor are offered as in any way exceptional. Poetry and music, well attested as pastimes of both upper and lower deck in the period concerned, come to us in rehearsals for a noisy and enthusiastic Messiah in which hierarchies are temporarily forgotten, in the verse-contests of two junior officers partial to odes, in the stamp of hornpipes and the therapy of farces and dramatic interludes and, pertinently, in the comments of the inartistic, like the complaint of Aubrey's cantankerous servant Killick, exasperated by the noise of a first attempt at 'Old Bach's D Minor double sonata':

> 'There they go again, tweedly-deedly, tweedly-deedly, belly-aching the whole bleeding night, and the toasted cheese seizing on to their plates like goddam glue, which I dursen't go in to fetch them; and never an honest tune from beginning to end.'[37]

The Romanticising of Fact

Patrick O'Brian's long sequence of sea-adventures gives the lie to the dogma that the genre does not allow for any real development of character. He has the advantage of having devised a series of self-contained but effectively linked novels, full of properly casual back-references, in which he can show his hero changing with circumstances from the exuberance of a young lieutenant, to whom personal courage, seamanlike skills and informed opportunism have brought reputation and wealth, to a middle-aged man still exuberant but oppressed with financial cares and by the continual malice of personal enemies. Aubrey's personality and in particular his approach to command are accounted for reasonably and naturally. With the robust acceptance of hardship and violence proper to his time, he is opposed to flogging and has an open demeanour towards his crew which makes him popular but still respected. There is nothing at all romantic about this sympathy for the underdog: as a midshipman, we are told, Aubrey had been disrated for an unsavoury escapade and had served a long period on the lower deck, an experience which he never forgot. Throughout the sequence of novels there is an element of inconsistency, of the unexpected and unpredictable, in Jack Aubrey, fostered in action and also in the varied comments of his shipmates and crew.

Most of all the unusual complexity of this particular hero is made possible by his friendship with Stephen Maturin, which begins when the doctor joins the *Sophie*, Jack's first command, as ship's surgeon. The special isolation of a naval captain means that an author looking for a confidant for his hero as an essential device of character-drawing is debarred from using a member of the ship's company. The surgeon, a special case in terms of employment and status, is useful as an exception. Besides, his professional duties allow the author greater variety of incident, and Maturin brings two extra dimensions to the stories, for he is a keen experimental naturalist and, at the same time, a secret agent for the British government. His given personality – passionate for freedom, eccentric in person and behaviour, sardonic and observant – is a foil for the traits in Jack which bring misfortune as well as success to his career.

In a sense Patrick O'Brian may be said to offer two heroes, each capable both of influencing events and being affected by them. Their public and private lives (and, with Maturin, the secret manoeuvres of espionage) are related to historical event skilfully and with perfect propriety. History can vouch for the kind of rapid change of fortune and geography which beset Aubrey and Maturin, nor are their actions ever allowed to be

45

improbable. In an Author's Note to the first book, *Master and Commander*, Patrick O'Brian assures us that '. . . very often the improbable reality outruns fiction' and offers enough information about his sources (in log-books, diaries and other contemporary records) to confirm the authenticity of the events through which he displays his characters. The long blockade of the French fleet, the shifting alliances in the Mediterranean and the Middle East, the war with America, the Baltic and East India convoys, the movements of power in the Caribbean, the capture of Mauritius from the French – in these and other historical situations Jack Aubrey and his surgeon are variously involved, always as unmistakable individuals, never in any way distorting the known course of history. Neither character could exist for the reader without the novelistic skill, the use of every fictional device to support them: nor would either live for the reader without their close relation to the fate of nations, the constant background of these magnificent tales.

One of the concomitants of O'Brian's writing, the blessed undercurrent of humour, by no means common in sea-stories, takes many forms. The relish in broadly comic scenes confirms his descent from Marryat, so evident in the tone and flavour of his books in general. To the interplay of character in its amusing aspects O'Brian adds a sense of the ridiculous which often relaxes tension and sharpens the reader's response to intricate action. In H.M.S. *Surprise* the difficulties the doctor endures in controlling one of his live specimens, an over-affectionate sloth addicted to alcohol, inspire laughter and add one more point of variety to a narrative of natural and man-made challenge. In *The Ionian Mission*, a hilarious account of the crew exercising a rhinoceros on deck has a serious point behind its absurdity: the animal is a diplomatic gift from the British government to one of the most tricky and desirable potential allies in the Eastern Mediterranean. Jack's inexorable, slow jokes (one about weevils crops up several times) and Stephen's reaction to them help to build up personalities which exist both independently and in relation to one another.

The resemblance to Marryat in O'Brian's novels is unarguable in general terms and may even be more than a broad likeness. It may be no accident that Jack Aubrey shares with Marryat himself a reputation for saving an unusual number of 'men overboard'. It is possible that the character and appearance of Stephen Maturin owe something to the friendship between Captain M. in Marryat's *The King's Own* and the surgeon MacAllen, a dedicated amateur naturalist who used the ships on which he served as convenient repositories for live and dead specimens from their ports of call.

It could be, too, that the unusually complex character of Captain Hawkins, an illegitimate son of Peter Simple's uncle, a man moved by obsessive jealousy, eroded by concealed cowardice and capable of the most intricate plotting against the young hero, has something to do with one of O'Brian's most impressive studies of character, the officer Lord Clonfert who, in *The Mauritius Command*, more than once frustrates Aubrey's plans and perplexes to the point of real suffering the open-minded captain with his extraordinary psychosomatic state. Both Marryat and O'Brian made the most of the peculiar circumstances of life in Nelson's navy, the enforced closeness of hostile personalities and the system of rewards and punishments which left much scope for personal vindictiveness. Maturin's secret missions and Aubrey's orders involved them in dangers very often due to the malice or ambition of individuals rather than to the fortunes of war. Both Marryat and O'Brian chose to write historical adventure rather than a more sober kind of historical fiction because of an abiding interest in human nature. In this, as in their treatment of fact, they are essentially realistic rather than romantic writers.

Novels in any genre reflect the temper of their times and, in practical terms, are affected by changes in popular taste. The 'Jack Aubrey' sequence – broad and bold in humour, sophisticated in narrative techniques, sardonic in tone, politically alert – is designed for adult readers with somewhat different expectations from those who, during the thirty years between 1937 and 1967 and afterwards, followed the fortunes of C. S. Forester's Horatio Hornblower in a series of novels describing in an unconsecutive but neatly planned order his career in the navy of the Napoleonic period from midshipman to admiral. Forester's fiction is as meticulous in detail and as active in plots as that of O'Brian, yet the Hornblower novels are basically romantic adventures, built on sentiment as much as on action and answering more directly than the Aubrey tales to the simplest conventions of the adventure story.

Forester's huge and enthusiastic public received Hornblower as a 'real' person. This is well enough attested by the existence of a Hornblower Club in which aspects of his life could be canvassed seriously and by C. Northcote Parkinson's 'biography', *The Life and Times of Horatio Hornblower*, with its elaborate statement of provenance (the lifting of a hundred-year-old embargo on three boxes of family papers). Far more than a 'companion' to the Hornblower novels, clarifying and extending the historical background and arranging the events of the hero's life in chronological order instead of in the irregular order imposed on readers by the dates of publication of the books, Parkinson's book is related in intention, though not in style and tone, to the amiable pamphlets published from time to time summarising the relationships and activities of the fictional inhabitants of Coronation Street.

Forester allowed himself a novelist's licence in *The Hornblower Companion*, where admirably executed maps with concise accompanying comment helped to establish the factual background of his stories. The useful information in this book is shot through with the engaging assertion that the books are biographical and that when he journeyed to some of the scenes of Hornblower's exploits the author was truly *following* in the steps of his hero. In a note on naval patrols off Cape St Vincent, referring to *Hornblower and the Hotspur* he wrote:

> Unfortunately the conscientious student who reads the official reports will find no mention either of the *Hotspur* or of the *Félicité* and may naturally experience doubts as to whether there ever was a Captain Hornblower, but if he once accepts Hornblower's existence he may at least agree that Hornblower's action in this case displayed remarkable self-denial as well as the clarity of vision worthy of a hero of fiction.[38]

This is the special pleading of an author thoroughly at home with his subject and satisfied with – indeed, enjoying to the full – his approach to it. Where in his character-drawing O'Brian touches the reader's imagination by the unexpected, Forester satisfied his readers by helping them to a complete acquaintance with his officers and men.

Familiarity can only be achieved by simple, direct and unchanging characterisation and this Forester provided. In uncomplicated prose he steered his readers through the episodes of his hero's life, repeating at intervals Hornblower's mannerisms (his repressive 'Ha-hm', his almost unseemly giggle in moments of crisis), his physical attributes (a homely appearance, an unfortunate tendency to seasickness) and the deeper, clinching duality of his nature. It is with this basic contradiction that Forester avoided sentimentality. Hornblower is not a romantic hero but a hero in spite of himself. He is capable of cold-blooded or berserk courage in desperate moments yet is constantly afraid of being cowardly. Quick and bold to seize the occasion for a night attack, an escape or a ruse, he suffers before and after any such action from painful self-doubt and exhausting self-analysis. When Forester first introduced him as captain of the frigate *Lydia*, in *The Happy Return*, he announced in plain terms the contradiction in his nature:

He had performed a most notable feat of navigation, of which anyone might be justifiably proud, in bringing the ship straight here after
eleven weeks without sighting land. But he felt no elation about it. It
was Hornblower's nature to find no pleasure in achieving things he
could do; his ambition was always yearning after the impossible, to
appear a strong silent capable man, unmoved by emotion.[39]

The paradox recurs throughout the sequence of novels.
Hornblower is no more comfortable with himself as an admiral,
commodore of a Baltic convoy, than he was as a junior captain.
In the full flush of eager planning, in the excitement of disciplin-
ing intuition by stern reasoning, he is warned by the response of
his subordinate to his behaviour:

There was eagerness and excitement in his voice at once, echoing
the emotion which must have been obvious in Hornblower's tone –
Hornblower took notice of it, and as he buckled his waistband he
reaffirmed his resolution to be more careful how he spoke, for he
must regain his reputation as a silent hero.[40]

Moved by the decorations of the chapel at Westminster and the
array of victorious, distinguished officers allied with him in the
Order of the Bath, Lord Hornblower is true to his distrustful self.
He 'felt a surge of patriotic emotion within him' but almost at
once he 'incontinently began to analyse his wave of emotion and
to wonder how much of it was due to the romantic beauty of his
surroundings'.[41]

Growing older, learning to conquer his diffidence as he wins
fame and fortune, still Hornblower does not change. It is in the
nature of Forester's aim that he does not. Nor is there any real
evolution, only the inevitable modifications of time, in his personal
feelings, the loyal determined affection for his drab wife Maria,
his jealous longing for Lady Barbara Wellesley and his brief
encounter with Marie de Graçay during his escape from France.
Here are none of the divagations and contradictions with which
Patrick O'Brian follows the course of Aubrey's life with Sophia or
Maturin's long, difficult passion for Diana Villiers. The course of
Hornblower's love for the forthright (and fictional) sister of the
noble Wellesleys, developed through his uneasy, self-tormenting
thoughts, plays the central part in the novels demanded by their
romantic tone and structure; in the way the two proud individuals
adjust to an intimacy which disturbs their essential need for
privacy of character, in Hornblower's emotional vacillations
when in perilous circumstances he meets Marie de Graçay again,
his behaviour and musings are consistent with his given character.
This is not to use the term 'romantic' in the pejorative sense

in which it must be used when speaking of the film made of *The Happy Return*, in which Lady Barbara, envisaged as a coy, magazine-cover blonde (and without the hereditary Wellesley nose) fluttered her eyelashes at Gregory Peck as an equally improbable Hornblower. Yet Hornblower's agonisings over thoughts of Barbara in the arms of her husband do verge on the sentimental and the hackneyed as Hornblower suffers 'a white hot wave of passion as he thought of her, slim and lovely, understanding and sweet'.[42] The progress of the affair, its curtailment and ultimately happy ending, is described in terms significantly different from the matter-of-fact reference to it in Parkinson's 'biography':

> Had he and his guest been lovers on board the *Lydia*? So far as one can tell from the scanty evidence available they had been something short of that. Hornblower could not afford a scandal nor could he dare to offend the Wellesleys, who were rapidly gaining importance. It would appear from the sequel that Lady Barbara would have been more reckless and that it was Hornblower's caution which prevented the friendship from becoming a romance.[43]

Love and honour, the pivotal themes of the Hornblower books, and essential to their success, are held in a balance which at times seems to hamper the essential directness of Forester's narrative technique. The escape from France described in *Flying Colours* offers him the chance of the kind of swift, concrete description in which he excels but too often the pace slackens overmuch as Hornblower's emotions are analysed with an almost sentimental thoroughness. It is, to be sure, the element of sensibility which has attracted many of Hornblower's readers but many more will remember with greater satisfaction the account of Hornblower's stand against four French ships-of-war, in *A Ship of the Line*, in which professional skill, emotional introspection and moment-to-moment physical behaviour are unerringly matched. At moments like this Forester writes within the conventions of the genre and uses them superbly. In such rapid alternations of mood he rescues his hero from the risk of monotony in the way he has chosen to reveal his feelings. We can only know these feelings from Hornblower's own unspoken soliloquies. There is none of the variety which O'Brian provides through the intimate or casual conversations of Aubrey and Maturin: although circumstances allow Hornblower a little more than a restricted relationship with his loyal and devoted lieutenant Bush, it is never a *personal* friendship.

Nor has Forester the weapon of humour at his disposal, except in occasional moments when he allows his hero to appear in an almost ludicrous light. We may remember with pleasure the picture of the skinny midshipman stuffing his stockings with oakum to give the impression of a properly gentlemanly leg. We may remember the unusual play on Hornblower's self-distrustful temperament in *Hornblower and the Atropos*, when as the official organiser of Nelson's funeral procession down the Thames he is beset by disaster. The barge carrying the body springs a leak, his ceremonial uniform is soaked as he frantically bales, he worries about the expensive watch which he has inadvertently left on the coffin, the ceremony leaves him with a bad cold which he tries, not altogether successfully, to hide when he is presented to the King. The poised, lively writing in this incident adds a different dimension, unfortunately a rare one, to novels which for all their scholarship and vigour seem for the taste of the eighties a little sedate, a little soft – in short, a little too romantic.

It was in fact somewhat of a surprise to see cadet editions of a few of the Hornblower novels published for readers in the early and mid-teens, since neither Forester's open, smooth narrative style nor his approach to sex and violence could be considered exacting or improper where young readers were concerned. In the apt selection of active incidents, the clear response of a hero to the challenge of danger and the support of interesting detail, Forester's books followed the conventions of adventure-story which had governed 'boys' stories' for two centuries and the undercurrent of irony in the presentation of Hornblower as reluctant hero was hardly insistent enough to perplex immature readers. Moreover, Forester (like most of his contemporaries and successors in the sphere of the naval sea-novel) offered enough young characters to reassure boys and girls engaging with adult fiction, since he rearranged historical fact to the extent that his midshipmen were invariably between fourteen and eighteen: those older, even middle-aged men, soured by repeated failure to pass as lieutenants, were not suitable for his purpose.

The junior adventure story has always had to reconcile two contrasting points. Action, and dangerous action, must be successfully encountered by heroes too young and inexperienced for such success to be guaranteed or even probable. The artificiality of so many boys' adventures is the result of miscalculation in this aspect of story-telling. Naval midshipmen, like their counterparts in the merchant service, may be authentically involved in vigorous, violent action in fiction, as they were in fact, at least until the recent past. When the author of *The Three Midshipmen* reflected that his three heroes, supposed to be his former schoolfellows at 'dear old Eagle House', had in a few years 'crossed swords with real red-capped or turbaned Mohammedans, fought with true Greek romantic pirates, hunted down slavers, and explored African rivers with voracious sharks watching their mouths, hungry crocodiles basking in their slimy shallows, and veritable negroes inhabiting their banks',[44] this rhodomontade, appealing to the eager youth of the mid-Victorian period, was entirely justified. Yet there *were* differences between the attitude of W. H. G. Kingston to his heroes and Marryat's to Peter Simple or Jack Easy in adult novels, differences reflecting the special constraints on fiction written specifically for young readers.

There can be no doubt that the prolific Kingston gave boys what they wanted. In a list of favourite boys' books compiled by Edward Salmon in 1888, Kingston came second to Dickens, and Salmon observed, 'Mr Kingston is Captain Marryat transformed from a novelist into a juvenile romanticist'.[45] As a juvenile romanticist Kingston, like his contemporary Ballantyne, used the device of the intrusive author accepted in his time and, besides, the didacticism expected in books for the young, didacticism made easier by the continuity and the extent of time afforded by serial publication in the boys' magazines of the period. As editor of *The Colonial Magazine*, *Kingston's Magazine* and *The Union Jack* (the last-named started in 1880, the year of his death, and taken over by Henty), Kingston could claim all the space he needed to express his views on the importance of colonisation and use the experience he gained from working for the Colonial Land and Emigration Board. His address to the prospective readers of the first issue of *Kingston's Magazine* in 1859 is significant:

> My great aim is to give you a periodical which you will not throw aside as soon as read, but which you will value and look over years hence as an old familiar friend, when you may be battling with the realities of life under the suns of India, in the backwoods of Canada or the United States, or the grassy downs of Australia, over the wide Ocean among the isles of the Pacific, or on the distant shores of Columbia.[46]

The imperialist attitude was accommodated in his books all the more easily because he put the emphasis on service and sacrifice rather than on nationalist domination or material gain: an approach that may seem hypocritical to present-day readers was sincere enough in a man who set out to be a philanthropist and reformer and became a best-seller. He was fortunate in that his choice of subjects and his robust story-telling were perfectly in tune with his reading public. Besides, such a prolific writer could hardly be ignored and his popularity moved through many decades by its own momentum, rather as Enid Blyton's has done in the middle years of the present century.

The appetite for travel tales was insatiable at a time when so many young people were taking the chance of good fortune in lands newly opened up, often in aided emigration schemes such as Kingston himself administered. He was a keen traveller and could write of many European countries, as well as Canada, the United States and Scandinavia, from personal knowledge. As for other parts of the world, he assured his readers that:

> . . . those countries which I could not visit in my proper person, I have so attentively read about, that as I turn round a globe I can almost fancy that I know the appearance and characters of the portions of the great world itself which lie mapped out under my eye, and observe all that is going forward on its surface. At all events, wherever I have wandered I have had my eyes open and my senses awake.[47]

Without indulging in passages of inactive description, he extended to his readers a panoramic view of the world, making good use of the duties performed by the navy in the aftermath of the Napoleonic Wars to keep up the colour and excitement of adventure.

Britain's role as Kingston described it could be called that of a peace-keeping force, and his stories of intrigue and skirmish are punctuated by anti-war sentiments. When Midshipman Jack Rogers, trying to identify a distant ship, hopes it may be a Frenchman and declares 'the French will never like the English till they have taught us to eat frogs, and have thrashed us on a second field of Waterloo, and I hope that time may never come', his friend Alick Murray defends French courage in war and laughs at Jack's belligerence. The author draws the conversation to a close with the comment that Murray was still too young to realise that 'fighting under any circumstances is a dreadful business, and that the person who gives the cause for the fight does a very wicked thing, utterly hateful in the sight of God. Never let that truth be forgotten.'[48] The complicated politics which lay behind expeditions against slave-traders, pirates or opium-traders, diplomatic missions to Indian potentates or corrective action against insurgents in South America and the Caribbean, are plainly stated rather than analysed or qualified. Once the national point of view has been established the decks are cleared for the exploits of three young heroes to whom battle is fun and orders exist to be cunningly circumvented when there is a chance of appealingly extraneous adventure.

This limited view is dictated by the convention within which juvenile heroes usually operate in fiction. Kingston's three midshipmen are carefully chosen to satisfy the contemporary patriotic line. Jack Rogers, son of a land-owning family in East Anglia, is sturdily English; Terence Adair (inevitably nicknamed Paddy) has been sent to sea to relieve the pressure on an impoverished though aristocratic Anglo-Irish family; Alick Murray, the necessary counterbalance to the impetuous courage and reckless exuberance of the other two, is soberly and morally Scottish. The schoolfellows had been appointed to the *Racer* together through the efforts of a family friend of the Rogerses, and they serve together for much of their time at sea, occasionally allotted to different ships so as to give the author freedom to range more widely in space and circumstance. Like Ballantyne, Kingston used the different temperaments of his youthful trio to keep their exploits within reasonable bounds. Obliquely flattering his readers by introducing them to boys near their own age involved in surprising and exciting events, he also invited them to wishful thinking, if not to identification, by emphasising the youth of his heroes and underplaying the responsibility and enforced maturity belonging to midshipmen in the early and mid-teens in reality. Adventure in Kingston's stories is fast and active but it is handled with a light touch. When Jack and Alick, after being shipwrecked and narrowly escaping murder, starvation and sundry other perils, are reunited with Terence on board a brig-of-war, he declares it is worth being lost when reunion is so pleasant and ends with a flourish: 'Old fellows, I knew you would come back somehow or other; I always said so; astride of a dolphin, if in no other way . . .'[49]

The operative word in the four books about this carefully selected trio is 'scamper'. Undoubtedly Kingston's favourite verb, it is used again and again to describe the alacrity with which his heroes rush into adventure: by contrast, their enemies often scamper as well, but away from danger rather than towards it, thus implying the superiority of the British race which is taken for granted in the yarns of the last century. As Jack and his friends grow older their pace necessarily slows a little but there is still an impetuous tone about their exploits as lieutenants, commanders and even as admirals, and their courtships as well as their warmongering are still basically 'fun'.

To avoid exaggerating this necessary aspect of the stories (necessary because the later books are not addressed to more mature readers but to those who, feeling they really know Jack,

Alick and Terence, would resent their becoming staid and solemn), Kingston introduced in the second book another trio of lads who filled the spaces left by the midshipmen now promoted in *The Three Lieutenants*, a sequel if ever there was one. We meet Jack's younger brother Tom, Paddy's nephew Gerald Desmond and Alick's cousin Archie Gordon. These three carry on the irresponsible practical jokes and illicit enterprises of their seniors, borrowing boats while in harbour and exploring themselves into danger, invariably rescued by improbably patient sailors. Temperamental differences operate once more with this new trio of junior heroes, whose elders, the three lieutenants, regard their pranks with mild amusement. Carrying out a siege in Brazil against rebels, Tom and Gerald, happy to be put in charge of cannon instead of their earlier muskets, describe their efforts against the stone walls of the enemy as 'very good fun' and are mildly reproved by Archie, who cries, 'I don't call that fun', as:

> . . . a round shot struck a seaman at one of the guns near them on the breast and laid him dead on the deck, before he had time to utter a groan. A grapeshot, the next moment, hit another man on the shoulder, and he was carried below. Two others were shortly afterwards wounded.[50]

Their light-hearted attitude balances the greater seriousness of events in *The Three Commanders*, for they still scamper into adventure as their respective ships operate against slave-traders off the African coast and when they carry troops and fight battles off the Turkish coast during the Crimean War. Their elders in more serious mood watch from a distance the Charge of the Light Brigade and, in the course of discussing the future of their young relatives, indulge in a dispute for and against the innovation of steam in naval vessels. Predictably, Irish Terence Adair believes that 'if steamers come into vogue, they will do away with all the romance once upon a time supposed to belong to a naval life' but the Scotsman's more practical view chimes in with Jack's opinion. When Alick Murray suggests:

> '. . . it will be a great thing not to have to depend on the fickle wind for making a passage, and still more to know that we may pounce down upon those rascally fast-sailing dhows whenever we can sight them in a calm, and be sure of overtaking them. . . .'[51]

sensible Jack determines to improve on his knowledge of engines.

All the same, the phrase 'pounce down upon', like the word 'scamper', is in keeping with the attitude to adventure which is still apparent even after the three commanders have found suitable wives and have won promotion to the rank of admiral as a result of successful expeditions in the Pacific. The use of coincidence, timely rescues and convenient accidents persists in the final book of the sequence, *The Three Admirals*. Indeed, the proliferation of adventures in the South Atlantic, Abyssinia, China, Japan and New Guinea, with the addition of the Maori Wars, shipwreck and the challenge of life on a desert island, earthquake and eruptions, suggests that Kingston was at last finding it difficult to adapt his exalted heroes to the kind of narrative his readers expected. The heroes of the next generation, now lieutenants, sustain most of the action, still able to regard as fun the missions which their elders discuss more seriously in terms of Britain's rule as a force for justice and peace in the world. This is of course having your cake and eating it, an achievement to which Kingston owed the enormous popularity of his naval as well as his other yarns. The facts of British intervention round the globe could, in his brief, be treated with a confident and (for many decades) an acceptable blend of sturdy patriotic fervour and romantic exhilaration. The formula was to be used, with suitable modifications, right up to and occasionally beyond the 1940s.

The trick, of course, is to give young heroes quick wits and ingenuity as well as an impetuous and opportunist temperament, so that any opening for individual enterprise against the enemy can be plausibly taken: at the same time the status and responsibility of a midshipman, however young, which allows him to direct his seniors in dangerous and often illicit exploits will also ensure that he will have the backing of those older men and the support of their common sense, experience and physical strength. It is far easier to convince readers of the courage and invention of a youth of fifteen or so when he is foiling the enemy with a clever disguise or a neatly gymnastic escape than when he is in grim and bloody action on board an enemy ship – not only easier, but more in keeping with the romantic excitement proper to adventure-story.

Showell Styles chose with acumen the incidents to make up four successive junior novels, beginning with *Midshipman Quinn*, which followed the fortunes of Septimus Quinn from his fifteenth to his seventeenth year. Writing almost a century after Kingston, he fulfilled the expectations of his readers with less melodrama in his plots and a more responsible attitude to life in his young hero, but Quinn is a very obvious descendant of Marryat's Peter Simple and Kingston's Jack Rogers in his lively opportunism and his youthful capacity for living in the present. He is introduced literally with a bang, explaining in his pedantic way an alarming explosion in his room to his clergyman uncle as 'a little experiment':

> 'It had occurred to me that if the substance known as Potassium Chlorate were to be contained in some small vessel with the right quantity of Sulphur, and the compound impacted – that is to say, if I hit it a pretty fair whack with a pestle – the result would be an explosion.'[52]

His uncle's testy interruption is followed by a more dramatic one as Admiralty orders arrive for Septimus to join the frigate *Althea* as junior midshipman; but, not to be diverted from his experiment, he uses a similar home-made bomb to good effect when the coach is held up by highwaymen on the Portsmouth road. Some months later he is still obstinately experimenting, in the stretches of inaction while the *Althea* is engaged in the blockade of Toulon. Reporting to the captain the reason for, and extent of, the explosion in the ship, the first lieutenant brings the culprit with him:

> The midshipman was dark-haired and studious-looking. Beneath a cocked hat somewhat too big for him his small face, pale despite the sun of a whole Mediterranean summer, was much more calm and composed than that of the man behind him. He was wearing a pair of steel-rimmed spectacles.[53]

Curiosity, quick wits and a degree of practical skill, presented in a measure appropriate to a precocious, solitary youth, make Quinn's exploits plausible. The escape, made possible in part by the chemical explosion in *Quinn of the Fury*, is followed by a series of independent forays in which Quinn seizes a French sloop carrying hides by following it into a secret harbour and pretending he and his men are drunken sailors returning on board, rescues Royalist prisoners from a castle by skulking and climbing, seizes another French ship by disguising the prize vessel under his command as French, and outwits a pirate ship by means of a collision (rescuing, by the way, a young Contessa who adds a romantic touch to the story). Any reader literal enough to doubt Quinn's success in those matters is likely to be diverted by the thrust and crackle of action rapidly described and by the element of chance so quickly exploited by the boy.

His is a temperament well calculated to flatter and intrigue readers in the early teens and to draw them into vicarious adventure. The need for reality is satisfied in that Septimus Quinn, for all his impetuosity, does not look upon war as fun, nor does he abdicate his responsibility for the men whom, from time to time, he is called upon to lead. Yet he is far from being a copybook hero. There is sly humour in the choice of an undersized, bespectacled, studious youth as the instigator of so much bold harassment of the enemy but it is humour grounded in a psychologically apt interpretation of his character. Like Hornblower, whose temperament was delighting readers with its contradictions at the same time as that of the Quinn adventures, Septimus has adopted certain measures of what could be called self-defence. Where Hornblower's cough is designed to give him time to avoid embarrassment or to get out of a tight corner, Septimus puts on his spectacles, which in fact he only needs for reading, when he needs time to think of a way out of a difficulty or the chance to seem more confident than he really is. It is a novelist's trick, useful for recognition when a character is used in a series of stories: it is also properly matched to the portrait of a youth who is intelligent but not physically impressive. Humour is a good way to stabilise a character which could be over-romanticised. There may be a certain exaggeration in the statement that Napoleon had offered a reward for the taking of 'the English incendiary "Kvinn or Quin" who had been responsible for the burning of three French battleships in the Gulf of Villefranche last year' but the sixteen-year-old's behaviour while in prison in Toulon is entirely in keeping with what we know about him:

> Septimus, who was a philosopher by nature and had been in a French prison before, made the most of his breakfast in a way peculiarly his own. He turned it into a four-course meal, thus:
> Bread.
> Bread washed down with coffee.
> Bread dipped in coffee.
> Coffee.[54]

It is a useful authorial device to offer readers an unheroic hero so as to escape romantic cliché. To a great extent this is the reason why Forester's self-deprecating Hornblower is more believable than Alexander Kent's Bolitho or Dudley Pope's Ramage. Showell Styles balanced the junior tales about Septimus Quinn with a sequence of adult novels built round a middle-aged naval officer who, at thirty-three, had moved only from midshipman to the unsatisfactory rank of acting lieutenant because of intermittent periods of unemployment at the end of the eighteenth century and a sad lack of useful patronage. The deliberately impassive front cultivated by Michael Fitton, hiding reckless courage and a talent for improvisation, provides a different example of the way a novelist can colour and intensify fact without falsifying it. The contrast between Fitton's studied calm and the bravura of his victorious naval actions is neither romantic nor realistic. Showell

Styles's sea-stories, moderately coloured by invention, provide entertainment in the broadest sense. If the events in each of his series did happen or could have happened, they come to us with the optimistic tone, the promise of a happy ending, which we expect of the classic adventure story. One could hardly find a more severe rebuttal of this convention than the latest contribution to the junior Napoleonic adventure, Jan Needle's *A Fine Boy for Killing*.

The 'fine boy' with the grim destiny is Thomas Fox, a boy of fifteen whose father, a small farmer, has entrusted him for the first time with a flock of sheep for Portsmouth market. Inexperienced in the ways of the world, the boy is tricked into accepting money from a plausible and (to Thomas) impressive midshipman, a year younger than he but already well instructed in ways of avoiding the various laws against press-ganging. In a day and a night of violence and imposture William Bentley, working for his uncle, the captain of the frigate *Welfare*, also succeeds in capturing Jesse Broad, a smuggler returning with a cargo from a French ship. The terrified farmboy, Thomas, miserably seasick but comforted by being set to tend sheep, calves and poultry in the depths of the ship, is protected so far as it is possible by the sturdy Jesse, but both are subject to the appalling cruelty of the captain, Daniel Swift. His sadism is satisfied, at least at first, within the permitted limits of naval discipline, but it is accompanied by unpredictable moods and actions which disturb and perplex the crew to the point of mutiny, terrified as they are by the hostile surveillance of the officers and the malicious spying which William Bentley the midshipman carries on by his uncle's order. The inevitable revolt shows only too plainly the helplessness of the seamen against the power of authority. As fighting on board goes first one way and then the other, the captain strikes Thomas Fox to death with a belaying pin in an access of rage because the boy, genuinely unaware of the seamen's plotting and almost insensible after hours at the masthead in icy weather, does not give him the names of the conspirators. Captain Swift and his party are set adrift but the good fortune customarily accorded to characters in the right is this time acceded to those whom we must call villains. Quickly picked up near Cape Town by a passing ship, Swift, in the confidence of sealed orders and of his own determination, persuades the captain to divert his passage to track down the *Welfare*. The mutineers, driven by weather to abandon their plan of escaping round the Horn into the Pacific, are intercepted and taken back to England, where Jesse and those of his comrades who have survived are tried and hanged.

The stark events of *A Fine Boy for Killing* are no more and no less authentic than the events of Showell Styles's novels or those of O'Brian and Forester. There is as much evidence for unhappy as for happy ships. The difference is in emphasis and in conclusion. Instances of cruelty and mania, in O'Brian and Forester, are not minimised, but they are subordinate to the drive of a story towards the traditional and expected ending in the triumph of right over wrong, of good over evil. The facts of sea-warfare are not ignored but there is no concentration on their gruesome aspects and, usually, plain statements do not extend to an analysis of the effect of conflict on individuals.

The contrast between the accounts of battle within the conventions of adventure-story and Jan Needle's deliberate departure from these conventions may be shown in two contrasted passages. In Marryat's *Percival Keene* the author, speaking through his hero, describes a moment after a battle against a Dutch ship when the young midshipman is sent below by the captain to report on casualties:

> . . . I got a lantern and commenced my examinations. I found fourteen wounded men waiting the doctor's care in the gun-room, which was almost a pool of blood. In the steerage there were nine who had been dressed, and four in their hammocks who had undergone amputation of the arm or leg. I then went down into the cockpit, where I counted eleven of our best men lying dead.[55]

Keene's matter-of-fact approach to the grisly scene allows for no introspection on his part, nor are the feelings of the wounded men explored. Marryat was not avoiding actuality: his authentic plots did not extend to emotional exploration. But a complete, inexorable account of violent suffering is essential to the deepening horror of Jan Needle's story. Statement is shot through with feeling in the long, passionately detailed account of the mutiny. At one moment the boatswain Jack Allgood comes out of a berserk rage to realise that he, a warrant officer, has allowed his hatred of the captain to lead him into mutiny; the points of physical detail enforce his emotional agony:

> There was between them and the quarterdeck a group of men who had left the fighting. They were standing about as if in a daze, gazing about at the littered corpses and wounded. Some held bloody cutlasses drooping in their hands. One or two were weeping. As the *Welfare* lurched and another thundering beating of canvas came from aloft, Mr Allgood emerged from the group. His face was covered in blood and one arm hung limp beside him. He stared aloft, then shook his head. Matthews hailed him.
> 'Ahoy Mr Allgood! Here by the cutter! Quick man!'

The boatswain shook his bull head again and began to walk towards them.

'Here man,' said Matthews, when he had arrived. 'We have got to get this ship under control. She will beat herself to pieces else.'

The huge warrant officer stared at him unseeingly. He blinked red-rimmed eyes. His face was livid and bloody. He looked beaten, hurt.

'Oh God,' he said at last. 'Oh God, what have I done? Oh God, the shame of it. To raise a hand against an officer. To start a mutiny in His Majesty's Navy . . . The man is a villain, double-dyed. But to mutiny, Jesse Broad, to raise a hand against an officer of the King.'[56]

The extreme realism in this tragic adventure (realism, that is, in the sense of a deliberate emphasis on the unpleasant aspect of adventure) constitutes a reaction against the essentially optimistic approach to violent events which can be seen in many other branches of adventure-story. Noticeable in the last decade or two in fiction, it is a reaction that could be called political. Jan Needle's story shows inexorably the workings of a system in which power could corrupt.

It is not only the exaggerated violence and horrific detail of the book that marks it as a portent of change within the genre. As the title suggests, this is the tragedy of Thomas Fox; the narrative draws out the disintegration, physical and mental, of an innocent boy caught up in a world of inexplicable rules and inescapable brutality. But it is also the tragedy of William Bentley, a tragedy because he too is a boy caught in circumstances which he is incapable of understanding and which will, finally, leave him totally unfit for the life he has been trained for. For all his arrogance, William Bentley is still at heart an innocent boy, a fourteen-year-old brought up to believe himself superior and privileged and flattered at receiving the trust of his uncle, whom he admires for his firmness of purpose. As the youngest midshipman, William is especially concerned to demonstrate his toughness and capability in rivalry with his messmates. Accepting without question his uncle's explanation that, as captain, he cannot be too directly concerned with the minutiae of shipboard life, the boy eagerly agrees to spy on the seamen and find out their weaknesses and their delinquencies.

He is boy enough to enjoy, though with misgivings, a brutal practical joke against the ineffectual tutor who is supposed to educate the group of youths. He is bitterly humiliated when he is beaten in a fist-battle with Thomas Fox, arranged by the captain as the climax to a day of races and contests organised to keep the hands occupied while the ship is becalmed. William is humiliated not because he is defeated (he had half expected this) but because of the shepherd boy's refusal to go on hitting him. William orders:

> 'You must fight, Thomas Fox. You must hit me, you know.'
> 'No,' said Thomas. 'Your poor face, Sir. I have hurt you, child, and I am very sorry.'
> A silence fell over the ship's company that was appalling. Not a man stirred, hardly a breath was drawn. William Bentley's face, already pale, drained slowly of blood until it was glaring white. His mouth opened, his eyes glittered with rage.[57]

The roar of laughter that burst out was something he never forgot. This bitter education continues through the increasing violence of the voyage in the Atlantic. Doubts assail the boy. Knowing as he does that his uncle has to hold down by discipline a crew with an unusual number of criminals and malcontents, he is still disturbed by the flogging of Jesse Broad and Joyce and the masthead punishment of Thomas Fox. Acting bravely and with initiative during the mutiny, he is oppressed with shame when he remembers certain arrogant and cruel actions of his against the crew. In part he is swayed by fear of his fate at the hands of the enraged seamen: in part he is driven by an awakening of conscience as painful as the circulation returning to the frozen body of Thomas Fox when he is brought down from the masthead.

At the end of the book the two 'heroes' are dead but Bentley, who has been obliged to watch the hanging of Jesse Broad on the day of his fifteenth birthday, is left to come to terms with his life and his position. Jan Needle leaves us to imagine the boy's future. He has said enough to ensure that we will take his point. What he has done, in fact, in this remarkable book is to cut across the basic acceptance of 'good' and 'bad' characters. He has shown good in Allgood and even in the evil captain, bad in the intermittently cowardly surgeon, a mixture of impulses in William Bentley. He has implied by his character-drawing that adventure stories need not be concerned with absolutes. This is, again, a decisive change in the genre in our time and one which is likely to have lasting effects on it.

3. Honour and the Unattainable Ideal

The romantic element in adventure stories is one of several processes of selection by which a writer takes from his raw material – from real life, if you like – what he needs for his particular fiction. But the word romance has for most people the immediate association of love and, in the main, of heterosexual love. In this sense the particular manipulation of reality found in the adventure story, at least until the past two or three decades, has been away from the practicalities of extended cohabitation, whether in or out of marriage. The wedding bells that sounded on the last page of so many 'romantic' novels of the last century are still sounding in certain genres but in the adventure story they seldom sound at all. For at the heart of that dominant form, the quest-story, there lies very often a denial of fulfilment. Man seeks a distant, passionately desired ideal: often, he is happiest when he fails to find it.

The most significant stories of man's quest for woman in this genre – like Rider Haggard's 'She' novels, Masefield's *Odtaa* and *Sard Harker*, William de Morgan's *Joseph Vance*, Hilton's *Lost Horizon* – override the convention of the happy ending in a conclusion of happy pessimism, an almost cherished melancholy, a sense of emotional growth coming from loss and failure. The special, complex mood communicated to the reader through this kind of romantic adventure has as its literary results a particular intensity of emotion fostered by a constant shift of pace, tension and suspense. At its best it satisfies the sense of hubris in all of us and helps us to forget the inevitable contrast between real and ideal, in human love as in every other human impulse.

This happy pessimism is a far more compelling element in adventure stories, to my mind, than the cheerful man-gets-girl conclusion of the general run of romance-adventures. Certainly the word 'romance' cannot be tied down to any one meaning. This is very clear in the swashbuckling tale given that very title, compounded by Conrad and his close friend Ford Madox Hueffer (afterwards Ford Madox Ford) in what may surely be called the Golden Age of the classic adventure story.

The novel *Romance* can almost be read as a series of definitions designed to emphasise the elusive, personal nature of the word. The young hero, John Kemp, grows up with the ardent expectation of rose-coloured, agreeable adventure:

> It was, I suppose, what I demanded of Fate – to be gently wafted into the position of a hero of romance, without rough hands at my throat. It is what we all ask, I suppose; and we get it sometimes in ten-minute snatches.[1]

'Rough hands' and brief snatches of pleasurable exhilaration alternate in an intricate tale of innocence threatened by evil. In trouble after a smuggling affray, early in the nineteenth century, John Kemp escapes to Jamaica and works his way to prosperity as a plantation owner. Before long he is involved, through loyalty to a Spanish relative, in the vexed affairs of old Don Baltasar, whose seaboard estate is being used as a refuge for pirates secretly commanded by James O'Brien, a villain with a front as a respected official in the Jamaican government. To the still ardent John Kemp the old Don is a romantic figure, while Don Baltasar for his part dreams of England as a glamorous country, free from the political pressures of his own adopted land. The constant dangers and perplexities that beset John Kemp arise from the ferocious enmity of O'Brien, whose hatred of anything English is increased by his hopeless love for the Don's daughter Seraphina, for whose sake he moderates from time to time his evil power over the old aristocrat. To John Kemp Seraphina becomes the beloved ideal as well as the victim of persecution whom he vows to rescue.

The authors of this perfervid, crowded adventure use the first-person device to plot the course of Kemp's feelings concurrently with the bold actions in which he is conventionally heroic. The mood of this unusual story is alternately sentimental and active, its hero alternately introspective and confident, but the predominant note is one of 'romance' in its most popular sense. Of Seraphina, John confesses:

> . . . she remained to me always unattainable and romantic – unique, with all the unexpressed purposes of love such as no world had ever known. And naturally, because for me hitherto the world had held no woman. She was an apparition of dreams . . . and yet I was permitted to whisper intimately to this my dream, to this my vision.[2]

There is no sense of possible anticlimax when reality cuts across Kemp's idealistic view of the girl. Escapes involving desperate small-boat journeys, tramping over difficult terrain, the physical distress of thirst and hunger, show Seraphina as a courageous young woman but, still, as the idealised beauty. Kemp looks at her as they shrink within a dark cave, besieged by O'Brien and his men:

In the guise of a beggar-maid, and fair, like a fugitive princess of romance, she sat concealed in the very heart of her dominions.[3]

During their subsequent separation and his long sojourn in an English prison, where he is saved from the gallows only by a last-minute reprieve, his vision of her becomes intense and idealised. At this point in the tale most readers would expect a tragi-heroic ending, and indeed in the hands of Rider Haggard or Masefield this would almost certainly have been the case. But having viewed the past in romantic terms through the eyes of their hero, the authors bid farewell to him in his retrospective old age as the husband of the refound, finally-won love. In doing so they offer, it seems, their most conclusive definition of the word that has inspired their fiction:

> And, looking back, we see Romance – that subtle thing that is mirage – that is life. It is the goodness of the years we have lived through, of the old time when we did this and that, when we dwelt here or there. Looking back, it seems a wonderful enough thing that I who am this, and she who is that, commencing so far away a life that, after such sufferings borne together and apart, ended so tranquilly there in a world so stable – that she and I should have passed through so much, good chance and evil chance, sad hours and joyful, all lived down and swept away into the little heap of dust that is a life. That, too, is Romance![4]

A bold assertion of reality indeed and very far from the idealised approach to love in adventure in another collaboration. In *The World's Desire*, Rider Haggard and his close friend Andrew Lang presented as it were their thesis of romance in a turgid tale based on certain theories of their time concerning possible trafficking between Achaean Greece, Crete and Egypt under the Ramessids. Archaeology was only an excuse for a highly personal interpretation of myth in which Odysseus, seeking ideal beauty, finds it in Helen, surviving in Egypt as a seemingly immortal, ageless goddess. Although a plot of sorts involves the intrigues of the Egyptian Queen, whose enfeebled brother and consort has no power to break her obsessive love for 'the Wanderer', the story turns on the simple fact that Odysseus must for ever love an unattainable ideal. He is promised that he will enjoy Helen, but only in death:

> For though here on earth she seems to live eternally, it is but the shadow of her beauty that men see – each as he desires it. In the halls of Death she dwells, and in the garden of Queen Persephone . . .[5]

His consolation has to be that although she is, as an ideal, constantly changing, 'yet she dies only when the race of men is dead – then to be gathered to the number of the Gods.'

The unattainable ideal woman was to become something of an obsession for Rider Haggard, idealised but hardly ideal, for the strange being he introduced in *She* was both good and evil, goddess and witch. Though he allowed himself no fewer than four books (*She*, *Ayesha*, *She and Allan* and *Wisdom's Daughter*) in which to analyse this character, he never seems to have decided exactly what she was meant to represent or how far she was intended to be a symbol of the 'world's desire'.

There is a difficulty here. *She* and the sequels have suffered far more from changes in social attitudes and literary expectations than the rest of Rider Haggard's adventures have. The extraordinary decadent sensuality of the books and their moral and sexual elusiveness seem nowadays a particularly unpleasing example of social hypocrisy. Besides, Rider Haggard's attempt to present 'She' as a kind of divinity seems nowadays either absurdly grandiose or ludicrous. The fact that 'She' appears to those privileged to see her as a *veiled* figure and that her lustrous orbs, dazzling limbs and perfect ankles are revealed with tantalising slowness, has a rather different effect on today's readers than it no doubt had when the book was first published, very nearly a century ago, in 1887, to be greeted with a storm of ecstasy or alternatively of appalled disapproval, which lasted for many decades. (I can remember, when I was a child, watching with amazement as my book-loving grandmother burned a copy of *She* on the sitting-room fire.)

Rider Haggard's heroine (if such a general term can be applied to her) is introduced in terms that were to become very familiar in his fiction, as a fabled white goddess-figure ruling over an unknown tribal kingdom in unexplored Central Africa. The difference between 'She' and the similar female figures in *The Ivory Child*, *The Treasure of the Lake* and *The Holy Flower* is that 'She' has, it appears, already lived for three thousand years when two travellers, handsome Leo Vincey and his guardian, Professor Holly, discover her in a volcanic fastness, once the ancient kingdom of Kôr. A priestess of Isis, the beautiful Ayesha had broken her vows for love of a Greek soldier Kallikrates who, in his turn, was in danger because of his love for the Egyptian princess Amenartas. Failing to win his love, Ayesha had killed him and had been condemned by Aphrodite to an eternal existence of longing and jealousy. Amenartas, escaping from Ayesha's

66

wrath, had borne a child whose line persisted through the centuries to end with Leo Vincey, who is as much a descendant of Kallikrates as he is a reincarnation of him.

The extraordinary background of this veiled beauty is at first revealed only in hints and large generalisations as Ayesha woos Leo Vincey as her reincarnated lover, and the story was not extended significantly until thirty-six years later when Rider Haggard indulged his passion for Ancient Egypt and for the occult by giving Ayesha a family and a local habitation in *Wisdom's Daughter*. This crowded historical panorama of war and the power of beauty describes the birth of Ayesha as the mortal daughter of noble Arabian parents but suggests in recounting her long train-ing in mysticism under an Egyptian priest and her guardianship of the Fire of Immortality in the shrine at Kôr that she is to be regarded in part as a spiritual being. The first, brief account of her long love for Kallikrates which Ayesha gives to Leo Vincey and his guardian in *She* is expanded in *Wisdom's Daughter* to emphas-ise this spirituality and to excuse her sin as being due to the inexorable power of love. When Kallikrates and Amenartas, in their life of exile, seek refuge in Kôr and are confronted with Ayesha, he argues his case:

> 'I love Amenartas with my body and am bound to her, but it is not so with my spirit. Our souls, I think, are far apart. Oh! hear me witness that my heart is set on higher things; it would sail into far seas unvisited of man, but always there is this anchor of the flesh chaining it to its native shore.'[6]

In an agony of choice between human and ideal love Kallikrates tries to kill himself: he refuses to enter the fire in which Ayesha has already achieved immortality and the force of her spiritual power kills him.

It seems clear that Rider Haggard intended Ayesha in part to embody a moral distinction between physical and ideal love. Leo Vincey is forced by the events of *She* towards the same decision as the one which destroyed his counterpart Kallikrates. While he and Holly are exploring the caves and valleys of Ayesha's African kingdom, Leo loves and is loved by Ustane, whose human warmth and generosity provide a contrast to the exalted claims and petulant jealousies of Ayesha. Using her temporal power to have her rival killed, Ayesha easily overcomes Leo's horror by the unconquerable combination of physical beauty and mental dominance. Holly, watching as his ward is seduced, comments:

> I looked up again, and now her perfect form lay in his arms, and her lips were pressed against his own; and thus, with the corpse of his

dead love for an altar, did Leo Vincey plight his troth to her red-handed murderess – plight it for ever and a day. For those who sell themselves into a like dominion, paying down the price of their own honour, and throwing their soul into the balance to sink the scale to the level of their lusts, must win deliverance hardly. As they have sown, so must they reap and reap, even when the poppy flowers of passion have withered in their hands, and their harvest is but bitter tares, garnered in satiety.[7]

Punishment for sin comes quickly. Revealing her inmost secret, Ayesha leads Leo and Holly by a perilous mountain route to a cavern where the Fire of Immortality appears intermittently. In what seems a somewhat specious argument, she urges Leo to bathe with her in the fire so that their mortal sins may be purged: but although the fire at first seems to do her no harm as she shows him the way into it, the self-seeking nature of her love becomes evident as her ageless beauty is destroyed:

Smaller she grew, and smaller yet, till she was no larger than a monkey. Now the skin had puckered into a million wrinkles, and on her shapeless face was the stamp of unutterable age. I never saw anything like it; nobody ever saw anything to equal the infinite age which was graven on that fearful countenance, no bigger now than that of a two months old child, though the skull retained its same size; and let all men pray they never shall, if they wish to keep their reason.[8]

Rider Haggard's mouthpiece through this turgid mixture of heightened passion and exalted mysticism is a middle-aged but still susceptible university professor swayed by Ayesha's beauty but still detached enough to observe her effect on Leo (who is, it must be confessed, a bone-headed and highly conventional aristocrat-hero) and her wilful inconsistencies of mood and intention. There would of course have been no story if the author had not given Ayesha enough of human frailty and caprice to bring about certain changes in the circumstances of her rule over the cannibalistic Amahaggar and her relations with Leo Vincey. Yet Rider Haggard seems to have been dissatisfied with his presentation of the character (and naturally he must have been influenced, as a professional novelist, by the enormous popularity and sales of *She*) and he did not resist the temptation to give his readers a further insight into her. In an Author's Note to the second book about this strange being, *Ayesha*, he wrote:

Not with a view to conciliating those readers who on principle object to sequels, but as a matter of fact, the Author wishes to say that he does not so regard this book.

Rather does he venture to ask that it should be considered as the conclusion of an imaginative tragedy (if he may so call it) whereof one half has been already published.[9]

The unearthly, mysterious aspect of beauty is emphasised at the end of a book which is in many ways a repetition of its predecessor. *Ayesha* reintroduces the central figure reborn from the apparent death at the end of *She* and now the sole survivor of the cult of Isis, living in a volcanic mountain fortress, this time in Tibet, and with some difficulty holding her power against a wild tribe in the valley, partly consisting of survivors from Alexander's army, under the control of Queen Atene, who proves to be a reincarnation of the Egyptian princess, Amenartas, beloved of Kallikrates.

To this hidden land come Leo Vincey and Holly after twenty years of wandering in search of the goddess woman and here the pair of them are involved with the rebellion of Atene and her husband against the secret ruler Ayesha, now called Hes (or Isis). Victorious in war, and victorious also against the wiles of amorous Atene, Leo is taken to the ruler, who reveals herself to him as Ayesha and challenges him to view her in her hideous age. In a fairy-tale scene he kisses her and she becomes beautiful, but after their betrothal she confesses her past sins and the weakness of her nature, imploring Leo to love her only in a spiritual sense. His reply is immediate and definite:

'But, Ayesha, I am no god; I am a man, and as a man I seek the woman whom I love. Oh divest thyself of all these trappings of thy power – that power which strews thy path with dead and keeps me apart from thee. If only for one short night, forget the ambition that gnaws unceasingly at thy soul – I say forget thy greatness and be a woman and – my wife.'[10]

Tempted by his ardour, Ayesha warns him of the danger if she does as he desires. When she kisses him as a woman, he dies: she casts herself into the Fire, taking his body with her: and Holly seems to see her alive and radiant, a woman whose sins have been compounded.

Nothing could be less conclusive than this sensational ending to a turgid and inflated romance, nor does Rider Haggard's elaborate initial paraphernalia of the letter and package coming to the author from Holly after the old man's death convince one any more successfully of the 'tragedy' of the lovers than does the equally elaborate account of the 'letter and two packets' containing Leo Vincey's family history and Holly's account of the events of *She* which, we are asked to believe, reached the author a few years after he had first seen Holly and the golden-haired hero Leo Vincey in a Cambridge street.

There was perhaps a better chance of enlisting the reader's belief in Ayesha in involving her with that most believable hero, Allan Quatermain. *She and Allan* has, so far as the plot goes, the look of an afterthought, with a patchwork plot full of echoes of Quatermain's other adventures and placing Ayesha in the same kind of danger from rebellion and rivalry which made up the story lines of *She* and *Ayesha*. But whether Rider Haggard wanted to move his mysterious veiled woman somewhat further from the realm of allegory near which she certainly appeared to reside in *She* and *Ayesha*, or whether he was merely exercising the husbandry of a writer who had created in Quatermain a remarkably useful narrator and wanted to make the fullest use of him, the fact remains that the 'She' of *She and Allan* is more shrewdly realised as a woman than in the two preceding books, even if her self-centred mysticism is still as grandiose and woolly as it was.

The link between Allan and the beautiful Ayesha is not altogether satisfying. The intervention of the unsavoury witch-doctor Zikali, who appears to be in mental communication with Ayesha as she rules in Kôr, in a way diminishes her immortal, all-powerful aspect, yet it is easy to believe that Allan, always tormented by memories of his two beloved wives, Marie and Stella, should be persuaded by Zikali to visit Ayesha and win through her power a glimpse of the lost ones. It must be admitted, too, that sceptical Allan, who resists Ayesha's sexual dominance except in one brief moment, gives us a far less exalted and unreal portrait of her and a more active, interesting view of her circumstances than the sententious scholar Holly did. The cover picture of a paperback edition of *She and Allan* published for popular consumption in 1960 implied that this was a 'romantic' novel, but the orthodox young, handsome 'hero' depicted there bears little relation to the 'insignificant and withered hunter' whose presence, helped by that of the warrior Umslopagaas, coolly acceptant of mystery, pulls this tale of Ayesha round into the robust atmosphere of Rider Haggard's most typical African adventures.

All four books about Ayesha, defined by courtesy and by their subject-matter as adventure stories, contain in fact relatively little action. Although in each one Ayesha is engaged in military as well as emotional conflicts, the sequence of events is suspended on endless dialogue as Ayesha defines or defends her amorphous philosophy. In *She and Allan* a substantial subplot concerning the kidnapping of half-Portuguese Inez Robertson by the Amahaggar and her rescue by Allan and Umslopagaas, and the tremendous duel between the Zulu warrior and Ayesha's gigantic adversary Reza, lightens the inflated, intense musings of the goddess-woman. Moreover, Allan offers a description of her which seems more explicit than any offered through another mouthpiece. When he is first led into her presence she is veiled 'but with her draperies so arranged that they emphasised rather than concealed the wonderful elegance of her tall form' and 'two plaits of glossy, raven hair', each ending in a 'single large pearl', appear beneath her veil. The feminine beauty so parsimoniously revealed is, almost always, taken calmly by the sardonic, fatalistic hunter but he does see beyond the woman:

> Mystery seemed to flow from her; it clothed her like the veil she wore, which of course heightened the effect. Beauty flowed from her also; although it was shrouded I knew that it was there, no veil or coverings could obscure it – at least, to my imagination. Moreover she breathed out power also; one felt it in the air as one feels a thunderstorm before it breaks, and it seemed to me that this power was not quite human, that it drew its strength from afar and dwelt a stranger to the earth.[11]

Rider Haggard offered this strange combination of a Gibson Girl and an embodiment of ancient divinity as the nucleus of adventure stories in his characteristic mixture of vigorous narrative and personal philosophy but his portrait of a distant ideal, strongly affected by his own reticences and sublimations and those of his time, is hard to take seriously today.

The fact that the adventure story has always been very largely the province of male writers does not necessarily mean that the female characters in such fictions will be less 'real' than the heroes or villains. Convention dictated, however (and still does to some extent), that dangerous physical action is the part of heroes, not of heroines. In the kind of fiction under consideration here, the quest draws on the traditions of chivalry, traditions which are romantic in the sense that reality is softened, that a heightened emotional response to a *distant* ideal is interposed between the hero's initial motive for action and his expectation of reward. This is very clear in Masefield's analysis of one such romantic hero, the almost impossibly self-denying Captain Margaret, who has vowed his life to the service of a woman long loved and now married to a villain:

> It was a great nature, checked by some hunger of the soul, which (this is the source of all beautiful desire) would perhaps have destroyed the soul, had it been satisfied.[12]

As Rider Haggard's novels about Ayesha presented her in part as a symbol of the ideal woman, so Masefield showed Olivia Stukeley in this light, as Charles Margaret saw her:

> He felt that human beings were all manifestations of a divine purpose. Perhaps that lovely woman was an idea, an idea of refinement, of delicate, exquisite, right grace, clothed in fitting flesh, walking the world with heavenly intention.[13]

The captain's love remains on this exalted plane throughout scenes of action in which idealism is not always satisfactorily integrated. Set in the late seventeenth century, this story of a three-cornered relationship depends on active events vigorously described but ill supported by very generalised characters. Captain Margaret is the owner of the privateer *The Broken Heart* with which he intends to open up trade in the Spanish Main with the Indians whom he hopes to rescue from the harsh exploitation of Spanish settlers. His love for Olivia obliges him to take her, with her husband, as passengers to Virginia, where Stukeley hopes to escape from debts and the legal action of certain victims of his villainy.

The idealised concept of Olivia requires that she must be impossibly innocent. Where Charles Margaret is moved by the chivalric ideal of honour towards women, Olivia's sense of honour requires of her a complete loyalty to, and trust in, her husband. The only way Masefield can make this credible is to present her as a kind of child-bride, a happy innocent; necessary as this may be to both the theme and the plot of the book, it does not allow her to develop beyond the limits of a type-character. This is very evident when we compare the actual words Masefield uses when he describes the moment when Olivia is forced to accept the warnings of the Governor of Jamestown about her husband's past and to face the destruction of her romantic view of their marriage. The words in fact are intended to reflect her night-time, miserable feelings but they only reflect Masefield's failure to render her as a human being:

> All her nerves shook with it, as though the blow struck her in her face. He had sworn at her, jeered at her, called her a lump of cold batter, told her to get to the devil, told her that he was sick of the sight of her, that he had married her for her money, that if she gave him any more of her canting preaching he'd hit her one that she'd remember. Later in the night, as she lay crying at his side, he bade her for God's sake to stop snivelling, so that he might get to sleep. As she could not stop, he had arisen, telling her that she might cry

herself sick, but that he was going to Mrs Inigo, a woman who wasn't quite such a cold poultice. She had not stopped him. She could not stop him. He had gone from her, leaving her life too empty for her to wish even to kill herself.[14]

The character of Olivia carries no more conviction when after dangerous conflicts and escapes on the Spanish Main and after Stukeley's treacherous dealings with the Spanish government on the Isthmus of Darien and his death from yellow fever, she falls into Charles Margaret's arms. The happy ending seems as much a contradiction of the melancholy, idealistic tone of the book as the ending of Conrad and Ford's *Romance* did. *Captain Margaret* is about ideals, about aspects of love described in terms of three very generalised figures (for even Stukeley, vigorous though his idiom and behaviour may be, is not a 'real' villain in the sense of that tongue-in-cheek villain, Abner Brown, in the fantasies *The Midnight Folk* and *The Box of Delights*). Like *Multitude and Solitude*, it is an early exploration of the quest-adventure, man's search for beauty as an ideal in human form, which Masefield was to bring to fruition in two later novels, *Sard Harker* and *Odtaa*.

As a setting for these adventures Masefield invented the 'Sugar States', somewhere in Central America (a place used again in his fantasy-adventure for children, *The Midnight Folk*, as well as in a sea-adventure, *The Taking of the Gry*). Here two men, a ship's officer and a gently born younger son sent from England to make his way in the world, are involved in certain events which are, as it were, by-products of civil war. In the province of Santa Barbara, in 1887, as we learn in *Odtaa* (chronologically the first book, though written and published second) a mad dictator, Don Lopez, withstands a determined but seemingly hopeless attempt by a heroic friend of the people, Don Manuel, to overthrow his tyranny. Ten years later, as *Sard Harker* relates, Don Manuel has become dictator and is establishing order and prosperity in the ten provinces of the Sugar States. Justifiably defined as romantic adventures, the two books follow their quest-plots to very different conclusions, but each is a poet's novel, with the pursuit of ideal beauty as the ultimate goal and with the chivalrous service of a man for a woman as its motive force.

The tragic heroine of *Odtaa*, as she appears to the other characters in the story, is idealised in two senses. Carlotta de Leyva belongs to one of the liberal families opposed to the dictator Lopez and as the betrothed of the leader of that opposition, Don Manuel of Encinitas, she is to some extent a figurehead, a political symbol: moreover, to the youth of eighteen, Highworth Ridden, who is introduced to her soon after his arrival in Santa Barbara, she is an ideal because she is in effect the first woman who has ever touched his love, as someone to be served, not someone to aspire to. Looking back on the bitter, dangerous adventure he undertook in her service, years later, Hi Ridden still sees her in a romantic light:

> It is difficult to set down what she was to me. 'Calf-love', I suppose most people would say. Well, there is a generosity in calf-love that gives it a grace: not that mine had any grace. I saw her on only one day twenty-two years ago: I have thought of her every day since; not as a lover of course (for years past) but as a spirit apart, unlike anyone else that ever was . . . She was the most exquisite thing: in life marvellous, in the unspeakable end, heroic: and always so beautiful, so gracious. All who knew her felt this: she had cruel enemies, the mad, the diseased, the godless, the savage and the greedy hated her.[15]

The active, courageous aspect of Carlotta and her lover Don Manuel is suggested now and again in the echoes of the conflict heard by the reader before they are heard by Hi Ridden. Passionately anxious to serve Carlotta, he undertakes to take a message from her to Don Manuel, at a time when he and his followers are seriously threatened by the dictator. Hi's desperate overland journey is interrupted by weather, by bandits, by the hazards of terrain: finally captured by Lopez's Reds, he learns that even while he was pressing forward with his message, Carlotta had been seized by Lopez and, after refusing to pray to him as the God he declares himself to be, had been brutally slaughtered by the public hangman.

This intensely concentrated yet spacious journey-tale gives an impression of urgency by Masefield's typical 'and-then' pattern and the energetic sequence of dangers and escapes which comply with the title (Odtaa is 'One damned thing after another') – not as flippant a title as it might sound but an example of Masefield's virtuosity in the way he can mix humour, tension and deep emotion without self-consciousness. The tragic ending of Hi's chivalrous mission is proper to the emotional tone of the book: his feelings, his anxiety and longing, his anger and impatience, his hope and fear, run along with the concrete, forceful adventure-plot and give it purpose. As well, Hi's reflections on Carlotta establish her as a real woman as well as an ideal of love and beauty. Hardly operating as a character in the story, Carlotta is always vividly present in it.

The tensions of *Sard Harker* lead ultimately to the uniting of lover and beloved rather than to tragedy; the prevailing note is not foreboding but a painful and frustrating postponement, again by the hazards of an overland journey. Romance, in this book, is a very different matter from the heightened, chivalric tone of *Captain Margaret*. Masefield's choice of his central characters, at least in his later novels, was always a little unexpected, and there is a particular piquancy in the seemingly inappropriate nature, as a romantic hero, of Chisholm Harker, nicknamed Sard 'because he was judged to be sardonic' and defined as a proud, reticent, austere man. But we are soon warned that the young officer in the *Venturer* hides in his memory the image of a girl met years before, so that his response to a strange night-vision seems entirely logical. On his first sea-voyage, as the ship lay in the harbour of Las Palomas on its way to Santa Barbara, he had woken to the sound of words in his ear perhaps inspired by the strange familiarity of the house of Los Xicales, glimpsed from the ship, perhaps indeed a prophecy that he would meet the girl of his memory in that very house.

The interaction of chance and personal agency is of great importance in Masefield's adventure novels: dogged by ill fortune, by evil coincidence, by accident, his heroes face the odds in a way that is both practical and ideal. Sard Harker cherishes the vision of the flower-encompassed house for ten years before, in 1897, he revisits it, to find it empty and shut up, and resolves to forget the distant figure of the girl he has always hoped to find. His resolve ends when again he wakes at dawn with prophetic words in his ears. The ship is due to sail that day: on shore with the captain at a prize-fight, he overhears a plot to kidnap a certain American lady visiting Los Xicales with her brother, and rides out on a bicycle to warn them but also expecting that this will be the moment foretold for that second meeting. A feeling of mystery irradiates the scene at the house which he has so far only glimpsed from a distance:

> A woman stood at the door of the French window, half in the verandah. He could not see her face, since it was turned from him, but there was something about her that made his heart stand still. She spoke as he closed the door:
> 'I will water the xicales, Hilary,' she said, 'and come back when you are alone.' Her voice rang in his brain like a memory: she closed the glass door behind her, and passed by the verandah steps into the garden out of sight.[16]

He does not see her face: it seems that she is not the Juanita he has kept in his mind: yet he is haunted by an inexplicable likeness and is perturbed by the young American's cool reception of his warning. The dangerous journey in store for Sard is not in fact in

75

pursuit of the ideal woman, but a prosaic attempt to get back to his ship before it sails, an attempt frustrated by the theft of his bicycle and by wanderings that involve him with a silver-train and a period in gaol, the traverse of an appalling desert and a rock-strewn mountain. The immediate physical obstacles in the way and the suppressed anxiety about the threat of kidnap merge in the implied soliloquy which does half the work of describing the journey, intensifying the sense of danger and of nightmare slowness.

Masefield's continuous narrative method depends on internal changes of pace, on stresses in the placing of words and phrases. In *Sard Harker* there is a complete change of tempo when Sard, finally reaching Santa Barbara, is told that Miss Kingsborough has already been found. Before he discovers that this is a lie put out by her enemy, he has various practical duties to perform in connection with the wreck of the ship he should have joined. The result is that the final confrontation with the evil Sangrado, the melodramatic scene of occult horror from which Margarita is rescued and the revelation of her true identity, take on a particular sharpness of surprise, a tone of active, romantic effort quite different from the tensions of Sard's wanderings. Yet it is a logical ending, a romantic ending, if you will, but one drawn into reality because of the almost casual, incidental humour, the personal tone of dialogue and the secret, passionate, poetic feeling that moves Sard all through his adventure.

Masefield's unique narrative style is at its most sustained in these two novels. The brilliant clarity of his prose, the steady forward pace, bring the reader close to the actions and moods of the travellers. It is as if the writer were drawing, in words, one of those pictorial maps where each point of approach is represented by a picture, each landscape captured on the page in one carefully selected view described in a concrete, unfussy, immediate way. No description is inorganic. Each time action is halted for the sake of a picture, it is a picture coloured by the mood of the viewer and confirmed by concrete detail. The romance of ardent feeling and eager endeavour never becomes cloying or sentimental because it is sustained by, included in, that movement in space and time which we can call the action of a story. Masefield held a balance of action and emotion in his adventure stories which has never been equalled.

I have called *Odtaa* and *Sard Harker* poet's novels. Almost always considered secondary to his poetry, Masefield's fiction has the same basic theme, man's search for beauty – in nature, in ideas and, often, in the ideal of womanhood. The physical beauty of Carlotta de Leyva and Margarita Kingsborough is important in the novels, not as a snare in the way that Rider Haggard sometimes seems to imply that Ayesha's beauty was, but as an embodiment, an example of the ideal. The chivalrous impulses of Hi Ridden and Sard Harker are natural and human as well as idealistic: if they had not been, the novels would have lost much of their vigour and point.

Many novels of adventure have been based on the chivalric theme of service to women. This theme reflects the concept of chivalry deriving in the mid- and late nineteenth century in part from the Gothic revival and defined in the seminal work of Kenelm Henry Digby, *The Broad Stone of Honour*, published in 1822 and 1823 with the significant title 'Rules for the Gentlemen of England'. The concept of honour as it appears in the adventure stories of the late nineteenth century was at least partly an artificial code belonging to the ruling or leisure classes, requiring a dedicated loyalty towards women, family honour and masculine comradeship which owed little to common sense or practicality. It was essentially a masculine code, and those who often find it unacceptable in fiction may find some support in the comment of the Duchess of Omnium, regarding her noble husband's often inconvenient scruples, that 'Men shouldn't be made of Sèvres china, but of good stone earthenware'.[17]

Certainly the theme of honour in an adventure story has to be accepted in an historical context and if possible with a determined suspension of disbelief. How many of the popular novels of the past evoke derision rather than appreciation if we read them in too literal a spirit! We have to think ourselves back into a social system and culture very different from our own if we are to respond, in the way P. C. Wren required, to the improbable events and exalted sentiments of the three Geste brothers who, to serve their adored aunt and their fraternal obligations, vanished into the Foreign Legion, taking upon themselves the imputation of having stolen the blue diamond which she had long ago sold and replaced by a fake for the sake of her extravagant husband. How cruel, to present-day ears, sounds her final comment on the misguided heroism of the brothers – 'a beau geste indeed'. The self-imposed exile of the handsome *flâneur*, the Honourable Bertie Cecil, hero of Ouida's *Under Two Flags*, and his secret, heroic service with the French against the Arabs in North Africa, depends in the same way on the reader's acceptance of social and military codes of honour strained to the limit to provide a sensational story.

Fiction reflects the changes in the concept of honour, personal or institutional, sorting out the basic scruples of conscience and the natural feelings of compassion and devotion which must be newly defined for each and every period in time. Paul Girouard in *The Return to Camelot* pointed out that the chivalric code of conduct 'never recovered from the Great War partly because the War itself was such a shattering of illusions, partly because it helped to produce a world in which the necessary conditions for chivalry were increasingly absent' and that the absence of so many men at the Front 'had put women in a position of responsibility which made many of them distrust chivalry as a form of concealed slavery'.[18] It is still possible to adapt oneself to the atmosphere of the romantic, chivalric adventure provided we can be genuinely captured by the characters. This may mean ignoring the frequent assertion by critics that in adventure stories character must be subordinate to action. By this dogma, Conrad's novels should be regarded as outside the conventions of the adventure genre because of the dominance of self-analysis in them. Lord David Cecil wrote of Conrad:

> His ideal hero was a knightly hero who besides being brave and loyal was dignified, chivalrous, compassionate and vowed to the service of a rigid standard of personal conduct, the slightest violation of which is an unappeasable torment to his conscience. It is a stain on his inner ideal of himself, his honour; and the conception of personal honour is the centre of Conrad's moral system. The man who preserves it is saved, the man who loses it is damned.[19]

Personal honour will affect us in so far as we can believe in the man or woman who defends or loses it. The Geste brothers are stereotypes and may be laughed at with impunity: but Charles Wogan, as A. E. W. Mason saw him in *Clementina*, and the ingenuous John Ridd, self-revealing narrator of *Lorna Doone*, exemplify the intricacies of love and honour in a way that transcends period and social niceties.

The particular combination of dignity and personal pride which governs John Ridd's behaviour through his many years of devoted service to Lorna Doone is carefully related to the social attitudes of rural Somerset at the time of the Restoration. Indeed, the romantic flavour of the story depends in part on the tantalising yet inevitable growth of love between the yeoman farmer, proud of his physical strength and family background yet accepting his place in society below the squirearchy, and the girl, supposedly one of the Doones, aristocrats in exile after the Civil

War, but in fact the kidnapped daughter of noble Scottish parents. John Ridd's sense of honour is practical as well as idealistic and his motives are relevant outside their historical context. Besides, his robust narrative voice carries with it a quiet irony as the reader sees more than he realises of this attractively vigorous and unaffected hero. It may be as much for the homely, recognisable nature of this particular hero as for the energy and drama of the story that *Lorna Doone* has remained a classic for more than a century, and a classic adopted by the young for their own reading.

It is mainly to adult adventure stories that they must look for the romantic and chivalric manifestations of love towards which they reach in adolescence; such feelings are by convention regarded as unseemly and unsuitable in books written specifically for the young. Isabelle Jan surmised that the lack of 'the essential emotional outlet of erotic passion'[20] in children's literature led to 'more or less disguised and distorted substitutes for adult love' but goes on to point out that passionate feeling can be, and is, expressed strongly in family relationships. Such relationships belong to problem novels, rather than to novels of action, to fiction where a place is not the scene in which action develops but a certain spot where characters place themselves in order to talk. Dialogue or soliloquy come first: action is confined to minor stage directions concerning gesture or the kind of movements called, by biologists, displacement activity.

When young people play central parts in adventure stories, their motives and actions are as a rule suitably moderated nor are they expected to concern themselves with elaborate points of honour. Yet this is an area where the emotional strength of junior adventures, so often timid and inadequate, could be deepened if the concept of honour in its universal sense were to be recognised. A remarkable film of 1955, *Rebel without a Cause*, claimed as 'new realism' when it was first screened, showed delinquent boys and girls in the mid-teens proving their worth in 'chicken' contests whose violence, distorted as it is by social pressures, does express a genuine personal pride: the dares and challenges of the groups of Hell's Angels today, leading to criminal actions, have a distant debased origin in the concept of honour. The remarkable novels of S. E. Hinton – for instance, *The Outsiders* and *That Was Then, This Is Now* – describe the operation of honour as it exists within American city gangs with a passionate conviction one looks for in vain in many similar contemporary adventure fictions. The concept of honour, artificial as it can often seem, can be an abiding emotional force in fiction, but only when it is demonstrated fully and specifically through believable characters as well as believable action. To take a particular example, loyalty to a cause and to an individual is demonstrated with great variety in a body of fiction which has come to be known generically as Ruritanian romance.

4. Ruritania

The barrister Anthony Hope Hawkins was walking back from Westminster Crown Court to the Temple on 28 November 1893, having won his case, when the idea of Ruritania came into his head:

> Arrived at my chambers, I reviewed it over a pipe and the next day I wrote the first chapter. Though sometimes interrupted by law work, I sat tight at the story, sometimes writing as much as two chapters a day. I was only once seriously 'stuck up'; I seemed to have got 'The Prisoner' so tightly shut up in 'Zenda' that it was impossible to get him out of it. But that difficulty was in the end surmounted and, on the whole, the writing was easy and pleasurable.[1]

A light touch, no excessive ambition but an evident enthusiasm, produced a masterpiece. With *The Prisoner of Zenda* and its sequel, *Rupert of Hentzau* (and with the less well-known novels, *The Heart of Princess Osra* and *Sophy of Kravonia*) Anthony Hope created a subspecies of the adventure story and a useful literary adjective. Taking the ingredients of the cloak-and-dagger historical novel current in his time, he gave his imaginary country certain recognisable Central European characteristics but only one or two passing references to Vienna and Dresden gave it anything like a real location. Ruritania and its dynastic problems remain separate from the complexities of Europe at the end of the nineteenth century. Dorothy Sayers, discussing the literary tastes of one of her characters, the Russian exile Paul Alexis, said of the Ruritanian type of story that 'the greater European powers of the League of Nations had nothing to do with the matter':

> The rise and fall of governments appeared to be a private arrangement, comfortably thrashed out among a selection of small Balkan states, vaguely situated, acknowledging no relationships outside the domestic circle. No literature could have been better suited for the release of the subconscious.[2]

Anthony Hope's detachment meant that his story could be free from contemporary political overtones: if he was expressing any apprehensions about the state of Europe, they were not visible in his books as they are in Erskine Childers's thriller, *The Riddle of the Sands*, or in Buchan's 'Ruritanian' novels. To the conventions

81

of the romantic historical novel, then, Anthony Hope added the colour of society in his day and the pattern of love and courtship which appear, in a far less interesting way, in his novels of his own London society, and he drew in a more general way from the Victorian version of medieval chivalry, with its idealisation of woman and its desire for service to an ideal. As Paul Girouard puts it:

> Anthony Hope's inspired invention of Ruritania allowed him to move his English hero straight from modern clubland into a world of castles, kings, beautiful women, and feudal loyalties.[3]

The invention of Ruritania led to many descendants, all declaring their ancestry in the 'a' suffix, from Buchan's Evallonia and George Birmingham's Lystra to countries invented for young readers like Frances Hodgson Burnett's Samavia, Noel Streatfeild's Livia, Serraillier's Silvania, Adrian Alington's Rumelia and Harriet Graham's Zoraya. The likenesses and differences within this unique group of adventure stories are illuminating from the point of view of both social and literary change.

Anthony Hope would hardly have supported any grandiose claims for his tales of Ruritania. He himself said that the root idea of *The Prisoner of Zenda* was 'the old and wide-spread theme of "mistaken identity" as a starting-point for the writer's development of "characters, emotions and incidents and his exploration of dramatic possibilities".'[4] Modestly he suggested:

> I think that the two variants which struck the popular fancy in my little book were royalty and red hair – the former is always a safe card to play, and its combination with the latter had a touch of novelty. . . .[4]

and he could be pleasantly practical about the craft into which he channelled his surplus energies. The writer, he said:

> . . . reminds me – more than anyone else – of a village cobbler sitting alone in his little shop, cross-legged and considerably absorbed in patching an old shoe to make it fit for more service.[5]

The Prisoner of Zenda and its sequel certainly bear witness to their author's craftsmanship. His skill in exploiting the idea of mistaken identity ensures that there is no slackening of interest in two novels which are in fact extremely simple in structure, combining lateral movement (on foot, on horseback and, rarely, by train) from the city of Strelsau to the castle and hunting lodge of Zenda and back again and with dialogue through which the motives of these movements are explored and explained. Both plot and character depend for their effect on the theme of honour which underpins the two books. Without this theme, the novels might not have survived, let alone become minor classics; but without characters properly created to promote the theme, there would have been no organic life in the books either.

The starting-point, then, is the idea of identical men of very different environments and the hereditary reasons why English Rudolf Rassendyll so strikingly resembles Rudolf, King of Ruritania. As the narrator of *The Prisoner of Zenda*, Rassendyll is at first inclined to be deprecating about the relationships between 'the palace at Strelsau or the castle of Zenda and Number 305 Park Lane, W.'[6] He is well aware that his brother, Lord Burlesdon, prefers to forget the misbehaviour, in 1733, of Rudolf the Third of Ruritania and the Countess Amelia, wife of the fifth Earl of Burlesdon and twenty-second Baron Rassendyll, which resulted in the transmission of certain characteristics ('long, sharp, straight noses and a quantity of dark red hair'[7] as well as blue eyes rather than the dark hue more common to the Rassendylls) in several generations of the family.

It was to satisfy a roving disposition and an idle curiosity rather than any deep ideal that Rudolf Rassendyll, man-about-town, decided on impulse while travelling in France to visit Strelsau for the coronation of Rudolf the Fifth. The fact that he had been given the Elphberg name of Rudolf by a Royalist father was of small importance to him, nor was he at first more than casually intrigued when he woke from a strangely prophetic dream in the forest of Zenda to hear two men discussing the remarkable resemblance between him and the King. He was respectful but unalarmed when the King appeared and after a moment's silence he chose to laugh at the likeness and the revelation that they were distant cousins; indeed, so little was Rassendyll impressed that he noted that the King's mouth lacked 'something of the firmness (or obstinacy) which was to be gathered from my close-shutting lips'.[8] This was the first of many hints by which the reader would come to understand, before Rassendyll himself, how deep and important the difference in character was by contrast with the 'striking, salient, wonderful'[8] physical likeness.

The neat, symmetrical plot turns on just this physical likeness. Invited to join the King, with his companions the Chancellor Colonel Sapt and his aide-de-camp Fritz von Tarlenheim, on the ruler's last night of freedom before he takes up the burden of the Crown, Rassendyll is conveniently available to step in when the monarch collapses, drugged by wine presented by his jealous brother Black Michael. Rassendyll accepts the plan in a spirit of adventure and with some reluctance sacrifices his beard to the need of the moment (a practical detail which helps veracity at the right time).

The impersonation so lightly undertaken proves necessary for more than one day, for the King becomes the 'Prisoner' of his ruthless brother. It is renewed (in the sequel, *Rupert of Hentzau*) for a further period when, after an interval of some years, the machinations of Michael's nephew Rupert lead to the King's death and loyal Sapt appeals to Rassendyll once more for help. The plot of each book is built on the physical fact of impersonation: the emotional content depends on character, as the Englishman in effect proves himself worthy to be a king in more than mere appearance.

This does not imply that Rassendyll is developed as a character in the round. His role is to exemplify the theme of the two novels, the conflict between love and honour. Introduced initially as an agreeable aristocrat, he faces his first real challenge when he falls in love with the King's cousin and destined bride, the Princess Flavia, with chivalric self-denial. When circumstances have revealed his true identity to Flavia, and she has reaffirmed, with some maidenly shame, her own love for him, he accepts exile from her in terms which are general and romantic rather than individual:

> '. . . your ring shall be on my finger and your heart in mine, and no touch save of your lips will ever be on mine. So, may God comfort you, my darling.'. . .[9]

and he renounces all but one annual link with her, at which time he meets von Tarlenheim in Dresden and receives from him:

> . . . a little box; in it a red rose, and round the stalk of the rose is a slip of paper with the words written: 'Rudolf – Flavia – always' and the like I send back by him. That message, and the wearing of the rings, are all that now bind me and the Queen of Ruritania.[10]

Three years later, after a letter unwisely sent by Flavia has fallen into the hands of the bitterly ambitious Rupert of Hentzau, Rassendyll has a harsher temptation to withstand. The King's death must be concealed if the throne is to be secured for Queen Flavia. He could fall in with the desire of Sapt, marry her secretly and fill the empty place in the Elphberg dynasty. The struggle with his conscience comes to the reader at second-hand as the narrator, von Tarlenheim, watches him pacing in the garden and guesses at his thoughts. This puts any deep analysis out of the question and Rassendyll can remain the conventional, generalised *preux chevalier* which the story demands, dying with his honour intact but with his love unachieved. His courage and nobility are innate rather than acquired through circumstances; he is no commoner swept into lofty office but an Elphberg by inheritance. The contrast between the two men of near-identical appearance is shown in a less formal, more novelistic manner in the character of the King, depicted in *The Prisoner of Zenda* as a weak, pleasure-loving young man trying to equip himself for his destiny and in *Rupert of Hentzau* as a man ill in body, wearied by matters of state, gradually coming to resent his obligations to the man whose courage and energy have twice saved his position for him and burdened by jealous suspicions of his wife's fidelity.

Brief though von Tarlenheim's account of the King's behaviour is, it is enough to establish a genuine emotional situation and to explain the change in the Queen, from the regal figure of *The Prisoner of Zenda*, proud in the confidence that the honour of Ruritania will be safe for ever with her, to the woman weary of renunciation who, in *Rupert of Hentzau*, breaks the compact of silence with her dangerously imprudent letter. If Flavia's passion and occasional petulance in the second book diminish her from the dedicated Elphberg to a woman of lesser breed, she becomes more individual, a more positive key to the course of a story which, as compelling as *The Prisoner of Zenda* in its chases and escapes, its dark streets and darker forests, and as strongly tied by the theme of honour, is subtly more human than its predecessor. There was no room in either of the two books for more than a suggestion of the way a woman might be changed by a complicated political and personal dilemma. The subtle and interesting studies of personality in *The Heart of Princess Osra* and *Sophy of Kravonia* show what Anthony Hope could do when he decided to shape his fiction wholly round a feminine concept of honour.

If the two novels were to be recast in late post-Freudian terms it would be clear how completely our attitudes have changed towards amatory and social matters: it is difficult to read the Ruritanian stories now in the way Anthony Hope's first readers did and not to dismiss them as mere escapist romances. To read them in an historical frame of mind is to see the death of Rassendyll, by an assassin's bullet, not as a fortunate escape from prolonged misery but as the formal seal on a pact of honour. Von Tarlenheim shows the way to a proper assessment of the theme of *Rupert of Hentzau*, as of *The Prisoner of Zenda*:

> To me it seems now as though all had ended well. I must not be misunderstood. My heart is still sore for the loss of him. But we saved the Queen's fair fame, and to Rudolf himself the fatal stroke

came as a relief from a choice too difficult: on the one side lay what impaired his own honour, on the other what threatened hers. As I think on this my anger at his death is less, though my grief cannot be. To this day I know not how he chose; no, and I don't know how he should have chosen. Yet he had chosen, for his face was calm and clear.[11]

If Rassendyll escapes being a sentimental hero it is because of the spare, simple plots and the headlong speed of the narrative which carry his idealistic musings along. The importance of speed and simplicity in stories of this type and theme is evident if we compare Rassendyll's moments of decision with the amorous niceties of some of Jeffery Farnol's heroes who offered succulent romance to the readers of a later decade through elaborate problems of honour.

The unique atmosphere of Anthony Hope's Ruritania, its compound of energy and idealism, of courtly formality and personal passion, has never been precisely evoked in any of its numerous imitations. Parody can sometimes get to the heart of the matter in a way that imitation cannot, and George Birmingham's *King Tommy* is genuinely Ruritanian in its quirky way. Whether this ebullient novel of 1923 is to be considered as a parody or just as a light-hearted analogue of *The Prisoner of Zenda*, the resemblances are too close to be mere coincidence.

The cast of characters is evidence enough of the approach: a fashionable young baronet intended by his ambitious politician uncle to marry the Princess of Lystria; an exiled king running a fashionable London restaurant; two pretty dancers, one royal and one plebeian; a curate on holiday who strikingly resembles the baronet – with such components, the square dance performed through Central Europe is both neat and exciting. It allows for gentle but shrewd mockery of Ruritania, most of all when Tommy Norreys, mistaken for Lord Norheys, is actually crowned King of Lystria. The plan meets the garrulous approval of the exiled monarch Wladislas, who calls himself 'a middle-class professional man' and who is relieved to escape from the rivalry of priests and nobles and the expense of entertaining courtiers of extravagant tastes who 'love dressing up in uniforms, putting on swords and attending state balls' and whose appetites are such that 'a bullock roasted whole and a couple of pigs go no distance at a supper table in Lystria'.[12]

The gentle mockery of Ruritanian dignity continues in the account of Tommy's reception at the palace by the Patriarch and his entourage:

The other two held aloft a kind of canopy made of embroidered silk, not unlike a huge two-handled umbrella. If they had held it, as they should, over the Patriarch's head, it might have kept the dew from settling on his mitre. Held crooked, a little behind him, it served no useful purpose. But it was highly striking and ornamental. . . .[13]

and in the entertaining glimpse of the new King:

Tommy had been fitted out by Count Albert Casimir in a very handsome crimson silk suit with a jacket laced hussar fashion, with gold. I noticed that he wore one of his own clerical collars round his neck. Perhaps this was his idea of full dress for a ceremonial occasion. Perhaps he did it to please the Patriarch.[14]

The phrase 'fitted out' neatly underlines the attitude of the narrator, the curate's Uncle Bill (whose voice is, of course, the author's). The verbal pinpricks are shrewdly administered in a story indulgent to the conscious flippancy of the early 1920s; from our own angle of vision it seems as though one socially artificial and isolated world is being used to comment on an earlier, equally artificial and isolated one.

The courtly side of Ruritania which George Birmingham happily played with gave another writer in the 1920s, Dornford Yates, a way to embellish thrillers which were basically unoriginal. In his 'Chandos' novels he created a kind of private Ruritania in sundry duchies and noble estates within the borders of Austria, combining a high idealistic approach to women and active physical courage in a setting of noble families and ancient domains which offer in some ways a post-war version of Anthony Hope's novels, though his plots concerned private theft and murder rather than matters of state. However convenient the conflict of love and honour may have been to Anthony Hope as the motive force of his books, he treated it seriously within their emotional climate. Dornford Yates expressed his idea of honour in a tone of heightened sentiment and suggested sexuality, an obverse perhaps of the permissiveness of that post-war society. He seems to have found it more difficult to extrapolate remote, romantic adventures from the complex, changing world of the 1920s and after than Anthony Hope found it to transport a late-Victorian man-about-town to a small Central European kingdom. At any rate Dornford Yates's highly artificial, mannered prose style, which may have spelled 'romance' to his first readers, moves his books further from us today than Anthony Hope's active style and his very moderate use of courtly language.

The prose of Dornford Yates, intended to evoke the codes and idiom of chivalry, has been described as 'Lincoln's Inn prose laced with Jacobethan'.[15] His characters never wash their hands but 'lave' them; his robust heroes are 'gentle' and 'debonair'; feet are 'shod', fields are 'meadows' and pigs always 'swine', while tags from the Bible and Shakespeare encrust the tales further. Such mannerisms muffle the cleaner, more direct prose that carries splendidly compelling descriptions – static, of dungeons, thickets, wells and tunnels or active, of fist- and gunfights, sieges or car chases.

His proper names show the same self-conscious striving for a romantic atmosphere. Within Carinthia (itself a province sufficiently remote from the Austria known to the 1920s to seem Ruritanian) lie the castles of Littain, Hohenem, Varvic, Midian, Reichtenberg and Gath; the noble heroines make their champions free of such Christian names as Leonie, Olivia and Marya; pseudonymous villains like Barabbas, 'Rose' Noble, Pluto and Orion Forecast cast their shadows forward to the works of Ian Fleming and the only truly villainous female glares at her enemies as 'Vanity Fayre'.

All this is top-dressing. There is no genuinely heroic tone in the books. In *Blind Corner* Dornford Yates condemned his characters to days of digging for the Wagenburg treasure in a well so deep and cold that Richard Chandos comments on the absurd situation in which he and his comrades, who have bought the castle under the noses of their villainous rivals, live in constant dread of discovery, while their enemies, in possession above, come and go as they please. A reader has pencilled the following comment in a library copy of the work:

> But in that case, why could they not have called in the authorities and have the other fellows cleared out? – only this would have made but a tame end to the story.

A timely point and one which could be made into a test of this kind of narrative by which an author may be seen to have succeeded or failed to create the necessary suspension of disbelief. It is the emotional and dynamic tug of a story which must prevent us from reading in too literal a spirit.

Chivalry is a dominant thread in the Chandos thrillers rather than a serious theme. This is partly to say that Richard Chandos and his frequent companion-in-arms, George Hanbury, are commonplace adventurers compared with Rudolf Rassendyll, in spite of the resonance of Chandos's name. More important, the code of honour is hardly consistent. The claim of the 'good' characters to the Wagenburg treasure is no better justified than that of the rival party under Ellis, even if his murder of a secret service man does inspire Jonathan Mansel, who makes a third with Chandos and Hanbury, and who heard the dying man's last words, to engage upon the adventure:

> Whether the lust for gold had mastered us, whether a hatred of the thieves suffused our outlook, whether their attempts to thwart it had not toughened our resolve I cannot say: but I know that after the bomb had been thrown into our midst, we would, one and all, have died in agony rather than let the treasure fall into the enemy's hands.[16]

The buccaneer impulse revealed in these artless words accounts for the vigorous campaigns against other villains in other castles, though the immediate object is almost always the traditional one of help for a distressed damsel.

Ruritanian romance, like any other kind of adventure story, has the prime duty of making the artificial seem real, of establishing validity for a studied, carefully composed sequence of events. It is perhaps in part a matter of date which makes Dornford Yates's novels seem high-flown and absurd to us where we can accommodate ourselves to the formalities of Anthony Hope's Ruritania. The society in which Dornford Yates's chivalrous heroes ride out in their Rolls-Royces to combat evil is too near to our own to be viewed historically. The beautiful, high-born maidens who wait to be rescued, or who in chaste comradeship help in their own rescue, are too readily recognised as akin to the heroines of our own time. Anthony Hope wisely avoided set-piece descriptions of his noble ladies: in Dornford Yates's portraits chivalry becomes ludicrous. Idealising his tall, slender ladies, he dwells lovingly on tiny feet from which their champions remove dainty shoes. He ignores the fact that tall girls would probably have feet of commensurate size: foot fetishists would not find size-seven brogues as attractive as court slippers several sizes smaller.

On a less superficial note, the chastity which is an essential part of the chivalric code is presented in terms of sentimental sensuality disguised in a semblance of courtly love. In *Perishable Goods*, Jonah Mansel's restraint in concealing his love for Adèle, wife of Boy Pleydell, is made more difficult when the villain Rose Noble uses stolen letters to force Mansel into submission. Chandos, as narrator, describes the two who have agreed to remain loving friends with the luscious approval that 'suddenly faced with life in the midst of death, two natures so alike and so peerless should have comforted each other';[17]

they have in fact exchanged a kiss. Mansel lies wounded and apparently dying:

> Upon the great bed sat Adèle, steady-eyed as ever, but very pale. She might have been Eve, as Milton has pictured her, sitting upon the green bank, looking into the pool. Her left arm propped her, and she was sitting sideways, after the way of a child: one ring of the broken handcuff was still about her slim leg. Her hand was in Mansel's, and their two hands lay in her lap: her beautiful head was bowed, and her eyes never left the eyes of the man she loved.
>
> On her other side lay Testa [Mansel's terrier], close up against his lord. Mansel's left hand was upon him; but though, I think, he would have licked it, the poor scrap never moved, but lay as still as an image, with his chin on his little paws and his eyes upon Mansel's face.[18]

It is only too easy to isolate the hectic emotionalism and artificial situations in the Chandos novels at the expense of their considerable virtues as thrillers, ingeniously varied in scene and skilful in the use of pace and tension. Yet because Dornford Yates did to some extent invoke Ruritania in plot and mood it is fair to point to the way in which the code of chivalry has been debased and sentimentalised. This is all the more apparent when the Chandos stories are compared with three linked novels – *Huntingtower*, *Castle Gay* and *The House of the Four Winds* – in which John Buchan at the same period explored the code of honour through the fortunes of Saskia, a distressed maiden, and the dynastic troubles of the fictitious kingdom of Evallonia.

Although there is much in these three books to put them in the category of Ruritanian adventure, Scott may be a stronger influence. It is significant that Buchan gave his middle-aged hero, the Glasgow grocer Dickson McCunn, a literary ancestry: the dedication to *Huntingtower* explains that McCunn can claim descent from Baillie Nicol Jarvie in *Rob Roy* and that 'he can count kin, should he wish' with Rob Roy himself through 'the auld wife ayont the fire at Stackavrallachan',[19] while a secret fervour for the lost cause of the Stuarts helps to equip the sedentary, fifty-five-year-old grocer of the 1920s for unexpected challenges. The development of Dickson McCunn as a hero will be considered more fully later. At present his status in the three books is relevant because it serves to establish Buchan's particularly energetic version of Ruritanian adventure and the irony and humour with which he tempers the romantic colour of his fiction.

Three men of traditional type act as foils to McCunn. John Heritage, an avant-garde poet, reveals the heart of a Rassendyll when Saskia appears to call forth his chivalrous pity; her absent fiancé Alexis, toughened by circumstances as an exile in Australia, is as regal and remote a figure as the villain Paul Abreskov, impelled to crime through the bitterness of physical imperfection but magnificent as a 'lost angel'. The contrast between these three characters with their orthodox ancestry in story and the plain, middle-class grocer is a piquant one. Buchan chose to express it indirectly through the musings of the young Russian princess Saskia:

> 'I have been back among the fairy tales . . . Mr Heritage? He is youth . . . and poetry, perhaps, and a soldier's tradition. I think I know him . . . But what about Dickson? He is the *petit bourgeois*, the *épicier*, the class which the world ridicules. He is unbeatable. The others with good fortune I might find elsewhere – in Russia perhaps. But not Dickson.'[20]

Alexis replies in the voice of British patriotism and political awareness:

> 'You will not find him in Russia. He is what they call the middle-class, which we who were foolish used to laugh at. But he is the stuff which above all others makes a great people. He will endure when aristocracies crack and proletariats crumble. In our own land we have never known him, but till we create him our land will not be a nation.'[20]

Huntingtower, a story of exotic intrigue, is Ruritanian in tone if not in geography, with the exiled princess imprisoned in an ugly pseudo-Tudor mansion at the instigation of Paul, who needs the jewels she has guarded for her fellow-exiles for his plots against the Evallonian government. It is her gallant courage as much as the danger she is in which impels Heritage and his chance-met companion Dickson McCunn to rescue her from her prison and, eventually, to defeat her persecutors. The novel departs clearly from Anthony Hope's tale in this element of the power politics of the 1920s. Buchan used Evallonia as an image of the great power which he feared and the fictitious kingdom, into whose affairs McCunn stumbles more completely six years later (in *Castle Gay*), is allowed convincing links with reality:

> It will be remembered that a republic had been established there in 1919, apparently with the consent of its people. But rifts had since appeared within the lute. There was a strong monarchist party among the Evallonians, who wished to reinstate their former dynasty, at present represented by an attractive young prince, and at the same time insisted on the revision of Evallonian boundaries.[21]

But in fact the fortunes of Evallonia are not of prime importance in the novels, either as romantic or actual politics. The moves and countermoves of Republicans and Royalists in two rented Scottish mansions, Castle Gay and Knockraw, are directed by Buchan to one point, the apotheosis of a middle-aged man, Thomas Carlyle Craw, who has risen by his own efforts from a poor background to become the millionaire owner of an influential newspaper group. He has built up a reputation for naïvely self-important pronouncements on the state of the world and for a determined shunning of personal publicity, but circumstances force him to stand by his words when the Evallonian Royalists seek his support. The troubles of kidnapped, intimidated Craw are central to the book but not in the usual romantic way, in spite of the Jacobite overtones of the plot and the brief appearance of the Republican leader, the Communist Mastrovin, 'the most subtle and dangerous mind in Europe today'. *Castle Gay* is not primarily a thriller in spite of its lively excitements. The gleeful irony in the tale dominates it as it explores the character of a testy, vain man of sedentary habits changing into a comparatively humble, sensible and useful citizen. High adventure drew from Dickson McCunn a latent heroism: Thomas Carlyle Craw had buried his sense and courage far more deeply but they are at least glimpsed at the end of an adventure story which interprets the concept of honour in terms of individual rather than of chivalric motives.

A castle, a mansion and an inn in Austria provide a more directly Ruritanian setting for *The House of the Four Winds* but the coincidental meetings and puzzles of identity which engage Dickson McCunn and other characters from *Castle Gay* are worked out with a somewhat mechanical expertise. The groups in Evallonia – the supporters of the romantic Prince John, the Juventus league of disaffected youth and its leader, the dashing Countess Araminta Troyos, the sinister Mastrovin and his anarchic associates – serve almost too obviously to express once more Buchan's fears for the post-war world of the 1920s and after. Randal Glynde, as a secret agent, analyses the situation formally:

'We are now in the midst of the retarded liquidation of the war. I do not mean debts and currencies and economic fabrics, but something much more vital – the thoughts of man. The democracies have lost confidence. So long as they believed in themselves they could make shift with constitutions and parliaments and dull republics. But once let them lose confidence, and they are like children in the dark, reaching out for the grasp of a strong hand. That way lies the dictator. It might be the monarch if we bred the right kind of king . . . Also there is something more dangerous still, a stirring of youth, disappointed, aggrieved youth, which has never known the discipline of war. Imaginative and incalculable youth, which clamours for the moon and may not be content till it has damaged most of the street lamps.'[22]

The important point about disillusioned youth is somewhat slackly followed up in the book. Its champion, Countess Araminta, is conceived as a woman of the calibre of Hilda von Einem in *Greenmantle* but she never fulfils this introduction, while Mastrovin, that 'survivor of old black days',[23] is helpless against the common sense of McCunn and the elementary cunning of the diplomat Archie Roylance. The status of royalty comes in for summary treatment when one candidate for the throne of Evallonia, offered the support of the young revolutionaries, declines the honour. Count Jovian, after three years at an English university, has no mind to sit on a throne:

'. . . in such a thing I do not trust myself. Your wretched England has spoiled me. I do not want pomp and glory. I should yawn my head off in a palace, and I should laugh during the most solemn ceremonies, and I should certainly beat my Ministers. I desire to remain a private gentleman and some day to win your Grand National.'[24]

In the end it is left to Dickson McCunn to further the romantic element of the book when he impersonates the chosen royal candidate, the elderly and ailing Archduke Hadrian. There is a peculiar appropriateness, especially to readers of today, in the use of the Glasgow grocer to reconcile the mixture of Ruritanian romance and political forecast in this late Buchan thriller, whose emotional direction is never entirely clear.

Another romantic element is introduced intermittently through the attachment of the aristocratic Alison Westwater and humble Jaikie Galt, a rugby player of international repute whose light-hearted approach to Evallonian politics deepens as he listens to Alison's analysis of the situation. If the Ruritanian tributary was to flow into the country of junior fiction, it could only be in a narrower channel. Of the two aspects of chivalric honour, love and patriotism, the former would be misplaced in an adventure story for children. By the time the permissive climate of the late 1960s had come to allow boys and girls to admit tender feelings for one another, the first faint notes of anti-sexist protest ensured that girls would no longer be content to be victims awaiting rescue by dauntless boys. Politics, however – at least in the sense of nationalist feeling – had for many decades been an important and even a dominant theme in children's fiction, and we would expect to find Ruritanian stories using nationalistic honour as a theme at least in books where adventure made any pretence of being more than a game. Even so, that mixture of emotion and social need, of personal pride and territorial inspiration, which we call honour, is not easily brought to life for young readers. Frances Hodgson Burnett found a way by describing how a father handed on his code of honour to his son.

The honour of Samavia, the restoring of the true monarchy after five centuries of unrest and tyranny, provide the theme of *The Lost Prince*, underpinning a plot which in its own way echoed the rags-to-riches pattern of other novels by Frances Hodgson Burnett, for adults as well as for children. *The Lost Prince* is in more than one sense a transitional book. Samavia is represented as a small country, unstable in government and under pressure from stronger neighbours. The story takes place at an unspecified date but clearly in the years immediately before the First World War. It was written during the latter part of 1913 and the first half of 1914 and for part of that time the author was travelling in Austria. The situation in Europe and especially the history of Serbia must have influenced her in her choice of subject and in this sense her book looks forward to Buchan rather than back to Anthony Hope. There is, though, no overt mention of current international affairs. This romantic tale casts back to Ruritania especially in the implied distinction between city and country. It is shepherds and mountain folk who have remained loyal over the centuries to the true royal line. In caves and hill-strongholds the legend has persisted of the Lost Prince, Igor Fedorovitch, said to have survived the assassination of his father; and it is mainly among 'simple, pastoral folk' that the Forgers of the Sword have been slowly gathering support for the restoration of the rightful king, after his existence and identity have been discovered.

The defence of honour as a theme gives emotional and moral substance to a book that has also the ingredients of a junior adventure story. A journalist living in straitened circumstances in London, Lorestan has brought up his son Marco to feel an intense loyalty to the country from which they are exiled. When the story begins Marco, a strong, handsome lad of twelve, is beginning to see more meaning in the oath he has so often sworn on his father's sword, brought out from its hiding-place under the floor-boards of their lodging:

'The sword in my hand – for Samavia!
The heart in my breast – for Samavia!

94

> The swiftness of my sight, the thought of my brain, the life of my
>   life – for Samavia!
> Here grows a man for Samavia,
> God be thanked!'[25]

Explaining, now, more of the past history of Samavia, Lorestan
reveals that the Lost Prince has been found, the time has come
for the corrupt government to be overthrown and the message
must be carried through Europe that 'the lamp is lighted'. The
years of training in which Marco has learned from his father to be
brave and loyal, to be secret and silent, are now to be proved: he
is to be the messenger.

Education is dominant in all Frances Hodgson Burnett's novels.
The Lost Prince in particular belongs to a long tradition of didacticism in stories for the young while in its rapid pace and direct style it
looks forward to the growing body of junior adventure stories of the
late 1920s and the 1930s when children were to play a leading, active
part in important, often great events. Marco has been brought up by
his father in a way designed to fit him for the future. Dramatic irony
allows the reader to know that he is in fact the son of the 'Lost
Prince', and a lost prince himself, rather than, as he supposes,
one of many Samavians of high birth long in exile. Beside this
deliberate, purposive teaching the author has set a second kind of
education which is just as moving and as important to the story.

On his way home to Philibert Place one day, Marco wanders
through an alley to waste ground where a hunchbacked boy
pushing himself on a makeshift trolley is reading to his ragged
companions from a newspaper – about Samavia. This first
encounter between Marco and the boy known as the Rat is not
friendly – at least not until the two lads, each with his own
particular air of authority, have confirmed their direct loyalty to
the disturbed country and have begun to work out for the 'Club' a
youthful but intelligent strategy for revolution.

The Rat, rough and aggressive as he is, has been, like Marco,
educated by his father, but in a random way:

> . . . his wretched father, who had each year sunk lower and lower in
> the underworld, had been a gentleman once, a man who had been
> familiar with good manners and had been educated in the customs
> of good breeding. Sometimes when he was drunk, and sometimes
> when he was partly sober, he talked to the Rat of many things the
> boy would otherwise never have heard of. That was why the lad was
> different from the other vagabonds.[26]

The boy's natural intellect had somehow survived and grown
in unpromising circumstances. He had added to the crumbs of

education thrown to him by his father an ambition of his own focused on Samavia – not, to him, a real place so much as a symbol of satisfying large issues to take him out of a drab world. Marco's father realises that the quick wits developed in the London slums and the boy's everyday, practical good sense make him a perfect companion (aide-de-camp, as he likes to be designated) for the quietly ardent, reflective Marco. He offers to Samavia a loyalty as warm as Marco's but deriving partly from hero-worship as he comes to find in Lorestan a father-figure.

The two boys become in a sense a composite hero, complementary to one another and useful to the story in a purely formal way. For the dialogue needed to reveal character there must be two people and in many scenes on the journey through Europe two questers are needed to enhance tension and to shape events plausibly. Besides, Marco is in something of the position of Anthony Hope's Rassendyll: he is a representative, the royal candidate, as well as a boy of twelve, and we need to feel that he stands a little apart from the stance of an ordinary boy-hero. There is a significant difference, and I do not feel it is only a class and an age difference, between the spare dignity of the oath Marco has learned from his early years and the oath which the Rat has devised as part of the game he has created for his Club:

> 'To swear to stand any torture and submit in silence to any death rather than betray our secret and our King. We will obey in silence and in secret. We will swim through seas of blood, fight our way through lakes of fire, if we are ordered. Nothing shall bar our way. All we do and say and think is for our country and our King. If any of you have anything to say, speak out before you take the oath.'[27]

Marco's devotion to Samavia, given his reflective nature, could easily have seemed priggish if he had not had the Rat as a foil, with his quick memory and his youthful ingenuity. Lorestan has equipped his son, over painstaking months, with tools for the journey – maps, languages, portraits of individuals to be assimilated. He has equipped him, too, with a moral certainty which the Rat recognises and envies. To him it is like magic, but Marco explains it as laws of nature as seen by his father:

> 'You have to be either on one side or the other, like an army. You choose your side. You either build up or you break down. You either keep in the light where you can see, or you stand in the dark and fight everything that comes near you, because you cannot see and you think it's an enemy.'[28]

The practical street-boy had, as it were, foreseen what the enterprise would need while he was developing what his gang enjoyed as a game:

> 'To all the Secret Ones in Samavia, and to the friends of the Secret Party in every country, the sign must be carried. It must be carried by someone who could not be suspected. Who would suspect two boys – and one of them a cripple? When my father is drunk and beats me, he does it because I won't go out and beg in the streets and bring him the money I get. He says that people will nearly always give money to a cripple. I won't be a beggar for him – the swine – but I will be one for Samavia and the Lost Prince. Marco shall pretend to be my brother and take care of me.'[29]

The final plan, as it is adapted and developed by Lorestan, has less of a boy's melodrama in it but it is the Rat's plan, and it is the Rat who advises Marco to pose as a poor, insignificant boy so that the two of them can reach Samavia without attracting attention.

The contrast between the two boys, fruitful as it is for the novelist, is strong both in the early part of the story, when they are in training, and in the second phase when they work their way from Paris to Rome, to Salzburg, to Vienna. Shrewd and observant, the Rat is the perfect aide-de-camp, keeping guard at a theatre in Munich where Marco is in danger from kidnappers, watching in the rain under a bush in the garden where a certain prince sympathetic to the cause is to be given the sign.

There is one particular reason why the Rat must be given the role of alert guardian and subordinate. All through the book there are two points of expectancy for the reader. First, when will Marco be recognised as the Lost Prince and, secondly, when will *he* realise his identity? Though the successive events of the journey are exciting in themselves, dramatic irony adds an edge to them, becoming more telling as the Rat begins to guess the truth. When an old woman on the mountain curtseys to Marco, when a priest takes the boys to the cave where loyalists have gathered and shows them a portrait of the historic Ivor, the story rises to a climax, but not to the final climax. This comes only when, after a lowering of tension, the boys are summoned from London to the newly constituted Samavia and Marco, expecting to see his father as a loyal subject near the throne, is rewarded to the full for his devoted service, as he realises it is his father who is the restored King.

Even when *The Lost Prince* was first published it was often criticised as sentimental but the richness of the story depends on its emotional tone, on the strands of love, devotion and dependence in Marco's love for his father and on the underlying sense of honour which is communicated in different ways by Lorestan, Marco and the Rat. It is true that Frances Hodgson Burnett probably also put into the character of Marco, as she did with that of Cedric Errol, something of her own feelings for her dead son Lionel. Ann Thwaite, in her biography *Waiting for the Party*, suggests the relevance to *The Lost Prince* of a certain incident in October 1913. When two friends, travelling with Mrs Burnett, returned from a visit to an art gallery and showed her a photograph, Mrs Burnett wrote to her sister Edith:

> When I looked at it, I cried out in spite of myself. It was a photograph of a portrait by Van Dyck – the portrait of a boy about fifteen – a young Prince Ruprecht von der Pfaltz of Bavaria and he was so like Lionel that it brought one's heart into one's mouth. The head, the eyebrows, the shape of the face, the eyes were Lionel's very own. It gave me strange things to think of when I found myself looking at my own boy's face in a picture painted three hundred years ago![30]

So Marco, as a character, may carry an intimate image for the author as well as the romantic aura of hidden royal descent.

All the same, he is a boy and not a symbol. His reactions to a challenge and his mode of speech, his capacity, are all those of a boy trained for a certain duty but not distracted from his natural instincts and responses. His behaviour is in strong contrast, for instance, to that of Kingston's three swashbuckling, scampering apprentices whose exploits delighted readers of an earlier generation. The serious backing for the adventure of the lost prince, compounded as it is of romantic but genuine love of country and an equally genuine love of son for father and father for son, gives Frances Hodgson Burnett's tale a richness of texture and an emotional maturity which is not easily matched in later stories for children adopting a similar subject.

If there is any true successor to Frances Hodgson Burnett in her shaping of Ruritanian adventure-romance for young readers that successor is surely Violet Needham, whose linked tales of an unlocated 'Empire', the neighbouring kingdoms of Flavonia and Monte Lucio and the duchies of Ornovitza and Trollac, were published between 1939 and 1956. The nearest to a map-reference which Violet Needham ever gave for her fictional countries may be found in a casual conversation between two schoolboys, one of whom has recently visited:

'. . . a queer little place called Ornovitza, tucked away in an eastern corner of Europe, it's rather of the Republic of San Marino type, only it isn't a republic, it's a Duchy.'[31]

Hugh goes on to describe the country:

'. . . very flat, all canals and marsh land and big meres; pretty dreary in winter, I expect, though I believe there's very good duck shooting there.'[31]

Unlocated, then, as far as the stories go. Hilary Wright, in an article on Violet Needham, points out that the various countries are 'clearly recognizable as pre-1914 Austria-Hungary, with contributions thrown in from France and the Netherlands',[32] and that it was a world in which Violet Needham had lived herself. Her father, 'a younger . . . and illegitimate, though much loved, son of the eccentric 2nd Earl of Kilmoray',[32] served in the First Life Guards and was military attaché in Rome from 1895 to 1901; her mother was the daughter of 'a Dutch nobleman of ancient lineage who had made a fortune out of East Indian tin'.[32] Born in 1876, Violet Needham was educated at home with a governess like any other conventional girl of her class in the late nineteenth century and grew up 'to think as a European'.

Hilary Wright feels it would be wrong to call her books 'Ruritanian' since they were authentically based. Yet their geographical characteristics follow the needs of the adventure-plots, with woodland for concealment, canals for transport, mountains where peasants remain loyal to exiled royalty, cities where intrigue is fomented; the association with Anthony Hope's Ruritania seems clear enough. Precise dating of events is no more necessary than precise locations. Internal evidence in regard to such details as the use of motor cars or the social idiom and manners of the characters suggests the first two decades of our century but the wise reader will accept a certain anonymity as an integral part of the fiction.

The stories are distanced from any recognisable reality by the tight pattern of codes and relationships proper to the exalted status of the characters and by the tone of the story-telling. Paradoxically this makes the moral and dynastic problems in the books less taxing to young readers, because they are isolated from the pressures of their own time. Unfamiliar, clearly posed, these problems are made accessible not quite as history nor yet as fantasy but with something of the acceptable plainness of fairy-tale challenges. These are transitional novels. In plots and themes they form a bridge from *The Lost Prince* to the more obviously juvenile world of adventure which Arthur Ransome and others opened up in the 1930s. Hilary Wright places the works clearly in period:

> Her first published work, *The Black Riders*, was originally told as bedtime stories to her four small nephews and written down at their insistence, in 1918. When it was shown to publishers, however, it was rejected as 'too difficult', and indeed its young hero has to resolve the different claims of loyalty to an oath and his friends or his duty to his country as represented by the autocratic but not tyrannous government. The story was put aside for twenty years, then rescued by the wife of one of the now adult nephews, shown to a publisher relation, tried out satisfactorily on his own children and brought out to resounding success. Violet Needham was by then sixty-three, but for the next eighteen years she produced on average a book a year; not until she was eighty-one did her last book, *The Sword of St Cyprian*, have to be turned down because her powers were failing.[33]

The moral problems which Violet Needham set for her heroes and heroines, the points of honour appropriate to their royal or aristocratic heritage, belonged to an earlier society than that of her eventual readers, but the exhilaration of adventure was there to help them. It was possible for a middle-class reader to sympathise with a girl, even if she were a countess, when she entered upon the search for an ancient royal treasure in a thoroughly youthful way, or with a boy who, even if he were a king or at the least a count in eclipse, faced danger and responsibility with the doubts and the dutiful idealism of a public-school upbringing. Generalisations about dates and trends are always subject to reservations. Adventure stories overlap in their subject matter, attitudes and characters in a way that can be confusing. There are constants, all the same, and it is in tracing the way the attributes of adventurous children – their courage, their resourcefulness, their loyalty – change yet remain the same, that the traditions of the adventure story can be verified.

The most obvious link with *The Lost Prince* (I do not suggest it was a conscious one) is *The Emerald Crown*, the story of fourteen-year-old Alexander Valesciano, brought up in England by his mother's people and taken after her death to Flavonia, a kingdom usurped from his paternal ancestors seventy years earlier. The circlet of gold and jewels is a potent symbol of the Vallens dynasty which is re-established through diplomacy and through the wishes of the nation: the acclaiming of the 'lost prince' by mountain families, hereditary guardians of the Crown, is strongly reminiscent of the recognition of Marco in Frances Hodgson Burnett's story. But Alexander and his friend Christine (who performs something of the Rat's role as aide-de-camp) carry on the quest in the spirit of the junior adventure of the 1930s, with the equipment proper to their years of curiosity, keen eyes and perseverance.

Moreover, Alexander faces a moral problem which Marco, dedicated from his youth to a service in Samavia, did not have to face. Brought up in an English public school, Alexander is introduced very suddenly to his new destiny and he reacts predictably; when he examines the documents attesting to his birth he feels 'a sudden thrill of pride':

> Flavonia might not be one of the great powers, but still the name of Vallens had stood, for generations, as a shining example of honour, chivalry and known to all the world. . . .[34]

but the idea of becoming a king seems absurd and increasingly distasteful as Count Trollac, leader of the movement for restoration, explains his obligations:

> 'I won't be a king,' he muttered to himself; 'they can't force me to; I'm free to make my own life. I mean to live in England and be a Master of Hounds, not a rotten little king of a rotten little country. If my father had wanted me to be a king, why didn't he become king himself? He chose to be an English country gentleman.'[35]

The boy had never been told that his father was killed in battle in Flavonia, in an earlier attempt to seize the throne for the Vallens dynasty. He accepts the acclamation of the mountain men as a way of saving his playmate from rough handling, after she has found the Crown. It is not until he sees the motto 'Quit you like men' on the Vallens tombs in Flavonia that 'the burden of fear and foreboding slipped from him' and he sees the task before him not as that of a king struggling after an impossible ideal but as that of a man playing a man's part:

> . . . he might be young, lonely and not a little bewildered, but the way was clear before him at last; he had taken his orders and been given the pass word, he could win through.[36]

The conclusion, grandiloquent as it is, is consistent with the honest fears of a young hero who belongs as much to the junior fiction of the 1930s and early 1940s as to the climate in which Frances Hodgson Burnett was writing.

The behaviour of Violet Needham's young characters and the patterns and manners in her books make them period pieces nowadays; her prim, earnest, winning girls and ardent, courteous boys are as alien to our times as Marco Lorestan is. We may find a common denominator in one particular character who plays central or peripheral parts in seven of her 'Empire' books. We first meet Richard Faucenbois as a boy approaching his twelfth birthday in *The Black Riders*; *The Stormy Petrel* and *The House of the Paladin* return to the boy at fourteen and fifteen, when he has already earned his nickname of the Stormy Petrel, and in *The Betrayer* he moves into his sixteenth year with agonising decisions to make; in three later books (*Richard and the Golden Horseshoe*, *The Red Rose of Ruvina* and *The Secret of the White Peacock*, he is in his mid-twenties and the chases and escapes of youth have been put aside for the role of diplomat and teacher. If the boy Dick is recognised in the civilised, thoughtful young man, it is only in one constantly mentioned physical trait, his steady, 'unwinking' eyes, and in his sense of responsibility towards the Empire and the allies whose support he helps to win. The later books have very much the air of contrived sequels, with young conspirators or princes in training cut from the same pattern and taking, one by one, the centre of a story, none of them capturing attention as the Stormy Petrel had done as a boy.

Dick Faucenbois is a character who lives in the memory, an individual in his eager response to adventure, exciting sympathy for his loneliness and admiration for his courage and his quick wits. With much that is traditional in the traits and circumstances he is given in the story, he is none-the-less real to the reader, partly because the three earliest books in which he appears are so fresh and vital, so full of striking incidents and unusual settings. In part, too, it is because of the entirely natural way in which Dick's thoughts and feelings are interwoven with his activities. His father had died serving the Empire as one of the Black Riders and as the boy looks down on the great imperial road from the quiet house of his foster-parents he listens to tales of the powerful Count Jasper, Governor of the Citadel and commander of those orthodox forces.

He suffers a first conflict of loyalties when he helps the strange man who calls himself Faraway Moses to escape from the Riders and learns that a confederacy is working in secret to reform a government that favours rich against poor, 'not with rifle and sword', as the conspirator tells Dick, but:

> '. . . with pen and ink, printed pamphlets, anonymous articles in newspapers, a speech here, a word there, a message given or sent.'[37]

With the ardour of his age Dick agrees to carry a vital message across the frontier into Flavonia: delighting in unexpected action, he is afraid only of being late and failing in his mission and it is the free resourcefulness of a boy that ensures that in spite of accidents the message does get through. A lonely childhood, a youthful longing for adventure, made it easy enough for Dick to lay aside his devotion to an almost legendary father and to dedicate himself to the service of a man who gave him the emotional security and incentive he had lacked for so long. Later he had a sterner challenge to face, one which more closely affected his personal sense of honour.

When Faraway Moses, who was once Count St Sylvain and a Black Rider, is captured and imprisoned, Jasper the Terrible, who has made himself responsible for the boy in his own household, offers to release the man who has become like a father to Dick if he will reveal the names of the other Confederates. Tried almost beyond endurance, Dick keeps silence. There is another lesson to add to this bitter one. As Dick comes to know Count Jasper he no longer sees him as a villain and realises that this inscrutable man is in his own way working for the same ends as the conspirators. Events which begin by offering the boy exciting adventure end by teaching him – about people, about statecraft – and confirming in him the steadfast loyalty to the Empire which is evident in his later exploits.

The adventure stories which last longest and date least are, I believe, those in which the hero at least, and perhaps other characters as well, develop as a result of the challenges offered to them. This applies particularly to stories designed for young people but because they are still growing and changing themselves, the moral and psychological lessons must not be rigid or overstrained for these young readers. If the Stormy Petrel does not seem priggish it is because his appetite for action and mystery is always as evident in the stories as his steadfast loyalty and his intelligence. Already in *The Black Riders*, though, he has begun to grow up and Violet Needham has begun to equip him for the role of teacher and mentor even as he is still meeting the challenge of danger with the eager opportunism of a boy. When he appears again in *The Stormy Petrel*, part of his duty is to encourage the prospective King Carol, a timid boy under Count Jasper's Regency – a boy who, as Dick complains, knows 'a lot out of books' but nothing about 'real things', which he defines as:

> . . . the everyday sort of things, finding one's way in the dark, using a compass, picking a lock, making up one's mind quickly, the sort of things that one wants if one's in a hurry or a tight corner.[38]

Similarly, education and adventure are mingled in *The House of the Paladin*, when Dick, on holiday in the Duchy of Ornovitza, is swept into a conspiracy against the young Duchess Anastasia. There is an element of humour in this story as the eleven-year-old girl, brought up by a cynical, unloving father to be arrogant and self-sufficient, is helped by the bracing company of Dick and his holiday companion Hugh Vallens to relax and enjoy a little fun. All the same, the theme is still national honour and personal loyalty, the lessons which Dick teaches to Anastasia as successfully as he had taught them to the weak but responsive Carol.

In these three first 'Stormy Petrel' stories the theme is supported by skilful narration, sensitive character-drawing and carefully controlled settings supporting the accepted tone of high adventure. Sometimes we seem to be in an almost oriental land of Byzantine decoration, sun and olives; at other times sleighs and snowy mountains provide the backing for action. In *The House of the Paladin* waterways and boats are skilfully used to prolong tension in a country which Hilary Wright thinks derives from the author's knowledge of Holland. In subsequent books the landscapes are less vivid and Dick's intervention in times of stress seems less precisely motivated, though he still flies over troubled waters as his guardian, Count Jasper, supposes he always will. There is even an echo of the testing time of his twelfth year in the fourth book in the sequence, *The Betrayer*, when he has to find a way of helping one of the Confederates, involved in a misguided conspiracy against the young Emperor, without being disloyal to his ruler. Not yet sixteen, Dick still has a youthful attitude to adventure and the new challenge makes him feel, as he says, like a tightrope walker; but, to the reader, the impetus of personality has somehow been lost.

Certainly the young man who plays the part of mentor in later books – to Jasper's young son Richard caught up in a conspiracy against the Duchess Anastasia in *Richard and the Golden Horseshoe*, to schoolgirl Rosamond in similar straits in *The Red Rose of Ruvina*, and to the orphan Laurette, guardian of dangerous knowledge, in *The Secret of the White Peacock* – is little more than a mouthpiece for various expressions of the wish for peace within the Empire and a device by which conspiracy and danger, the like of which the boy Dick had defeated by his own efforts, could be frustrated seemingly by a younger generation of gallant boys and girls. The last book confronts Dick with an opponent less believable than the political enemies of earlier days. Laurette's guardian, Count Schillingin, has forced from the girl a scientific formula hidden by her father which would give him world power. The melodramatic vagueness of the plot reflects on the characters and makes even the indomitable Dick seem unreal; in moving

104

from the neo-Victorian flavour of the earlier books to a more modern idiom, Violet Needham lost something of the clear moral purpose and the emotional reality of her fiction and, in particular, the special honest warmth of her young hero.

Even while Violet Needham was using the theme of honour in countries which distantly recalled Ruritania, other writers were using the associations of Anthony Hope's fiction simply to give a new impetus to the kidnap and escape formula. Adrian Alington's Rumelia, with its mixture of European and Middle-Eastern scenery, is really Buchan country. The hero of *The Boy King* is a young ex-army captain who casually applies for the job of escorting a boy from his English school to the Rumelian capital in time for the coronation of the young King Boris. This 'Story of an Adventure' was published by Blackwell in 1935 (antedating Violet Needham's *The Black Riders* in publication but not in composition) in a series designed to provide boys with more up-to-date tales than the hardy survivors of Percy F. Westerman or Herbert Strang. The series, now forgotten, had a curiously mature tone, as though the commissioned authors (they included Rex Warner and C. Day Lewis) were not trying over-hard to pitch their voices to any particular audience. Adrian Alington's ingenious and astonishingly slow-witted hero is reminiscent of certain Dornford Yates men-about-town as he wrests his young charge away from his kidnapper, a sinister doctor, using his sanatorium for his nefarious ends, and there is a Buchanesque relish for disguise in the revelation that one persistent pursuer is no enemy but a reporter and that the boy whose coronation they watch is in fact an actress used as a decoy, while unsuspecting Captain Langdale has had the true king in his charge all the time.

A similar urbanity of style took Ian Serraillier's 1950 adventure story, *There's No Escape*, away from formula-writing. The hero, a young scientist-turned-secret-agent, has an impetuous courage and a talent for improvisation which ally him to the boy and girl heroes of innumerable travel-tales (Viola Bayley's, for example) published a decade or so later, and a gallant country boy who provides practical help in moments of extreme danger, on the frontier of beleaguered Sylvania, directs the book just as firmly to young readers. All the same the 'nine-and-over age-range' recommended for the Puffin reprint of 1975 seems to me over-optimistic; the book belongs properly to the 1950s when there was more trafficking, usefully, in the no-man's-land between junior and near-adult fiction, in the matter of style and approach, than there seems to be now. For all the ease of manner in

Serraillier's book and the statutory backing of chase and escape, forest and mountain, honest peasant and brutal soldiery, there is an adult edge to it as the preoccupations of the post-war years show through, and a faint echo of Buchan's clubbable heroes which readers of the present generation might miss, being conditioned to expect a less heady mixture – such a mixture as they could find in Noel Streatfeild's romantic adventure, *The House in Cornwall*, where four dauntless children rescue the nine-year-old King of Livia from sinister political kidnappers.

The elements which appealed to the first readers of the book in the early forties could still appeal to readers today, provided they did not expect much more than cardboard cutouts for characters. The saving grace of this predictable thriller is the humour which creeps in as Noel Streatfeild's shrewd understanding of children edges in to the improbable plot. The story leaps into life suddenly when the children work out a way for Sorrel to carry coffee to royal Rudi, to counteract the sleeping draughts administered by the wicked doctor, in a water-jug corked with a dirty sock belonging to Edward and wrapped in an old hot-water-bottle cover found in the wardrobe of Uncle Murdock's gloomy house. Edward is as proud of his ingenuity as he is critical of the cover:

> 'It's an awful thing, really, with a rabbit on it, but it's dark green and we can carry the rabbit inside where it won't show.'[39]

Touches like this make up for a wild climax when the children hold off a villain axing Rudi's door (Sorrel bites his hand) and another on a ladder outside the window (Edward smashes his hand with a brass bedknob) until the police and embassy officials land outside with reinforcements.

Humour might seem an unlikely ingredient in the true-bred Ruritanian adventure, yet the humour or wit of incongruity, the lightening of menace or of emotional tension with practical detail of a bathetic kind, is one of the most effective, and rare, methods of adapting romantic adventure for young readers. In *The Ring of Zoraya* Harriet Graham, a few years ago, made good use of the Ruritanian formula and period in a third story about a conjuror and the two orphans in his care. By setting her tale in 1894 and linking it to the death of Czar Alexander III she gave her plot a certain authenticity; if Michael, Crown Prince of Slovadia, and his villainous uncle, are fictional, the conspiracy and the involvement of the boy and girl are plausible enough. But this is skilful pastiche in the mood of the 1980s. The prescriptive elements of the story (exotic uniforms, the rumblings of anarchy, royal arrogance and pride and all the grandeur of the Orient Express) are

106

balanced by characters defined with subtlety and humour, faithful in behaviour to their Victorian background but reaching out to the present in their mature sympathy for the frightened boy-Prince. The responsibility they assume for Michael is their kind of honour and they sustain it while answering his insolent conceit with their own brand of offhand humour. In the same way a scene in a Vienna hotel where the conjuror Rowlandson conducts a one-sided conversation with a deaf and totally unknown German guest, as his Aunt Louise, to divert the suspicions of the villainous Count, lightens the story at the right moment, lessening the tensions of the railway journey so that the climax, the rescue of young Michael from a hunting-lodge and the wild carriage journey to St Petersburg, may make the right, strong impression.

The deflatory humour belongs to our own time: the romantic trappings of the story and the operating of a personal sense of honour suggest that *The Ring of Zoraya* is a true descendant of *The Prisoner of Zenda*. None-the-less it has the hallmarks of a story allowing for the relative experience of situations and emotions which is usually assumed in readers between ten and fourteen; nor is there much in the way the plot is worked out of what we could call political awareness, such as Ian Serraillier introduced, albeit sparingly, in his *There's No Escape* thirty-five years ago.

Political sharpness is a concomitant of John Rowe Townsend's gently mock-heroic Ruritanian romance, *A Foreign Affair*, the latest descendant of Anthony Hope's novels to be offered to the young. We must of course heed the author's prefatory warning – 'This story has no message and no hidden meanings that I am aware of. Don't take it seriously. It is for fun.' It is fun, undoubtedly, but it is the contrast between the romantic nature of the imaginary European principality of Essenheim and the modern adjuncts of so-called civilisation (coveted by some Essenheimers but not by others) which determines the tone of the book and perhaps directs it to readers in their teens who can detect and enjoy a touch of irony and satire as well as relishing a stirring adventure. Here is a Ruritanian situation of an ageing ruler, the Laureate, threatened by unrest from soldiers, government officials and students but (as it seems at first) not from a docile peasantry. The situation is not to be resolved by swords, fast horses and heroic gestures: international finance, military coups and unexpected moves from the grass-roots will settle the matter. The romantic longing which English Kate, sardonic daughter of a foreign correspondent, develops for the dashing Crown Prince Rudi can hardly survive her shrewd observation of his philandering. Common sense and practicality replace cloak-and-dagger heroism. Secret passages are revealed in the most casual manner and the rebellious army is defeated not by arms but by the timely gift, by Kate, of the key to the Laureate's well-stocked wine-cellar.

In the past decade or so adventure stories have been changing to suit young readers of the television age. How far these changes go, and how deeply they probe human nature, will be a matter of further discussion. John Rowe Townsend's neo-Ruritanian tale demonstrates one aspect of this change.

5. The Jacobite Rebellions

The conflict which is the necessary basis of adventure stories rises naturally and fruitfully from the theme of honour preserved against the dangers of intrigue, betrayal and the clash of loyalties. Historical novels have explored the theme in such periods as the Wars of the Roses, the Civil War and the Jacobite rebellions of the eighteenth century. Changes in historical interpretation are reflected very clearly in fiction. The hunchback image of Richard III, the attitude to 'right but revolting' Roundheads and 'wrong but romantic' Cavaliers have gradually been reversed, to create fresh generalisations. The lost cause of the Jacobites has always imposed its particular ambiguities on fiction. However romantic and ardent a novel on the subject may be, it will inevitably be darkened by the sense of disillusion and failure. 'Romantic' remains in most instances the dominant adjective.

A century and a half ago Scott put into the mouth of Baillie Nicol Jarvie firm economic reasons for his prediction of the 1715 rebellion. A new world had 'come up wi' this King George', he told young Francis Osbaldistone, and the pensions granted by Queen Anne to the Highland chiefs had ended:

> '. . . they haena the means o'mainteening the Clans that let them up . . . their credit's gone in the Lowlands; and a man that can whistle ye up a thousand or feifteen hundred working lads to do his will, would hardly get fifty pounds on his band at the Cross o' Glasgow – this canna stand laing – there will be an outbreak for the Stuarts – there will be an outbreak – they will come down on the low country like a flood, as they did in the waefu' wars o' Montrose, and that will be seen and heard tell o' ere a twelmonth gans round.'[1]

Persistently ignoring this approach for one more directly related to character, novelists have isolated clan loyalties and the personal charm of the son and grandson of James II from the complex political background of the two risings. Yet it cannot be said that historical adventure fiction was wholly responsible for the romantic image of Bonnie Prince Charlie which persists to this day in portraits on biscuit-tins, in haunting traditional songs and in the significant shape of certain drinking glasses.

As the first and greatest of those who presented the aims and loyalties of the Jacobites in fictional narrative, Scott offered no romantic portraits either of the Stuarts or of their adherents. With a sturdily sardonic view he collected material within living memory and used it to explore the effect of a lost cause on a variety of temperaments. Most Scottish readers of around sixty years of age, he observed, could remember men who had been 'out in the Forty-Five':

> Those who remember such old men will probably agree that the progress of time which has withdrawn all of them from the field, has removed, at the same time, a peculiar and striking picture of ancient manners. Their love of past times, their tales of bloody battles fought against romantic odds, were all dear to the imagination and their idolatry of locks of hair, pictures, rings, ribbons, and other memorials of the time in which they still seemed to live, was an interesting enthusiasm; and although their political principles, had they existed in the relation of fathers, might have rendered them dangerous to the existing dynasty, yet, as we now recollect them, there could not be on the earth supposed to exist persons better qualified to sustain the capacity of innocuous and respectable grandsires.[2]

Thus distanced in time, the Jacobite atmosphere was further complicated by being filtered through the eyes of young heroes whose particular preconceptions of the Highland rebels were to be in various ways corrected by experience. Darsie Latimer's leaning towards adventure was defined with some anxiety in a letter from his friend Alan Fairmond, who contrasted his own rational courage with Darsie's:

> '. . . intellectual courage, highness of spirit, and desire of destruction – impulses which render thee alive to the love of fame and deaf to the apprehension of danger, until it forces itself suddenly upon thee. I own, that whether it is from my having caught my father's apprehensions, or that I have reason to entertain doubts of my own, I often think that this wildfire chase of romantic situation and adventure may lead thee into some mischief . . .'[3]

Like Edward Waverley, whose expectations of life were built on poetic romances, and Francis Osbaldistone, rebelling against a mercantile future, Darsie Latimer found the realities of Highland Jacobites more extreme and less picturesque than he had expected.

Later novelists were to fall in with Scott's way of diffusing his view of the Jacobite risings through individuals as a safe way of combining historical fact with imagination, though (with the exception of Stevenson) few were to match the pervasive ironies of Scott's Jacobite novels. Consciously or not, he did pass on to later ages certain settings and atmospheres which were to be increasingly romanticised, the colour of his own Celtic revival being softened both in style and emotion. Scott's descriptions of Rob Roy, Fergus MacIvor and Redgauntlet, of the wild, remote country where they lurked and from which they conducted their guerilla activities, were a major source of later pictures of the eighteenth-century Highlands adapted to softer, more 'literary', more civilised demands made on the adventure-story genre; the change can be seen clearly in Neil Munro's *Doom Castle* of 1901, for example, and in the popular trilogy by D. K. Broster published in the 1920s.

Even the potent landscaping of Stevenson shows clearly the passage of time and the smoothing out of Scott's Gothicism. Stevenson's debt to Scott was especially obvious in his careful handling of genealogies, his understanding of the operation of clan loyalties and the peculiar complexities of honour among the Jacobites. His own Scottishness made it obvious that he would assimilate Scott's picture of the Highlands and merge it with his own conception. There is much of Scott, for instance, in the description of the exiled chief Cluny in *Kidnapped* (filtered as it is, of course, through the eyes of sensible, dogged David Balfour) but, in addition, there is a prevailing, pointed, mischievous humour which is vastly different from the harsh, dangerous sense of comedy in *Waverley*. David describes how he was sheltered for a time by the chief:

> On that first day, as soon as the collops were ready, Cluny gave them with his own hand a squeeze of lemon (for he was well supplied with luxuries) and bad us draw in to our meal.
> 'They,' said he, meaning the collops, 'are such as I gave His Royal Highness in this very house; bating the lemon juice, for at that time we were glad to get the meat and never fashed for kitchen. Indeed, there were mair dragoons than lemons in my country in the year forty-six.'[4]

The adventure story depends for its validity on a special balance of real and imagined detail, whether we are concerned with a totally believable character adrift in a world of fantasy, even of magic, or an improbable sequence of events taking place in a precisely defined place. David Balfour's adventures are confirmed for the reader by the meticulous mapping of his journeys in and around Edinburgh and in the Highlands, in *Kidnapped*, and by the legal details (documents, interrogations, court scenes) through which the introduction of a fictitious character into the notorious affair of the Appin murder is eased in *Catriona*. This is a matter of technique. Deeper in intent is the balance, in the two books, between the character of David Balfour and the Jacobite exile Alan Breck Stewart. The enmity of David's uncle Ebenezer, his direct and his proxy efforts to murder his nephew and protect his dubious claim to the House of Shaws and all that accrues to it, seem almost domestic and ordinary compared with the dangers which the youth faces after he has been involved, not altogether willingly, in the affairs of Alan Breck and that more devious, less romantic Jacobite, James More Drummond, whose clan name of McGregor had long been forfeited and proscribed.

As stories, *Kidnapped* and *Catriona* are as active, varied and pictorial as any young reader could wish and the prominent position given to *Kidnapped* as a serial in *Young Folks* between May and July 1886 suggests that the editor was confident of its appeal for itself as well as because the popularity of *Treasure Island* ensured a receptive public. With memorable scenes, strongly selective description, an illusion of pace even in the most extended sections, the books have congenial plots of chase and escape within a firm lateral structure. In *Kidnapped* David is fleeing from justice as a suspected ally of Alan Breck; in *Catriona* he is struggling, against restraints imposed on him by various interested parties, to reach Edinburgh in time to testify in defence of James More for the sake of his daughter. None-the-less these are not solely 'children's books'.

Certainly David Balfour is suitably drawn as a hero of adventure and a young reader meeting the books for the first time may accept him merely for what happens to him. Yet he is not a hero in the most obvious sense – certainly not a romantic figure, as Alan Breck is – and this hypothetical reader, growing older, may see and admire the way Stevenson has drawn a very ordinary young man, slow in thought and provincial in outlook, a Whig by upbringing and a supporter of law and order by inclination, a young man whose honesty blinds him to the perfidy of others and whose loyalty, once given, is unwavering.

These are all traits which lend themselves to adventure-story: in other words, David's fortunes result from his character, a character entirely convenient for a story-teller. Yet Stevenson handled the character so skilfully and with such intuition that he took it far beyond fictional convenience. Too far, M. R. Ridley has suggested; in his introduction to the Everyman edition of the two books he writes:

> . . . preoccupation with character is apt to handicap a teller of stories. Of course any story must have characters who are live human beings and not puppets, or the reader will care nothing what

happens to them and lay the book down. But granted that they are alive there is little loss and probably considerable gain if they are straightforward and obvious, with perhaps an odd quirk or two to enliven them. Anything like subtlety of characterization, any invitation to the reader to become interested in a 'character-study', either slows up the progress of events or distracts the reader from it, because he is gripped by the character's reaction to the events rather than by the events themselves.[5]

Whether this principle be accepted or not (and it will come up again in connection with many books), there can be no doubt that it is just those depths in David's character, the evolution through time and experience, which sustain two novels in which the remaining characters are drawn rather differently. It is the balance of romantic exhilaration and inspired common sense which make them classics of their kind.

Beside the brilliant set-pieces (of Rankeillor, of the hard Advocate, of James More and others) and the mistily attractive portrait of the titular heroine Catriona, stands the lively figure of Alan Breck Stewart, an outline (but a firm one) based on traits which are 'Jacobite' in the romantic sense and developed from the points of view of various people involved with him. Visiting Scotland officially as a courier to receive money for the cause of the exiled Prince Charles Edward, Alan Breck has a strong personal compulsion towards his native mountains and valleys. The reader's (and David's) first sight of him may even suggest that this man, rather than the callow orphan, is the real hero of *Kidnapped*:

> He was smallish in stature, but well set and as nimble as a goat; his face was of a good open expression, but sunburnt very dark, and heavily freckled and pitted with the smallpox; his eyes were unusually light and had a kind of dancing madness in them, that was both engaging and alarming, and when he took off his greatcoat, he laid a pair of fine silver-mounted pistols on the table, and I saw that he was belted with a great sword. His manners, besides, were elegant, and he pledged the captain handsomely. Altogether I thought of him, at the first sight, that here was a man I would rather call my friend than my enemy.[6]

Any such impression is soon corrected. David's admiration of him when he and Alan have routed the rascally ship's officers, and after they have been reunited as shipwrecked fugitives, is enhanced by his discovery of Alan's talents in pipe-music and poetry, his literary tastes and physical skills, but he also realises his faults, 'his childish propensity to take offence and to pick quarrels'[7] and his strong conceit of himself, and after the murder in Appin has driven the two friends into the heather, he takes a clearer, more adult view of the matter:

> . . . taking things in their proportion, Alan's society was not only a peril to my life, but a burden to my purse.
>
> But there was no thought of the sort in the honest head of my companion. He believed he was serving, helping, and protecting me. And what could I do but hold my peace, and chafe, and take my chance of it.[8]

The lawyer Rankeillor offers a view of the situation hardly new to David when he comments that 'Mr Thomson' seems 'a gentleman of some choice qualities, though perhaps a trifle bloody-minded' and a 'sore embarrassment'[9] to his young client. All the same Rankeillor, if a little cynically, concurs with David's resolve to be loyal to his friend. The relationship between David and Alan Breck, essential as it is to the working out of the stories, is also the most important of the many aspects of honour illustrated in them, from the mean villainy of Ebenezer Balfour to the ambiguous self-seeking of James More and the dilemma of the Lord Advocate as a private man of some honesty and a public figure under intense political pressure. One may surmise that Stevenson in these two books was taking a shrewd look at the emotional and nostalgic aspects of Jacobitism as he felt them in himself.

Kidnapped and *Catriona* are adventure stories romantic in texture and plot but with a bite to them. They are in no sense the kind of escapist adventure which one might expect the lost cause of the Stuarts to inspire. It is surprising, indeed, how many novels on this subject are sardonic, offering a very different view from that of Scott's dedicated grandsires. Stanley Weyman's *The Wild Geese*, for example, romantic in the deployment of his favourite pride-and-prejudice formula, is in another sense an anti-war sermon. His hero, Colonel John Sullivan, who has fought in Europe as a mercenary for many years, puts an end to the plan formulated in a wild corner of Ireland to send men to support the rebellion of 1745, setting against the ardent inexperience of Flavia McMurrough the superficial ambitions of her brother and the cunning manipulations of the bishop and the Spanish admiral, his own experience of the devastation of war and the suffering of innocent folk, and a strong foreboding of disaster for the Stuart cause.

Again, there is marked irony in the appearance of the Old Pretender in Andrew Balfour's vigorous adventure story, *To Arms!*, seen as he is through the eyes of a surgeon, Alan Oliphant. A lukewarm supporter of the House of Hanover, Oliphant is captured by the Jacobites and pressed into service, on one occasion being summoned to Peterhead to treat the defeated King for an attack of ague.

The medical gloss on the occasion serves to intensify the feeling of doom and discouragement which affects the men who are pledged to new efforts for the just-landed Chevalier:

> In a chair by a glowing fire of peats sat the Chevalier: black-haired, sallow-faced, and all in a sweat and a shiver. He had an air of the most depressing melancholy, and looked as though he would weep upon the slightest provocation. His spare frame was huddled up as if to gain warmth from itself, and he had a cup of mulled, steaming wine within reach of his hand. His features were handsome after a fashion, but his expression was listless and sad, and his dark eyes had a weary worn look in them as he raised his head and looked at me.[10]

The young prisoner prescribes sulphur mixed with treacle and a 'warm footbath with mustard-powder'[11] and is well aware of the mingled tragedy and homeliness of the occasion:

> The clansmen were chilled by this dark, solemn, melancholy mortal who had come to lead them, or rather to mislead them, and for whom they had been willing to lose life and lands. He was so silent, they wondered if he could speak at all, while he was of a peevish, vacillating nature, and scarce knew his own mind two weeks together.[12]

This dismal portrait (Oliphant finds only one trait, his religious fervour, for which to praise James III) is in strong contrast to the main story line in which Oliphant fights a private enemy, and Buchan's picture of the old age of Prince Charles Edward in his short story 'Companions of the Marjolaine' is as melancholy in tone.

The tone most natural to adventure-story is one of buoyancy and optimism and this is likely to be best satisfied when the disastrous mistakes and internal dissensions of the '15 and the '45 are kept in the background while loyalty to James or his son becomes the moving force of private, fictional individuals. Buchan would certainly have called his *Midwinter* a serious historical novel but it has the same chase and escape form as the books which he styled 'shockers'. In spite of the accuracy and the confident period atmosphere of the book it is an adventure story of the classic kind, the tale of a man taking dangerous journeys for a practical cause and a personal ideal. A young Highlander,

Alastair MacLean, is sent to probe the intentions and assess the possible support of English Jacobites, increasingly important as Prince Charles Edward advances into England. Travelling as a merchant, Alastair is benighted in Wychwood Forest and is helped to reach the house of Lord Cornbury on Otmoor by the strange being, Midwinter, and his lurking band of lawless men. Homesick for his native hills and ill at ease in an unfamiliar country, Alastair is almost at once involved in a double mystery, the disappearance of the beautiful heiress Claudia Grevel and the identity of a traitor whose trail the young Jacobite picks up through intercepted papers. Since these papers contain details of levies expected from Wales, Alastair journeys north to intercept the Prince on his march to Derby but is delayed by weather, accident and the action of enemies.

Buchan does not suggest that the delays of this winter journey or Alastair's final unmasking of the spy in any way affect the course of history. The Prince's army remains in the distance, a matter of rumour and report and a potent emotional addition to the quest-plot. Even before the retreat of the Jacobite army begins the Prince is described to Alastair as 'Sad and reflective – like a man who has staked much against odds and does not greatly hope',[13] and the young courier, reaching Ashbourne, realises that this part of his journey at least has been in vain:

> So that was the end of the long song. Gone the velvet and steel of a great crusade, the honourable hopes, the chivalry and the high adventure, and what was left was this furtive banditti slinking through the mud like the riff-raff of a fair . . .[14]

Alastair's travels in England have been a bitter education to a young man nurtured on unquestioning loyalty and fervent hope, a young man whose given character, opaque and generalised, allows Buchan to indicate the various influences which change his attitude to events. A meeting with General Oglethorpe, a Hanoverian general liberal in mind by contrast with the brutal Cumberland, opens Alastair's eyes to a new idea of the Prince and his cause:

> 'He is the young gallant, a figure from an old chivalrous world. Oh, I do not deny his attraction; I do not doubt that he can charm men's hearts. But sir, there is a new temper in the land. You have heard of the people they call Methodists – humble folk, humble servants of Almighty God, who carry the Gospel to dark places at the expense of revilings and buffetings and persecutions. I have had them with me in Georgia, and they fight like Cromwell's Ironsides, they are tender and merciful and brave, and they preach a hope for

the vilest. With them is the key of the new England, for they bring
healing to the sores of the people . . . What can your failing Prince
say to the poor and hungry?'[15]

The companion on the young man's travels, the shambling,
stammering tutor seeking his lost pupil Claudia Grevel, whose
fervent Jacobite sympathies are moderated by an unexpected
dour wisdom, is none other than Samuel Johnson, boldly introduced into the story on the strength of a single fact, that in the
summer of 1754 he had walked to Elsfield from Oxford to take
tea with Francis Wyse, then squire of Elsfield Manor and
Bodley's librarian. Local and national history provided Buchan
with a past for the manor, which he had bought in 1919, and a
doorway into the lonely marshes and small villages of Otmoor
and Wychwood.

At that date (and as late as the 1930s) this part of Oxfordshire
could still be felt as ancient and mysterious and *Midwinter* is,
above all, a celebration of 'Old England' as it is epitomised in the
woods and pastures through which Alastair blunders, in which
the enigmatic Midwinter and his 'Naked Men' operate with their
network of information and their robust independence. Alastair's
actions are compelling for the romantic colour of his loyalty to the
Prince and for the excitements of this enterprise but perhaps most
of all because whether he is on horseback or on foot, in thicket or
on moorland, in summer heat or winter chill, the place *where* he
is can be seen in the mind's eye, can be felt as a factor, almost a
character, in the story.

This does not mean that a setting, though an integral part of
any adventure story, can sustain that story on its own. The
necessary motivation of the young hero of *Midwinter* seems
adequate for its purpose when it is compared with Robert Neill's
tale of the '45, *The Devil's Weather*, where a brilliant exploiting of
routes, storms, journeys on horseback or on foot, trade secrets
and ambushes, is not supported by the stereotyped characters.
The delicate balance of elements in this type of story is seen at
its best in A. E. W. Mason's romance of 1901, *Clementina*, which
looks forward to the twentieth-century interest in personality and
motive as surely as it looks back to Scott in the vigour of its
narrative style and setting. Mason gave his friend Andrew Lang
the credit for setting a new, economical style for tales of adventure towards the end of the last century, but the credit belongs as
much to him, and to Anthony Hope and Seton Merriman also,
for taking certain elements of pace and richness from earlier
decades while moving away from the density and the authorial

interpolations which discourage many readers of today. The 'new style' recognised by A. E. W. Mason a century or so ago is remarkably unchanged today as regards story line and verbal economy.

The plot of *Clementina* has a classic simplicity. Charles Wogan, the hero, has been chosen to escort Clementina Sobieska, daughter of the King of Poland, to the Chevalier de St George (or, as Wogan and others think of him, the exiled and rightful James III of England). The marriage is to gain support for James in Europe against the Hanoverian ruling house. The enterprise is threatened, first when delays in the journey from Poland have given the chance for the Emperor of Austria to have Clementina captured and then because James has meanwhile sought permission from the Pope for marriage to his nobly-born Italian mistress Maria Vittoria. Committed to the marriage politically and also by his admiration for Clementina's courage and her strong loyalty to the Stuart cause, Wogan determines to bring the Polish princess to the King against any odds: because he falls in love with her on the journey, the adventure becomes a test of honour. A. E. W. Mason struck out from the historical facts of the marriage of the Stuart king to Clementina Sobieska into a romance which is plausible, intense and redeemed from sentimentality by a kind of irony of accident, most of all shown when Wogan stands as proxy in the marriage ceremony. The conflict between love and honour gives special point to a precisely defined and vigorously described journey from Innsbruck to Bologna.

Roger Lancelyn Green, an illuminating commentator on Mason's work, takes a critical view of *Clementina* as a romance:

> . . . once more he produced a story with swift action, told with the skills and finish of which he was by now a master, and made more notable by one or two touches of psychological interpretation applied to the motifs of pure romance – notably the love which springs up between Wogan and the Princess and their struggles between duty and desire. The spiritual battle is still not quite real enough to bear with it that pleasure of both intellect and emotion which is so much fuller and, in a sense, higher than the effects produced by the thrill of the purely outward context which is the theme of the ordinary adventure story. Truly though the adventure still carries the book, it is undoubtedly there, striving for mastery. From this unconscious contest proceeds the slight feeling of dissatisfaction which *Clementina* produces in retrospect; the characters have too much individuality to let us abandon ourselves wholly to the exciting rush of the story, and yet they are not real enough for us to look at the story wholly through their eyes. And the struggle between the two methods in the author's mind seems to

be reflected in a certain discomfort in the style, a discomfort which makes the adult reader wish regretfully from time to time for the lightness and wit of *Parson Kelly*, foreign though such a style would be to such a book as *Clementina*.[16]

This is personal comment and my own would be different. There are many ways of creating character and Roger Lancelyn Green would seem here to be requiring that a certain depth of personality be defined. It seems to me that A. E. W. Mason was creating Wogan and Clementina not through any intricacy of personality (indeed, the course of their love is described in general terms which at times almost amount to romantic cliché) but by precisely and strongly indicating their observable *reactions* to circumstances, using setting, weather, time of day and other such novelistic mechanics to draw the reader into the emotional vibrancy of the story.

The scene in the mountain hut, with its compelling dialogue, the strong sense of place, the evocative references to the tragedy of Königsmark, the very simple, almost stark definition of the posture and movements of Wogan and Clementina, do the work of character-drawing in a way that is a valid alternative to the more direct descriptive method used, for instance, by Buchan. A passage like the following leaves something for the reader to do:

> The curtain between them was down. Wogan had patched and patched it before, but it was torn down now, and they had seen each other without so much as that patched semblance of a screen to delude their eyes. Clementina did not answer him or raise her head. She went quietly into her room. Wogan did not move until she had locked the door.[17]

Such clues to character, with the motive power towards exciting action, are part of the whole, together with the framework of historical fact working on the reader with all the associations of the Jacobite rebellions and with honour as a motive force of individual loyalty.

There is a choice for the reader, in fact, between abandoning himself to 'the exciting rush of the story', as Roger Lancelyn Green puts it, and responding to those deeper demands which I feel are fully allowed for in *Clementina*. The choice is more or less made for the reader in the romantic trilogy by D. K. Broster which uses the second rising of 1745 and its aftermath as a framework for personal relationships. The three novels published between 1925 and 1929 – *The Flight of the Heron*, *The Gleam in the North* and *The Dark Mile* – together provide a study of

119

honour in which character dominates and largely determines action.

Action there is in plenty in these latter-day examples of the traditional adventure-romance. Chases and escapes reminiscent of *Kidnapped* are strongly rendered in the first two books, while *The Dark Mile* is built on the recurring theme of frustrated love, as a young Scot falls in love with a member of a rival clan. It is mainly for these two elements of love and escape that D. K. Broster's trilogy filtered down to young readers.

There was also the consideration that it offered to the teens a maturity of subject and style unsullied by any sordidness or explicit sex. The books seem to have been adopted during the 1940s and 1950s as a halfway house between junior and adult fiction. They were included in Penguin's Peacock list for young adults, in 1963, 1968 and 1974, where they constituted something of an equivalent to the swashbuckling tales of Stanley Weyman and Seton Merriman and others which had provided a halfway house for the adolescents of earlier generations.

But if D. K. Broster was aware of past traditions when she worked out her interpretation of the Jacobite rebellions, she was also looking forward. The loyalties to nation, king or clan which she explores are a matter of history but her approach belongs to the post-war period. These are novels of character as much as they are novels of action; one sign of this is the predominance of dialogue, the characters being allowed space to explore their beliefs and circumstances in some depth.

This is especially true of *The Flight of the Heron*, where both the plot and the emotional tone depend on the change from enmity to friendship in Ewan Cameron, involved in the '45 rising under Lochiel, head of his clan, and Captain Keith Windham who leads a Hanoverian regiment on reconnaissance in the Highlands. Foreshadowed by a riddling prophecy from Ewan's foster-father, delivered with all the force of a Highland seer, the relationship between the two men is an intense one. If the book had been written half a century later the homosexual overtones might have been more obvious, but this would not have served the book well, for its point is one of the principles of honour tested in action; each encounter involves Ewan and Keith in opposed loyalties as each tries to save the other without betraying the cause he serves.

The friendship developed through argument and through the attitude of each man to the other is used to suggest the implications of the Jacobite cause and to contrast the clan rivalries and mismanagement before and after Culloden with the passionate loyalty to the Prince which overcame doubts and fears in Ewan and his elders. Windham is introduced as a professional soldier whose lonely childhood and adolescence have led him to assume a pose of cynicism, intensified when he is transferred from a conventional campaign in the Low Countries to the bewildering mountain passes of the Highlands. His journal, written while he is a prisoner on parole with the Cameron clan, comments bluntly that the 'Pretender's Son' is a 'very personable young man . . . they all appear crazy about him'[18] and when Ewan Cameron puts himself in danger in order to save Windham's reputation, during an imbroglio in Edinburgh, he notes:

> The days of chivalry were over; one did not go about in this century behaving like the knights in the old romances. An enemy was an enemy – at least to a professional soldier – and it was one's business to treat him as such.[19]

Gradually Windham's view changes. Through growing affection he relaxes his assumption of being in the right; he comes to see and value Ewan Cameron's essential honesty and to understand at least some of the motives behind the rising, while his death, ironically caused by the man who would most have wished to avoid it, means that he escapes having to choose finally between friendship and the honour of a soldier.

The theme of honour in the novels could have struck the reader as strained and finicking, particularly in the complex loyalties and obligations invoked in *The Gleam in the North*, which centres on the fate of Lochiel and his brother Dr Archie Cameron. But the scruples explored in all three books depend not only on their historical context but also on the firm character-drawing which holds action and motive in partnership, and show the Jacobite cause, the foundation of the trilogy, in terms of individuals.

An interesting clue to changes in readers' expectations may be discerned in Naomi Mitchison's approach to the subject two decades later in *The Bull Calves*. Published two years after the end of the Second World War, this interpretation of the history of certain of her Haldane ancestors shows individuals facing the bitter tensions of divided loyalties and debts of honour after the '45 in a way which strongly relates the past to the post-war period in which she wrote, a period when 'relevance' was considered to be desirable in historical fiction.

These novels were adopted by readers in the teens looking for a congenial blend of emotion and action in stories. They could be expected to accept the concept of honour in its historical context. A different, simpler, perhaps more distanced way would have to be found in presenting the conflicting loyalties and clan rivalries of the Jacobite rebellions to those younger boys and girls, eager for tales of action, needing the motivation which alone can truly activate action in narrative yet with less emotional experience and fewer associations to bring to their reading. The impulse towards adventure, in readers no less than in the characters they are invited to meet, is a complicated compound of instinct and conditioning. No writer for the young can afford to limit style or material too strictly to what they can be expected to understand actively and at once: that way, the impulse can be interrupted or even lost. A context must be found in which children can read and understand at their own pace and with understanding at more than one level.

Olivia Fitzroy found such a context for a time-slip adventure, *The Hunted Head*, with Prince Charles Edward as the focal point and emotional stimulus. When Jamie Stewart, as a result of a blow on the head, is whisked from 1946 to 1746, he has no recollection of his former self; he has been translated not only into the body of an ancestor but into his passionate adherence to the Stuart cause. As the earlier Jamie he takes on the dangerous role of messenger, travelling from the family home at Carrick to Knoydart, where the Prince is in hiding while waiting for news of the ship that is to carry him to France: at the same time Jamie's sister, disguised as a boy, dodges Hanoverian soldiers on her way to warn the ship's captain of the Prince's plans.

The parallel enterprise of brother and sister is one clue to the author's approach to her material. As the children scramble over hill-passes, wade through streams, ponder over the prophecy that the Prince's safety is threatened by a man with white hair, suffer cold, hunger and fear, their behaviour and attitudes (especially because of the neutral tone of the dialogue) belong to the chase-adventure of twentieth-century children rather than to the Highlands of 1746. Even the climax of their meeting with the Prince is oddly perfunctory:

> Fiona, standing respectfully against the wall, knew she would never forget that scene. The flickering light from the many candles that Ludovic had lit and stuck in cracks in the walls . . . Jamie kneeling by the Prince and carving him pieces of mutton with his dirk and spreading butter on scones . . . And the Prince himself with his large sad eyes and the brown fairish hair and the long white fingers now smeared with mud and unwashed for many days. And in spite of that and of his dark ragged coat and haltered plaid and the brogues worn through with walking, he had an air about him that turned the cave into a palace and the Highlanders to courtiers.[20]

122

The anxieties of the young messengers, and their clan loyalties, have to be sensed by the reader from authorial statements which seem flat because the characters hardly fill them out. Skilfully though the mechanics of the tale have been managed, there is no suggestion that this unexpected extending of family history has changed Jamie or Fiona noticeably.

Of all the didactic elements introduced into books for the young, the growth into maturity accelerated by unexpected happenings is most acceptably accommodated in adventure stories. Here, in a special way, the events of the past can be related to the present in a general way without hindsight or false emphasis. For example, in *Charlie is My Darling* Jane Oliver used the Prince's triumphal entrance into Edinburgh in 1746 and the optimistic start of the journey to London as her story line, linking the trick at the Netherbow Gate by which the Prince found a way into the strongly guarded city with the Macdonald family and most of all with Sandy, whose eager longing to prove his loyalty to the cause is turned in a more useful direction after he has worked with Dr Archie Cameron in the terrible aftermath of a battle and decides to train as a doctor. Young readers of today should find it easy to accept that a boy of fifteen could find a new incentive and could wake up to the realities of civil conflict in this particular way: the emotional pattern is, after all, a universal one.

Mollie Hunter's tale of conspiracy, *The Lothian Run*, is set in 1736, midway between the two major Jacobite risings, when an atmosphere of danger, uncertainty and confused allegiances could be rendered in accurate period terms but brought close to young people of our own time. Here a boy of sixteen, bored with his apprenticeship to a dry lawyer, eagerly agrees to use his knowledge of Edinburgh and its environs on behalf of a special investigator in the Customs Service, following the activities of a thief escaped from prison, a timid minister committed to the Prince's cause and a time-serving nobleman secretly returned from exile. Sandy cheerfully engages in eavesdropping and uses a boy's cunning in escaping from his enemies; but when he reflects that danger, 'an unpleasant, almost a nauseating thing at the time of its happening', was 'exciting . . . in retrospect',[21] the official corrects him:

> 'It is an acquired taste . . . only suitable for those who have the physique to tolerate it, and the intelligence to know how far to indulge it.'[21]

When Sandy's excursion into adventure is over he knows what he wants to do with his life and, besides, he has been shaken out of an unpractical, romantic view of the issues of the day.

Both these stories in a sense contain lessons on how to be a useful citizen. Iona McGregor's *An Edinburgh Reel* looks behind the heroic devotion of the Prince's supporters to the unhappy aftermath of 1751, the year of amnesty for the Jacobites of the '45, but historical circumstances are peripheral to the theme of the book, the making of a relationship. The central character, Christine Murray, is sixteen when her father returns from the Continent under the amnesty. Her memory of him has been overlaid with a certain ardent feeling for the heroic past. Forgetting that Red John Murray had been betrayed and sent to the hulks before escaping to France, she expects to see him in the French uniform he had described to her in a letter, a vigorous man in the outward semblance of a hero. Meeting the mail coach, she supposes her father had not travelled by it after all:

> There was one man who did not seem to know where to go. He was quite short and small, and stooped a little. He wore a green coat, short cut in the French fashion, and a dark pigtailed wig. Underneath it, his hair showed grizzled and sandy. He had no sword, only a small cane. As he came near, she saw a livid scar on his right cheek. He had a disturbed, elderly likeness to her father.[22]

The relationship between father and daughter develops through events typical of historical romance. After the first shock Christine becomes in effect her father's protector, although the respect due to a father, and John Murray's vacillating attitude to life, make it difficult for her to save him from disaster when he is persuaded by an old friend to involve himself in plans for a new anti-Hanoverian plot. The search for her father's betrayer allows Christine and her friend Jamie Lindsay to lurk and contrive in the way of hundreds of fictional children but it is the change in the emotional balance between a girl and her father at a crucial stage in her growing-up which gives tone to the book, with a timely attention to motive and personality that is as rare in such books as it is desirable.

Adventure stories like this encourage active rather than passive readers by giving them enough unexpected, stimulating ideas to exercise their wits on – ideas, in the present instance, of the way people behave and change in unusual situations. The story comes first but it is the interaction of character and event that makes the essential demand on the reader. The ironic note heard in so many adult novels about the lost cause of the Stuarts carries a seemingly simple junior tale of mistaken identity, *The Young Pretenders*, to an unusual depth. Barbara Leonie Picard's Jacobite tale has at its centre a boy of fourteen, Francis Rimpole, and his younger sister Bella, children of a Whiggish family in Yorkshire who have individual reasons for favouring the rebel cause. Francis's admiration for a young neighbour who has gone to join the Prince in Scotland (as he is too young to realise, for decidedly selfish reasons) makes him 'all in a matter of twenty seconds, an ardent Jacobite',[23] while Bella, learning from her governess of the Prince's landing, visualises:

> . . . the handsome young Prince, stepping out from a little cockle-shell boat which tossed on a stormy sea, on to the wild and inhospitable shores of Scotland with his seven companions – such a magical, evocative, and legendary number seven! – to regain his father's lost crown.[24]

When a little later the children find a wounded man hiding on the estate they jump to romantic conclusions in which the fugitive, not unnaturally, encourages them:

> The stranger glanced again from one to the other of them, then he smiled wryly. 'Faith! And what alternative have I but to admit that I am a Jacobite, and I with nothing but the pair of you between me and the gallows.'[25]

Idiom and detail support the dramatic irony by which the reader quickly recognises the mistakes: the stranger's true identity as the thief Seamus MacDonald, gradually explained, is plausibly kept from the enthusiastic children, with the help of a surname equally suitable for a Scot and an Irishman and of certain convincing anecdotes which the glib but shamefaced Seamus spins for his rescuers after they have established him secretly in the empty Dower House.

The situation is skilfully developed on more than one level. The children, as they smuggle food and face awkward questions from their elders, might well have been drawn like a boy and girl of the present in fancy dress but the period details chosen are far more than stage properties. The problem of finding enough food for their protégé brings the brother and sister, sheltered as they are in the privilege of their class, to a certain understanding of the way other people live. Francis, reserved and unpopular with the family servants, is forced to find a new way of speaking to them and both children are shocked and embarrassed when a young servant is accused of stealing food and they have to find a way to exonerate her without revealing their secret.

The disillusion which these two young aristocrats have to face is just as carefully described in terms of their time and circumstances. Francis's entry to Eton has been deferred by illness but by temperament and training he has already absorbed the required attitudes. He reacts naturally at first, with a mixture of wounded pride and mortification, when he discovers that their heroic Jacobite is a petty criminal wanted by the law but he realises in a cooler moment that he still has a duty towards the man:

> . . . from somewhere among the bitter, shaming memories that jostled each other in their eagerness to torment him, there came into his mind the picture of himself looking down at Seamus in the ditch below the stone wall of the park and swearing on his honour as a gentleman that not for any consideration whatsoever would he betray him. Not for any consideration: not for revenge, not even to see justice done on a deserving criminal. And yet, Seamus MacDonald to whom he had given his word was not the James O'Leary who was a coin-clipper and a thief. Or was he? Was not the man the same, unchanged in himself – unchanged in his corrupt, deceiving heart? To whom, Francis began to wonder, did one make a promise: to a man himself, or to the man one believed him to be?[26]

One of the most valuable offerings Barbara Leonie Picard made to young readers in this far from simple adventure is the differentiation between brother and sister. Both are angry when they find they have been deceived but they face the situation as individuals. The scruples Francis feels are those of a gently nurtured, reflective boy; he decides on abstract grounds that Seamus must still be protected, since he is not yet fit to walk. Bella agrees for more emotional reasons; young as she is, she senses that Seamus is unhappy at his ingratitude and she finds herself as ready to daydream about the thief as she was to romanticise her role towards the supposed hero. Her vision of 'a Highland home and a tall Highland woman wearing a tartan shawl which was blowing in the wind, looking out into the sunset, watching and waiting . . . would he be her son or her husband?'[27] merges into the vision of a man reformed by her noble generosity:

> . . . she saw herself and Francis, a few years hence, being thanked – with all his old charm, now no longer misapplied – by a happy, hard-working, and honest Seamus, for having been the ones to set his feet on the path of righteousness.[28]

Brother and sister discuss seriously and with a total lack of experience whether Seamus shall be encouraged to become a shopkeeper, a publican or a thief-taker, and the stratagem eventually carried out in which Seamus is taken to Bristol by their unsuspecting uncle is confidently expected to lead to an equally suitable career as a seaman. They never find out that after one voyage their protégé has returned to his former activities and their anxieties about him slowly subside. A few months later:

> . . . such is the resilience of youth, the careful efforts which they had at first made to forget, were now no longer necessary: they forgot, for long periods, with no conscious effort at all.[29]

The moral obligations recognised by this gently bred pair of two centuries ago should not be impenetrable to responsive young readers of today, given a story so liberally endowed with pace, incident and humour. The young may use this and other studies of honour, if they please, in order to decide how far they relate to their own codes of conduct and how far such scruples and pre-scripts are now fossilised. What have Ruritanian allegiances or Jacobite loyalties to say to them? Does the concept of 'a gentle-man' have any meaning to them now? Although it has become permissible, even to some extent obligatory, for historical novel-ists to exercise a certain measure of hindsight in order to give their books relevance, yet we do at least expect them to exercise historical imagination and to reflect the attitudes of their chosen period. Equally, novelists should expect us, as readers, to accept the honour of a Rassendyll or an Alan Breck in their particular context, with everything that is implied about morality in that honour.

6. The Querying of Morality

The emotional motives and moral values of novels set in the past can be simplified and isolated: distance makes for clarity. The challenge for both author and reader is more formidable when we come to adventures arising from the conditions of contemporary or near-contemporary society, and most obviously when the conflict necessary to form a plot is found in some aspect of crime – murder or petty theft, sabotage, terrorism, espionage. The reader rightly expects in such novels a reasonably accurate reflection of his own social culture and, besides, he will expect to recognise in the characters something of his own sense of life, his own fears and wishes. Buchan picked up unerringly the forebodings of his contemporaries, as Graham Greene has touched on the nerves of the early thirties, as Le Carré probes the anxieties of the seventies and after. In doing this they have extended the range of the genre which Buchan liked to call 'shockers' and Graham Greene 'entertainments', names which can hardly be accepted as literal definitions.

We have to distinguish between books which are simply danger-games, designed as pastimes and no more, and adventure novels, thrillers if you like, in which beyond plot lies something extra which I will call *direction*. This direction, this extra element, could be an anti-war theme or a thread of social analysis; it is more often perhaps (certainly more successfully from a literary point of view) a direct relating of character to action. The line between danger-games and adventure novels of this more complex kind is a narrow one but it does seem to me a reasonable way of putting Ian Fleming and Len Deighton on one side of a line and Graham Greene, Le Carré and Buchan on the other.

The interaction of character and event is crucial to any kind of novel, though critics have been trying for many years to assure writers of adventure stories that this is not their concern. It is especially crucial to tales describing the confrontation of good and bad in our society. Some thrillers make a stand on simple distinctions of good and bad and go no further: others explore in a way suggested by a reviewer of new novels by Nicholas Freeling and P. M. Hubbard in 1969. Commenting on the 'heroic genre' of such books, he pointed out that the crime novel 'acts within a

128

chosen concept of right morality and often queries what this should be'.[1] It is in this querying of morality that the reader is taken from plot to direction, as the attitudes and responses of characters to events are canvassed. John Le Carré was aware of a change in his writing with his third novel, *The Spy Who Came In from the Cold*:

> I really wasn't satisfied with that kind of writing – that's to say, fitting characters into a preconceived plot. And although *The Spy* is very tightly plotted, I was determined with that book to make characters organically move the plot and it's true that the more I've gone on writing the more contemplative, I suppose, I've become.[2]

Demonstrating in the character of George Smiley, developed in the course of several novels, the querying of morality, the interaction of plot and character, Le Carré has proved most forcefully the capacity of the adventure story to go beyond any chase or mystery formula.

The formula-thriller takes a simple method of satisfying readers by exposing their secret fears or aggressive fantasies in such a way that their fears are assuaged and their fantasies flattered. A publisher reflecting, ten years ago, on the popularity of spy-stories, commented that 'the spy as an anti-establishment symbol has his own contemporary appeal, across boundaries of ideology and class'.[3] Still a best-seller in its most sensational form, the spy-story owes its popularity to its now alarmingly topical aspect. But defections from West to East over the past years have not only meant a search for novels which by their artificiality and sensationalism make it possible for us to avert our eyes from the unpleasant facts about treason. Any reader of fiction is moved by a curiosity, superficial or passionate, about the springs of human nature, and the more layered and perceptive the novel, the more we realise our kinship with the characters, whoever they may be. Specifically, the nature of treason is a subject so emotive, calling on what seems to be an instinctive revulsion and a correspondingly morbid curiosity, that it would seem hard to treat it in anything but a serious manner.

This does not alter the need for pace and action in adventure stories. It would not be right to expect in a spy-thriller an analysis like that of Elizabeth Bowen's *The Heat of the Day*, in which with cool, deliberate, cruel veracity she analysed the suburban background which formed, created and nurtured a man who was to betray his country. More often than not the 'why' of the case will seem, at least initially, to be less prominent in the narrative of a thriller than the 'how'.

The novel of action was slow to respond to the increasingly probing analysis and the half-tones of good and bad in the problem-novels of the 1920s and after. Erskine Childers, writing in the years before the First World War, put into words the political apprehensions of his time as surely as Buchan and Le Carré were to do later, yet *The Riddle of the Sands* almost seems to have been written with the intention of distracting the reader's attention from the man who (as the narrator surmises, because of some disgrace) abandoned his identity as an officer in the British Navy and became the German Dollman, engaged ostensibly in some mysterious diving operations on the North Frisian coast. Purporting to be the 'editor' of his narrative, Erskine Childers explained in a preface that 'the whole story should be written, as from the mouth of a man whose name has been changed to "Carruthers", with its humours and errors, its light and dark side, just as it happened',[4] saving only that the year and the identity of the characters should be disguised. We do not get to know Dollman; that is, we do not find out why he had used his knowledge of naval matters and the north-east coast of England to work out and forward to the German government an elaborate plan for an invasion of England from the Frisian dunes and water-courses. We see him entirely from the point of view of the two Englishmen who share the status of hero in the book, Carruthers of the Foreign Office and Davies, a solicitor's clerk and a friend from Oxford days.

Very much the man about town, Carruthers regrets that he has agreed to share an autumn cruise to shoot duck on the Baltic coast when he joins Davies at Flensburg and finds craft and owner far below his accustomed standard of sailing at Cowes. His suave, self-deprecating complaints lighten the deepening seriousness of the story. We are aware all the time that he is changing, that he is learning to respect his diffident friend for his skill in handling the yacht and, more, for his courage. For Davies is afraid. A chance-met German sailing with his daughter, a man of fifty or so with a reserved but friendly air about him, has apparently tried to murder him by giving him a lead through dangerous sandbanks during a storm and abandoning him there.

It is in the intertwining of humour and suspense that the brilliance of the book lies. As the friends explore the sands, meet associates of Dollman and by surveillance, deduction and socialising gradually discover the truth about the man, Carruthers remains detached and even mildly satirical about Davies's fears and only casually sympathetic when he realises that his friend has fallen deeply in love with Clara Dollman and is determined to rescue her without letting her realise her father's true purpose and identity. For both young men, in fact, the situation is a romantic one, an adventure of knight-errantry, and for Carruthers an enjoyable one:

> My philosophy when I left London was of a very worldly sort, and no one can change his temperament in three weeks. I plainly said as much to Davies, and indeed took perverse satisfaction in stating with brutal emphasis some social truths which bore on this attachment of his to the daughter of an outlaw. Truths I call them, but I uttered them more by rote than by conviction, and he heard them unmoved. And meanwhile I snatched recklessly at his own solution. If it imparted into our adventure a strain of crazy chivalry more suited to knights-errant of the middle ages than to sober modern youths – well, thank heaven, I was not too sober, and still young enough to snatch at that fancy with an ardour of imagination if not of character; perhaps, too, of character, for Galahads are not so common but that ordinary folk must needs draw courage from their example and put something of a blind trust in their tenfold strength.[5]

So, through Davies's anxious devotion to Clara and Carruthers's youthfully romantic approach to adventure, the enigmatic figure of Dollman appears and disappears, changing from Davies's first sight of him as 'a tall, thin chap, in evening dress . . . with greyish hair and a short beard' . . . and 'a high bulging forehead'[6] to the sight Carruthers has of him, in the starboard sidelight of a launch, as the friends sustain a pretence with difficulty at a crucial stage of their enterprise:

> . . . those fruitless green rays . . . you know their ravaging effects on the human physiognomy – struck full on Dollman's face. It was my first fair view of it at close quarters, and, secure in my background of gloom, I feasted with a luxury of superstitious abhorrence on the livid smiling mask that for a few moments stooped peering down towards Davies. One of the caprices of the crude light was to obliterate, or at any rate so penetrate, beard and moustache, as to reveal in outline lips and chin, the features in which defects of character are most surely betrayed, especially when your victim smiles. Accuse me, if you will, of stooping to melodramatic embroidery; object that my own prejudiced fancy contributed to the result; but I can, nevertheless, never efface the impression of malignant perfidy and base passion exaggerated in caricature, that I received in those few instants.[7]

As Carruthers says, the man remained the centre of everything for him. While Davies, intent on saving Clara from pain and disgrace, saw him as 'at most a noxious vermin to be trampled

on for the public good', Carruthers was trying to understand
the origin of his treason, 'noting the evidences of great gifts
squandered and prostituted' and wondering 'whether he was
open to remorse or shame; or whether he meditated further
crime'.[8] Dollman remains a mystery, in his association with his
German fellow-conspirators, in his suicide at sea and in the
Editor's Epilogue in which, as 'X', the traitor's invasion plan is
quoted.

Artistically, the oblique method of characterisation is totally
successful. The elements of the book – the precise, enthralling
descriptions of small-boat sailing, the slow tracking-down of
Dollman and the resolving of the puzzle of his various activities,
the changing relationship of Carruthers and Davies and their
contrasting reactions to danger, the brief but intense revelations
of Davies's passion for Clara, the urbanity cast over the narrative
by Carruthers's unmistakable voice – are unified in diversity in a
story that seems slow, leisurely and even rambling but which is in
fact superbly organised towards its climax and anticlimax. As for
the implicit warning of invasion, coming a decade before the start
of the First World War, this is something which must have a
different emphasis for readers of today than it had when the book
was first published.

In the political context, the treason of the ex-naval officer may be
said to be treated seriously: in the psychological sense Dollman is
an *example* of a traitor, not an individual. Childers directed his
narrative towards the effect of one man's perfidy on his fellow-
countrymen, Carruthers and Davies; through their reactions to a
dangerous adventure a general warning of enemy intention is
expressed. The reader is free to take his own view of the traitor's
personal motives and will decide whether or not the author's
method seems justifiable. John le Carré has used the same
oblique method of depicting a traitor in *Tinker Tailor Soldier
Spy*, but he scrutinises his character far more closely. The course
of history and of literary techniques between 1900, the date of
The Riddle of the Sands, and 1974, when Le Carré's book was
published, has necessarily changed the expectation of readers;
this, if nothing else, placed a responsibility on Le Carré to probe
the motives behind the years during which Bill Haydon manipulated the intelligence organisation known as the Circus for the
benefit of his Soviet masters.

This is not to say that Le Carré's readers would be likely to
expect any concise, logical, final explanation of Haydon's behaviour. Warned by the actual circumstances of Philby, Burgess

and Maclean, accustomed to the evasions, smoke screens, contradictions in their life-styles and their defections, those readers looking for something more than the pantomime-villains of railway-bookstall spy-stories will not have been surprised by the ignoble, dislocated, manic sentences which Smiley recalls from Haydon's rambling apologia or the open expression of his colossal vanity (coming, significantly, from a man who 'to Smiley's eye . . . seemed quite visibly to be shrinking to something quite small and mean'):

> He was touched to hear that Ionesco had recently promised us a play in which the hero kept silent and everyone round him spoke incessantly. When the psychologists and fashionable historians came to write their apologies for him, he hoped they would remember that that was how he saw himself. As an artist, he had said all he had to say at the age of seventeen, and one had to do something with one's later years.[9]

The structure and emotional shape of the book comes from the way Haydon is seen through the eyes of his colleagues, friends, associates, and through their eyes undergoes a diminishing from the brilliant, dominating polymath and leader to the nose-bleeding, disreputable wreck who still affects to despise the man whose painful and patient investigation has brought him down. The circumstances of Haydon's recruitment as double agent and, finally, as a mole hidden in the Circus are in terms of politics very clear from their obvious topical connotations. Connie Sachs laments the situation of a generation 'trained to Empire, trained to rule the waves'[10] and finding all its security taken away, and Smiley notes that Bill in the past 'had proposed all sorts of grand designs for restoring England to influence and greatness'.[11] Smiley wonders with bitter, reluctant sympathy whether Haydon's treason does not belong to the public domain rather than to the man, for was Haydon not himself betrayed:

> He saw with painful clarity an ambitious man born to the big canvas, brought up to rule, divide and conquer, whose visions and vanities all were fixed upon the world's game; for whom the reality was a poor island with scarcely a voice that would carry across the water. . . .[12]

and he feels 'a surge of resentment against the institutions he was supposed to be protecting', for the complacency, greed and mendacity of his masters. Even when faced by the defeated Haydon, Smiley cannot deny him a measure of heroism, any more than Guillam, for whom Haydon had been 'the torch-bearer of a certain kind of antiquated romanticism',[13] can entirely forget in his furious disillusion that Haydon had had greatness in him.

Haydon's iniquity is perceived gradually, by implicit comparison with Bland's crude opportunism, Alleline's arrogance, Esterhase's time-serving vanity, as each in turn comes under scrutiny as the possible mole. Because each of these men is seen to have his own limited loyalty, his own impure sense of honour, Haydon's betrayal, because it is more extreme, more intelligent and more warped, is thrown up in harsh lines against their paler, minor weaknesses. Defined as a thriller, legitimately classified as an adventure story, *Tinker Tailor Soldier Spy* has an intricacy of motive and attitude which far outdoes the intricacy of its thriller-plot.

As far as method goes the book is in fact conceived as an interrogation (or a series of interrogations) with the action almost always reported rather than direct. There is none of the noisy violence with which best-selling spy-stories of a more trivial kind conceal their emptiness of real passion. Rather, intensity depends on an infinite variety of movements, from car-drives or walks to small alterations of posture, facial expression or gesture within a room, a car, a restaurant, indicated within or between motions of dialogue. The double-illusion of happenings external or within the minds and the changing attitudes of the characters is far more powerful than the illusion of the James Bond kind of danger-game, not only because it is based on a veracious rather than a fantastic view of society but also because it reaches beyond the simple, aggressive impulses we all share to deeper, more complex patterns of behaviour.

The generalised 'foreign spy' favoured for so long by novelists has been like any other fictional character affected by changes in society and in international politics and, as a consequence, by the altered demands of readers in successive decades. They will no longer accept the villain of danger-games who is working for 'the wrong side' or believe that the methods by which the hero counters the enemy are justified because he is on 'the right side'. The blurb for Pan's paperback edition of the James Bond tales naïvely explains and justifies the hero:

> The licence to kill for the Secret Service, the double-O prefix, was a great honour. It had been earned hardly. It brought James Bond the only assignments he enjoyed – the dangerous ones.[14]

As a role for the hero this differs conspicuously from the intellectual pleasure which Le Carré's George Smiley finds in his profession of intelligence officer, an 'academic excursion into the mystery of human behaviour, disciplined by the personal application of his own deductions',[15] especially as it is balanced by personal scruples against violence and a nagging doubt about the concept of any absolute moral-national code. As the indirect cause of the death of Dieter, a former colleague and friend whom he has proved to be a spy, Smiley reflects on his responsibility:

> They had come from different hemispheres of the night, from different worlds of thought and conduct. Dieter, mercurial, absolute, had fought to build a civilisation. Smiley, nationalistic, protective, had fought to prevent him. 'Oh God,' said Smiley aloud, 'who was then the gentleman? . . .'[16]

Behind the documentary richness of Le Carré's books and the persuasive professional jargon of moles, lamplighters, baby-sitters and so on (some invented, some borrowed from KGB usage), which gives his readers the illusion of entering a secret world, there are characters who are not the psychopaths of the James Bond tales, the stereotyped heroes and villains of scores of spy-dramas, but ordinary people trapped in unordinary situations, forced to corrupt the normal human pleasures (what the spy Leamas called 'that simplicity that made him break up a bit of bread into a paper bag, walk down to the beach and throw it to the gulls'[17]) by using them as protective coloration. Bill Haydon the traitor, Karla the KGB spy and spymaster and Smiley, his antagonist, are spies in a new kind of fiction, a fiction that moves as close as it can to reality with a close look at the duties of an agent:

> Assimilation is his highest aim, he learns to love the crowds who pass him in the street without a glance; he clings to them for his anonymity and his safety. His fear makes him servile – he could embrace the shoppers who jostle him in their impatience, and force him from the pavement. He could adore the officials, the police, the bus conductors, for the terse indifference of their attitudes.[18]

Like his predecessors (his ancestors, almost) Conrad and Graham Greene, Le Carré has given the spy-thriller new dimensions by looking behind the type to the individual, by extending Cold War situations into an examination of motives on both sides of the conflict, replacing melodrama by a careful, thorough documentation of everyday. It is the method of Greene's *The Confidential Agent* whose hero-spy, bleakly named 'D', has chosen the people he will fight for – 'certain people who've had the lean portion for some centuries now'[19] – but who realises it may be the 'wrong side' and wryly comments that 'In melodrama a secret agent was never tired or uninterested or in love with a dead woman'.[20] It is the method of Conrad's seminal novel,

The Secret Agent, with its thicket of confused motives and beliefs and ambitions and the sardonic mingling of chance and character by which Adolf Verloc's self-loving, lethargic, insensitive, stupid behaviour, as *agent provocateur*, revolutionary and government snooper, brings about its own destruction in an atmosphere of sordid domestic banality. Here are none of the fantastic exaggerations, the super-ingenious hardware which hide the emotional emptiness of danger-games. Le Carré, Greene and Conrad exploit the elements of everyday – a cigarette case, an overcoat, a bread-knife; it is the ordinariness that produces, activates and intensifies the passion and the passion transforms the traditional shape of adventure stories.

How much of this passion, this awareness of the human condition, can be contained in a story for the young? Can they be asked to consider, in any degree at all, the isolation of a spy, the problems of conscience, the 'duress of the lie'[21] as Arthur Hopcraft put it? Like any other kind of novel the adventure story can be a superficial game of action or it can examine action in a way that is emotionally stirring and enlightening. But a story designed for young readers has one inescapable limitation, however maturely an author approaches it. The tone as well as the structure of most junior adventure stories depends on the placing of a child at the centre and the observing of a consistently (though not necessarily a totally) youthful point of view. In the genre of the spy-story this means a double standard in the drawing of characters and their interaction with circumstance. The child-hero (for this is the role he is given to play) may be drawn realistically and set in a background socially and domestically veracious: the spy-villain, seen through the child's eyes, will more often than not appear as a stereotype, a sinister unmotivated figure.

How can this be avoided? A quarter of a century ago Margaret Kennedy in *The Outlaws on Parnassus* commented that 'a strong degree of detachment' is valuable in presenting a villain in fiction. 'An outstandingly bad man', she wrote:

> . . . is not easy material, if he is to be three-dimensional. He generally appears merely as the villain of the piece, as a mechanical contrivance, and as soon as he is foiled he is done with. To present him entire is not within the power of every writer. The yard-stick of ethics will not altogether measure him; he is not exactly like ourselves, only worse. He also may have a different way of looking at things.[22]

In practical social terms a spy is someone who betrays his country: in the personal sense he 'may have a different way of looking at things'. It is this 'different way', the spy's motivation, that is so often missing in junior spy-stories, which are usually an awkward mixture of reality and fantasy. The author, having given up any idea of making his villain an individual, relies on domestic detail to make his story 'real' and 'relevant' and carries over the fantasy treatment of his villain to his young hero by giving him an improbable allowance of power and luck.

Emotionally empty as a consequence, such books deny their readers any kind of stimulus in their aridly conventional, generalised moral stance. The spies whom children detect and expose in superficial danger-games are wicked, the agents of a 'foreign power', and that is all that the young hero, and the young reader likewise, is required to know. If the moral angle of an adventure story is to have any value it must be active within the plot and not merely a matter of bald statement by the author. This is particularly difficult to achieve in bringing the complexities of treason within the understanding of the young because of their limited area of experiences. It would be natural to expect a relatively light, generalised handling of the subject four decades ago, when junior fiction still had a sheltered tone, a certain prescribed attitude expected of an author. In this respect Antonia Forest was ahead of her time in her adventure stories and particularly in *The Marlows and the Traitor*.

As far as the plot goes this tale of danger and rescue seems much like the scores of tales which introduced certain preoccupations of the 1940s in the spirit of holiday-adventure. A boy of fourteen and an older sister, with two younger twin sisters, staying in a seaside town, have their suspicions aroused by the unaccountable behaviour of a British naval officer; heedlessly investigating, they are captured and three of them are imprisoned in a disused lighthouse; through the escape of one of the girls and the professional activities of their elders the enemy is defeated and the children saved. Unlike most stories of the kind, *The Marlows and the Traitor* describes a genuinely dangerous situation. The incidental realities of the background, idiom, weather, coastal contours, sailing techniques, terrain and so on, are matched by a plot which works out favourably not by chance or luck but with a logic that depends ultimately on character.

Antonia Forest has drawn individuals in her four Marlow siblings and the traitor Lewis Foley. In the case of Foley she has provided clues to his behaviour not through omniscient statements from above but disseminated in the reactions and comments of the people involved in his activities, adults as well as young. Because this *is* a plausible story, the tracking and defeating of a spy cannot be left to the young, as it all too often is in junior spy-stories, and Anquetil, a young intelligence officer who has known Foley from boyhood, usefully indicates some at least of the man's motives as he explains his suspicions and his reasons for them. Foley is not, as Anquetil sees him, 'an ardent Communist' but he has accepted the role of spy for them 'because he gets a peculiar kick out of being on his own against the rest of us. He always did.'[23] Anquetil's superior officer builds, from records and memory, the picture of 'a wild, slapdash young man, with a life-and-death temperament. Plenty of courage, but no discipline. No loyalty, either. No idea of working as part of a team.'[24] It is appropriate that Foley's downfall, and indeed his death, are to a great extent due to the uncommitted, impulsive, accidental activities of children, for Foley has an immaturity which makes his selling of his country's secrets, as well as being part of a financial bargain, seem like the exhibitionism of a self-centred, disaffected child at odds with the prosaic adult world.

So far, then, Foley's motives have been seen intellectually: their impact on the young Marlows is an emotional one which gives true depth to the book. Peter Marlow, a cadet at Dartmouth, has been reprimanded, harshly and in public, for an error of judgement, by Lewis Foley, one of his instructors and the object of his ardent admiration. When Peter and Nicola, walking on the esplanade in the rain, are cut dead by Foley, the shock to the boy is a sharp one and helps him to admit to a doubt in his mind about the lieutenant (whose behaviour towards Peter's best friend at Dartmouth has also seemed odd to this honest boy). When the four children stumble on Foley's house by the sea and find a cache of naval documents which the man's bluster does not adequately explain, Peter accepts the truth with bewilderment. Later, from the lighthouse island, the captive children watch destroyers going past – Nicola with her 'midshipman look', Peter with his eyes on Foley:

> He wondered how it felt, to be a naval officer watching those ships and at the same time knowing yourself to be a person who was doing his best to destroy them; it was queer how little people's thoughts showed in their faces.[25]

The boy plays his part in the stratagem intended to prevent Foley from joining the enemy U-boat in a spirit of misery and rage. Nicola, whose heroes are Nelson and Hornblower and whose temperament responds naturally and simply to the naval traditions of the Marlow family, regards Foley as an enemy but is sensitive enough to be unexpectedly distressed when he is drowned. Through Nicola we watch Foley's actions as an enemy in story-book tradition, but through thirteen-year-old Ginty, who has always found anger and abuse terrifying and who, besides, suffers from claustrophobia, we see the man as someone really dangerous. The youngest Marlow, Lawrie, who combines a flair for mimicry with a strong tendency to self-dramatisation, manages to escape from Foley and get back to the town but she plays a less useful part in the action than her more sensible twin Nicola would have done; her entertaining mixture of terror and conscious heroics lightens the tension of the story and brings it now and then almost into the mood of the routine holiday-adventure which it could so well have been.

The contrast between the inexperienced views that the children take of Foley (and fourteen, thirteen and twelve were relatively unsophisticated years when the book was written) and the detached comments of his peers makes the traitor come to life in the emphatic yet mysterious way of any human being. We do not see Foley alone, nor do we enter into his thoughts, but we see him reflected through a number of points of view, canvassed at various stages of the story and combining to provide its emotional basis.

Antonia Forest's breadth of moral reference and the convincing behaviour of her characters are all the more remarkable because she was writing at a time when the optimum age for young heroes and heroines had changed from the late teens to the years between ten and thirteen. In the 1940s the convention of children acting on their own, without the benefit of adult guardians, dominated the sphere of the spy-thriller as of other types of junior adventure. This particular domestic emphasis was obviously useful in freeing characters for exploits unlikely in real life. This is a legitimate liberty for a writer to take but if he does little harm in ignoring some of the sanctions of childhood (mealtimes, school discipline and so on), he gives himself a heavy problem in making his plots plausible.

It is easier to believe in the successful campaigns waged by Percy F. Westerman's schoolboys and cadets against the enemies of their country a decade or two earlier because they are legitimately given the technical experience and physique of near-manhood. Two such heroes, pupils at a West Country school, become assistants to a professor engaged in secret scientific research and are swept into a dangerous encounter with the evil plots of Nessian dictator Schlanger and his spies. The initial definition of their characters suggests that they are at least old enough to bear themselves creditably in a crisis:

Rupert Redmayne, the elder of the two, was a tall, well-set-up lad of seventeen, with clear-cut features, dark-brown eyes and closely-trimmed auburn hair; he had the appearance of what he actually was – a typically healthy and athletic schoolboy.

His chum, Donald Daintree, was a year younger, and quite different in build and colouring. Three inches shorter than Redmayne, he was stockily built, with square shoulders and massive limbs. His dark hair, deep grey eyes and features tanned by sun and salt-laden gave him an almost swarthy appearance.[26]

Nothing in the approach or behaviour of these predictable heroes takes them outside this formula description. If their age and education gives them a certain credibility demanded by the story, it ensures as well that they will not question either the justice of their cause or the possible motives of their enemies. Younger characters, set against spies and secret weapons, can hardly operate so easily without benefit of adults nor can they be expected to offer such heartfelt pledges to their country as Westerman's young men do, actual or potential servicemen as they are.

One author who explored the suitability of the spy-thriller during and immediately after the Second World War for a wider and younger readership found her own solution to the problem. In her Bunkle series (twelve books, half of which concerned children and spy-hunts) Muriel Pardoe created a family within which the various political and structural demands of the subject could be to some extent satisfied. Major (later Colonel) de Salis, secretly employed in Army Intelligence, carries on some of his investigations during family holidays, at home or abroad, which provide a useful screen; his only attempt at an actual disguise, in *Bunkle Began It*, when with the help of a monocle he affected the manner of a vapid upper-class gentleman, failed to deceive the German agent met by chance in the Shropshire hills. The serious aspect of the tales (particularly noticeable in the three earliest books, written before or during the war) is vested in de Salis and, in a different way, in his supportive wife; equally, the dangerous moments of confrontation, the physical apprehending of the enemy agents, are handed over to de Salis and his colleagues. Violence is in any case kept to the minimum – this is the period of the safe middle-class adventure, after all – but one difficulty of involving children in spy-activities has been neatly avoided.

The three de Salis children are carefully placed as regards action. When it is necessary for them to be alone to make important discoveries their parents are removed temporarily and plausibly from the scene, but the safety-net is always there when it is

140

needed. Their characters, too, are defined, in outline but firmly enough, so that their particular contribution to spy-detecting is believable. When the sequence begins in 1939 with *Four Plus Bunkle*, Jill is nearly fifteen, her brother Robin a year younger and Bunkle (nicknamed by his elders because of the nonsense he talks) is in his tenth year. Sent to school on the Riviera for a year for his health, Bunkle is joined by his parents and siblings during the summer holidays of 1938 and here, while their parents are away, the three children pick up signals from a room opposite their hotel and discover a young Intelligence officer with a broken leg who implores them to deliver an important package to the British Consul – 'the whole difference between war and peace in Europe, and the safety of England, may depend on that packet getting into the right hands'.[27] Train journeys provide the movement and tension in the story, in which Bunkle's part seems mainly to provide comic relief, with his frequently inconvenient devotion to food.

Gradually the stories include more useful elements. Observant and incorrigibly inquisitive, with the self-confidence of a rather spoilt youngest child, Bunkle is almost always the first to notice a vital clue. In *Bunkle Began It* it is he who knows that Mrs Wetherby is a spy and not the mad old woman his father remembers from his youth, because she has *not* lost the tops of two fingers. It is natural to him to poke into old cellars and detect the one keyhole that has been oiled, to crawl into an unpromising roof-route to the hotel's cisterns; nobody but Bunkle would have thought it unusual to find a large portion of a plastic bag hanging on a wild raspberry bush in a Scottish field but Bunkle worries at the oddity in time to expose a large-scale poaching organisation. The natural gifts of a small boy for lurking, overhearing and observing are commonplace in junior adventures but they are neatly fitted into the good-humoured and relatively individual portrait of Bunkle, who is cheerfully aware of his position in the family; as he assures his friend Belinda:

> '. . . this kind of adventure always seems to be happening to me, and I'm getting sort of used to dealing with them. It must be my destiny, you know, nothing ever seems to happen to the others if I'm not there.'[28]

His character is effectively established through contrast. His sensible older brother Robin acts as moderator to his enthusiasm, for Bunkle's discoveries are nourished by an addiction to such thriller-clichés as ammonia-pistols, secret passages and sinister strangers; his sister Jill meanwhile maintains the security of domestic routine from which the small boy can range into adventure, his cockiness corrected now and then by his father, who after one particularly bold effort of Bunkle's in rearranging people's lives:

> . . . proceeded to wallop him cheerfully across his latter end with a wooden spoon.[29]

By deliberately containing this young hero within a conventional middle-class mode of life, Muriel Pardoe gave greater credibility to the moment when his guesses prove to be right. At one end we have the believable successes of youthful curiosity: at the other, glimpses of the serious and dangerous career of an army officer who establishes through the stories his own robust and orthodox political and social attitudes.

A similar cross-fertilising of adult and youthful points of view characterises John Pudney's 'Fred and I' thrillers, transmitted as radio serials in the late forties and 1950s before appearing in book form. Crackling, rowdy, yet pertinent to their times, the yarns are told by 'I', a boy of eleven or twelve who is never named; he is under the guardianship of his Uncle George and conducts his life with his friend Fred, a neighbour in the Sussex village near Ashdown Forest from which they rush out to adventure. Uncle George's exact position at the secret Fort X and its associated station at High Standing is a matter of national security; the author leaves himself free to deploy him as both inventor and counter-spy and so to add variety to a genre which even in the late forties was still being overworked.

Uncle George is called upon to forestall 'the enemy' in the exploiting of dangerous chemical and technological discoveries or to prevent them from seizing for their own ends the formulas for advanced weaponry or the control of new mineral or chemical substances. The 'enemy' consists of predictable foreigners from countries whose Ruritanian names (Lovelia, Poldana, Fragovinia, Aranoctia) and mid-European locations offer all the identification that is needed; even when John Pudney does specify an actual country, as he does in *Tuesday Adventure*, it is by way of a conveniently vague but powerful international organisation known as L.E.L., consisting of disaffected Latvians, Lithuanians and Estonians. His villains keep their forces in subjection through political blackmail, brainwashing or drugs, and they often work through British or allied scientists who have either been suborned or else kidnapped and turned into malleable zombies.

As with scores of similar tales, 'good' and 'bad' are taken for

142

granted. The popularity of the series rested on no originality of attitude or plot, probably not even (at least for the average reader) on the special zest of Pudney's prose style. To the clichés of secret formulas and thievish foreign agents he added an extra dimension which almost took his books into the category of Jules Verne science-fiction. Instead of the well-worn stage-properties of submarines, binoculars and microdots of run-of-the-mill adventures, he satisfied his listeners and readers with such ingenious hardware as a jet-powered hedgecutter with sinister potential, innumerable electrically-powered cars and submersibles, jet-propelled skis, an early and complex closed-circuit television system, a force-field, a superior modification of inter-floor lifts in a London store and an internationally operated radio transmitter rising out of a peaceful Sussex valley on a huge pole. These and other adjuncts to villainy, keyed though they are to nefarious activities, seem like an extension of the kind of train-set, whether clockwork or electrical, which fathers notoriously filch from their children: Pudney manipulates them with evident enjoyment and with a certain tongue-in-cheek gaiety.

Rumour is certainly as important in the books as action. Indeed, it serves to distract the attention from a rather monotonous arrangement of scenes which do little more than plot the movements of the characters from one tunnel, secret passage or vehicle to another, with an occasional chase, tussle or explosion by way of a change. Certainly the books reflect indirectly the preoccupations of the Cold War years concerning nuclear development and the sources of essential raw materials. Pudney makes good use of an imaginary mineral 'Quassium' in several of his stories as a goal for Uncle George's antagonists. If in *Monday Adventure* it is little more than an incidental explosive and in *Autumn Adventure* an ingredient in a snow-melting compound, it is valuable enough for both sides to compete in raising a cargo of the substance from a wrecked ship off the coast of Malta, in *Wednesday Adventure*; the bid by an Aramoetian dictator for world power, in *Friday Adventure*, depends on it; and the mineral deposits under a Norwegian mountain competed for in *Tuesday Adventure* are, as a chance ally suggests, 'not in great quantity, but enough to alter the whole international balance of power if it is got out by wrong hands'.[30]

None of these considerations is pressed very hard. There is far less political underpinning in Pudney's tales than there is, for instance, in John Verney's stories about the Callendar family in which a rather similar material, 'Caprium', is concerned, and it is perhaps significant that the attendant adult in these books,

Augustus Callendar, enters upon espionage as a roving, investigative journalist rather than as a somewhat detached scientist.

The ingenuous narrator of the 'Fred and I' stories has a proper respect for his uncle's work but he and Fred abstain from questioning Uncle George at least in part for fear of provoking one of his irascible explosions; when on one occasion they ignore the embargo on Uncle George's desk, for good reasons, their search for a key reveals unexpected secrets:

> We had always imagined that the desk contained top security papers, revolvers, and all kinds of exciting gadgets and equipment. We were surprised, therefore, to discover dozens of old pipes and tobacco tins, heaps of foreign coins, a set of false teeth in cotton wool, wine catalogues, tyre gauges, paper clips, and old spectacles. We knew that Uncle George was inclined to hoard things, but never realised to what extent. When we came across our old school reports, Fred suggested that it was evidence against us which ought to be destroyed.[31]

The degree of danger in the stories is indicated by the gusts of humour which ease tension and relieve difficulties. There is fun with recalcitrant pet donkeys in *Spring Adventure* and with a flock of geese in *Autumn Adventure*, and Fred's impersonation of a stout housewife in *Friday Adventure* balances an awkward moment when it looks as though Uncle George, imprisoned in the seemingly innocent store Merryworth's, will be whisked overseas by rocket and disposed of by the agents of Aramoetia. In fact Uncle George is rescued by the boys as often as he rescues them and although there are officials ready to deal with the enemy in every book, the usual youthful attributes of impetuous curiosity and sharp eyes, together with the necessary good luck and an extra measure of technical skill, account for enough of the success of the 'good' characters to flatter young readers.

John Pudney clearly enjoyed working out a mixture of ingredients to suit a particular audience but there was no condescension in this. His books have an urbanity, a stylishness in description, which could only come from an adult novelist who did not believe in scaling his work down for junior readers. This generosity in craftsmanship may be found in other writers of thrillers who cater for young as well as adult readers (Joan Aiken and Peter Dickinson, for example, and Lionel Davidson as 'David Line') but it is by no means invariable and it is one of the best claims for junior adventure stories to be considered as mainstream literature.

From the point of view of the story, in the 'Bunkle' and the 'Fred and I' series, the enemy agents are devices of the plot, providing the initial conspiracy needed to supply motive power. The villains exist for what they are, not for what they believe or feel, and their 'good' adversaries are able to assume that their aims are 'bad' and their patriotism, if any, wrong-headed or corrupt. A simplistic treatment like this, accepted by readers in the 1950s and long before, was to seem inadequate in the next two decades. If there were still plenty of yarns for the young in which enemy agents were no more than stereotypes, the opportunity was there to extend the emotional range of the spy-thriller, if only by a hint here and a touch of character-drawing there. Gradually the adults who had been excluded as significant characters in the child-oriented stories of the immediate post-war years crept back to life, not just as mentors but as co-actors in the perplexities and dangers of adventure. Communications, educational psychology, social patterns have all contributed to the new expectations of the young about the books they read and the characters with whom they might want to identify. In stories about criminal events the writer who does not satisfy these expectations nowadays with a proper degree of realism and emotional depth is offering a product inadequate to their needs.

As the lessons of the Second World War were assimilated, the simplistic attitude to treason and espionage in fiction had to be altered for new generations of young readers responsive to social change and ready to accept characters drawn in moral colours other than the statutory black-and-white. When K. M. Peyton chose the first year of the First World War as the period for *Thunder in the Sky* she brought the past in touch with the present as she described the dilemma of a boy of fifteen who had to face the knowledge that his older brother had been passing information to the enemy.

Young Sam Goodchild, who serves as mate on a sailing barge carrying freight between Yarmouth and London, has the pre-judices of his time. He distrusts the new skipper of the *Flower of Ipswich* after he has heard him express unorthodox opinions during an argument about mine-laying. A man who refuses to agree that the Hun tactics are a swindle and who suggests that the British will soon follow suit; a man who asserts:

> 'Young men'll always go to war. They go for the sheer hell of it. You can call it patriotism or honour or what you like. But honour doesn't win wars. It's cunning and brute force that wins wars. That's what we want, not claptrap about honour.' . . .[32]

– that man must surely be a traitor; and when the next voyage is scheduled for Calais, Sam is convinced that Bunyard will reveal his villainy. Eventually the skipper's common sense begins to make an impression on the lad. It is not too hard for him to admit his mistake. The real test comes when his eager spy-hunting brings him to the revelation of his brother's guilt. He never entirely understands the motives or the social blackmail which led good-natured, impressionable Gil into trouble but he does come to accept that Gil is not the preconceived villain he had imagined; growing up, for Sam, means admitting that human understanding is a necessary but difficult goal to achieve.

Human understanding and the correcting of prejudice is the theme of another junior novel set in the months before the declaration of war in 1914. The sober purpose of Dennis Hamley's *Very Far from Here*, published in 1976, is made clear in the dedication to 'Class No 2 of Denbigh School, Bletchley, Milton Keynes' and to 'Peter and Mary for listening to this story as it was being written and giving helpful and constructive criticism'. The author's presence is strongly felt as he looks at the hidden xenophobia and the dangerous power of mass hysteria within a small closed community.

Two boys provide the medium for his message – Eddy Sparrow, who is twelve, and his friend Tim Elphick. Life in the south coast resort of Harold's Bay being monotonous, the boys are only too easily affected by the forebodings which Mr Foskett, the local intellectual and recluse, passes on to Eddie concerning a German invasion. But this is not a case of a mistaken choice of villain. There is no spy in Harold's Bay – not Mr Foskett, whose posters, books and maps at first exercise Eddy's suspicions, and not Mr Brown at the bicycle-shop, the newcomer with a foreign accent and a friend whose large house, expensive car and foreign surname are enough proof of complicity for the boys.

As Eddie tracks Mr Brown on his mysterious journey to Eastbourne, the train-wheels seem to be hammering out the phrase 'catching a spy', but as the train slows down to enter the station the beginning of doubt seems to be hammering out a new rhythm, 'What if he's not?' The boy's imagination is only momentarily checked for there are enough anomalies in the conversation and actions of Mr Brown (who is in fact an Austrian refugee) to assure him that it is his duty to outwit an enemy who, dangerous in the months before war is declared, must be doubly so after Eddie has seen the first of the Harold's Bay Territorials drafted to the Front.

The lurking and spy-hunting of Eddie and Tim are misguided but not in themselves malicious. Mr Foskett's more serious campaign against the supposed spy is at least understandable, even if his predictions are eccentric; he is convinced that the Kaiser plans

146

to send his troops to the south coast equipped with bicycles. It is in the effect of Mr Foskett's beliefs on the community, and especially on men like Eddie's Uncle Bill, a man frustrated by his age and excitable by temperament, that the point of the book lies. Stirred up by fear, Uncle Bill and his pub friends are easily persuaded to attack unpopular Mr Brown in the coward's way by smashing the windows of his shop and finally by assaulting him. The mob is restrained by Eddie's hero George Naylor, whose experience in the trenches has given him the sense to see Bill as a stupid egotist and his supporters as sensation-mongers. Mr Brown's explanation of his situation satisfies Eddie and the boy has clearly learned something from the unpleasant scene. But the story is not merely concerned with the escapade of two school-boys. Although Uncle Bill decides to lie about his age and get into the army, there is an uneasy feeling that the mistake about the spy has only meant disappointment to this blinkered indi-vidual, as it has to wayward Mr Foskett also. Because he has extended the action of his story in the direction of the adult as well as the young characters, Dennis Hamley has posed a serious question within a lively and uncomplicated period adventure.

These two schoolboys are still in an early stage of moral reason-ing; we can expect only that they should be mildly shocked to find human beings more complex than they had supposed. Robert Westall in *Fathom Five* has set for a boy of sixteen a more severe test, at the moment when a friend is shown to be an enemy. Chas McGill, the central character of an earlier story, *The Machine-Gunners* (see p. 368), now takes a serious attitude towards the possibility of spying activities in the Northumberland coastal town where he lives, but he is still young enough to jump at adventure for its own sake. In 1943 the destruction of merchant shipping was a serious matter but it is another aspect of the case that Chas finds disturbing when he reads of the execution of a seaman who had sold information to the enemy. The face in the newspaper does not fit his comic-cut preconceptions:

> Chas stared and stared at it, trying to find some kind of comfort. Stared at the blurred photo of the dead spy; a pale, cocky young face with Brylcreemed hair and turned-up greatcoat collar. He didn't *look* wicked or a traitor. That was the terrible thing. He looked like somebody out of the *Garmouth Evening News* who had won a prize for ballroom dancing or got married, or been killed doing his duty against Rommel. Like somebody down your street . . .[33]

Another romantic aspect of spy-catching is abruptly changed when the boys conduct an experiment to prove that messages are being sent out to lurking U-boats in enamel bowls launched from under an extended pier and carrying electronic equipment; sending out experimental bowls from a dinghy, the boys narrowly escape drowning in the wash of a freighter, besides rousing the wrath of the Maltese families in the socially ostracised Low Street area.

Disaster only makes Chas more determined to catch the spy but there is no satisfaction when he succeeds in identifying him. He could have enjoyed the triumph if his blundering activities had revealed fat Mr Kallonas or the disturbing woman in the pawn-shop as the secret agent, but when the U-boat is captured, partly as a result of his actions, he faces the shocking fact that the guilty man is a seaman on a local tug who has presented himself as an eager ally in the search:

> He couldn't take his eyes off Sven's face. A nervous twitch had developed on Sven's forehead, making his beret twitch up and down. Sven kept swallowing, swallowing. And jerking his head sideways, then back, as if some fly was bothering him. But there was no fly. He could even smell Sven now. Like the daddy-long-legs Chas had seen one evening caught between an electric light bulb and its shade. It kept beating itself against the hot bulb, *ping, ping*. Then one of its legs broke off, then another, then there suddenly wasn't very much left of it. But it still kept pinging against the bulb till it died . . .
>   Like Sven now.
>   And he was doing it to Sven.[34]

For only Chas knows that Sven, hastily disguised, is a spy deserving death, and not one more U-boat sailor destined for a prison camp; and Chas keeps his counsel, confused by a touch of sympathy for a friend-turned-enemy and full of rage against the Establishment figures who somehow add an unpleasant gloss to the scene. The shock of finding that Sven is not in fact the victim of Nazi oppression in Norway is less terrible for the boy, even at its worst, than the unhappy memory of his blundering investigations which may have led to the murder of the enigmatic Nellie Staff, the Madam of Low Street, who from an impulse of affection had agreed to make enquiries on his behalf. Reason tells Chas that as a small actor in a large drama he need take no responsibility for events: emotionally, he takes the responsibility on himself. The story does not end on a sentimental or a sensational note; we do not see Chas overcome by remorse or thrown into a state of nervous prostration by his experience. He remains the sturdy product of his environment. All the same he is not unaffected by events and in this respect the book reflects the deeper emotional tone which has changed the scope of the adventure story in our time.

Although these heroes and heroines are more aware of interests other than their own, rights and wrongs are still laid out directly and simply. The conflicts in which they engage are between nation and nation rather than between one ideology and another. As a subject, international politics has been largely untouched or skirted round in junior novels, at least until recent years. During the 1970s two writers challenged this particular omission and in doing so they took the thriller to extreme limits – extreme, especially, in the sense that the subject of terrorism in the context of today might even be considered inadmissible in the genre of the adventure story. Yet there seems good reason for authors to present, in the format of action-stories which young readers can take at a pace suitable for their emotional judgement, certain issues which they will also meet in the more hasty and ephemeral media of newspapers and television reports.

The media can name and even describe individuals concerned in terrorist activities: fiction alone can probe the motives and personal pressures behind an ideological issue. The particularisation of a story can guide the young towards some understanding of large issues. At the same time, these young readers have a right to demand the pleasures associated with adventure-fiction – pace and tension, verisimilitude, atmosphere and an absence of overt moralising.

This is partly a matter of technique. To produce a story and not a sermon an author must organise his material so that his final commitment and the direction of his work do not hamper the story line. Buchan's novels, to take one example, show considerable variation in the success with which this kind of balance is achieved; so do the 'entertainments' of Graham Greene. Peter Dickinson was obviously well aware of the problem when he planned the structure and set the symbolic framework of *The Seventh Raven*, which is above all a brilliant piece of narrative. The plot is simple. In a prosperous district of Kensington a committee of men and women, known to the narrator ironically as the Mafia, are organising rehearsals of an ambitious annual opera, to be performed by children but with theme, music and technique addressed to their elders. The libretto is based on the conflict between Elijah and Jezebel; it includes Elijah's exile in the desert and the horrific death of Jezebel. Both words and music emphasise the dilemma of a weak king, 'in a muddle in the middle' between the stern conviction of Elijah that Jehovah's rule must prevail and the fervent support of Jezebel for the cruel rituals of the god Baal, both ideologies implying force, violence and antagonism echoed in the clashing musical motifs allotted to each. In a well-bred, artistically accomplished manner the conductor and committee set themselves to express the conflict through music: philosophy is to be painlessly, even elegantly, expressed in performance.

Reality intrudes, abruptly. To satisfy a government plan for détente with a South American dictatorship about to change leaders, the committee reluctantly agree to include as an extra raven the young son of the Mattean ambassador in London. Terrorists plot to seize young Juan as a hostage, to achieve freedom for political prisoners in Matteo. Failing to snatch the boy before he enters the church for the first dress rehearsal, the four terrorists hold more than a hundred adults and children in siege; a long period of argument and tension ends in a counterattack from outside and, seemingly, the defeat of the terrorists.

A physical victory, certainly, a successful strategic coup in which the terrorists are captured and given over to justice: in terms of right and wrong, no victory but a series of questions posed in verbal argument and never more than tentatively answered. Has music the right to remain abstract and detached or should composer and musician serve a particular ideology? Has anyone the right to stay in the middle? The narrator herself is in the middle in some ways. Doll at seventeen is now too old to perform in the opera which has absorbed her energies for several years but she can act as a useful liaison between the 'Mafia' of parents and their offspring, trying to bring some kind of order into costumes and groups of singers. More dangerously, she becomes the liaison between besiegers and besieged and has to try to reconcile uncomfortable ideas with her comfortable middle-class assumptions.

Through Doll we listen to the arguments of two of the terrorists – Danny the schoolteacher and Chip, who has escaped imprisonment in an Amnesty exchange, and to the informed explanations of international power politics from Mrs Dunnett, a dedicated Communist whose search for justice for the individual seems a hopeless one. We notice that Doll calls the invaders of the church 'bandits' but feels she is unfair to do so. Meanwhile through her eyes we watch in close-up, sharing her mixture of amusement and apprehension, the ingenious efforts to hide Juan, the stolid common sense of the child whose name, Elizabeth Windsor, has inevitably become Queenie and the exhibitionism of a more

150

precocious one, the self-contained nervous tension of Doll's musician mother, the improvisations of the terrorists and the barely concealed aggressiveness of the girl Angel, who represents one extreme of the rebel attitude as Danny's reasoned stance stands for the other. Angel's deliberate pose with a machine-gun, her beaded plaits and military costume, her set expression ('guerilla chic', Doll thinks) come near to melodrama:

> Suddenly she shook her head, like a horse pestered with flies, so that the beads rattled as they whirled and settled. The noise made the children turn, and she did it again for their benefit, a deliberate signal of danger, like the rattle of a snake when the cameraman gets too close.[35]

Yet the final impression left by the book is neither terror nor relief but the sense that questions of great importance have been properly and firmly posed and may perhaps one day be answered. As an event the siege ends with little physical harm and the opera is safely, even splendidly performed: nobody in fact remains untouched by it.

This is one way to make a topical point, alleviating violence with moments of humour, relaxing tension with quirks of personality, making a kaleidoscopic pattern of mood and atmosphere. As a contrast to Peter Dickinson's graceful, assured style Robert Cormier's prose in *After the First Death* is hard, concrete, a style of serious reportage transferred to narrative and retaining some of its formalities. Yet this, too, is a story intended to expose the dangers of ideology through the crisis, mental as well as physical, of individuals. Not far from Boston a bus full of small children on their way to a day-camp is hijacked by four terrorists and held captive on a disused railway bridge during negotiations with a military force sheltering in a building on one side of the ravine. The scene is photographically clear as a sectional narrative moves from one group to another, now probing the actions and abortive plans of Kate, who is driving the bus for her sick father, now moving from her impressions of the four terrorists and her agonised speculations about their plans to the perplexities that come unexpectedly to Miro, at sixteen not much younger than Kate but in bitter experience of hardship far older. Miro is desperately disappointed when his specified duty to kill the driver is postponed, for this was to have been his initiation to adulthood and his way of assuring his teacher and leader of his dedication. As he guards Kate and watches her comforting the children he begins to see her as a human being as well as an enemy; the shock of her attempt to escape drives him to a confusion of hatred which in the end makes her death inevitable – his first death, though in the brutal sequence of events not the last.

The physical violence in the book, horrifying as it is, is less disturbing than the reasons for it, laid bare with surgical precision. The target of the terrorists is not primarily the anticipated demands for money, safety and the release of political prisoners. This is one move in a complex campaign to reveal to the public the existence of American Inner Delta, a secret investigative organisation within the regular army post which works in the belief that the end justifies the means. As he did in *I Am the Cheese*, Cormier in *After the First Death* denounces the trend in governments to regard crime as permissible, to see individuals as expendable in the national interest; ultimately he is setting the final aim of the terrorists to regain their lost homeland against the blind patriotism which General Briggs has been brought up to support. Remembering the day when he joined up in 1941, the General reflects:

> 'We were poorly trained in those days, Ben, but trained superbly in one thing – patriotism. There are all kinds of patriotism – ours was pure and sweet and unquestioning. We were the good guys. Today, there is still patriotism, of course. But this generation is questioning. This generation looks at itself in a mirror as it performs its duties. And wonders: Who are the good guys? Is it possible we are the bad guys? They should never ask that question, Ben, or even contemplate it.'[36]

At the end of the story it is clear that the General has been forced to contemplate it. He has offered his young son Ben as a messenger at a crucial stage of negotiating. The boy believes he has betrayed his country when after being tortured he gives the terrorist leader the time when the army is due to attack; before he dies of a wound received in the final battle he has realised that this betrayal was intended, that his weakness was to divert attention while the army prepares for earlier and successful action. Innocent in his patriotism, which is in fact loyalty to his father, Ben has been betrayed by an ideology, a nationalism as dangerous as the methods by which Aitkin and his allies fight for the right to have a country of their own. Between the two bodies of brutal, disciplined conviction the three young people are crushed. Miro, living from hand to mouth in refugee camps, nameless and stateless, has never really been a child; yet after years of training in which he has learned to deny the normal desires for love, sympathy, human contacts and to become an instrument of war, he has a terrible innocence that matches Ben's blind loyalty and

Kate's practical, untried courage. These three characters are the central symbols of Cormier's surgically sharp narrative. Pawns in an enormous, inexplicable power-game, their situation concerns us all. The struggle in our time to equate individual rights with national needs cannot fail to be reflected in any story with such a subject if the writer believes that he owes his readers honesty as well as skill.

What we seem to be seeing in the thriller, adult or junior, is a move from a phase when a conventional distinction between good and evil, or hero and villain, was generally accepted to a phase in which the moral basis of any situation has to be more closely scrutinised. Ambiguity has taken the place of certainty. It has become permissible, even necessary, to show that individual and socio-national interests are not necessarily the same and that a conflict of loyalties and beliefs can be fatal to an individual, whether physically or emotionally. As regards the adventure story, this does not imply that entertainment has to be submerged in social philosophy but that the formula-plots and stereotype characters of past decades will now be less than satisfying to young readers aware of the conflicting issues of their time. Faced with the querying of morality which, as a normal activity of adolescence, has been intensified by modern communications and the interdependence of world affairs, writers have to modify certain conventions which have previously set limits to realism in junior adventure stories. In particular certain mechanical and artificial aspects of the domestic thriller, often cheerily called the cops-and-robbers tale, are likely to be strongly affected.

7. Cops and Robbers

Domestic crime has been a fruitful source of material for writers of junior stories for well over a century. The cops-and-robbers situation, with the tension and conflict necessary to adventure, is especially congenial to young readers because they can see their fictional counterparts not only solving mysteries but also exposing and defeating criminals where their adult guardians have failed. Burglars and blackmailers, kidnappers and smugglers have been staple antagonists for the young for decades but the very elements which have sustained the popularity of this kind of story have imposed on it certain necessary conventions. There are two issues to be considered here. First, the writer must determine according to the social and cultural climate of his own time the degree of seriousness proper to his readership. Can he present sordidness, violence, lawlessness in proportion to the apprehensions of children without distorting or diluting reality in a way that might mislead them or make them insensitive to the manifestations and the effects of criminal activities in real life? Secondly, how can the inexperienced young of fiction be seen plausibly to triumph over antagonists older, more powerful and less innocently motivated than they are themselves?

A long-standing convention dictates that the children who are opposed to criminals in orthodox, formula-stories must not be subjected to real danger but only to a literary arrangement of danger calculated to produce the necessary suspense and tension: luck, coincidence or the ineptitude of the criminals will ensure that the children do not meet the fate only too likely to overcome them in reality. Beyond this arrangement of danger we also have to accept in the good characters – that is, the crusading children – an over-generous allowance of brain and brawn; an improbable self-confidence, a certain rigidity in their attitude to other people.

The moment the young characters become in any way individual they introduce differing points of view which inevitably call into question the end result of their actions. The characters in the stereotyped cops-and-robbers tale approach danger with the effrontery of ignorance; in this lies their chance of success. As they exhibit no thought of being mistaken or misguided, so they suffer no effects from the dangerous situations they have to

154

endure; surviving imprisonment, rough handling, hunger and thirst, the very contact with evil, they remain unchanged. In fact their adventure is lacking in any emotional content.

This enormous area of omission is all the more noticeable when the accepted artificiality of character and action is supported by a realistic setting. If you know just what a character is wearing or exactly where he is hiding, it is natural to want to know also what he is thinking and feeling: to be denied this is to have the kind of annoyed surprise that comes when one brushes against a person in a shop and realises it is a dummy. The lack of any emotional response to a situation reveals the lifelessness of the characters and the reader's response is likely to be as lifeless.

How far does artificiality matter, though? Formula-writing may seem more distressing in some areas than in others. A light-hearted, good-luck approach to the area of crimes against children would certainly seem callous and misguided. The central character of Bernard Ashley's *A Kind of Wild Justice*, a boy of twelve whose father has been forced into crime by East End gang leaders, illustrates the distinction between one type of fiction and another in what purports to be a distinction between real life and fiction, an authorial device justified in this case because it is no gimmick but a strong emotional comment:

> Life might be a load of games for the rest of them, playing after school, having birthdays, watching telly, going to scouts on Fridays: but for him it was different. He didn't play cops and robbers, and talk about watching thrillers on the box: he was on the near edge of being part of the real thing; and a nasty accident, to him, could never be someone falling off the P.E. apparatus; it was the thought of a pick handle across the brittle of his back.[1]

Lacking the panache and self-confidence of most fictional children opposing criminals, Ronnie Webster does play a hero's part in helping the law to catch the Brewster brothers, but it is not a happy triumph, for the boy's investigations bring trouble to his schoolfellow, Pakistani Mirza; her problem is not solved but intensified. Skilfully cast as an exciting mystery, the story is interpenetrated by social comment, as indeed all Bernard Ashley's books are. It is no new idea, to use the pace and tone of adventure to forward a social idea: what is new in the past two decades or so is the degree of reality behind the idea and the greater demand made on the response and intelligence of young readers, who are expected to attend to the motives behind the action rather than the action itself.

It follows that the attitudes and reactions of the characters must be appropriate to their age and circumstances but, within these limits, as lucid and as honest as the writer can make them. Prudence Andrew has treated the subject of baby-snatching with a humour and a narrative zest which does not minimise its seriousness; yet the social comment in *Una and Grubstreet* is kept within the capacity and experience of the child of eleven who stands at its centre and so within the experience of readers of similar age. The essential points are made consistently through this central character rather than through a voice-over from the author; the device of implied soliloquy helps to establish Una's motives for stealing Mrs Heaven's dirty but attractive baby.

Una has two companions in her loneliness. One is her neighbour and friend Lee who, though two years younger, has for a small boy a great deal of common sense. The whole stratagem depends on Lee's practical help, in smuggling food into Una's hiding-place in a deserted house and keeping watch at critical moments, and it is through Lee's very natural fears and his objections to a long, uncomfortable exile that we see the literal side of the adventure. The other companion is Grubstreet, a small wooden bear which Una's mother had given to Una before she died. Grubstreet listens to Una's dreams, fantasies and complaints; through the toy we glimpse the compulsions which lead the girl, still missing her mother and the baby brother who died with her five years before, to plan a better deal for the youngest Heaven child than life with a cruel and slatternly mother.

This, at least, is the picture which Una passes on to her confidant Grubstreet as she defines her role of rescuer: her more sensible self replies, as if through him, with a certain ruthless candour which balances her fantasy. Defeated by facts (baby Christopher may be attractive but he is also perpetually wet and noisy and soon falls ill from cold and wrong feeding) but also defeated by her own good sense, Una comes out of hiding and has to face certain consequences of her actions, not least the knowledge that she has misinterpreted the marks on the baby's back and that Mrs Heaven is in her way a good mother. The crime proves to be no crime at all. Una is consoled by her father's unusually affectionate manner but it has been a hard lesson for her to learn.

A similar misunderstanding of a young mother's behaviour towards her baby is explored in greater depth by Noreen Shelley in *Faces in a Looking-Glass*. Her heroine, a girl of thirteen, is

156

growing up in a socially mixed suburb of Sydney with a widower father, an Inspector of Primary Schools, accustomed to talk freely to her about his work and its implications. Kylie MacFee's broader terms of reference mean that the author can explore the implications of her impetuous actions more deeply and can engage her emotions more seriously than Prudence Andrew could do with the child Una. When a baby is snatched from outside the launderette Kylie is almost glad that the bad-tempered young woman she has been watching has been punished for treating her child so roughly. Her father's judicious replies to her questions, and the comments of her class-teacher about looking-glass images, make her think again. She has to accept that the woman whose behaviour had shocked her was the same distraught girl interviewed on television:

> She could hardly believe what she saw and heard. The thin face was carefully made-up; the greasy, straggling hair was neat and smooth, fresh from the attentions of a hairdresser – and the voice! It wasn't the loud, angry voice that had made her feel as though she were in a nightmare. Now it was soft and timid as she answered the questions that were put to her, and described her baby and the clothes she had been wearing when she was abducted.[2]

Kylie does not give up her idea that the baby was badly treated and there was some justification for those first impressions. Similar conclusions had in fact led to the kidnapping; a lonely middle-aged woman living opposite the launderette, imprisoned by the care of a bedridden mother, had been driven to take baby and pram into her house after brooding over the slaps and rough words she had observed. The attitudes of social workers, police and neighbours to pathetic Miss Claypool are as confusing to Kylie as her own mixed feelings about a young woman obviously out of her depth in life. Noreen Shelley has worked the threads of her narrative together so that message and mystery support one another. The observant eyes of Kylie and her friend Beth pick up discrepancies and odd details which lead to the discovery of the baby; the common sense and sturdily practical attitude of Kylie's younger brother, her father's experience, the wisdom of their friendly neighbour Mrs Merryweather, the careful explanations of the police, all provide support for the girl's feelings of anger and distaste, a certain excitement at being the centre of the affair, surprise, unwilling sympathy, which establish the emotional tone of the story in a way consistent with the adventure-plot.

Nina Bawden has used the subject of a child in danger in a similar way, to show how a misconception is corrected and an

apparent crime is shown to be a more complex matter than at first
appeared. Her method differs from that of most writers for the
young, though, for she does not take the customary path to
simplicity by choosing one character – prescriptively, a child – as
focal point. She has always transferred her attention from adult to
junior fiction easily and with little obvious change. Always lucid,
plain and concrete, her prose style is virtually unaltered when she
writes for the young; her story lines are as uncluttered in both
spheres of her writing; her character-drawing is consistently a
matter of small, telling details of behaviour, opinion or preoccupation, her sense of class, period and circumstance consistently
acute. And though in her junior novels she sets the emotional
tone and emphasis in relation to the children whose adventures
she is describing, she never uses stereotypes for the adults
involved in the action or minimises their part in it. This close
correspondence in technique between her adult and junior books
is evident in her children's stories in the quasi-dramatic method
by which she divides her attention between several characters of
equal importance, using this shifting of emphasis to give emotional
colour and variety to scenes which are firmly based on domestic
reality.

The range of her children's books and the peculiarly persuasive
way she presents and develops her characters is apparent in three
books whose differing approaches to the subject of kidnapping
may serve to show the constraints operating on junior fiction
at various points on the scale. *The White Horse Gang* is a game
of kidnapping but one which appears more complicated to its
initiators at the end of the adventure than at the outset. Abe
Tanner, in effect the centre and leader of the gang, has a disorganised life with a blind grandmother, reputed to be a witch;
his casual attitude to school and other demands on his time, and
his claim to an old horse, once a Grand National winner, are as
much the envy of the other children in the Shropshire market
town as they make him suspect to adults. His independence of
authority encourages the other children in their plot to kidnap
Percy, a spoilt child of seven whose parents, well-to-do incomers
from Birmingham, are disliked by the locals.

Confident that the Mountjoys will pay a ransom for Percy that
will help homesick Rose to join her parents in America, the
children organise the affair with the peculiarly practical logic of
the young:

> They laid out all the money they had between them. They spent
> sixpence on glue and the rest on chocolate and packets of mixed

nuts and raisins and half a dozen sherbet dabs. Sam wanted to buy baked beans, his own favourite food, but Rose said it would be foolish to buy that sort of thing. 'They'd guess there was something up,' she said.[3]

The glue is used for the traditional anonymous note; the cutout words, arrived at after long argument, are eloquent of the age and the preferred reading of the children – 'Your son has been kidnapped by professional criminals. Swift action is necessary to save his life.' In spite of differences of opinion the conspirators arrive at the moment when they are to seize Percy only to be disconcerted by the small boy's delight in the whole enterprise. Not only does Percy beg to be snatched but he becomes a petty tyrant, ordering his gaolers not to quarrel and, when the children lose their nerve, refusing to be returned to his distraught mother – 'I'm having a lovely time and I don't want to go home.' Percy has tasted freedom: the gang have felt their own freedom in danger. The situation is amusing but, as Nina Bawden develops it, devastatingly true. It is people who concern her first; events are there to reveal people, to themselves and to the reader. Her stories hold the attention more surely because of the characters and their extraordinary reality rather than by plots which, in bald terms, are cut from old cloth – quarrels, escapes, changed circumstances, the material of everyday life and, equally, of formula fiction.

The kidnap of Percy Mountjoy was a piece of fantasy which was overcome by reality, but in proportion to the motives that lay behind the enterprise. The kidnap plan in *Squib* has far more serious motives. A determined child not yet six meets a pale, timid little boy in the park and resolves to protect him; for Sammy and his sister Prue are convinced that Squib is in danger from the woman he lives with, the ogress (as they see her) whom they had watched as she hit him and strapped him into a laundry basket. Their sensible older brother Robin tries to curb their half-pleasurable fears of the ogress but his friend Kate, though she believes that Squib's foster-mother will not seriously harm him, is moved by a secret sorrow in her family to fantasise that Squib is her dead brother, mysteriously saved from the sea and once more in danger. When the children have actually witnessed a violent quarrel between the woman and her husband they feel compelled to steal into the caravan and rescue the little boy.

Here again the situation is turned from the general to the particular by the actions and reactions of the children. This is not a social case-history but a conjunction of individuals, of a man

159

violent of temperament and frustrated by circumstances and a wearily combative, overworked woman, saddled with a child through accident and incapable of dealing with him. Kate comes near to realising how far from the truth their limited experience has taken them when she overhears the man's 'God damn this rotten life' and watches him slump off to the pub, 'shambling and heavy like a tired, old bear'.[4]

Life is not simple for Kate and her friendship with Robin is not without its uncertainties. She can hardly match his casual acceptance of the social gap between them, the difference between the airy spaces of the small house where she lives with her artist mother and the noisy, crowded terrace house opposite where Robin's redoubtable mother, once a Channel swimmer, rules over her family. When Robin says casually to Kate, on her way home, 'Tell Mom I've put the potatoes on':

> . . . Kate nodded, looking vague. It embarrassed her that Mrs Tate should work for her mother, cleaning a house with only two people in it, when she had a family at home waiting for their dinner. Robin grinned, as if he knew this. 'Tell her to get a move on,' he said.[5]

The distinction is important not as social comment but as an expansion of the characters, illuminating the story in the simple but perceptive way proper to its direction towards readers of ten or so, sensitive but inexperienced, who can be invited to reach out in some degree towards the troubles of their elders.

The conflict between good and evil which is one base of the adventure story has probably been most thoroughly changed in the past decade or two in the kind of story I have been discussing where the conflict is between crime and society (that is, selected supporters of society). The ambiguities arising from present attitudes to crime, the search for motives in environment and circumstance and the perpetual discussions about types of punishment and their efficacy have forced a wider division between reflective, properly argued thrillers or detective-stories and best-sellers, and the division is as obvious in the sphere of children's fiction. Nina Bawden has brought reality into her junior adventure stories not by sensational plots or violence but by a steady look at certain situations in which children could find their comfortable suppositions and their considerable capacity for wrongdoing thrown into a different light by circumstances for which they are partly responsible. In a paper entitled 'Emotional Realism in Books for Young People' she affirmed that for her the most important kind of realism needed by children was 'the realism of the emotional landscape in which the book is set' rather than in terms of plot and setting, which in our day means the sordid and sensational. Children, she said:

> . . . feel as violently – if not more violently, since they have less self-control than adults. They love, or hate, their parents, their brothers and sisters, their teachers, their friends. They feel guilt, despair, as well as wild and sudden joy, they are aware of self-deception as well as other people's lies. I wanted to write about children who felt passionately, as I knew that children did, and set those feelings down as honestly as I could manage in the framework of an exciting plot that would make them want to turn the pages.[6]

If the idea of passionate feeling might at first seem inapplicable to Nina Bawden's junior novels, a moment's thought would bring to mind Sammy's frantic championing of Squib, the frustrated hostility of Carrie and her young brother to the meanly tyrannical Mr Evans in *Carrie's War*, the energetic indignation of Fred and his friends when old Mrs Blackadder's savings disappear with her smooth-talking lodger, in *A Handful of Thieves*. Fred's answer to this theft is a counter-burglary at the hostel where Mr Gribble had gone into hiding, a burglary planned with an entirely convincing mixture of practical cunning and youthful glee which deserved better success than it achieved. It was the glee that led a bookseller to attack Nina Bawden at a publisher's party; she had failed in her duty to society, he insisted, in describing children planning a burglary and allowing them to *enjoy* it. She defended herself, though without changing her critic's attitude:

> . . . it seemed totally unrealistic to pretend that my characters were not thrilled by the idea of being burglars, of breaking into a house at night. But I also thought I had written about it in an extremely moral way. My little thieves knew exactly what they were doing. They knew it was against the law. But they had discussed the situation – touching, along the way, on the conflict there often is between law and morality – and decided that it was, in the circumstances, the right thing to do.[7]

They had discussed the situation. It is in the discussion that Nina Bawden's most conspicuous gift to junior novels can be seen. She achieves the emotional realism which she regards as essential by letting us overhear the discussions between groups of children, siblings or friends, and making sure by a selection that is completely unobtrusive as far as the reader is concerned that we learn what each child is like and how each one subtly influences the actions and feelings of the others. Through the unaffected talk of children a particular crime – theft, fraud, blackmail – is shown from a personal rather than a legal point of view; in each case the 'why' as opposed to the 'how' comes through the relative experience of the children. It is in this angle of vision and the tone of style, rather than in the style itself, that her adult novels differ from those written for the young.

The difference in technique is shown clearly in *Devil by the Sea*, a novel in which a kidnap leads to child abuse. The book was published for the adult market in 1957 and reissued in 1976 by Gollancz in the same format as their junior novels, in the young-adult section of their list. The original story of a seaside town and the murder of a child was shortened for republication but the changes were such that they did not soften the passion and the horror of the story; while it might be salutary for readers over fourteen to think about the situation, the material and the emotion would be far beyond the understanding of anyone much younger. The central character is self-centred in the way of a child but she is viewed entirely from an adult point of view; her feelings are analysed in plain, deliberate prose from the same novelistic stance as the feelings of her father and mother, her stepsister and the sad, tormented murderer. Technically the book is a thriller but only in the sense of having a crime-mystery plot. In its exploration of the reactions of a girl and the adults in her life to a sordid tragedy it is a logical extension of Nina Bawden's treatment of the relationships in her junior books – of Carrie with the repressed Mr Evans and his meek sister, for example. Writing always with a sense of proportion, she satisfies the expectations of young readers with an element of mystery and surprise while opening their minds to the extra mystery and surprise of human nature.

Character is the focus and motive power of Nina Bawden's adventure stories. The emphasis becomes very different in that formalised subsection of the genre, the detective-story, which offers a special version of the general illusion of fiction. The detective-story is first and foremost a puzzle. The author sets up a mystery, introduces a crime by a person or persons unknown and invites the reader to solve the mystery and identify the criminal before it is authorially explained. This is done within certain conventions of fair dealing even when, with writers like P. D. James, Amanda Cross or Ruth Rendell, the intellectual pleasure may well be disturbed or distracted by an extension of emotional truth that strains the formula to its limits.

The reader's participation in a detective-story, even if it is casual and intermittent, has in it a special pleasure, a subtle flattery beyond the enjoyment of vicarious adventure. In the junior detective-story, a genre at least half a century old by now, the flattery has a double function. It is directed not only to the reader but also to the characters, who are challenged, often quite specifically, to try their hands at solving a puzzle which has baffled the professionals and to demonstrate their particular talents in the adult field. The flattery is especially persuasive because of the formal element of detection, the emphasis on the working out of a conundrum rather than on the actual confrontation with danger and villainy found in other kinds of junior thrillers.

Because the puzzle must be the first consideration, such intricacy of character or depth of emotion as the author wishes to include must be entirely relevant to the puzzle. Most such books, adult or junior, have a deliberately restricted area of feeling and motive so that the traditional form and conventions are observed. That it is possible to drive deeply into the human condition without endangering the form (and this is, of course, part of the bargain with the reader) is amply proved when one sorts the good from the indifferent – proved, for instance, by a novel like Amanda Cross's *The Theban Mysteries* or, in the junior sphere, in an interesting group of detective-novels by Stephen Chance.

'Stephen Chance' is the pseudonym of Philip Turner, an Anglican parson who has published under his own name several treasure-hunt tales for children. Under his pseudonym he has built four junior mysteries round an amateur detective particularly well suited to the role. Septimus Treloar, rector of the Fenland parish of St Mary's Danedyke, had previously been a London policeman on the beat and later a police detective before he was dropped into occupied Europe as an underground fighter in the 1940s. A specialised background has always been one of the most useful tools by which the writer of detective-stories gives them validity and Treloar's character is properly established through details of church observances, architecture and scholarship. He fits so well into his background and his contacts with his parishioners are so natural that the reader can readily accept him as an individual and can appreciate that his training and experience as a policeman have been as effectively transferred to the pastoral care of a country parish as his physical strength and courage transfer to the detective enterprise, which unexpectedly vary his normal routine.

The two first books about Septimus Treloar, arguably the best of the four, are in every sense parochial. The simple, pictorial setting and firmly outlined characters are in the detective-story tradition, distributing the elements of a mystery through a substantial and absorbing social and domestic documentation. The opening of *Septimus and the Danedyke Mystery* is masterly in its direct, compelling style. Miss Mary Crowle, middle-aged schoolmistress and organist, is practising for a forthcoming wedding when she hears a movement in the Relic Chapel and bravely investigates, being too sensible to believe that she is hearing the ghost of Abbot John, the last abbot of the old monastery, seeking the Grail-like cup he was reputed to have hidden in the chapel. Marching across the church in her sensible shoes, Mary orders mischievous Jimmy Bates, whom she suspects of playing a trick on her, to come out:

> A shape came rushing at her out of the blackness and an arm lashed across her face, hurling her aside so that she fell backward with a scream over the altar rail, the oak rail crashing painfully into the small of her back.
>
> She rolled over and struggled to a sitting position, leaning against the altar itself, conscious of both the pain in her back and the curious incongruity of sitting on the altar step with her skirt round her waist. As her eyes focused she saw a dark shadow vanish beyond the reach of the choir lights down the centre aisle. She could hear running feet and then a fumbling, and then the north door opening, and then the crash as it closed.
>
> She was shaking as she struggled to her feet, pulling herself up by the altar frontal. Her back was very painful, and she had to retrieve her spectacles from the corner of the sanctuary. She stood with her hands on the altar and smiled weakly at the brass cross. At least it had not been a ghost. It had not been Jimmy Bates either.[8]

With the touches of personality, the plain drive of the action through Mary's senses, the easy references to place and time, this is a style set well within the comprehension of young readers but giving that little extra which could turn those readers from a passive to an active response to the words. It is an effective way into the story, for Treloar will obviously be involved as custodian of the church and shepherd of his flock – involved also as a man with some literary and historical knowledge, for thieves are after the lost Danedyke cup and the clues to its hiding-place lie in a certain sequence of illuminated pages in an old book. Septimus sets out to trace the marauders with the skills of a policeman, the interest of a scholar and the concern for church and people proper to his cloth.

The second of his investigations, *Septimus and the Minster Ghost*, is more directly concerned with people; his deductions which identify the destructive ghost in the minster as a man

164

trying to right an old wrong draw on his experience of men and affairs. There is nothing ostentatiously doctrinal and certainly nothing sentimental in the overtones of the two books but Treloar's compassion and commitment give them a substance and a maturity which extends the scope of traditional plots.

It was presumably for the sake of emotional maturity and a measure of reality that the author chose to present an adult detective in a story for young readers. Escaping the inherent improbability of the child-detective, he compromises so far as to give Treloar junior allies – an ingenuous young assistant teacher and her fiancé in the first book and, in the second, the schoolboy son of the Dean of the minster who brings the natural instinct for snooping, lurking and chasing into play, usefully as regards the plot and also because it introduces an element of humour and sheer fun which, typically, Treloar encourages.

Henry Treece used a similar compromise in his tales of a needy investigator, Gordon Stewart, tales of deduction and danger written in the late 1950s and sixties which clearly show the influence of Buchan's thrillers. The schoolboy son of old friends who determinedly involved himself in Stewart's pursuit of spies and thieves in *Ask for King Billy, Don't Expect Any Mercy, Killer in Dark Glasses* and *Bang, You're Dead!* in the same way broke tension with slapstick comedy or ingenuous comment and contributed enough guesses and interrogations to each story to make young readers feel personally concerned.

Personally concerned and also, in a sense, edified. The junior detective-story has inherited from the adult version a formal structure and a circumscribed approach to character but the genre has also by right and prescription found room for that measure of moral instruction which seems inescapable in every branch of children's literature. Certainly the adult detective-story has its moral, as the Western romance has: the wicked are caught and punished, the detective wins in the end. Until recent years the moral has never been pressed very far; it has remained a matter of statement and assumption behind the dominant element of mystery and puzzle. It cannot but be formal when characters are formal.

The writer for the young has a responsibility beyond the purveying of an exciting story, though this need not affect the essential virtues of good story-telling or discourage readers from legitimate enjoyment. Both Henry Treece and Stephen Chance seem to me to have recognised this responsibility in their way, setting their angle of vision somewhere between a young person and an adult and including within active and exciting scenes a

165

sincere concern, a sense of the value of individuals which goes beyond a puzzle-formula.

This is noticeable if we contrast their books with the formula-stories of Franklin W. Dixon and Carolyn Keene, stories in which the angle of vision at first appears to be, similarly, shared between adults and young people. The Hardy Boys and the Nancy Drew series reflect the values of supposedly average middle-class, tax-paying, law-abiding American citizens in a way that has no real meaning but is merely part of the formula which allows Frank and Joe Hardy and Nancy Drew to operate with the blessing of the law and without having to think for themselves beyond the facts of whatever fraud, theft or usurpation they are trying to bring home to a perpetrator.

The Hardy Boys and Nancy Drew tales represent the ultimate in formula-writing – and in two stages. Leslie McFarlane described in a cheery autobiography, *Ghost of the Hardy Boys*, how he became Franklin W. Dixon. After toiling with some parts of the Nat Ridley Rapid Fire Detective Stories, the Dave Fearless and Roy Rockwood series and the adventures of the Rover Boys, he drafted a letter to Edward Stratemeyer, the founder and outliner of these popular series, protesting that he had had enough of Dave Fearless:

> His moral character is impeccable. His courage in the face of impending disaster cannot be questioned. I have conducted him through Arctic wastes and tropical jungles, in and out of the damnedest perils ever conceived by the mind of man. But dim-witted bravery is not enough. Fearless has the mind of a cretin; in fact, he is such a dull, insufferable bastard that I can't stand him any longer.[9]

The astute Stratemeyer offered McFarlane instead the setting and characters for books which he hoped would be pulled along in the slipstream of Van Dine's popular detective-stories.

He sketched the setting, the town of Bayport on the Atlantic coast, and named the two lads who were to be heroes of the tales, together with friends whose attitudes were clearly devised to provide physical support or comic relief – greedy Chet from the farm, athletic Biff Hooper, and Tony Prito, who, as McFarlane shrewdly remarked, 'would presumably tag along to represent all ethnic minorities'.[10] Frank and Joe Hardy were allotted girl-friends but relations 'would not go beyond the borders of whole-some friendship and discreet mutual esteem'.[11] The series was to work on the principle propounded by the journalist Frank

Packard – 'You get your hero into a hole, and then you throw rocks at him' – [12] but the rocks were to be as American as the characters. As 'Franklin Dixon' realised, the Hardy Boys would be popular because of their familiar, non-exotic background:

> They didn't go wandering all over the seven seas, pursued by imbecile relations. They stayed at home, checked in for dinner every night like other kids. They even went to school. Granted, they didn't appear to spend very much time at school; most of the outline seemed to be devoted to extra-curricular activities after four and on weekends. [13]

The ghost-writer was to be confined not only by a given setting and characters and a ban on swearing, smoking and drinking (except by the villains) but also by a given plot for each book which included scenes, subplots, confrontations and movements. Nevertheless he decided to make room for some quality of writing and a measure of individuality and humour in the drawing of character. He described scenes in the classroom where the Hardy Boys, after a tough night pursuing criminals, would fall asleep at their desks and lay themselves open to practical jokes. He developed in cranky, opinionated Aunt Gertrude a comic character for whose interruptions his readers were to wait eagerly. Between *The Tower Treasure* in 1927 and *The Phantom Freighter* in 1946 McFarlane wrote within Stratemeyer's outlines but stretched his writer's limbs as far as he could. When prosperity made it possible for him to hand over the Hardy Boys to another ghost-writer (and, naturally, to hand over his pseudonym as well) he did not reread the books; they remained on a bookcase shelf 'under glass, like a row of embalmed owls, so the dust wouldn't get at them'.

Outside their author's study, though, the books were not embalmed. Immensely popular with one generation, in the 1950s they were revamped to suit the times, and McFarlane read a note in a new edition of *The Tower Treasure* that:

> In this new story, based on the original of the same title, Mr Dixon has incorporated the most up-to-date methods used by police and private detectives.

It seemed reasonable enough that the Hardy Boys should be allowed to move from roadsters to fast convertibles, that helicopters, modern radio communication and other examples of advanced technology should increase the topical appeal of the stories. On McFarlane's own admission it was not until the early seventies that he realised, while he was being interviewed for a

167

magazine article, that the books had been completely rewritten, not brought up-to-date so much as totally gutted.

It might perhaps have been expected that the cases offered to Frank and Joe Hardy, which so often had political and even international aspects, would have to respond to changes in social attitude and perhaps to show a greater awareness of the importance of lost formulas or industrial espionage. But this was not in fact the purpose of the alterations: they were stylistic. Humour had gone almost entirely and the inorganic but pleasant subscenes which had allowed characters to display themselves; description had been reduced to the minimum, action telescoped, reflection cut short. Robert Still in his article gave a telling example:

> A man whom McFarlane had described in *The Missing Chums* as 'an unsavoury-looking fellow, unshaven, surly of expression . . . and bareheaded, revealing a scant thatch of carroty hair so close-cropped that it seemed to stick out at all angles to his cranium' had now become just 'a huge man with a bald head'. In the new books, the stories move perhaps a touch faster because there is hardly a place to stop and linger, never a scene to wallow in. They have been written for a less literate generation of children and they are the sort of books which can themselves engender a less literate generation.[14]

It seems clear that this drastic revision was designed to bring the books closer to the speed and generalised confrontations of television rather than to relate them in any genuine way to the social scene of today. Robbed of the small amount of humour and verbal vivacity which McFarlane had managed to give them, the stories stand out in all their baldness. They fail as adventure stories because the reader quickly tires of the monotony of a thrill in every chapter. Equally, they fail as detective-stories. Frank and Joe Hardy may be semi-official, trusted by their detective father and respected by the police, but in fact they do not detect. The distance between detectives and clues, clues and interpretations, is minimal. Their successes come more often through luck and coincidence than by any effort of thought on their part; the villains are known and recognised, or at least suspected, from the first moment, so that the invitation to the reader to participate in a puzzle is unappealing. Nothing is left to hide the total unreality of the tales, the one disaster which the story-teller must avoid.

Possibly the Nancy Drew tales, conceived by Edward Stratemeyer as a series to match the Hardy Boys series, have a better chance of stirring or at least tickling the imagination. More domestic and personal in approach than the cases of the Hardy

Boys, the revision they suffered to commend them to present-day readers was less drastic. With the late-Victorian flavour of their plots, concerning long-lost heirs and impersonations, documents stolen, forged or faked, they must always have had something of the period piece about them, and indeed something of the fairy-tale. In *The Lady Investigates* Patricia Craig and Mary Cadogan point out that the puzzles in the Nancy Drew stories are usually centred on a romantic object which not only directs the plot but also gives something for the imagination to work on:

> The old albums, stage-coaches, dancing puppets, scarlet slippers and so on, are sufficiently quaint and intriguing to produce an instantaneous effect. They're all, of course, objects with a traditional appeal for girls – stagey or sentimental – unlike the twisted claws, sinister signposts and broken blades of the corresponding boys' series, which belong to an order of symbols distinctly masculine. The Hardy Boys would be embarrassed by a case which started with a ballet dancer's shoe.[15]

The comment is a shrewd one and suggests one reason why the recent attempts to bring red-haired Nancy into partnership with sensible Frank and excitable Joe proved to be ludicrous. Nancy may be tough and self-reliant, fearless in the face of ghosts, confidence-men or charging bulls, technically adept and consistently resolute, but she is never less than feminine and her preoccupation with hairstyles and clothes belongs to the world of teenage magazines rather than of women's liberation pamphlets.

The link between the two series is the compromise by which the young but accomplished detectives are supported by adults and work freely in the adult world. They are old enough to drive cars, speedboats and the occasional aeroplane but young enough to accept the authority and help of their parents – Carson Drew the lawyer and Fenton Hardy the detective – when they get near real trouble. Given this background and the fact that they never stop to notice any ambiguities or social paradoxes in the cases they investigate, the reader can, though I hope with some reluctance, accept the way these young sleuths remain consistently ahead of the police without seeming to interfere with them.

But can the convention that young detectives can succeed where their elders have failed still win belief? Was it ever expected to convince readers at all? As long ago as 1948 the ebullient young heroes of *The Otterbury Incident*, while earning (and losing) the money to pay for a broken window, had stumbled on a gang of counterfeiters. The boy who tells the story is overjoyed when the police inspector, at a full school assembly, admits '. . . it's quite clear to me that Scotland Yard couldn't teach some of you youngsters very much about the elements of crime detection'[16] and that 'I consider you all acted with resource and initiative and courage':[16] but he is brought down to earth, even if he still does not grasp the inspector's irony, when the officer concludes his speech:

> 'That's about all I have to say. Except that, when you young terrors next embark on a gun battle with a gang of crooks, you might let me in on it. *And*, if ever again I hear of you so much as raising a water-pistol against anyone, I'll clap you in the cooler as sure as eggs are eggs! But seriously, no more taking the law into your own hands, see? Promise?'[17]

Behind the tongue-in-cheek, urbane manner of this rousing tale the point is clear. Beyond the basic artificiality of the detective-story genre there is for writers for children the additional problem of the success of their young heroes.

Every writer must find a way to get over this. C. Day Lewis used pace and humour to disarm the most literal-minded reader. Roger Pilkington set problems for his Branxome children, in *The Isembart Mystery* and other books, and gave them a certain technical expertise because their highly communicative father was a Scotland Yard detective; there was safety also in the fact that their deductive skills were called upon to find long-lost treasures rather than to identify and frustrate criminals; finally, any tendency in the reader to doubt their success and even the opportunities they found for adventure was likely to be disarmed by the agreeable tourist background of sailing along the canals of Belgium and Holland and the rivers of France and Germany. A policeman father was also useful to Dorothy Clewes in *The Lost Tower Treasure* and other books when she offered the Hadley children certain problems of theft or kidnapping and she made sure that it was their youthful curiosity and quick eyes that were in question and not their physical strength or endurance. These capable stories in sequence had a domestic tone which suited readers in the late fifties and early sixties, just as the more racy, colloquial style of Roy Brown's tales of Chips Regan, son of a London policeman, whose enthusiastic detective enterprises are hindered more than helped by Mitzi, an Alsatian disqualified as a police-dog, suit the wider reading public of the seventies and eighties.

Books like these do not set out to offer a wholly realistic

picture of contemporary society, nor do their readers demand this, but they do not retreat into sensational absurdities as the Hardy Boys and Nancy Drew stories do. Any degree of seriousness or of social point that may arise can be absorbed by the attendant adults, leaving the fun and the flattery of working out a puzzle for the young characters, and the young readers, to enjoy. Eventually, though, it may seem that the safest way to avoid improbability and, more seriously, a flippant or superficial approach to crimes against society in our own time, is to choose subjects (at least for an under-twelve readership) of a domestic and relatively safe kind. While the junior detective-story at its upper limits (in Roy Brown's *The Swing of the Gate* and *The Siblings*, for example) enters upon questions of motive and social circumstance with enough energy to remove it from stereotyped characters and situations, the detective-puzzle may be left to exercise the minds of young readers of nine or ten rather than their emotions.

When Erich Kästner began the genre of the junior detective-story, as I believe he did, he worked on the basis of the skills proper to children. He knew that they were naturally curious and observant and that the small details they were apt to notice might be overlooked as trivial and meaningless by their elders, however professional they might be. So in *Emil and the Detectives* the thief Mr Grundeis almost escapes retribution because his word is naturally taken against the word of mere kids but he is caught because of the holes left by the pin with which Emil's mother had fastened the three notes in the pocket of the boy's jacket. Just in time Emil remembers the pin and lays it on the counter of the bank with the entirely natural comment, 'And I pricked myself as well'.[18]

Walter de la Mare observed in his introduction to the first English edition of this classic tale, 'There is nothing in it that *might* not happen (in pretty much the same way as it does happen in the book) in London or Manchester or Glasgow tomorrow afternoon.'[19] A gang of children under the leadership of Gustave and 'the Professor', with their knowledge of the street system of Berlin, would be well equipped to trail the thief from pavement to café and from café to hotel – well equipped as regards speed, unobtrusiveness, confidence and communication, that is, but always with the hazard that they might run out of train fares or be obliged to relinquish their surveillance because of a stringent home timetable. The reality of character and setting is perfectly balanced with the excitement and stimulus which keys up the energies of the gang and keeps the pace of the story going.

171

Walter de la Mare added to his praise of the book's universal authenticity:

> None the less, Emil is just like the youngest of the three brothers who goes out to seek his fortune in the old folk tales – and gets it, in spite of a mistake or two on the journey. In other words, it is a tale of adventure and romance.[19]

Kästner belongs, certainly, to an old-established tradition but he added something of his own at once peculiarly local and also recognisable anywhere in the world – the ability children have to compensate for their apparent lack of power by organising, pooling their resources and skills and so proving their worth against the advantages of the adults who may be engaged in the same enterprise. Kästner's recipe – a group of children born and bred in a particular environment and acquainted with it in the thorough, uncritical, alert manner of their age; an equally authentic, unexaggerated background of parents and school, shops and organisations, local landmarks and local gossip – his successful recipe has served his successors for half a century and writers like Paul Berna in France with *A Hundred Million Francs* and its sequels or L. H. Evers with the brilliant Australian detective-adventure *The Racketty Street Gang* have maintained Kästner's standards of pace, inventiveness and veracity.

The recipe was used by E. W. Hildick in England at first with something of a crusading intention. He knew his children and had shrewdly assessed attitudes in them which could make them social nuisances just as easily as social benefactors. When his first story, *Jim Starling*, appeared in 1958 some critics (I was one) suggested that it was unlikely that four secondary-modern schoolboys of twelve or so could have identified and put to flight a gang of lead-thieves. We were smartly, and justifiably, corrected by the author, who described the genesis of his story in an article:

> Have you ever helped to capture a couple of armed hold-up men? Seven years ago, when I was teaching in a boys' secondary modern school in a Northern industrial town, a boy in my class did just that.
>
> The men had already robbed a sub-post-office after threatening to shoot the postmaster and his wife with a sten gun. The police had found no useful clue. The public were wondering where the men would strike next. Then this thirteen-year-old boy happened to notice something gleaming in a hole in a stone wall.
>
> He investigated – and ran straight to the police station! The dismantled sten gun had been put there ready for use on a second

raid, but because of this clue the police were able to trace and capture the criminals before they could do any further harm.[20]

The implicit flattery of the young in the tone of this piece does not alter their most important attribute, the undiscriminating, unselective observation which seldom survives the cluttered minds and lives of adults. Undoubtedly the Hardy Boys would have scooped up the criminals themselves. The more realistic approach of the boy in Hildick's anecdote, continued in the fictional investigations of Jim Starling and other Hildick heroes and heroines, has proved to be a better proposition for writers and readers.

Jim Starling was written, as Hildick said, to prove that 'youngsters in grimy industrial towns can have adventures every bit as exciting as those that commonly happen on a mountain or the edge of a jungle'. There was undoubtedly something of a political motive in the book as well, for at the time it was written the children who had not passed the selective eleven-plus exam and those who proceeded to grammar school were divided educationally in a far more emphatic and undesirable way than they are now in the more flexible organisation of the comprehensive system. Jim Starling and his mates, pupils of the Cement Street Secondary Modern School in Smogbury, were a good deal less artificial as characters than the definition of their environment might suggest. Whatever social point the books were supposed to make, these are properly individual boys – Jim with a managerial kind of brain, Terry Todd ready with encyclopedia-information on any and every subject, Goggles Grimshaw contending with a disturbed home background, Nip Challons recklessly brave as though to deny his small stature. Flushed with the success of deductions which led them to identify the cloakroom thief at school, they were very ready to follow up the accidental discovery of plans to rob local Godwell Hall of its roof-lead and then to form themselves into an official agency – official, that is, in having a title, the Last Apple Agency, and an office under a railway arch.

In *Jim Starling and the Agency* the aspiring detectives compete against one another in finding and solving particular cases, with results varying from farcical failure to relative success; the author allows himself a hint of satire as he shows how easy it is to make the wrong deductions from hastily collected facts. For a time, indeed, the Last Apple Agency confines its energies to peaceful areas of boyish competition but in two more of the seven books in the sequence, *Jim Starling and the Spotted Dog* and *Jim Starling Goes to Town*, they play detectives once more, with the same ungrammatical, boisterous vigour but with a more disciplined approach to the problems they meet. The trip to London promises to be a disaster, when they are persuaded by a con-man to exchange the tickets they have been given for the Cup Final at Wembley for four offering allegedly better seats which prove to be forged. When they recover from the blow the Last Apple investigators decide to get their revenge; they do so with a mixture of intelligent guesswork, skilful surveillance, tenacity and luck. The book proves once and for all that a writer who is prepared to give his novelist's attention to such matters as structure, logic and description, and to work at technique so that it seems effortless, will have more to offer than the writer who is content to rely on a formula, however popular it may be. Besides his technical skill, Hildick has struck a balance between excitement and prosaic detail which is comfortable for readers around nine and ten; the subjects chosen are such that they can be pursued in a light-hearted way without setting up dangerously false pictures of society.

In this first group of detective-adventures Hildick showed that the neighbourhood tale could be made exciting by certain devices which he was to develop in later books, particularly twists of narrative by which he could diversify an hour-by-hour story and still keep a clear direction for the plot. His expertise as a story-teller has perhaps never been shown more clearly than it is in *The Boy at the Window*, which was published in the same year, 1960, as the third and fourth Jim Starling books.

There is a trick in this book which in less skilful hands could have overweighted the story. David Case, recovering from polio, whiles away the time before his friends Stop and Scratch visit him after school by watching the row of shops opposite his house and their proprietors. Each of the first eleven chapters begins with an italicised passage referring in oblique and tantalising terms to the climax of the story. Before Hildick begins to describe the shops (piecemeal as bedridden David amuses himself by itemising their fascia, window contents, architectural styles and so on) he makes use of an ancient but useful authorial privilege:

> You may say: 'There was this boy at the window, with nothing to do but look out all day. Why didn't he realize what was going on in the sweet shop over the street? Why did it take him so long to discover who was the ringleader of the crooks?'[21]

The last of the eleven chapters ends with the advice that 'David now had all the basic information about the plotted crime, the criminals, the victim and even the time when the crooks were likely to strike. But it was still mixed up. It still needed sorting out. Could you have sorted it out?'[22]

And so on. Hildick plays fair. David is alerted to a possible crime only after his sister has retailed a conversation between her mother in her soft-goods shop and a commercial traveller and after talking to a visitor of his own, one of those drifting old men who hoard information about their neighbours. Even then David makes some wild guesses, veering between the possibility that Ralph Nellace is a private detective and is not systematically robbing his aunt's sweet-shop, the theory that mean old Enoch Grubbard at the junk-shop is being pursued by associates in crime whom he has cheated and that skinny Mr Taplett has something more to live on than the proceeds of his out-of-date men's outfitters' establishment. Sorting the evidence in his mind, considering the behaviour of the people he is watching through the window, arguing with his friends, David finally arrives at the truth and in a surprising (and surprisingly plausible) dénouement the boys foil the villains. The fact that their means of doing this are a white mouse and sundry glass and china jugs hurled at the getaway car is in line with the veracity of the tale.

The mouse is in fact useful in another way, providing comic relief and a subplot which neatly parallels the main mystery. 'Will Nicholas be caught in Mrs Case's trap?' is in its way as vital a question as 'Will David work out in time what villainy is being planned across the road?' The difference in degree, the double tension, add a special piquancy to the book. The puzzle is fairly stated and fairly worked out. If the action takes place outside the window it is seen entirely within David's restricted view; if his friends and his family help to confirm his suspicions, the working out is his and his alone, a fact which makes it all the more likely that readers will be drawn into the mystery along with him.

One of the unwritten laws of the detective-story is that every detail must contribute to the proposing and resolution of the puzzle. Hildick's propensity for description, often in the semi-comic form of cumulated lists, might seem to break this particular rule, but in fact the concrete details with which he satisfies one of the special demands of young readers are scrupulously chosen to forward the plot and to provide clues with which the reader might with a little effort arrive at the truth as quickly as David does. As our eyes, with David's, rove round the room and pick up details of furniture and accessories, we are looking at certain objects which are to play a part in the story.

Hildick's books are all directed to a particular readership and conceived in a particular way in which the emotional overtones of serious crime have no place; instead, there is an implicit social code and a security of domestic circumstance to support the understated reality of the books. The limited but sharp local atmosphere is never allowed to become artificial or perfunctory; the puzzle-element, the posed, contrived plot, is supported by credible details of character and place.

From the purlieus of Smogbury and the country town of the later 'Questers' series, Hildick has moved in recent years to what could be called an average suburbia, to one of those semi-urban rows of houses where there can be plenty of variety but nothing extreme. The familiar setting of front doors and dustbins, milk-floats and newspaper rounds translates readily into an American equivalent and the McGurk mysteries have been published in both countries with suitable modifications. The system of concurrent publications, books being planned for two markets and separately rendered in what amounts to two different languages, has made some difference to the typical Hildick style. The humour is as lively as ever, arising out of plausible everyday accidents and confrontations, but it is at times a little strident and it is a good deal swifter than it was in his earlier books. This may be at least partly due to the increased influence of television on stories for Hildick's preferred readership, nine-upwards, an influence apparent in the use of shorter, often one-sentence paragraphs and in the pace of the stories. The leisurely tone of the Jim Starling books is absent from the McGurk tales, in which the reader is given little space to ponder over a situation or a character.

None-the-less the two elements with which Hildick has set his personal mark on the puzzle-tale are still present – the ingenious but apparently casual structure and the well-devised characters. Each of his latest junior sleuths is firmly defined in relation to his particular contribution to a new detective bureau set up by ten-year-old Jack McGurk as a channel for his hyperactive desire to make things happen, his natural bossiness and his enormous admiration for the methods of Sherlock Holmes. *The Nose Knows*, published in 1974, introduced McGurk with his first associates. His friend Joey Rockwell's flair for words makes him an obvious choice for the role of recorder and archivist. Logically, he becomes the narrator for the series; in this way Hildick places the books firmly in a middle-years readership but does not allow first-person narration to sink into a consciously juvenile voice or to impede it with an authorial voice-over; with literary tact he makes sure that the voice of the boy is balanced by a proper, varied narrative pattern.

The third member of the organisation, Willie Sanders, is introduced in this first book when his particular attribute, an acute sense of smell, is exercised on the problem of a lost baseball glove. McGurk and Joey watch with astonishment the behaviour of the skinny boy newly arrived next door as he dives into each of the boxes and packing-cases strewn in the garden:

> With the small and medium boxes he'd do it standing up. I mean he would stick a box over his head, and turn from side to side, and maybe bow a little, and sometimes go right up on tip-toe, and then he'd groan. Yes, groan. All hollow and echoey, inside the box. I tell you, it was kind of spooky the way he did this, like something out of a horror film. Like the Man Without a Head. Or the Thing in the Iron Mask.[23]

When he emerges from the boxes and sniffs gently round their edges McGurk and Joey can bear the suspense no longer and accept an invitation to move next door and hear the explanation; complicated by McGurk's insistence on a proper detective plan, the search for the glove is carried through with a good deal of diverting detail.

The same method is used to bring a fourth member into the gang in *Dolls in Danger* when Wanda Greig makes a place for herself with a mixture of effrontery and blackmail and quickly proves her worth with her quick wits and her talent for tree-climbing. The fifth associate, 'Brains' Bellingham, makes up for his youth (he is only nine) by his scientific flair, abundantly proved in the ingenious machinery which drives McGurk to a frenzy of bewilderment in *The Case of the Invisible Dog*.

The five children operate successfully as a gang, four of them submitting with occasional complaints to McGurk's barely concealed vanity and his rash reliance on over-hasty deductions. Pooling their individual talents and the resources they share as children – the exact knowledge of local people and places, the propensity for noticing trivial things and making use of them – they cheerfully surround themselves with the machinery of detection which comics and television serials suggest are essential – identification-cards, a primitive computer or Kalamazoo devised by Brains, filing boxes and so on, conveniently housed in an office in the cellar of the ex-vicarage McGurk home.

The cumulation of circumstantial detail essential both to the background and the working out of any detective-story is not only a matter of amusing imitation by these Holmes devotees; it arises naturally from the neighbourhood nature of the books. Most of the crimes the McGurk gang investigate are simple neighbourhood puzzles – kidnapped dolls, a baby-sitting job worked into melodrama by McGurk's fertile imagination, a cat wrongly blamed for a wrecked garden. In the rare circumstance of adult crime being involved, as it is in *The Case of the Secret Scribbler*, the involvement of the children with the public is kept at a sensible and moderate level. Reality has been manipulated by rearrangement, by a careful degree of hyperbole, by order imposed on the disorderly sequences of day-to-day life and a colour and pace added to the monotony of everyday. Above all the seeming artlessness of the first-person narration is sustained by a neat structure, a planned interaction of dialogue, comment and action which makes each book a rounded whole, answering to its purpose as a tempting puzzle and a persuasive story.

The formally structured detective-story, the cops-and-robbers tale, will probably continue to serve pre-teen readers well enough provided it deals with subjects of a suitable scale and motives which such readers can appreciate. The serious social considerations raised by writers like Bernard Ashley and the late Roy Brown fall into a different category. New terms of reference have been seen over the past decade or two in the adult novels of Ruth Rendell and Amanda Cross, who have adapted a detective-structure through which to look at aberrations of character in certain communities, or in Nicholas Freeling's later novels, in which the high-ranking policeman Henri Castang's urban problems illustrate aspects of justice and human rights. The junior thriller seems to be separating in the same way into two sections, the mystery which explores human nature so far and no further and a narrative more flexible in plan and more taxing to the understanding which, like the terrorist stories I have already discussed, take the adventure story to new frontiers. Even in this more probing type of book there will remain a division between adult and junior books. For younger readers there will still be a distinction not so much in style or structure as in the degree of inference, of emotional response, of moral comprehension, which can be reasonably expected of them.

People

8. The Hero

Writing twenty years ago on the state of the novel, Nathalie Sarraute complained that psychology had affected the novelist's approach to character to a dangerous extent:

> Only reluctantly does the novelist endow him with attributes that could make him too easily distinguishable: his physical aspect, gestures, actions, sensations, everyday emotions, studied and understood for so long, which contribute to giving him, at the cost of so little effort, an appearance of life, and present such a convenient hold for the reader. Even a name, which is an absolutely necessary feature of his accoutrement, is a source of embarrassment to the novelist.[1]

Perhaps this pessimistic view has not been entirely justified. At any rate, it does not hold with regard to the characters in an adventure story. In a genre which depends on a firm definition of events, there has to be an equally firm definition of those who initiate or suffer from such events. The 'convenient hold for the reader' consists of various stylistic devices by which we can recognise and appreciate the people involved in events which are moving at an extreme and unrealistic speed; without the people the events could not exist or, if they did, they would have a different kind of interest. An impersonal account of an earthquake or an eruption might interest a scientist; the reader of fiction will require humans to be centrally involved.

The need for *firm* definition of character could become as threatening to an author as the psychological images referred to by Nathalie Sarraute. Critical dogma has asserted for a long time that the adventure story depends on action and that character needs only to be in outline. This view would tether the adventure story very strictly to the myths and legends from which it derives. It would imply, for example, that the hero of an adventure novel should remain an archetype, conforming in the most general terms to such dictionary definitions as a man 'of superhuman strength, courage, or ability, favoured by the gods' or, more prosaically, 'one who does brave or noble deeds', 'A man who exhibits extraordinary bravery, fineness or greatness of soul, in connection with any pursuit, work, or enterprise; a man admired and venerated for his achievements and noble qualities.' A

Superman does not have a character as such: he is particularised by circumstance, his reactions are prescribed by the fact that he is a hero. Reading myths and legends, we accept as hero the superman who either, as the embodiment of good, faces and conquers evil (like Beowulf against Grendel) or who compounds his aggressive self-seeking by redressing some social balance (like the Robin Hood of popular legend or the knight who rescues the damsel in distress – usually a feat carrying a worthwhile reward).

Even as we read, though, we are rearranging the archetypal hero in any way we choose: some may feel that Grendel had territorial rights or that damsels were often out of the frying-pan but into the fire. The writer of adventure stories, while relying on the foundation, and the universal associations, of the archetypal hero, will have to take him out of legendary anonymity to something more particular. And something more human. Supermen are not intrinsically interesting and if readers are to be properly engaged with the hero, fearing for his safety and hoping for his success, they will have to be given more than a mere sequence of events. The hero who will bring about real tension and will concern us, as readers, will be fallible enough to be recognised as in some ways like ourselves. Discussing junior adventure stories, Ivan Southall expressed the current demand for a move away from stereotypes. 'Real adventure,' he declared:

> . . . cannot happen to super-heroes; by nature they would have to be insensitive to it; real adventure belongs to us . . . Adventure is simply experience; the mistakes often enough meaning more than the successes.[2]

The adventure story shows the hero in action: it is not a study in character for its own sake but the demonstration of the way one person behaves in a situation of stress and danger. We are expected to get to know the hero first of all for what he actually does rather than what he thinks or feels, and his thoughts may be expressed actively, as plans and stratagems, rather than as emotional revelations. He is on the side of the right against wrong and so whatever he does is acceptable even if it seems technically to be wrong. As Jerry Palmer puts it, writing of the thriller-hero:

> . . . since we are on his side, and believe that he is justified, we are free to enjoy the sensation of suppressing the obstacles that confront us/him. Descriptions of violence practised by the villain are intended in a different way; they are clearly supposed to nauseate the reader . . .[3]

In this way the hero clearly shows his derivation from the archetypal hero of legend. Yet almost every writer of classic or 'high adventure' story whose work has endured or deserves to endure has deviated in one way or another from these established conventions.

Stanley Weyman, whom I take as a striking example, added a particular twist to tales in which romantic heroes overcame great odds in the service of the oppressed. His heroes are so far coloured by the cloak-and-dagger atmosphere of sixteenth-century France or Regency England that they may seem at first to be stereotypes but in fact the force and tension of the action, the duels, chases, escapes and intrigues compel attention because of the particular nature of the hero's involvement in them and the personality which directs this involvement.

History served Weyman well, both in the matter of background and of character. In his romantic adventures he contrived situations in which private individuals were caught up in national events but since he was writing adventure stories rather than historical novels, those events remained as background and the great figures of history were only glimpsed – Richelieu in *Under the Red Robe*, for example, Charles IX and Henry of Navarre in *Count Hannibal*. The use of the word 'background' does not imply that Weyman underestimated the importance of the events he chose. He is not concerned with the political implications of the infamous Massacre of St Bartholomew's Eve in 1572 except in so far as certain of his characters in *Count Hannibal* and *The House of the Wolf*, being Huguenots, could be placed under particular threat in Paris on that night. He has used this event to build up an intense atmosphere of danger and violence in which a group of people, isolated and with attention intently focused on them, cannot fail to inspire sympathy and anxiety in the reader. Beyond the simple fact that Louis de Pavannes is in danger and that the Vidame de Bezers rescues him, the narrative of *The House of the Wolf* turns on one of many versions of the pride-and-prejudice theme which Weyman uses to relate character and action and to make historical romance more than a series of swashbuckling scenes. He specialises, one might say, in the villain who turns hero.

There is no doubt that Raoul de Mar, Vidame de Bezers, has the hallmarks of the stereotype villain. This is all the clearer because this brief but compelling tale is told by Anne de Caylus, one of three young brothers devoted to their beautiful cousin Catherine and committed to the defence of her betrothed, the Huguenot Louis de Pavannes. The three lads fear their powerful neighbour de Bezers, whose attentions to Catherine are becoming embarrassing; it is a fear deriving both from his power in their district and his appearance:

It was not so much his height and bulk, though he was so big that the clipped pointed fashion of his beard – a fashion then new at court – seemed on him incongruous and effeminate; nor so much the sinister glance of his grey eyes – he had a slight cast in them; nor the grim suavity of his manner, and the harsh threatening voice that permitted of no disguise. It was the sum of these things, the great brutal presence of the man – that was over-powering – that made the great falter and the poor crouch.[4]

With the reputation of a duellist and an employer of bravos, de Bezers remains a sinister figure though he takes on the role of rescuer: through the eyes of a lad caught up in the terrors of the night of massacre we come to realise that the traits that belong to villainy could also be heroic. As de Bezers with a handful of his own soldiers defends the wounded Louis de Pavannes against a howling mob, the young narrator as he makes his escape compares the two men:

> . . . surely in all his reckless life Bezers had never been so emphatic-ally the man for the situation – had never shown to such advantage as at this moment when he stood confronting the sea of faces, the sneer on his lip, a smile in his eyes; and looking down unblenching, a figure of scorn, on the men who were literally agape for his life. The calm defiance of his steadfast look fascinated even me. Wonder and admiration for the time took the place of dislike. I could scarcely believe that there was not some atom of good in a man so fearless.[5]

Meanwhile Louis de Pavannes, who according to the conventions of the adventure story should be considered the hero, plays a noble but subordinate role:

> The face which I had known so bright and winning, was now white and set. His fair, curling hair . . . hung dank, bedabbled with blood which flowed from a wound in his head. His sword was gone; his dress was torn and disordered and covered with dust. His lips moved. But he held up his head, he bore himself bravely with it all; so bravely, that I choked, and my heart seemed bursting as I looked at him standing there forlorn and now unarmed. . . there was a quietness in his fortitude which made a great difference between his air and that of Bezers. He lacked, as became one looking unarmed on certain death, the sneer and smile of the giant beside him.[6]

The villain becomes hero, then, but not in the conventional sense. He restores his rival to Catherine while furiously rejecting Pavannes' thanks: to accept his gratitude would be to cheat him of his revenge, which is to preserve his hatred of the man and burden him with a permanent obligation to an enemy. Yet, the

narrator insists, in a retrospective ending to his story, the good
lives after his death and not the evil:

> . . . if all that good save one act were buried with him, this one act
> alone, the act of a French gentleman, would be told of him – ay!
> and will be told as long as the kingdom of France, and the gracious
> memory of the late King, shall endure.[7]

The definition 'cloak-and-dagger romance' implies a measure of
critical scorn in our time, but Weyman's skill as a writer carries
him beyond stereotype and sentimentality. Few of the authors
writing in those golden years of the historical adventure, the
1890s and early 1900s, can equal him in describing scenes of
mob violence, of ambush and chase, with the constant colouring (sometimes muted and sometimes positive and striking) of
costume and physiognomy, landscape and city purlieus. Yet
everything of narrative and ancillary detail is arranged to throw
into relief the behaviour of individuals – the confrontation and
conflict of personalities dominate the story and determine the
action.

In *Count Hannibal* Weyman played still more boldly on the
ambiguities of personality, using third-person narrative to take an
authorial view of three people whose emotional changes are of
equal importance – a villain/hero, a hero proved coward and a
heroine/victim. A simple story line, the flight of Mademoiselle
de Vrillac, a Protestant, from the terrible night of massacre in
Paris to her estates in Brittany, provides suspense and excitement
in terms of action but, far more, the tension and surprise of
character as we gradually realise how the heroine's handsome,
gallant lover de Tignonville belies his role as hero as surely as
the dark-visaged, hectoring villain Count Hannibal shows that
passion can be disciplined by gentleness and respect. Fast horses,
flashing swords, the desperate anxieties of pursuit and siege are
serving something far more than the needs of an adventure-
plot.

Technically adept as *Count Hannibal* is, Weyman's particular
version of the historical adventure is perhaps seen at its best in
Under the Red Robe. His manipulation of historical event is, in
this book, both bold and simple. He sets his story in the reign of
Louis XIII, early in the seventeenth century, and uses the
changeable fortunes of Cardinal Richelieu to activate his plot. Gil
de Berault, whose nickname of 'The Black Death' is occasioned
by his nature as bravo and ruthless duellist, condemned by his
master the Cardinal for the last of his illegal sword-fights, is given
a chance to save himself from prison and the gallows. He is to

seek out an enemy of the Cardinal, Monsieur de Cocheforêt, now exiled in Spain from his estate near the Pyrenees. An enterprise which seems to demand action and no close scrutiny becomes a different matter when de Berault has arrived at Cocheforêt and has found in the sadly neglected house a wife and a sister determined to protect the head of the household, who is in fact hiding not far away.

The fate of Monsieur de Cocheforêt is the mainspring of the plot: the emotional (I would almost say spiritual) effect of the enterprise on de Berault is its moving force. In moral terms it might seem, as in Weyman's other books, that de Cocheforêt is the hero and de Berault the villain. But our concern is not whether de Cocheforêt will escape Richelieu's agent but how his escape or capture will alter de Berault's fortunes, and (more important) how the staunch behaviour of Mademoiselle and the shame of his deceit will affect de Berault's actions. Will the good in him override the ill or is he in fact simply the arrogant bully which he seems at the outset to be?

Two elements of technique contribute to the quality of *Under the Red Robe*. The structure of the story is extremely direct, with no subplots and with two settings, Paris and Cocheforêt, used in neatly interlocking scenes. More significant is the method of narration. De Berault tells the story himself and he is allowed with no self-consciousness to define his own feelings as he describes the two ladies whose behaviour forces him to examine his own. Determination and doubt, shame and vanity alternate, as he sees his ruffling past in a different light and wonders whether he is turning into 'some Don Quixote from Castile, tilting at windmills and taking barbers' bowls for gold'.[8] The use of soliloquy, or private communing, can seem forced but Weyman skilfully limits the moments of stillness and solitude for his hero, so that we are hardly aware that action has momentarily stopped. He poses de Berault in the darkness of an inn, the luxury of Richelieu's lodging, on horseback in the dry wastes of the Spanish border, in the formal garden of Cocheforêt or its forest glades and ridings, with such pictorial vigour that the man seems to be thinking and planning on the move, with self-doubt and self-realisation as the spurs to action.

When de Berault has denied his master's assignment and given the captured de Cocheforêt his freedom, out of love for his sister but also out of distaste for his former self, he rides towards Paris to take the punishment which he has, after all, not been able to compound. He sees meaning in the contrast between the smoky sky over the city and the open air of the moor and pasture over which his prisoner will be riding, and so glides into more abstract thought:

> A man in middle life does not strip himself of the worldly habit with which experience has clothed him, does not run counter to all the hard saws and instances by which he has governed his course so long, without shiverings and doubts and horrible misgivings, and struggles of heart. At least a dozen times between the Loire and Paris I asked myself what honour was, and what good it could do me when I lay rotting and forgotten; if I were not a fool following a Jack O'Lanthorn; and whether, of all the men in the world, the relentless man to whom I was returning would not be the first to gibe at my folly?[9]

The decision to face the consequences of his actions is rewarded: Richelieu, temporarily in eclipse, has neither the power nor the inclination to punish de Berault. But the decision was made while punishment, death, seemed inevitable and the emerging of de Berault as hero remains the theme of the book, with Mademoiselle de Cocheforêt's change of heart the means to de Berault's triumph in love, rather than a separate emotional change of equal importance, as it is in the conclusion of *Count Hannibal*. Among Weyman's adventure romances, *Under the Red Robe* stands out for its particularly tight structure and firm emotional pattern. But in all his books he shows that for this kind of fiction to have any lasting value there must be a proper relationship between character and action.

The extent to which Stanley Weyman turned the traditional hero into an individual is clear when we compare his use of the hero-villain device with that of Rafael Sabatini. Sabatini's romantic stock-in-trade depends largely on the idea of the Misunderstood Hero, the Hero in Eclipse. He took a man respected and fortunate and placed him in a dangerous situation from which he could only escape by playing the villain. The central character in *Captain Blood*, an Irish physician condemned by Judge Jeffreys for helping a wounded supporter of the rebel Monmouth, escapes from slavery in Jamaica by turning pirate, and a Cornish landowner, Sir Oliver Tressilian, his good name similarly blighted by false evidence, becomes in *The Sea Hawk* Sakr-el-Bahr, the most dreaded of Mediterranean rovers. *Scaramouche*, perhaps Sabatini's best-known romantic novel, describes the return from self-imposed exile of a young lawyer caught in the complexities of the French Revolution and turning himself into 'a sort of Scaramouche – the little skirmisher, the astute intriguer, scattering the seeds of trouble with a sly hand', in order to discover his true identity and reveal his enemy's deceptions. Sabatini's piquant version of the traditional hero seems to have been forgotten until recent years; Dorothy Dunnett has revised it with particular brilliance in her character, Francis Crawford of Lymond, Master of Culter.

The hero, by tradition and definition, is expected and assumed to be combative and to prove his courage in combat against one or other of the enemies (national, political, fantastic, personal) which happened to be relevant at this or that date. Yet novelists, who most often find their best subjects in the exceptions to a rule, have often been successful when they have chosen a hero who doubts his own courage. There is emotional depth and colour to be found here to give the sequence of adventure a direction that will alert the reader to the unexpected in human behaviour; there is, besides, a subtle flattery for the reader who engages actively in the dialogue with the author, in that he is helped to take a liberal and an informed view of a man who suffers from a mistaken idea of himself. It was perhaps no accident that the theme was used many times in the decade overlapping the turn of the century, a period when the British imperial idea was under threat from changing attitudes as well as threats of war. The fears and doubts which began to affect the nation as a whole were reflected and almost symbolised in two significant novels, A. E. W. Mason's *The Four Feathers*, published in 1902, and Buchan's early novel, *The Half-Hearted*, of 1900.

Roger Lancelyn Green summarises the theme which A. E. W. Mason had tried out in *Lawrence Clavering* and developed more fully in *The Four Feathers*:

> . . . the idea of a boy growing to manhood in the belief that he is a coward, forced into the army by tradition and by a father without imagination, losing his honour and with it his fiancée – not by fear, but by the fear of fear – and finding, when it seems too late, that his is that finest bravery of all which can endure danger and pain in spite of the vivid imagination which urges him to run away.[10]

For this book A. E. W. Mason set aside first-person self-analysis for a surprisingly successful mixture of direct explanation and a theatrical use of dialogue and quasi-stage-directions. As the story opens, General Faversham is entertaining friends on one of his Crimean nights and he and his close friend Lieutenant Sutch, who has been invalided out of the navy, are exchanging extremely stark reminiscences of campaigns they lived through together, while the General's fourteen-year-old son Harry listens. The General's character is encapsulated for the reader in the terse comment that 'Personal courage and an indomitable self-confidence were the chief, indeed the only qualities which sprang to light'[11] in the man. The contrast between father and son is stressed not by statement but by a description of Harry's appearance, posture, expression. The spotlight is focused on the boy:

> The curtest, least graphic description of the biting days and nights in the trenches set the lad shivering. Even his face grew pinched, as though the iron frost of that winter was actually eating into his bones.[12]

Sutch, who has known and loved the boy's mother and knows how well she would have helped him to manage his imagination, offers friendship to the boy but Harry, sternly inoculated with family pride, declines to alter his reserved manner.

The story moves from this overture to the year 1882, when Harry, a young man of twenty-seven, on leave from his regiment, announces to his friends his engagement to Ethne Eustace, daughter of an eccentric Irish landowner. Again the scene is treated in almost dramatic terms, as the author follows one or another of the characters towards the climax. A telegram is handed to Harry from a friend advising him that the regiment is to be ordered to Egypt at once and Harry reads it, crumples it and throws it into the fire:

> . . . the fire took hold upon the telegram and shook it, so that it moved like a thing alive and in pain. It twisted, and part of it unrolled, and for a second lay open and smooth of creases, lit up by the flame and as yet untouched, so that two or three words sprang, as it were, out of a yellow glow of fire and were legible. Then the flame seized upon that smooth part too, and in a moment shrivelled it into black tatters.[13]

The symbolism here is boldly allied to the mechanics of the plot. Harry's brother officer Trench, an astute man, has glimpsed the words thrown up in the fire and later he and his friends, assuming, as Harry has done, that his action was entirely cowardly, send him three white feathers; to these Ethne, hearing Harry's confession, adds a fourth from her fan. The same night she burns Harry's letters and the fire leaves 'in the end only flakes of ashes like feathers, and white flakes like white feathers'.

Resigning his commission for fear of disgracing Ethne as well as his regiment, Harry determines to redeem his honour by such private acts as will persuade his accusers to take back the feathers. During six years of disguise and danger in Egypt he achieves his aim in a way which leaves no doubt that he has the active courage expected of a hero. A first-person narrative would have been disastrous with such a subject. Harry Faversham's doubts and perplexities, his quiet tenacity and endurance, could only have seemed mawkish and artificial if these and other changes in him had been made the matter of soliloquy. As it is, the narrative ranges freely from one important character to another so that the central dilemma is seen first from one point of view and then from another. Harry's perilous years in the bazaars of the Sudan as a zither-playing Greek, the desperate weeks in the prison at Omdurman, are framed, as it were, by the meetings, discussions and apprehensions of the people who love him and who gradually come to understand him: his sense of honour is enhanced by contrast with the personal conduct of his best friend Durrance, who loves Ethne but declines to take advantage of her situation.

In one of his rare authorial comments, A. E. W. Mason sets Durrance firmly alongside Harry:

> He was a soldier of a type not so rare as the makers of war stories wish their readers to believe. Hector of Troy was his ancestor; he was neither hysterical in his language nor vindictive in his acts; he was not an elderly schoolboy with a taste for loud talk, but a quiet man who did his work without noise; who could be stern when occasion needed and of an unflinching severity; but whose nature was gentle and compassionate.[14]

By giving Durrance such a large part to play in the drama, the author has been able to move his story from emotional confrontations to scenes of exotic and dangerous action and to establish his hero's problem so meticulously in the context of army and society at a particular time that scruples of honour and conduct very far from the attitudes of today can still be realised by the reader as valid and important.

Lewis Haystoun, hero by title of Buchan's early novel, *The Half-Hearted*, suffers from a conscience as quick to fear cowardice as Harry Faversham's and, like Faversham, he redeems himself by a passionate exercise of determined courage in the face of extreme danger. This wealthy young Scottish landowner is no more a coward than Faversham was but a combination of social fastidiousness, a lack of ambition and a profound personal malaise put him at odds with his life and with his fellow men. His curious distaste for positive action keeps him from declaring the love he conceives for Alice Wishart until in pique at his reserve, and in genuine distress and bewilderment, this exacting girl has accepted the hand of a very different kind of man, a middle-class politician of drive and energy. Buchan defined Haystoun's weakness

as the attitude of an aristocrat without employment. In the words
of a politician of the same class and outlook:

> 'The vitality of a great family has run to a close in him. He is strong
> and able, and yet, unless the miracle of miracles happens, he will
> never do anything. Two hundred years ago he might have led some
> mad Jacobite plot to success. Three hundred and he might have
> been another Raleigh. Six hundred and there would have been a
> new crusade. But as it is, he is out of harmony with his times; life is
> too easy and mannered; the field for a man's courage is in petty and
> recondite things; and Lewie is not fitted to understand it. And all
> this, you see, spells a kind of cowardice: and if you have a friend
> who is a hero out of joint, a great man smothered in the wrong sort
> of civilisation, and all the while one who is building up for himself
> with the world and in his own heart the reputation of a coward, you
> naturally grow hot and bitter.'[15]

The passage is vital in linking the *fainéant* behaviour of
Haystoun at the outset of the story with his energetic pursuit of
the Russian spy Marker in the passes of the North-West Frontier
and his truly heroic death when he holds the invading enemy at
bay long enough for the British troops to arrive. Unfortunately it
is not enough for a character to be defined externally by the
author through the mouth of another: he must present himself
actively, clearly and unequivocally in his own words, deeds and
attitudes. Haystoun's self-examination is prolix, drugging the
reader with its excess, and his scruples of honour, when he and
Alice declare their love for one another, are far less convincing
than Alice's own utterances.

In all Buchan's books there is a striking difference between the
style he uses for the confessions and inward thoughts of his
characters and the forceful, compact yet essentially plangent
and poetic style with which he describes important moments of
action. Haystoun's apotheosis as the half-hearted man-turned-
hero is not to be found, for the reader, in the long passages of
self-communing as he waits for the Russian-organised army to
reach the pass he has been left to defend – in such abstract and
grandiose phrases as 'He had returned to the homely paths of the
commonplace, and, young, unformed, untried, he was caught up
by kind fate to the place of the wise and the heroic,'[16] but in
passages where concrete detail and intense emotion are welded
together by the rhythm and tone of the writing. Such a passage
brings the chapter to a conclusion in which Haystoun establishes
himself for his solitary vigil:

> He did the journey in an hour, for he was in a pitiable state of
> anxiety. Every moment he looked to hear the tramp of an army

before him, and know his errand of no avail. Over the little barrier ridge he scrambled, and then up the straight gully to the little black rift which was the gate of an empire. His unquiet mind peopled the wilderness with voices, but when, breathless and sore, he came into the jaws of the pass, all was still, silent as the grave, save for an eagle which croaked from some eyrie in the cliffs . . .[17]

and sentences of the same restrained simplicity proclaim his death:

Then there came a wild surge around, twenty bayonets pierced him, and in the article of death he was conscious of a great press which ground him into the earth. The next moment the column was marching over his body.[18]

This kind of stylistic reverberation is worth scores of pages of introspection. The adventure story has no room for a deep, probing analysis of character but it need not be assumed that it has no room for character at all. Action can produce its own kind of character-drawing. At certain moments of high tension and strong writing in adventure stories, an individual becomes apparent, becomes known imaginatively to the reader. There were times when Buchan achieved this special kind of particularisation with something not too far from the genius of Stevenson.

In her biography of Buchan, Janet Adam Smith records that he was once found reading *Greenmantle* and guiltily admitting that he thought it 'rather good'. She comments:

These books were pure pleasure to invent, no trouble to write, and they made a lot of money; no doubt he felt that they could not therefore be counted for virtue. He was lucky to have had the story-teller's gift, and does not seem to have questioned whether he could have made more of it.[19]

But why should he have made more of it? If the value of literary genres were to be measured by the degree of seriousness, or the evidence of effort, the style suitable for sermons or formal histories, for instance, would have to be preferred or exalted above that of well-crafted stories. We may be thankful that Buchan did not try to make more of *The Thirty-Nine Steps* or *Prester John* than the special synthesis of action and character that he made his own.

It is seen at its best, perhaps, in the adventures of Richard Hannay. Ostensibly Buchan constructed this character to suit the kind of story he had in his mind. He needed a man with some experience of crisis and danger. Hannay, he tells us, had fought in the Boer War, had some experience of ciphers as an Intelligence officer, had been a mining engineer with administrative as well as technical duties. As a Rhodesian, he has a certain 'colonial' aplomb and flexibility but at the same time he is a clubbable English gentleman with a sturdy, unsentimental adherence to the country which he came finally to view as his true home and with a genuine sense of adventure. When Leithen towards the end of his life thinks about his closest friends, he remembers with affection:

> Dick Hannay, half Nestor, half Odysseus, deep in Oxfordshire mud, but with a surprising talent for extricating himself and adventuring in the ends of the earth.[20]

Hannay's encounters with villainy in its various guises engage his wits and the detective instinct which is part observation and part inspired guesswork. He is ready to state his social and political attitudes with conviction and to explain how they motivate his actions, but with no elaborate analysis or soul-searching. There are no doubts in his mind – not even the double view of life held by Dickson McCunn, whose latent romanticism draws him into danger, not even the conflict between ill-health and mental energy which directs Blenkiron, of whom a friend commented that he 'would go through hell with a box of bismuth tablets and a pack of Patience cards'.[21] From his entrance into the world of espionage in *The Thirty-Nine Steps*, when he is thirty-seven, to his respectable middle-aged response to danger in *The Island of Sheep*, Hannay remains all of a piece, a character well qualified to deliver Buchan's fears of power-politics and the decay of civilisation in a sturdy, unaffected way perfectly in keeping with his class and temperament. He develops with time, but consistently.

We first meet him as a man bored with prosperity and aching for action:

> At Oxford Circus I looked up into the spring sky and I made a vow. I would give the Old Country another day to fit me into something; if nothing happened, I would take the next boat for the Cape.[22]

Something did happen. The American secret agent Scudder appealed to him for help, and not in vain:

> I am an ordinary sort of fellow, not braver than other people, but I hate to see a good man downed, and that long knife would not be the end of Scudder if I could play the game in his place.[23]

The use of the word 'game' reflects the phrase 'The Great Game' – whose overtones resound in adventure stories from the turn of the century; it is also an essential part of Hannay's half-deprecating, easy-going idea of himself. For the sake of the plot, if for no other reason, he must not be allowed to be too clever or too intense. His successes against Medina, Ivery and the powers of evil in their servants and disciples are due to his observant eye (which sees through disguises), his practical, hard-headed nature (he cannot be hypnotised, as more than one enemy discovers too late) and his quick wits.

Hannay's talent for improvisation serves the story-teller admirably. Sometimes his rapid plans work magnificently (for example, when in *Mr Standfast* he escapes pursuit by using a megaphone to reduce an army exercise to chaos) and sometimes they are disastrous (for instance, when he poses as a Free Trade radical in *The Thirty-Nine Steps*). Buchan gave his hero a characteristic mode of speech which alters very little in the course of his life, an almost offhand idiom which adds piquancy to the chases and escapes he is involved in. Words suggest character in this passage as Hannay prepares to escape Scudder's pursuers and the police wanting him for Scudder's murder:

> It was going to be a giddy hunt, and it was queer how the prospect comforted me. I had been slack so long that almost any chance of activity was welcome. When I had to sit alone with that corpse and wait on fortune I was no better than a crushed worm, but if my neck's safety was to hang on my own wits I was prepared to be cheerful about it.[24]

The man who responded to challenge with imagination and practical good sense, who classed himself with cunning cowards rather than with the truly brave, who was not afraid to admit to fear but who escaped fear through anger, who could live within a social framework but move outside it when he needed to – this was a character based perhaps on a conventional type, an Establishment figure and something of a macho-hero, but a hero with enough substance to sustain the weight of a series of adventures in which the feeling of being hunted and the acknowledgement of national obligation could be expressed easily, forcefully and individually.

Characters in fiction are, inevitably, defined by class as much as by temperament, and because Buchan is so clearly visible in many of his characters, the search for signs of snobbishness which occupies his detractors has pointed many critics to the three books in which Dickson McCunn, the well-to-do, middle-aged Glasgow grocer, is the key to both tone and plot. Janet Adam Smith defines McCunn as a 'literary character' and relates him to Buchan's experience in this way:

The Hero

With Dickson McCunn . . . Buchan is paying a belated tribute to the Glasgow bourgeois, such as had lived in Queens Park and attended the John Knox Free Kirk, and to whose virtues he had been indifferent when he lived among them and looked on 'an avenue of respectable villa-residences and a well-kept public park' as the essence of dullness. Yet Buchan himself had spent most of his boyhood in a villa near a well-kept public park, and it had not blunted *his* spirit of adventure; so the retired provision merchant, who is an elder of the Guthrie Memorial Kirk, whose wife's idea of bliss is a holiday in a hydropathic, is given the soul of a romantic. . . .[25]

and she quotes Buchan's own acknowledgement that McCunn was conceived on the lines of 'that other Glasgow hero, Baillie Nicol Jarvie of *Rob Roy*'.

We first meet Dickson McCunn, shaving in five minutes with a safety razor, new to him, and working out that 'in his fifty-five years, having begun to shave at eighteen, he had wasted three thousand three hundred and seventy hours – or one hundred and forty days – or between four or five months – by his neglect of this admirable invention'.[26] It could well be the introduction of a comic character but McCunn is neither a figure of fun nor the victim of patronising interest, as he sets off on a walking tour with spring and a sense of adventure in his middle-aged heart.

The balance between romance and common sense, between improbable events and realistic circumstances, is one of the many factors that keep Buchan's stories so fresh and engaging. McCunn's romantic yearning after the glamour of the past, as he sees it, is born of his reading, of Scott in particular, and from his reading he has selected and held to himself the flavour he needs to compensate for his own successful but not entirely satisfying life:

> He was a Jacobite not because he had any views on Divine Right, but because he had always before his eyes a picture of a knot of adventurers in cloaks, new landed from France among the Western heather.[27]

Yet when McCunn is swept into romantic adventure – in the defence of the Russian princess Saskia in *Huntingtower*, in the fight against Mastrovin and his conspirators in *Castle Gay* and *The House of the Four Winds* – he never loses his sturdy common sense. The element of comedy enters the stories through McCunn, not because McCunn is made a figure of fun but rather because so much of his part in the adventures is the part of reason, of sheer unromantic common sense and tenacity. His

195

careful organisation of his holiday, his capable planning and provisioning, support him in moments of fear or physical distress. When called upon to become a burglar in order to help Saskia, he finds both rational and romantic justifications for his illegal behaviour and he finally puts an end to Mastrovin's evil threats by invoking the power of the police (always a good way to keep the balloon of adventure tethered to the ground).

As the provision merchant is carried further and further from his respectable existence, he suffers from very natural doubts of his own capabilities. Wading through a stream minus shoes, socks and breeches, he is uneasily aware that he has discarded sartorial and emotional conventions. Six years after the enterprise of *Huntingtower*, he has moved from the city to the country and has changed with retirement. Balder but thinner, with 'the innocence and ardour of youth' still in his eyes, he has found his own style:

> When not engaged in some active enterprise, it was his habit to wear a tailed coat and trousers of tweed, a garb which from his boyish recollecting he thought proper for a country laird, but which to the ordinary observer suggested a bookmaker. Gradually, a little self-consciously, he had acquired what he considered to be the habits of the class. He walked in his garden with a spud, his capacious pockets containing a pruning knife and twine; he could talk quite learnedly of crops and stock, and though he never shouldered a gun, of the prospects of game, and a fat spaniel was rarely absent from his heels.[28]

Without a sense of his own importance (though with a sturdy idea of his identity), he accepts the idea of an interview to help his protégé, Jaikie Galt, during the excitements of *Castle Gay*, and his easy manner convinces the journalist that he is Thomas Craw, but with reservations:

> Before him beyond doubt was the face that had launched a thousand ships of journalism – the round baldish head, the bland benevolent chin, the high cheek-bones, and shrewdly pursed lips. The familiar horn spectacles were wanting, but they lay beside him on the floor, marking a place in a book. Now that he had Mr Craw not a yard away from him, he began hurriedly to revise certain opinions he had entertained about that gentleman. This man was not any kind of fool. The blue eyes which met his were very wide awake, and there was decision and humour in every line of that Pickwickian countenance.[29]

The reader, knowing of the mistake, readily appreciates the inner difference between Craw, who in adventure changes radically from pompous dishonesty to a measure of courage, and

McCunn, from whom adventure draws out courage and intelligence that were always present. The sheer boyish enjoyment of his adventures, in spite of moments of fear, takes away any sense of exaggeration from McCunn's romantic attitudes. When he escorts Prince John to his boat at the end of the *Castle Gay* adventure, he is sincerely caught up in his view of the Jacobite past. Discovering that the Prince is distantly descended from the Stewarts, he sees his masquerade dress of royal tartan and his Garter riband as the embodiment of a dream and receives an engraved ring as a reward for his help with a passionate conviction that one day he will be called upon to help the Prince again. There is no contradiction between his total delight in the world of adventure and his certainty about the moment when the extremes of adventure need to be disciplined. After he has seen a defeated revolutionary off the rambling premises of Castle Gay, he explains his methods to Jaikie:

> 'I got the idea . . . by remembering what Bismarck said during the Schleswig-Holstein affair – when he was asked in Parliament what he would do if the British Army landed on German soil. He said he would send for the police . . . I've always thought that a very good remark . . . If you're faced with folk that are accustomed to shoot it's no good playing the same game, unless you're anxious to get hurt. You want to paralyse them by lapping them in the atmosphere of law and order. Talk business to them. It's whiles a very useful thing to live in a civilized country, and you should take advantage of it.'. . .[30]

and he shrewdly comments on Mastrovin's lack of any sense of humour, observing that 'without humour you cannot run a sweetie-shop, let alone a nation'.[31]

Like Hannay, Dickson McCunn grows in stature and assimilates experience in the few years when he is involved in romantic events, but he remains the same honest, clear-headed citizen and the respect accorded to him by the friends he finds and keeps depends on their knowledge of the two sides of his nature. Alison calls him a poet. Dougal attributes to him 'the heart of a boy and the head of an old serpent'[32] and admires the way his obstinate idealism overcomes fear. In *The House of the Four Winds* McCunn is faced with a task more dangerous than any he has met before. As he impersonates the Archduke Hadrian and even allows himself to be presented to the people as the rightful ruler, his imagination carries him through; when the Archduke's death has achieved the purpose of the impersonation and he escapes with his friends from Evallonia, he feels the situation as the climax of his life:

He remembered something he had read – in Stevenson, he thought – where a sedentary man had been ravished by a dream of galloping through a midnight pass at the head of cavalry with a burning valley behind him. Well, he was a sedentary man, and he was not dreaming an adventure, but in the heart of one. Never had his wildest fancies envisaged anything like this. He had been a king, acclaimed by shouting mobs. He had kept a throne warm for a friend, and now he was vanishing into the darkness, an honourable fugitive, a willing exile. He was the first grocer in all history that had been a Pretender to a Crown. The clack of hooves on stone, the jingling of bits, the echo of falling water were like strong wine.[33]

Buchan was fortunate in being able with perfect reason to conduct his bourgeois hero out of Evallonia on horseback and wise to leave him finally in the sober self-knowledge of his confident but unassuming nature:

'I'm going to catch a wheen salmon, and potter about my bits of fields, and read my books, and sit by my fireside. And on the last day of my life I'll be happy, thinking of the grand things I've seen and the grand places I've been in. Ay, and the grand friends I've known – the best of all.'[34]

The comradeship which runs through all Buchan's stories, contributing no less to their firm character-drawing than to their emotional content, is traced perhaps most notably in the three books in which Dickson McCunn by his own nature steps over the barriers of class and circumstance to find and keep true friends.

Class distinctions come into consideration in a more subtle way when we come to the most determinedly unheroic of all heroes, Rider Haggard's Allan Quatermain. When we are first introduced to Quatermain it is as a hunter of fifty-three, hard up after a luckless expedition, on his way back to Natal to look for some new opening. Born a gentleman, as he tells us (his father was a missionary and he was brought up from young boyhood in Southern Africa), he has been 'but a poor travelling trader and hunter'[35] all of his life. We realise after a book or two that self-deprecation is one of his chief characteristics and that in fact he has been a great deal more than this. It is, though, as a professional guide that he meets Sir Henry Curtis, a handsome English landowner of thirty or so, who has come out to look for his brother George, vanished in Africa after a family quarrel, following a report furnished by Quatermain earlier to the family lawyer. With Sir Henry travels Captain John Good, a naval officer prematurely retired. Employee Quatermain may be, but he is conscious of being an English gentleman as well as a 'homely, half-educated hunter and trader'. After the adventure of *King Solomon's Mines* which the three men undertake together he buys an estate not far from that of Sir Henry Curtis and leads, at least for a time, a life not unlike that of the squire Rider Haggard himself.

Allan Quatermain's exact social and working position is important because it has freed him from the constraints of rank and class and has enabled Rider Haggard to relate him, in many books (eighteen, if one includes several short stories), to people of every type, class and colour – to relate him not only in the way of circumstance but *personally*, in a way that reveals many sides of his nature. There was a practical reason for this. Rider Haggard seems to have built Quatermain gradually from a two-fold model – a famous hunter known to him in his African days and his own temperament as he saw it. He may perhaps have enjoyed a wry joke with himself when he decided on a hero as different as possible from any prevailing romantic idea, a small, weatherbeaten man with scrubbing-brush hair and a matter-of-fact outlook (in very clear contrast to the elegantly imposing six foot of Rider Haggard). But if Allan Quatermain was no romantic hero in appearance, he was in character exactly what Rider Haggard needed. Late in his life, reflecting on his career as a novelist, he remarked:

> . . . I always find it easy to write of Allan Quatermain, who, after all, is only myself set in a variety of imagined situations, thinking my thoughts and looking at life through my eyes.[36]

Moreover, as a novelist he confessed to finding young men 'somewhat difficult to draw' with a 'painful similarity to each other' whereas he had no trouble with elderly men like 'old Allan Quatermain' . . . 'perhaps because from my boyhood my great friends have always been men much older than myself'.[37]

In this unpromising reluctant hero he had designed for himself the perfect mouthpiece for his views on South African life, on the Boers and the Zulu wars, an ideal medium through which to describe a varied and exotic land for his readers, a character who could be easily and convincingly involved in strange adventures and, in time, a man who was used to express Rider Haggard's views on hypnotism, telepathy, and other such subjects, which he studied in a passionate desire to discover the springs and the meaning of life itself. A fictional character used for so many different purposes might seem to be in danger of becoming a chameleon-figure with as little true substance as the most stereotyped macho-hero. In fact Allan Quatermain is an exceptionally rounded and believable character. The novelistic reasons for this include the transparent but persuasive trick of the 'editorial author'.

Rider Haggard is to be supposed to have edited, as literary executor, the tales which Allan Quatermain had written down at various times of his life. The 'Editor's Note' prefixed to *Marie*, for instance, purports to explain how the 'editor' had been in a position to publish stories (or, as he calls them, 'new chapters of the autobiography of Allan Quatermain') written presumably during the three years or so spent in England after the adventure of King Solomon's treasure. A letter from Mr George Curtis, Sir Henry's brother, on 'January 17th, 1910' explains that more than two decades after Quatermain's disappearance, when his death could legally be presumed, Curtis as his residuary legatee had found in a sealed cupboard in the hunter's English house 'a stout box, made of some red foreign wood, that contained various documents and letters and a bundle of manuscripts' with a note asking for them to be sent to Quatermain's friend and literary executor, to be burned or published as he saw fit'. Three of the manuscripts thus 'found' – *Marie, Child of Storm* and *Finished* – form in fact a trilogy dealing with the fall of the Zulu Royal House founded by Senzangacona. It would be absurd to suggest that the reader actually believes the story of the sealed cupboard and the red box, but the circumstantial air of this preface ensures that one *accepts* Quatermain as an actual person.

Finished opens with a masterly double bluff, as Rider Haggard is addressed by the man he has created:

> You, my friend, into whose hand, if you live, I hope these scrib-blings of mine will pass one day, must well remember the 12th of April of the year 1877 at Pretoria.[38]

This third book of the great trilogy about the Zulu Royal House describes the annexation of the Transvaal from the Boers by the English, the war waged by Cetewayo against them and the end of this Zulu dynasty. Rider Haggard himself had witnessed the annexation, as assistant to Sir Theophilus Shepstone, who initiated and carried through the event, and he appears in the book as Allan Quatermain saw him, supporting the Resident Mr Osborn, as he read the proclamation, 'a tall young fellow . . . scarcely more than a lad then, carrying papers'[39], a young fellow not lacking in nerve, for he outfaced the Boers who tried to embarrass him on this most delicate of missions. 'I like to see an Englishman hold his own against odds and keep up the credit of the country,'[40] Quatermain comments. The device at once authenticates Rider Haggard's material and Quatermain as a person.

There are also in the books occasional editorial notes of impeccable seriousness, explaining certain points. A casual quotation from the Bible, in *King Solomon's Mines*, calls forth the comment:

> Readers must beware of accepting Mr Quatermain's references as accurate, as, it has been found, some are prone to do. Although his reading evidently was limited, the impression produced by it upon his mind was mixed. Thus to him the Old Testament and Shakespeare were inter-changeable authorities. – *Editor*.[41]

By similar authorial devices the provenance of each of the documents 'left' by Quatermain and 'edited' by Rider Haggard is clearly explained. Sometimes author and character speak with one voice. Quatermain explains why he has written down the story of Mameena and other experiences in his life:

> In days to come they may fall into the hands of others and prove of value. At any rate, they are true stories of interesting peoples, who, if they should survive in the savage competition of the nations, probably are doomed to undergo great changes. Therefore I tell of them before they began to change.[42]

Rider Haggard constructed a background for his hero which would enable him to describe as though from first-hand the striking incidents in the reigns of Chaka, Dingaan, Panda and Cetewayo, which he had learned about from those 'older men' who had served their country through the 1850s and 1860s, as soldiers or civil servants (but with Quatermain he could achieve a more panoramic view).

Elsewhere, the origins of the various Quatermain tales are more personal to the old hunter and fill out his character. They are reminiscences, varying from after-dinner anecdotes like *Maiwa's Revenge* to self-communing confessionals like *She and Allan* or the valedictory narrative *Allan Quatermain*. The extraordinary adventure with the monster called Heu Heu is told in the smoking-room of Quatermain's manor house; his testy objections to the doubts expressed by his listeners at some of the wildest details interrupt the narrative from time to time. The old hunter's first and simplest narrative, *King Solomon's Mines*, was penned for several reasons – to while away the time while Quatermain was laid up after being mauled by a lion, to entertain his son Harry during his medical studies, and at the insistence of his comrades in adventure, Sir Henry Curtis and Captain Good. Some of his most exotic adventures (*The Holy Flower* and *The Ivory Child*, for example) were written down when he lived as a gentleman of leisure on the diamonds which he and his companions had contrived to bring back from the fantastic treasure-cave in Kukuanaland, and before the death of his son, from smallpox, which ultimately sent him back to Africa for his last adventure; and during that last adventure, as he lay wounded and waited for death, he recalled more of his past experiences, together with the legend *The Ghost Kings*, in which (for the only time in the Quatermain cycle of tales) he played no part himself.

The illusion in all his tales that the old man is recalling the past is very strong, especially in the sombre tones of *Marie*, where the sadness muted over the years mingles with the sharp agony of young manhood, warmly remembered. It seems far more natural to believe that old Quatermain had kept the secret of his first marriage for many years, from grief and the sustained shock of the tragedy, than to accept the prosaic fact that Rider Haggard was taking one more opportunity to contrive a gap in Allan's fictional life which could also usefully include an account of that most horrifying incident in the history of South Africa, the massacre of Retief and the Boer trekkers by Dingaan.

So real is Quatermain that we can easily forget that we are being manipulated into believing that these are true hunter's tales. We can forget that Rider Haggard worked out piecemeal a complete dossier for Quatermain, for he slips relevant details into the tales in a completely natural way. With his son Harry, now aged fourteen, he is just back from an abortive period of gold-mining when he sets out after ivory and encounters the animals described in *The Three Lions*. His involvement in the conflict between the brothers, Cetewayo and Umbelagi, described in *Child of Storm*, comes about through a series of encounters while he is hunting ivory in Zulu territory, trying to forget his dead wife Stella, his infant son being left in Durban. Coincidence and chance meetings link the similar and very striking adventure of *The Holy Flower*. Allan's fame as a hunter and especially as a crack marksman leads him into a Chinese-box enterprise which starts with a simple quest for a rare orchid on behalf of an eager and extravagant young Englishman and ends in a desperate campaign against an evil ape and the rescue of an Englishwoman and her daughter, kidnapped as priestesses for a secret cult.

Abortive experiments as gold-miner or store-keeper, pauses between routine hunting trips in search of ivory or on behalf of amateur game-seekers, provide the necessary impetus for undertakings which will involve Quatermain's special skill and will make a place for him, plausibly, in the history of Southern and South Africa in the mid-nineteenth century.

Rider Haggard used his created hero to the full. Quatermain's prowess as a hunter and his knowledge of Africa gives all the opportunities needed for convincing scenes of adventure; his patient fatalism and his homespun philosophy serve him better in dangerous moments than the reckless courage of a conventional 'hero' would have done; he has, too, a touch of mysticism and an explorer's sense of wonder which allows Rider Haggard to convey to the reader something of the awe and mystery which make the books so rich in atmosphere. For the position of hero Quatermain is of course far from orthodox. Since he acts as narrator, we are asked to accept his own estimate of himself, conveyed with a self-derisive air. Here is the young Allan recreated in an old man's memory, at the time when he was tormented by a love for the Boer Marie Marais which he despaired of fulfilling, poor and unsuitable as he felt he was. His rival, the vain Portuguese Pereira, remarks cruelly that the lad looked as though he could be blown away like a feather:

> Still I said nothing, only glanced up at this tall and splendid man standing above me in his fine clothes, for he was richly dressed as the fashion of the time went, with his high colouring, broad shoulders, and face full of health and vigour. Mentally I compared him with myself, as I was after my fever and loss of blood, a poor, white-faced rat of a lad, with stubby brown hair on my head and only a little down on my chin, with arms like sticks, and a dirty blanket for raiment.
>
> . . . and yet, and yet as I lay there humiliated and a mock, an answer came into my mind, and I felt that whatever might be the case with my outward form; in spirit, in courage, in determination and in ability, in all, in-short, that really makes a man, I was more than Pereira's equal.[43]

A pardonable pride in the contrast between his outward appearance and his exploits allows Quatermain to quote cheerfully the conversation he overhears between women at the Zulu town of Ulundi, when they marvel at Mameena's love for this 'ugly little fellow with hair like the grey ash of stubble and a wrinkled face of the colour of a flayed skin that has lain unstretched in the sun',[44] for he is well aware that the Zulus call him Macumazahn or 'Watcher-by-Night' out of admiration for his cunning. Towards the end of his life the guests, at one or other of the country houses he frequents, marvel that the wrinkled, mahogany-faced old man should be so deeply respected; they are quickly won over by the pace and flavour of his yarns. The short stories ('Long Odds', for example, or 'Hunter Quatermain's Story') begin with that engagingly casual fiction of a dinner-party at which or after which a certain gentlemanly bragging was in order and here an anonymous pre-story narrator adds to Quatermain's intermittent self-portraits in a most useful way.

Useful, because novelistic skill is called upon when a hero tells his own story. There is much that he can tell us himself about his attitudes and feelings, but much that must be implied in his mode of speech or in such details as he can include naturally in his narrative. Quatermain's courage is perceived to be in part a practical habit of mind which enables him to conserve his energy and remain cool in moments of danger. When he and his client Anscombe ride into Zululand in search of buffalo, they ride through a ghostly patch of timber:

> 'Did that bush give you any particular impression?' asked Anscombe . . .
> 'Yes,' I answered, 'it gave me the impression that we might catch fever there. See the mist that lies over it,' and turning in my saddle I pointed with the rifle in my hand to what looked like a mass of cotton wool over which, without permeating it, hung the last red glow of sunset, producing a curious and indeed rather unearthly effect.
> 'I expect that thousands of years ago there was a lake yonder, which is why trees grow so big in the rich soil.'
> 'You are curiously mundane, Quatermain,' he answered. 'I ask you of spiritual impressions and you dilate to me of geological formations and the growth of timber. You felt nothing in the spiritual line?'
> 'I felt nothing except a chill,' I answered, for I was tired and hungry.[45]

This matter-of-fact view of life also takes the form of a habit of deflating moments of high drama or danger, a characteristic in Quatermain which perhaps was intended to supply the comic relief for which Captain Goode had been the vehicle in the two first Quatermain books to be published. An old woman snatched by a marauding elephant at night comes out of the hole in her hut 'like a periwinkle on the point of a pin'.[46] An experiment made by the evil King Simba entails burying a dead man with his head out of the hole and leaving him for the power of Quatermain to bring to life; the pot placed over his head looked as innocent, to Quatermain, as 'one of those that gardeners in England put over forced rhubarb, no more'.[47] Asides of this kind are of course part of the story-teller's technique, but it *is* Quatermain's technique, not Rider Haggard's – that is, it is as much a part of his nature as the fatalism which helps him to endure the extremes of danger

204

and pain or the cunning (a matter of experience, observation and a practical mind) which enables him to find a strategy to match any situation.

As a lover and husband Allan Quatermain is cast in the conventional mould of his time – ardent, sentimental, devoted and chaste – and for many readers the best of his stories are those in which the love interest is either absent or of minor concern except as a catalyst (as in the case of Lord Ragnall and his lost wife, or of the rival queens in *Allan Quatermain*). If Quatermain is a conventional lover, he is sensitive to other aspects of love, in a way that deepens his character. When he describes one of the irregular passions which, disastrously for the most part, sway the fortunes of the people he tries to help, he recognises their validity. Although he is often endangered by intense devotions, such as that of Nombe the witch for Heda, in *Finished*, or of Hendrika the baboon-woman for Stella, he accepts them as genuine and important; and if his recognition of the doglike attachment of his Kaffir servant Hans seems in the present day uncomfortably paternalistic, he mourns the old man no less sincerely.

Predictably, his attitude to the black races he fights for or against is, again, the attitude of his times; but there is no affectation in his respect for the Zulu warriors and his constant reminder that customs that differ from his own are not necessarily foolish. He treats with equal seriousness the mysterious powers of Ayesha and the remarkable divinations of Zikali the witch-doctor. In this he represents Rider Haggard's own attitude, one which was more liberal than that of some of the men he worked for in Africa. Reflecting on the Zulu's perception of the true value of a man, Rider Haggard comments:

> True gentility, as I have seen again and again, is not the prerogative of a class but a gift innate in certain members of all classes, and by no means a common gift; it either is or is not born in a man, and still more in a woman. To the Zulu the rest are what he calls *um fagozana*, that is, low fellows . . . Like others, savages have their gentle folk and their common people, but with all their faults even those common people are not vulgar in our sense of the word. In essential matters they still preserve a certain dignity. Of course, however, I talk of those savages whom I know. There may be others among whom things are different. Also, in this respect as in others, matters in Africa may have changed since my day. I talk of a bygone generation.[48]

The dignity of the Zulu, of companions like Umbopa and Umslopogaas, is felt and valued by Quatermain. `

It is remarkable that a character who embodies so many of

Rider Haggard's traits and opinions should claim the reader's recognition as an individual in his own right. It is still more surprising, perhaps, when we remember that he was first conceived, and in a very firm and confident manner, in a story intended for young readers. Although Rider Haggard had already had two romantic novels published (*Dawn* and *The Witch's Head*), he might have continued in his chosen profession of the law but, he tells us:

> . . . as it happened, I read in one of the weekly papers a notice of Stevenson's *Treasure Island* so laudatory that I procured and studied that work, and was impelled by its perusal to try to write a work for boys.[49]

Written in about six weeks, the book was dedicated 'by the narrator Allan Quatermain to all the big and little boys who read it'. The unusual, unorthodox hero, Quatermain, accounted as much for the immediate and long-lasting popularity of the book as the striding prose, the magnificent descriptions or the romantic trappings of treasure and underground passages. Though *King Solomon's Mines* was published in that open market for family novels where 'big and little boys' could equally find entertainment, and though the subsequent African novels were more obviously for adult readers, the fact remains that Allan Quatermain captured the imagination of the young as few other characters in comparable fiction have done. Perhaps simply because he *is* a many-sided character, inconsistent and even puzzling, he is that rare fictional creature, a 'real' person.

Rider Haggard knew what he was doing when he made Allan Quatermain the central character in most of his African novels. The piquant contrast between romantic situations and exotic scenery on the one hand and a very direct, practical narrator on the other, could only please readers who had had plenty of more conventional heroes offered to them. Nor did Rider Haggard deny himself the right to use more conventional types of hero as foils to hunter Quatermain. The imposing figure of Sir Henry Curtis, the very epitome of an English gentleman (in mid-Victorian fiction, if not in real life), could satisfy any desire for the expected hero, especially when in *Allan Quatermain* he aspired to the hand of a queen and the position of her consort. But although Curtis behaves impeccably, he remains a two-dimensional figure. The only one of Rider Haggard's orthodox heroes who really convinces the reader is the unacknowledged son of the great Chaka, the magnificent Umslopogaas.

The genesis of this character affords an interesting example of a novelist's method. The richness of Quatermain's character suggests that, no matter how deliberate Rider Haggard's first concept was, the composite worked in the author's imagination and took on almost independent life. In Umslopogaas we can see a character taken from life and adapted, romanticised round one particular cluster of 'heroic' traits. Rider Haggard described how he first met the man when he was on the staff of the special Commissioner to the Transvaal, Sir Theophilus Shepstone, in 1876 and 1877:

> There was another individual attached to the Commission of whom I must give some account. He was Umslopogaas, or more correctly M'hlopekazi, who acted as a kind of head native attendant to Sir Theophilus. Umslopogaas, then a man of about sixty, was a Swazi of high birth. He was a tall, thin, fierce-faced fellow with a great hole above the left temple over which the skin pulsated, that he had come by in some battle. He said that he had killed ten men in single combat, of whom the first was a chief called Shive, always making use of a battle-axe. However this may be, he was an interesting old fellow from whom I heard many stories that Fynney used to interpret.[50]

Long after Rider Haggard had left Africa, this servant of the white administrators discovered in conversation with Sir Melmoth Osborn that his name and his person had been used in Rider Haggard's novels and hinted 'it is right and just that he should send me half the money'.[51] He sent to Rider Haggard 'a very fine hunting-knife with his name engraved upon it'[51] and his view of the situation changed in later years, for when in 1897, shortly before his death, Lady Hely-Hutchinson, wife of the Governor of Natal, asked if he was not proud to be a character in books read all over the world, he sighed:

> '. . . to me it is nothing. Yet I am glad that Indunda has set my name in writings that will not be forgotten, so that, when my people are no more a people, one of them at least may be remembered.'[51]

His death-mask comes near to the character as he appears in the novels, with its strong look of wisdom, reserve and determination, but it is clear that Rider Haggard built on the basis of the man he met, taking certain physical details (the pulsating hole in the forehead, the axe which earned the fictional hero the name of 'Woodpecker') and extrapolating from the man's appearance and his vivid and characteristic reminiscences the figure of an adventure-story hero.

When Quatermain is organising the expedition described in *Allan Quatermain* he is offered the chance to take over a group of bearers whose English employer has died of fever. One of them is a pure-bred Zulu with 'a great three-cornered hole in his forehead', 'a short woolly beard, tinged with grey, and a pair of brown eyes keen as a hawk's'.[52] Quatermain recognises him at once and Umslopogaas explains that he has had to leave his own country, having been betrayed by his wife. In the typical sonorous phrases of a Zulu warrior, he accepts the new adventure as being to his taste:

> 'Come life, come death, what care I, so that the blows fall fast and the blood runs red? I grow old, I grow old, and I have not fought enough! And yet am I a warrior among warriors; see my scars' – and he pointed to countless cicatrices, stabs and cuts, that marked the skin of his chest and legs and arms. 'See the hole in my head; the brains gushed out therefrom, yet did I slay him who smote, and live. Knowest thou how many men I have slain, in fair hand-to-hand combat, Macumazahn? See, here is the tale of them' – and he pointed to long rows of notches cut in the rhinoceros horn handle of his axe. 'Number them, Macumazahn, one hundred and three – and I have never counted but those whom I have ripped open, nor have I reckoned those whom another man had struck.'[53]

The picturesque exaggeration is typical of the second dimension of adventures in which Quatermain's cold courage and hunter's skills played the chief part. Quatermain's recognition of the man he had last seen twelve years before is deliberately vague but it is a useful piece of novelist's housewifery, preparing the way for the later *She and Allan* when the witch-doctor Zikali advises Quatermain to add a certain Umslopogaas, chief of the 'People of the Axe', to his expedition, as a notable fighter who wishes to consult the 'white witch' Ayesha about his future and to be put in touch with his lost love, the beautiful woman, who shares with him the centre of the passionate adventure of *Nada the Lily*.

Rider Haggard was clearly fascinated by this usefully heroic figure; he believed that his creation accounted for a great deal of the popularity of *Allan Quatermain*, which had quickly followed *King Solomon's Mines* to satisfy a demanding public. Umslopogaas, he said, was popular 'with all classes of readers and especially among boys'.[54] It seems that Winston Churchill as a small boy said his dearest wish was to meet the heroic Zulu and his magnificent defence of the Queen's stairway in Milosis was among the mental pictures which Graham Greene had preserved in later life from an enthusiastic boyhood reading of Rider Haggard.

Rider Haggard's technique in drawing this character is clearest in *Nada the Lily*. The narrative is distanced by the anonymous narrator, an old witch-doctor consulted by a white traveller in Natal who is in difficulties after a freak snowstorm. The story has many epic qualities. The plot turns on the Zeus-like custom by which Chaka allowed none of his male children to survive. The old witch-doctor uses an inflated, rhetorical style for his story; the vocative case, adjurations to gods and spirits, a tone of lofty generalisation, these and other literary devices serve to isolate the character of Umslopogaas, a survivor of Chaka's fear of rebellion, and to give it a superhuman tone. It is notable that although in both *Allan Quatermain* and *She and Allan* the warrior plays a subordinate part, his utterances are usually of a broadly dramatic kind, and he uses a consciously heroic tone to match the sensational nature of his death.

Besides the many epic touches in *Nada the Lily*, the Zulu hero is made larger than life by the unusual circumstances of his life – his royal blood and his long exile and, especially, his partnership with Galazi as leader of the pack of wolves (hyenas, that is) on Ghost Mountain. He is not only a notable warrior, winner of a legendary weapon which made him chief of the People of the Axe; he is also a mysterious night-figure, wearing a wolf-pelt which gives him control over animals and strikes superstitious fear into his enemies:

> . . . who were these two that came with the wolves, shapes of men great and strong? They ran silently and swiftly, wolves' teeth gleamed upon their heads, wolves' hides hung about their shoulders. In the hand of one was an axe – the moonlight shone upon it – in the hand of the other a heavy club. Neck and neck they ran; never before had we seen men travel so fast. See! They sped down the slope towards us; the wolves were left behind, all except four of them; we heard the beating of their feet; they came, they passed, they were gone, and with them their unnumbered company. The music grew faint, it died, it was dead; the hunt was far away, the night was still again!
>
> 'Now, my brethren,' I asked of those who were with me, 'What is this that we have seen?'
>
> Then one answered, 'We have seen the Ghosts who live in the lap of the old Witch, and those men are the Wolf-Brethren, the wizards who are Kings of the Ghosts.'[55]

Rider Haggard's use of the idea of a human allied to a wolf-pack is sterner and more dramatic than Kipling's which was partly derived from it. The ferocity of an animal and the aggressive ambition of a man combine in Umslopogaas. He is a natural warrior and though his love for Nada is as passionate and large-scale as any of his impulses, the loving comradeship with Galazi is more important in the end; epic again, their companionship-in-arms is that of Achilles and Patroclus, a likeness felt though never suggested in the book.

Umslopogaas lived to fight, and *Nada the Lily* is perhaps the most horrific of all Rider Haggard's novels. He sturdily defended himself against the criticism that he glorified war and death. Man is a fighting animal, he insisted, and some of his finest qualities, like patriotism, courage, obedience to authority, patience in disaster, fidelity to friends and a noble cause and endurance, 'have been evolved in the exercise of war'.[56] He accepted the code of his time, but in his own way:

> Personally, I hate war, and all killing, down to the destruction of the lower animals for the sake of sport, has become abominable to me. But while the battle-clouds bank up I do not think that any can be harmed by reading of heroic deeds or of frays in which brave men lose their lives.
> What I deem undesirable are the tales of lust, crime, and moral perversion with which the bookstalls are strewn by dozens.[57]

In the character of Umslopogaas, in particular, Rider Haggard expressed his own ideas in concert with the attitude of a Zulu warrior which he could perceive in historical event and in conversation with the man who was the model for his heroic character. From the general concept of a warrior he built up through hyperbole, through a style drawing from classical epic and saga and from the characteristic rhetoric of Zulu custom, a character far more consciously literary than that of Quatermain.

Umslopogaas serves the novels not as a person we regard as 'real' but as a huge embodiment of the 'heroic' man. The intense, extraordinary mingling of strong action and symbolism in the account of his last fight, in *Allan Quatermain*, shows emphatically the function he serves in the kind of adventure-romance which Rider Haggard made his own. When at the end of a battle for the supremacy of the good queen Nyleptha against her sister Sorais, Quatermain learns that Nyleptha is in danger, he and Umslopogaas set off in a frantic race to the palace, Quatermain on his matchless horse and Umslopogaas *running*; at the palace, the warrior holds the gap where the door has been torn down, until he has killed all the soldiers who come against him; fatally wounded by the captain Nasta, he staggers to the great hall of the palace and with a last mighty stroke shatters the sacred stone with his axe before falling dead, thus fulfilling an ancient prophecy. The dramatic scene is in deliberate contrast to the death of Quatermain, a man equally heroic and equally brought low by war. The practical, philosophical hunter and the aggressive warrior stand for two different aspects of adventure as Rider Haggard saw it, and it is in the contrast and combination of these two unforgettable characters that much of the enduring power of the African novels is contained.

These, then, are some of the types of adventure-hero who are chosen to suit particular kinds of plot but who nevertheless have enough individuality to be recognised and remembered by generations of readers. These are some of the heroes whose exploits I followed ardently for some years from about the age of nine or ten. The concept of 'identification' had not for my generation made it necessary to separate, or to postpone, the reading of adult stories. I do not remember having any difficulty in responding to Allan Quatermain, though I had no particular wish to *become* this or any other romantic hero. I do not think that I felt any particular difference between entering into the feelings of, say, Norah of Billabong, Mowgli or Edred and Edith Arden and of Quatermain, Richard Hannay or D'Artagnan. They represented somewhat different kinds of adventure, all exciting and all of them memorable as *people*. Fred Ingles points to a similar pattern of reading in his childhood and suggests that for the young reader of today there is likely to be a similar mixture of youthful and adult heroes, but he offers his parallel lists with his own reservations, for he is attempting a definition and defence of literary cricitism:

> If we attempt a roll-call of the mythic heroes of our literary childhood, what figures step out of the gloom? King of the Golden River, Robin Hood, Crusoe, Mole and Ratty, King Arthur, White Fang, Bagheera, Quentin Durward, Long John Silver? Perhaps, and if we were lucky. More likely, little Noddy, the Famous Five, Biggles, Jill and her ponies, the heroes of Stalag Luft III, Colditz, Mickey Spillane, and Ian Fleming. I prefer the first list to the second, and to state literary preferences can be taken as intellectual snobbery. But the preference is not snobbish, and the ability to discriminate justly between the first and second list is an important and serious one.[58]

This list suggests that 'heroes' for past and present generations are, more often than not, adults. On the face of it, the young can hardly be expected to be supermen or superwomen in the kind of situation explored in tales of high adventure; yet for almost two centuries young people have needed, wanted and been given tales of action with a child at the centre. They have been able to choose between young or adult heroes, although it is only in the past fifty years or so that the isolation, as far as literary criticism is concerned, between adult and children's books has altered the way the choice is made.

The *young* hero (using the word 'hero' in the formal sense of protagonist as well as of central character) has been introduced into adventure stories through a number of compromises by which the disadvantages of physical and emotional immaturity have been avoided or disguised. One of these compromises is the dual hero, an adult matched with a young person; the two share the action, each offering the talents proper to his age, and the younger character attracts from the older the aura of a 'hero'. This association is one of the many layers (though by no means the most important) in Stevenson's *Kidnapped* and *Catriona*. These two novels of adventure, contributed originally to *Young Folks*, have been appreciated by the young partly because David Balfour never loses the habit of dependence, the naïveté and the impetuosity which they instinctively recognise. In Ballantyne's *The Gorilla Hunters* and *The Coral Island* a trio of far more stereotyped characters became, as it were, a composite hero and the youngest of them, Peterkin, kept the role of mischievous child although he soon passed his fifteenth year and became technically an adult. The artificiality of this particular compromise makes it unlikely that the resulting hero-combination will show the true, unmistakable individuality of a Quatermain. Its special advantage is that it enables an author to involve a boy or girl in the middle teens or even younger in dangerous or sensational events with a measure of plausibility, a task obviously more difficult in relation to contemporary events than in a story of the past.

Arthur Catherall has written a number of well-judged adventure tales set in some unspecified post-war period for those readers of the middle years who enjoy reading of children their own age. The books in this 'suspense series' have been advertised as exciting stories for nine to twelve year olds which 'feature a girl or a boy in a thrilling predicament which calls upon all their resource and courage'. The phrase 'thrilling predicament' points clearly to the author's modified approach and, indeed, he judges skilfully the circumstances suitable for the age of his characters. His 'Bulldog' tales, however, have a more robust flavour and deal with situations that require a different kind of 'hero', and yet (since these are adventure-thrillers published in the juvenile market) a hero not yet adult.

Jack Frodsham, central character of ten books, is introduced in *Ten Fathoms Deep* as a youth of seventeen, with some training in diving and towing techniques, who is about to join his father, owner of the tug *Bulldog*, on various contracts in the China Seas. While off duty in Singapore, father and son are accosted by 'Husky' Hudson, survivor of the liner *Tenasserim* whose captain faces a court-martial for neglecting his ship while drunk. Hudson has just finished explaining his suspicions that the wreck is an insurance fraud when Captain Frodsham is shot by an unseen enemy and in the course of time Hudson becomes Jack's mentor and support, with the boy nominally in charge of his father's tug.

Catherall introduces Jack as a somewhat romantically-minded lad anxious for adventure but his father's training and example, and Jack's resolve to be worthy of his reputation, are enough to account for the remarkable speed with which he copes with danger as he and Hudson stand together against the envious rivalry of the villain Karmey, owner of two tugs, whose crooked captains abet him in various schemes to wreck *Bulldog* and her reputation. There is no subtlety in the way Catherall organises the adult/youth partnership in these tales. Jack's father, though recovered from his bullet-wound, finds the climate of Singapore does not agree with his health, and the tug is turned over to Hudson while Jack works under him for the necessary Master's certificate. Hudson, a tough and experienced man of a type familiar to the thriller genre, is at first inclined to behave like a nursemaid to Jack, but when together they have found the evidence to prove the truth about the *Tenasserim*, he admits his mistake:

'You've just taught me a lesson – maybe a lesson I needed badly. You get to looking on any youngster as being more or less useless. I've made a mistake with you – we're going to get along famously. You've got the Frodsham touch about you. If we get through this your father's going to be pretty chesty about you. I've heard him talk about "my boy Jack" more than once, and it sounded like the bragging of any father – well, I don't think he was bragging, that's all.'[59]

In this particular adventure Jack has stood up to ramming and capture by the rival captains, has worked out a scheme for hiding the sunken ship and its damning evidence by cutting off her masts and erecting them elsewhere, and has survived drowning after the communication cord on his diving-suit has been cut by a bomb from an aeroplane, by *walking* in to land under water.

The nine succeeding stories are, in the manner of most series-books, evasive about time. Jack Frodsham does not appear to grow any older and the sweep of the stories ensures that the most literal reader does not stop to wonder why so many sensational events happen in such rapid succession. Jack needs to remain young in order to allow his readers to feel in touch with his feelings and reactions. To the successful outwitting of Karmey and his unpleasant associates Gawse and Hardacre, Jack contributes physical strength, a measure of technical skill, quick wits and adaptability. The towing of a crane in *Jackals of the Sea*, the raising of a Japanese wartime vessel in the Java Sea in *Forgotten Submarine*, of a torpedoed British cruiser in the Straits of Macassar in *Java Sea Duel*, the rescue of the inhabitants of one island after an earthquake and tidal wave in *Sea Wolves,* of another island community devastated by a typhoon in *Death of an Oil Rig* – these and other enterprises are bedevilled by sabotage, gunfights, hijacking and other unscrupulous methods by which Karmey tries to steal business for himself. Supported by Hudson's experience and good sense, Jack survives. More than that, he has enough substance as a character, when complemented by Hudson, to hold the attention of readers who need to be concerned for his success as well as being held by the events of the stories.

As a composite, dual character, Jack and Hudson do very well, in a modern version of the adventure-hero. All the same, Jack is at bottom a traditional figure, a descendant of the lads who in stories by Henty or Westerman upheld British interests at home and abroad. In *Jackals of the Sea*, Jack discusses with his fellow diver Ahmat the chances of their being rescued in time by a crane half sunk in the sea after being abandoned on tow. Ahmat's fatalism is strongly criticised by the optimistic Jack, who refuses to accept as his excuse the Malay's apology that his race is idle compared with the brave and vigorous English:

> 'The difference between white and coloured people, especially the coloured people of Asia, is that when you see there is no chance of winning you stop fighting.'
> 'That is sensible,' Ahmat suggested. 'It saves trouble and bloodshed.'
> 'The white man never stops fighting – and we're not stopping now.'[60]

The mixture of true-Brit patriotism and economic necessity which sustains Jack and Hudson in their various conflicts will necessarily be viewed critically a quarter of a century after the books were first published, and the rather similar partnership of adult and youth in the series of stories about *Bailey's Bird*, a recent television spin-off concerning a contract flier and his son in Australasian waters, is far more acceptable to present-day tastes.

214

The 'Bulldog' tales remain a valid example of the way a particular compromise can be used to narrow the gap between adult and junior books, by a dual-purpose hero.

For the young hero who stands alone, the lad of fifteen or sixteen thrown into a situation of danger, a different kind of support will be needed. If reality is not to intrude inconveniently in the reader's mind an illusion must be provided, a distraction through the speed of events or an authenticity of detail, so that we do not notice how young a particular hero is to emerge from peril unhurt and triumphant. Even so, a discriminating reader, however young, may well become weary of the stereotypes whom Ballantyne and Westerman and many of their present-day imitators have offered as their central characters, however flattering and glamorous the image they present may be, offering as it does a kind of growing-up by proxy.

Without some element of growing-up in the young hero of an adventure, some apparent enriching of his emotions or stretching of his capacities, an adventure story can offer only a diminished and temporary satisfaction. The fresh-faced, robust young hero of Ballantyne, of Kingston, of Westerman, is still with us: the hero who changes as a result of experience we meet less often. Stanley Weyman, whose moderate depth of character-drawing I have already discussed, offers this latter type of hero in the only book he wrote for young readers, *The Story of Francis Cludde*, published in 1891. The events take place during the reign of Mary Tudor, where a young man reared as a Protestant but brought up by the head of the family, a Catholic landowner living on the Warwick-Worcester border, sets forth to discover the truth about his father, who had vanished after an inglorious career as a turncoat and informer.

Stanley Weyman introduces his hero at the age of nineteen but presents him as young for his age, a lad self-conscious, hostile to Catholic influence, impetuous and brave in the unreasoning, headlong way of a boy. This interpretation has an obvious advantage. Francis is easily deceived and so the plot, intricate as it is, allows the reader the extra bonus of dramatic irony; as Francis tells his story, the reader sees further into the mystery than the young man does and enjoys the sharpness of suspense and apprehension. Involved in private and political intrigues and in the pursuit of a powerful unknown enemy, Francis journeys through Holland, the German Empire and Poland, growing in stature and in self-discipline and finding the strength to endure imprisonment and the threat of death because of his resolve to defend his father's honour. When the bitter truth of his father's deceptions is revealed he accepts the consequences with the courage of a man and the generosity of a boy, using his knowledge to save the uncle who had sheltered him in his boyhood from the fate of a recusant:

> I gave the packet into the Knight's hand, my own shaking. Ay, shaking, for was not this the fulfilment of that boyish vow I had made in my little room in the gable yonder so many years ago? A fulfilment strange and timely, such as none but a boy in his teens could have hoped for, nor any but a man, who had tried the chances and mishaps of the world, could fully enjoy as I was enjoying it. I tingled with the rush through my veins of triumph and gratitude. Up to the last moment I had feared lest anything should go wrong, lest this crowning happiness should be withheld from me. Now I stood there smiling, watching Sir Anthony as, with trembling fingers, he fumbled with the paper.[61]

That elusive tone of nobility which justifies the great adventure stories is apparent in Weyman's story of a youth who perceptibly and plausibly grows up as a result of unexpected experience.

Every adventure turns on a test, a challenge offered to its central character. In junior stories the element of *rite de passage* enters, sometimes so strongly that there is a danger that the exploration of emotion and personality may overbalance the plot, taking a book out of the adventure-story genre into the genre of the analytical problem novel. Two of Kipling's young heroes seem relevant here – Mowgli, whose adventures are described in eight stories in *The Jungle Book* and *The Second Jungle Book*, of 1894 and 1895, and *Kim*, a novel of India and the 'Great Game', first published in 1901, in which the Irish boy Kimball O'Hara is the central character. Both of these young heroes serve as focal points for a whole philosophy of education, for studies of the training of a young person both like and unlike the experiences of Kipling himself in English schools. The effect of the 'schools' (the school of the jungle and the flexible but strict training for a Secret Service) is to sharpen and increase an innate intelligence without destroying individuality: for the purposes of fiction Kipling has used two boys to explore certain aspects of moral and emotional growth but has through craftsmanship developed them as believable, identifiable individuals.

The Law of the Jungle into which Mowgli is gradually initiated is, as Kipling developed it, a combination of observable animal behaviour and the codes of conduct obtaining in society at the time when he wrote the stories. There is no need to assume in him an understanding of jungle animals ahead of his time. The social behaviour within a wolf-pack, the sanctions that applied at any waterhole in a time of drought – these and other points which Mowgli learnt, by precept or by experience, were a matter of common knowledge, as were the natural habitats of the animals and the cycles of predation or territorial aggression, though in Kipling's day they were not yet a matter of behavioural science.

To link human with animal behaviour, Kipling humanised the individual animals contributing to Mowgli's education in a straightforward and appropriate way, developing them as characters from one or two natural points. So, Baloo the lazy brown bear and the black panther Bagheera with his leashed energy became teachers of different types: the monkeys, restless and disorganised, named the Bandar-log, represented certain raffish elements in human society seen from an Establishment point of view; the lame, embittered man-eating tiger Shere Khan and his hanger-on, the sycophantic jackal Tabaqui, fall easily into the shape of human types; while the internal hierarchies of the wolf-pack corresponded so closely to the group-patterns of middle-class education that Kipling's humanisation of Akela was quickly translated back again into the pattern of Cub-Scout packs.

When Mowgli is adopted by the wolf-pack, as an infant found wandering in the jungle after the destruction of his home and parents, he learns to live by the wolf code of family obligations and observances, while Baloo and Bagheera instruct him in the rules by which the jungle animals exist in a shifting pattern evolved for survival, and extract from each species the master words by which he can communicate with every jungle inhabitant. Certain human attributes grow alongside the animal-lore he absorbs from his tutors; in this respect Kipling's wolf-reared boy is obviously romanticised in contrast to the unhappy children taken in real life from a wild environment. Mowgli learns from his animal friends that there is a colony of wild bees in a certain gorge, at the same time as he learns that the occasional irruption of wild dogs into their part of the jungle is one of the greatest dangers they have to face. It is by human reason that he puts the two facts together and works out a way of destroying the ravening pack, his courage and intelligence being equally beyond the animals whose life he shares. Kipling works out his fantasy from two firm bases, of animal and human fact, and uses a writer's technique, in pace, colour and tension, to make the fantasy work.

It is never easy for a reader to define his reactions to a particular book and with the young, whether they are suggestible or anti-suggestible, the chance of reaching an honest and clean-cut opinion is pretty remote. Obviously, the stories about Mowgli will be read differently at different reading stages. Kipling shared with certain of his contemporaries who wrote for children (notably, Edith Nesbit, Mrs Molesworth and Frances Hodgson Burnett) a breadth in the emotional content of his tales which was to go underground, to a great extent, to surface only in the last two decades. Boys and girls who read, or listen to, the *Jungle Books* when they are eight or nine will probably think of Mowgli mainly in terms of his exotic and exciting life in the jungle. His character, for them, is likely to be that of a wolf-boy, to be envied by those in more staid situations. To the thoughtful older reader the stories present, through jungle-adventures of the most specific and believable kind, a cumulative picture of 'growing up'.

This is not a simple picture nor is the educational process that moulds Mowgli a single one. The instruction he receives from the animals teaches him how to coexist with them; as baby, child and young boy, he is virtually a wolf, though of slower growth than theirs. Kipling jumps from the introductory narrative, in which the feud with Shere Khan is established (the tiger, having killed Mowgli's parents, asserts his right to the boy and is only temporarily bought off by contract with the wolves), to Mowgli's twelfth year, when a second phase of learning begins. Now he must learn to know himself and, in the end, must decide whether he is man or animal.

When he shrugs off Bagheera's warning that the wolves may turn against him, the panther tells the boy to look him straight in the eyes, and quickly turns his head away:

> '*That* is why,' he said, shifting his paw on the leaves. 'Not even I can look thee between the eyes, and I was born among men, and I love thee, Little Brother. The others they hate thee because their eyes cannot meet thine – because thou art wise – because thou hast pulled out thorns from their feet — because thou art a man.'[62]

The panther's predictions are true. The wolves drive Mowgli out; weeping for the first time in his life, he goes down the hillside 'to meet those mysterious things that are called men'.[63]

Some of his difficulties as he tries to adapt himself to life in the village are practical. Helped by an affectionate foster-mother, for whose dead son he is a substitute, he learns to endure sleeping under a roof, to wear clothes, to use money, to discipline his unusual strength. Trained to recognise gradations in the wolf-pack, he ignores the caste system of his fellow men:

When the potter's donkey slipped in the clay-pit, Mowgli hauled it out by the tail, and helped to stack the pots for their journey to the market at Khanhiwara. That was very shocking, too, for the porter is a low-caste man, and his donkey is worse. When the priest scolded him Mowgli threatened to put him on the donkey, too, and the priest told Messua's husband that Mowgli had better be set to work as soon as possible.[64]

The job of herding buffaloes, a congenial one, leads first to a boyish fit of mischief, when he sets out to expose the beasts of Buldeo the hunter with the help of his pack brothers who are still loyal to him, and then to a well-devised plot by which he brings about the death of Shere Khan. But success turns against him. The villagers, far from being grateful to him for destroying the dangerous man-eater, stone him as a wizard, in unlawful alliance with wolves and perhaps with spirits, and he returns to the jungle – but to hunt alone, for 'Man-Pack and Wolf-Pack have cast me out'.[65] In his song of triumph, as he casts Shere Khan's hide on the council rock of the wolves, he expresses a painful new knowledge of himself:

'My mouth is cut and wounded with the stones from the village, but my heart is very light because I have come back to the Jungle. Why?

These two things fight together in me as the snakes fight in the spring.

The water comes out of my eyes; yet I laugh while it falls. Why?

I am two Mowglis, but the hide of Shere Khan is under my feet.

All the Jungle knows that I have killed Shere Khan. Look – look well, O wolves!

Ahae! My heart is heavy with the things that I do not understand.'[66]

Accepting these new, puzzling obligations of humanity, Mowgli sets about rescuing his foster-parents, who have been condemned to death by their fellow villagers for giving a home to a dangerous wizard. Mowgli's revenge is conducted in animal terms. He arranges for Buldeo and his associates to be hazed through the jungle by Bagheera and the wolves and persuades Hathi the elephant and his family to break down the village huts and trample the crops. 'Letting in the Jungle' is a story of the most telling, vivid and pictorial adventure, but the undercurrent of sadness, perplexity, mixed motives in Mowgli is very strong.

For a year or two longer Mowgli is able to live in reasonable comfort of mind in the jungle, using his human skills (in the defeat of the wild red dogs, for example) or learning at second-hand about the frailties of his kind – as when he steals the King's

Ankus from its guardian, the blind white snake, and observes the effect of its ancient curse as it works on human greed. He is surprised and scornful at Bagheera's definition of the Time of New Talk, the spring, and its effect on the animals he hunts with, until he begins to feel at odds with them and with himself. Has he been poisoned, he asks his seventeen-year-old self; why is he hot and cold by turns, weak and strong, sad and excited? He visits the village, to see how it has changed, and finds in his foster-mother a new respect and affection which tempts him, while the sight of a girl going to the well disturbs him. Most of all he is tormented by the thought that he has lost the friendship of his fellow animals. He has lost, in effect, his childhood:

> 'Why did I not die under Red Dog?' the boy moaned. 'My strength is gone from me, and it is not any poison. By night and by day I hear a double step upon my trail. When I turn my head it is as though one had hidden himself from me that instant. I go to look behind the trees and he is not there. I call and none cry again; but it is as though one listened and kept back the answer. I lie down, but I do not rest. I run the spring running, but I am not made still. I bathe, but I am not made cool. The kill sickens me, but I have no heart to fight except I kill. The Red Flower is in my body, my bones are water – and – I know not what I know.'[67]

Kaa the snake has the answer. 'Man goes to Man at the last, though the Jungle does not cast him out.'[67]

The theme that binds the Mowgli tales together, the idea of learning and growing up, has given them a more than merely contemporary significance. This in itself would be enough to attract readers from one generation to another, by inviting them to see something of themselves in Mowgli. This hero has the opacity, the general shape which makes it possible for that inexplicable process of 'identification' to take place; and yet, by the atmosphere, the detail, the dialogue and ultimately by the sheer magic compulsion of the tales, Mowgli is created as an individual.

Certain of Kipling's adult works – *Captains Courageous*, for example, and many of the short stories – have been read by the young (the early and mid-teens, that is, and capable readers at that) but *Kim* is a special case. This adult novel is densely written, with a plot at times buried in highly idiomatic dialogue, and with that oddly riddling narrative technique which was to make some of Kipling's later stories puzzling at first and even second reading. A reader who comes to *Kim* too early is likely to be so confused by the affair of the White Stallion and the stately utterances of the lama from the hills that he gives up and so misses the more direct, richly comic account of the discomfiture of the two spies for Russia as they stumble through the hills with the resourceful Babu, their supposed rescuer. *Kim* is a book that needs to be read and reread if its full flavour of sentiment, sense and style is to be tasted, but an intelligent reader of fourteen or so may find in the book what he has already found in the Mowgli stories, a portrait drawn in detail, gradually and forcefully, of a boy growing up and learning from experience; he will find as well, when he has some practice in steering through the allusive dialectal conversations, a magnificent panorama of Indian life in the context of that 'Great Game' played by Britain in India, and especially on the Northern frontiers, as the self-imposed guardian of peace.

That the spy plot is subordinate to the exploration of Kim's 'education' is evident from his central position in the book, as well as in the manipulation of the ludicrously stupid enemy agents; but the adventure aspect of the book is no less compelling because of Kipling's particular approach. He has drawn the character of Kim with such richness of humour and perception that he has made it possible for us to read the book as adventure, as philosophy or as *rite de passage*, or in all three ways at once.

Kimball O'Hara, son of a nursemaid and a colour-sergeant in an Irish regiment, has survived almost thirteen years, most of them as an orphan, with help from foster-parents and the friends he has acquired through his own inquisitive, independent, confident nature. Switching his appearance as easily as he switches from one language or dialect to another, he has educated himself by observing and tasting many kinds of life, always finding his chief nourishment in adventure and in freedom. His occasional involvement in personal intrigues, as messenger boy and go-between, have left him essentially innocent in spite of a great deal of theoretical knowledge:

> . . . what he loved was the game for its own sake – the stealthy prowl through the dark gullies and lanes, the crawl up a water-pipe, the sights and sounds of the women's world on the flat roofs, and the headlong flight from housetop to housetop under cover of the hot dark.[68]

We realise as the story unfolds that Kim's education has many facets but the most important lesson he has to learn is to give up part of his freedom in order to learn to love and depend on somebody else – the lesson, in fact, which Mowgli learned in a different context.

The narrative follows two parallel journeys, each of them clearly affecting and changing the boy. The actual journey begins as his own personal quest. His drunken father, with whom he had wandered in his early years, had left him as a legacy certain papers (which the untaught Kim could not read) and a vague story that one day he would be given a new life by a Colonel riding on a horse and by nine hundred first-class devils whose god was a Red Bull on a green field. Idling outside the Museum at Lahore, Kim has seen an old man in need of help, a priest with bad sight whose begging-bowl is empty. The lama from the hills accepts Kim as his new disciple and helper. He too has a quest, for a fabled River through which the Buddhist teachings may be restored to their original purity, and he and Kim set off on their respective quests, led by chance and faith, helped by the sympathy of people in all walks of life for the old man's impressive holiness and Kim's bold, impertinent youth.

It is not long before Kim finds the Colonel, the devils and the Red Bull, coming by chance to a roadside place where his father's old regiment is setting up camp. Once Kim has shown the papers he carries in an amulet round his neck, he is caught up in a conventional phase of education. Certain of the adventurous exploits he has performed for the horse-dealer Mahbub Ali have in fact been a test of his potential as a member of a Secret Service in which the Colonel of the regiment is also employed. For the next three years Kim is a pupil at a Government school in Lucknow, enduring routine because he respects the many-sided experiences of his fellow-pupils, the army drummer-boys and sons of civil servants who, equally, learn to respect him. Ostensibly Kim is being trained to become a surveyor. Under the mysterious Lurgan, he battles through a stern régime in which his powers of observation and memory are trained to the limit, his need for personal freedom being satisfied by escapes, from time to time, into adventures in disguise in the underworld of India, which his mentors accept as a valuable and necessary part of his education.

Like Mowgli, Kim finds it hard to transfer from one kind of life to another. When he is put on the train to go to school for the first time, he accepts philosophically the fate that is sending him from one place to another, but with a good deal of doubt:

> 'I go from one place to another as it might be a kick-ball. It is my *Kismet*. No man can escape his *Kismet*. But I am to pray to Bibi Miriam, and I am a Sahib' – he looked at his boots ruefully. 'No, I am Kim. This is the great world, and I am only Kim. Who is Kim?' He considered his own identity, a thing he had never done before, till his head swam. He was one insignificant person in all this roaring whirl of India, going southward to he knew not what fate.[69]

His self-confidence is restored as he becomes more deeply involved in the 'Great Game' of espionage and as, from time to time, he rejoins the lama and serves him as guide and protector, but there are moments of self-doubt still. When Kipling takes leave of his hero, now a youth of seventeen recovering from a mysterious part-physical, part-mental illness and eager to take an adult part in life, he confirms the underlying theme of his tale. Encouraged by the holy man's confidence in him, purged ruthlessly by the rich old woman whose common sense has been an important strand in the story, Kim, as it were, shakes off his past weakness and stands fast on his newly-recognised self:

> 'I am Kim. I am Kim. And what is Kim?' His soul repeated it again and again.
>
> He did not want to cry, had never felt less like crying in his life – but of a sudden easy, stupid tears trickled down his nose, and with an almost audible click he felt the wheels of his being lock up anew on the world without. Things that rode meaningless on the eyeball an instant before slid into proper proportion. Roads were meant to be walked upon, houses to be lived in, cattle to be driven, fields to be tilled, and men and women to be talked to. They were all real and true – solidly planted upon the feet – perfectly comprehensible – clay of his clay, neither more, nor less. He shook himself like a dog with a flea in his ear, and rambled out of the gate.[70]

The threads of his education, formal and informal, have come together. And as the old priest acknowledges how he has leaned on Kim, depending on his young strength, so we realise that the deepest, most lasting part of Kim's education, his growing-up, has been because the service he began in a light-hearted spirit of adventure has taught him to give part of himself in genuine love of the old man and respect for his wisdom. The bold, confident boy has learned humility: the 'Little Friend of all the World' has learned another kind of friendship. Because of the sweep of the story, the time-scheme, the leisurely development of the character of Kim, he has been established as Mowgli was, as a recognisable individual as well as an example, in more general terms, of an adolescent quest for identity.

A broad time-scheme will obviously help an author to establish a character effectively. If he undertakes to follow his hero over a period of years, he can afford to introduce traits and even inconsistencies, gradually and in a natural way which is less easy if a portrait has to be quickly drawn. This advantage is offered by series-stories, where growth and development can be especially plausible. Indeed, we can separate formula-writing from a more intelligent approach by discovering how far specific authors make

223

use of this advantage. Moreover, the reader will come closer to understanding a character if he himself notices points for himself than if he is offered a set-piece, a hard outline, a stated set of traits.

The reader cannot be directed to identify with a certain character: he may be invited to do so. Patricia Wrightson has offered a working suggestion about the person I am calling for convenience the 'hero':

> My theory is that main characters shouldn't be drawn or described very positively. They should just emerge, positively but unstatedly, through their actions and dialogue. I think I think this because main characters are the reader; he has to merge with them and be them, and he can do this best if they creep into him so that he never notices himself adapting to them. Minor characters, I claim, can be drawn. Main characters are Ego in the third person and should simply emerge.[71]

This raises the whole question of 'identification' and the ways in which the word can be and has been used.

As I suggested earlier, one of the reasons why the classic adventure story has been relegated in the literary hierarchy, at least in the last few decades, is because of the 'escape' label attached to it. The expansion of an everyday horizon, through the agency of imagination, has been widely considered to be an indulgence, an ignoble kind of pleasure; this curious assumption, not unrelated to the priggish anti-novel attitudes which roused Jane Austen to ironic amazement, has meant that a kitchen-sink novel of the crudest kind can be, and sometimes has been, accorded more importance than a well-turned romantic adventure. It has not been suggested that adults reading the adventure novels offered to them precisely 'identify' with the heroes or heroines therein but at least that they are taken into their orbit. In the case of junior stories, a more specific role-playing is assumed, a very personal contact in which the reader feels at one with the character – in which, as Patricia Wrightson has suggested, the character is 'Ego in the third person'.

She does not suggest that characters for this reason have to be simplified or diluted, only (and I think rightly) that they should be developed gradually and with moderation. Yet the concept of 'identification' has been taken sometimes as permission for an author to draw a character in outline, deliberately, so as to allow the reader more freedom. This is simply freedom to substitute, for the power of imagination, the flicker of fancy. One of the charms of formula tales, for passive, lethargic, uncritical readers, is that the characters, stated rather than developed and stated in the simplest terms, are so bland that any child anywhere will be able to substitute himself in the leading role.

But supposing an author wishes to involve his readers more positively than this? Must he assume (as some authors and certainly some critics seem to do) that children will only respond to characters like themselves – that for every reader there is a double, a *Doppelganger*, which alone will satisfy him? J. M. Marks considered this problem when, using his own experience of Borneo, he wrote a story in which an English boy brought up in Hong Kong was involved in a hijacking in the Burma Sea. He deduced from the reading tastes of his own son that besides an exciting story with plenty of action he would need memorable characters and 'above all, reader identification with the main protagonist.' Because of his plot and setting this was a problem he had to solve:

> I saw that a British boy might not find it too easy to identify with someone in a remote land with quite different customs and outlook. I accepted that this was a considerable handicap, but reasoned that it could be offset by other facets of the story – by plot, by action and by authenticity of background.[72]

In view of his earlier statement that a successful story would need 'memorable characters', it is a little surprising that he does not include this point among the 'facets' which he hopes will help to put his readers in touch with his main character, the boy Jason (James Wright, aged fourteen).

J. M. Marks does not invite his readers to daydream that they are escaping from and bringing to justice a group of terrorists. More significantly, he encourages them to recognise and to understand the way the various stages of the adventure affect a boy both like and unlike themselves. To do this, he has matched the realities of his plot (the Arab origins of the hijacking, the diplomatic complexities that bring Japanese and Thai ministers, police and detectives into the action, the untimely interference of a determined free-lance journalist) with a hero whose reactions are just as real.

The covers of two paperback issues of the story show a certain uncertainty on the part of publisher or artist. The edition using the original title, *Jason*, Oxford's paperback version of the original hardback of 1975, shows a figure in jeans and singlet who could be eighteen, gazing at the grounded plane with a combative, macho expression: the Puffin edition of 1977, with the more directly appealing title *Hijacked*, is far nearer to the author's intention with regard to his hero, showing the boy hiding in the reeds and looking at the scene with a suggestion of fear and doubt. This is the boy Jason whom the author has involved, plausibly and *gradually*, in a situation far too great for him to handle.

If we look at the story as it reflects the reactions of the hero, we can see that it falls into three parts. When the pilot is forced to land on a beach in the Gulf of Siam, by Japanese passengers suddenly revealed as gunmen, Jason is inspired to attempt an escape more by chance and boredom than by the artificial impulse to be a hero which formula-writing would have demanded. A rudimentary knowledge of technology shows him a way to force open a panel in the washroom, his prowess as a swimmer helps him to get ashore in spite of a determined pursuer: he is afraid, but the edge of fear helps him, and a faint hope that if he can get a warning out, he may still be in time for the important interschool swimming contest on which his present ambitions are fixed. The escape has been bold and opportunist; though he is afraid of being caught by the terrorist who swims after him, he has so far no real understanding of the danger he is in. But as he is pursued through the jungle edging the beach, he is forced to act in a way that prejudices the negotiations just beginning. To escape being captured by the hijacker who has tracked him down, he shoots him with a blowpipe found in a deserted village; soon afterwards he finds his way to the army camp set up by the Thai ministry, where he is interrogated and realises that he has almost certainly killed the man and that reprisals are likely. An act which, with the formula-hero in a formula-story, would have been assumed to be heroic, seems in his inexperienced but honest view a serious error of judgement:

> He began to curse himself for his rashness in escaping. He should have stayed and done the less romantic task of looking after those two children. He had abandoned them, and now he was going to pay for it. Miserable, he lay back on the rough blanket, staring up at the groundsheet above him, the sun's rays overhead shining through . . . What on earth could he do? . . . he lay endlessly turning over and over in his mind the dilemma he was in . . .[73]

Jason is not left for too long in his state of misery, for it turns out that a phrase overheard in the aeroplane, whose meaning had not been clear to him, provides a key to the identity of the terrorists and a way to defeat them. By a piece of neat narrative symmetry Jason makes a second swim, this time under orders and into a danger which he and the responsible adults fully accept.

The Hero

There is no sense of adventure and certainly no conscious heroism in this last physical effort before the situation is resolved; it is
clear to the reader that Jason has changed a little as a result of his
experience. The wounded pilot commiserates with him for missing the swimming heats which had loomed so large in Jason's
programme for the summer term:

> Jason looked at the bruised and bearded face without comprehen-
> sion. Then he remembered, and for a moment stared round at the
> wreckage and the survivors. The swimming heats were part of some
> life he'd lived in the past, some strange remote existence where
> television lights had seemed important, and the roar of the crowd
> the most desirable thing on earth.[74]

Events have forced Jason to look more closely at his actions than
he had in his comfortably extrovert existence. The point is not
pressed at the depth it would have needed if the story had been
cast as a problem novel rather than an adventure story, but the
point is made none-the-less and it defines the hero enough to
engage the reader's attention far more than the plot and setting
will, rightly, do.

9. Making Room for the Heroine

So far I have been using the generalised 'he' to refer to both boy and girl readers. It is time to consider whether the heroine of junior adventure stories is drawn to appeal to girls, or girls only, and in what ways the role of heroine may be considered satisfying, either for the most superficial 'identification' or for rousing a stronger and more lasting emotional response. In this context it is important to distinguish between adventure stories and domestic novels (even if the distinction will often be arbitrary or blurred). The domestic novel allows for a broader and more leisured approach to the heroine as such and an attention to her development which can move far away from sexist stereotypes. (One example that may illustrate this point is the character of Ruth Hollis in K. M. Peyton's Pennington stories.)

Girls looking for a model, a source of vicarious emotional enlightenment or a point of interest will hardly be drawn to the idealised goddesses of Masefield or Rider Haggard; and if they do entertain any feeling for the distressed damsel of so many adult adventure stories, it will probably be because they would enjoy (or think they would enjoy) being 'rescued' by a Scaramouche, a Ben Hur, a Rupert Rassendyll or some more modern male-model. But supposing they want to meet, in a story of action, a girl not too much unlike themselves who plays a more than passive role and exhibits an active, even aggressive rather than an enduring courage, where should they look? Will they find heroines who are whole, complete, recognisable individuals and not merely unisex dummies, received into an adventure as ersatz-heroes? Looking back at my own reading at twelve or so, I can remember only Norah of Billabong who was *active* in exploits that passed for adventure, and she was carefully de-sexed and cocooned in that oddly evasive concept of 'mateship' until she had reached an age when she was able to feel and behave as a woman (when, regrettably, her adventures became more domestic and less intriguing).

Can a heroine only qualify as such (in an adventure story, that is) if she behaves like a hero? Henty seems to have thought so when he departed from the childhood sweethearts who patiently waited, in most of his books, for their lovers to return from dangerous missions. *A Soldier's Daughter* has the special interest

228

of any exception. Nita Acworth is introduced as a girl of fifteen whose mother has been dead for a year or so and who is living with her father, a major in a regiment holding a fort on the North-West Frontier. An only child, she is a tomboy and a happy one. A crack shot, a reasonably strong boxer, a good cricketer, expert with the foils, she passionately objects to her father's plan to send her to England to learn to be a lady:

> 'I can behave like that now when I like, father, and I am sure I don't want to grow up a young lady like the Colonel's two daughters, who used to walk about as if their feet were pinched up in wooden shoes, and simper and smirk whenever anyone spoke to them.'[1]

She is reprieved from the dire fate prescribed for her. Her father is lured away by reports of a frontier raid, leaving her as his official representative, supposedly under orders from Lieutenant Carter, who becomes responsible for the regiment. To Nita, impatient and clever, Charlie Carter is slow and even feeble, and she assumes a tone of authority over him, modified by grudging moments of feminine submissiveness. Circumstances change her attitude. The fort is attacked and she and Charlie are taken prisoner, Nita as a supposed junior officer in the army uniform she has assumed as a defence against tactfully implied dangers to her sex. We can detect a note of relief in the author once he gets his heroine into masculine costume. He can now allow her to become a hero; she rescues Charlie from his prison after escaping from her own, and by various skills and strategies brings the two of them safely back to the fort.

She has become a 'hero' – yet she is careful not to assume leadership too crudely and gives her companion every credit for his own contribution to the adventure, which includes making careful sketch-maps of the unknown country they traverse (a skill quite beyond impatient Nita). There are moments in the story when Nita is in danger of becoming a real rather than a made-to-measure character but Henty passes over such moments and keeps his heroine within the bounds of a tale for the young to enjoy on a limited level. Resting between one crisis and another, the officer and the girls discuss their adventure. Nita speaks in schoolgirl terms:

> 'It has been a jolly time, hasn't it, in spite of the hard work and the danger? I know that I have had a capital time of it; and as to my health, I feel as strong as a horse, and fit to walk any distance, especially since my feet have got so hard.'

'It is a time that I shall always look back upon, Nita, as one of my most pleasant memories. You have been such a splendid comrade, thanks to your pluck and good spirits, and no words can express how much I feel indebted to you.'[2]

The tomboy image is continued, though Henty does not seem to be entirely sure what Nita is really like. Back at the fort, her father sends for a 'roll of Karkee serge' from the quartermaster's stores, at Nita's request: in spite of his assertion, at the beginning of the story, that she could not make a garment for herself to save her life, he confidently urges her out of the unseemly uniform:

'There, Nita . . . you can make yourself a skirt out of that, and with one of my jackets you will be all right, though I do not suppose you will be quite fashionably dressed. You will find needles and thread in that haversack.'[3]

Nita herself has suggested that he buy her some cloth, as she would not like to be seen wearing a man's uniform in the fort, and she has assured him, 'I can soon make up something in which I shall not mind appearing'; but her dressmaking expertise, miraculously acquired, does not entirely please her:

'Do you know, father . . . I feel horribly uncomfortable in these clothes. Of course I shall get accustomed to them in time, but at present they seem to cling about me in a most disagreeable way.'[3]

Wisely, the major makes no comment. Like Henty, he realises that there is only one way the adventure can end. After two years in England, Nita returns to marry Charlie Carter; if readers speculate about who wears the trousers then, there is no answer. In spite of teasing ambiguities in this story, Henty has hardly drawn a satisfying feminine alternative to the traditional hero.

Children's authors do eventually, if slowly, reflect social change, but in their own way. Changing roles of women in the present century are reflected in an ambiguous way in a whole series of heroines conscientiously aspiring to be heroes. It is an obvious recipe for stereotypes – *Worralls of the WAAF*, for example – hearty girls whose liberation is just as limited as the sphere of action allowed to L. T. Meade's *Merry Girls of England*, for instance, or the young ladies in Mrs Molesworth's family novels, *The Red Grange* and *Meg Langholme*, whose lives are bedevilled by lost wills and false claimants but who are not permitted to do anything active themselves to redress injustice. At first sight Bessie Marchant may seem to be under the same kind of sanction, as a writer for girls in the teens. Extracts from reviews used as advertisement for 'Blackies' Books for Girls' at the back of her *Daughters of the Dominion* might seem to imply that she is writing in the same tone of voice as Sarah Doudney, whose *Under False Colours* is defined as 'a charming story abounding in delicate touches of sentiment and pathos' or Ethel F. Heddle's *Strangers in the Land*, which a reviewer had praised in conventional terms:

> Apart from providing the best of entertainment, this book is noteworthy as stimulating high ideals of life and action, and renewing faith in lofty and chivalrous sentiment as a factor in human service.[4]

The air in Bessie Marchant's books is a great deal less enervating, though the values implied (and occasionally, though not always, didactically asserted) reflect just as clearly the conventions governing girls' stories in the early years of the present century. One reason for the refreshing note of independence in Bessie Marchant's tales, which fall definitely into the category of adventures, is her choice of exotic settings. In Hawaii, the Seychelles, Russia, New Zealand, her heroines could be plausibly confronted with the kind of challenge which boys met by right in their corresponding types of fiction. But Bessie Marchant did not disguise her heroines as heroes. Their courage, their resource, their energies, above all their *concern*, belong to their sex. Often involved in the kind of legal and financial tangles which beset their Victorian sisters and were still besetting their contemporaries at the turn of the century, they are not advised and cosseted by family lawyers and they accept help from admirers or fiancés only when they have beaten fraud, theft and malpractice by their own efforts.

In *Island Born*, for example, a romance-adventure set in Hawaii, a girl of seventeen is left to cope with young siblings and an unhappy, inexperienced stepmother, after her father's death. Instead of falling in with Rose's timid advice and transporting the whole family to England, Violet Greville sets herself to clear her father's name and prove that the missing business documents with which he appears to have absconded were in fact lost by some hostile agency. She wins her fight against injustice not by aggressive tactics but by determination and endurance. Keeping the family afloat by taking over her father's secretarial work for the business, she wears herself out with difficult journeys, the last of which traps her on a volcanic island during an eruption, when she organises a perilous escape for herself and for a young man caught in the disaster who has come to admire her tenacity. There is no sensationalism in Bessie Marchant's plain, idiomatic prose, or in her view of her heroine. The particular kind of 'New Woman' who belongs to the first three decades of our century is, in these family adventure novels, an ordinary girl dealing with adverse circumstances as they arise.

The challenge that calls forth resource and endurance from orphan Nell Hamblyn in *Daughters of the Dominion* is one of poverty. The grandfather who has brought her up sells their shanty home without telling her and disappears to escape from the law, leaving Nell to contend with the new tenant, a bullying woman who expects her to stay as an unpaid servant. Facing the fact that she has nobody to help her, Nell sets out on a thirty-mile walk to the Canadian border and soon finds work to do, first as nurse in a family that has befriended her and then as a telegraphic clerk in a railway office. Domestic trials are interrupted by more dangerous events when Nell, sent to a lonely outpost, overhears a plot to rob the depot and boldly tackles the thief, after climbing a telegraph post to send a request for help when she has found the office wires cut.

Once more this is a heroine who acts with determination in a crisis, inspired by professional loyalty and womanly compassion. With all the freedom of action and independence of mind allowed to Bessie Marchant's heroines, they are in no way what our own times would denote as feminists. Nell quickly gives up her desire to take on advanced training when the man she has come to love urges her to be herself, and perhaps the most characteristic scene in the book is the one where she tends her dying grandfather, revealed as the railway robber and, into the bargain, no blood relation of hers after all.

Bessie Marchant found a formula by which she was able to offer to her girl readers enough action and suspense to lure them, at least temporarily, from the boy's adventure stories which many of them certainly adopted, while keeping prominently in her novels the womanly virtues. It is significant, for instance, that Tatna Sobieski, heroine of *A Dangerous Mission*, survives dangers in Moscow and on a country estate during the immediate pre-revolutionary years mainly by doggedly continuing her vocation as a teacher, while the claim of Sylvia Elliott, central character of *Sylvia's Secret*, to be a heroine is largely satisfied by her devoted nursing of her sick father; it is through strength of character rather than by acts of aggression that Sylvia saves the family estate in Jamaica and re-establishes its finances, in spite of the plots of a peculiarly unpleasant, fraudulent interloper.

The particular kind of family responsibility vested in women passes from Bessie Marchant's young women to the girls who perform suitably modified parts in certain of her junior stories. Here once again she makes good use of the advantage of foreign settings as against the school-and-home settings which so often hamper junior adventure or else increase its improbability. The perils of shipwreck in *The Unknown Island* hardly daunt the girl of fourteen who finds food for her young brothers on a rock in the Seychelles, tends an unconscious girl who alone survives the wreck of a liner and floats messages on leaves inserted into hollow stalks, one of which finally brings help to the children. While Tom Tit, who is ten or so, is delighted to be involved in a Crusonian adventure, Winnie Gravely feels guilty because their disappearance will bring anxiety to her stepbrother, a doctor on whose behalf the voyage has been made. Like other girls whom Bessie Marchant involves in difficult situations, she does not, as so many young heroes do, regard adventure as a game but as a challenge to her common sense and her local knowledge. Her attitude is couched in the moralistic terms of the 1920s:

> 'I think if we just go straight on trying to do our best, our mistakes get turned right way round for us. It is the trying that matters.'[5]

Through the next sixty years or so, the heroines of junior fiction would divide naturally into the same two camps – the surrogate boy, the kind of heroine for whom Enid Blyton's George is perhaps the ultimate stereotype, and characters like Ransome's Susan Walker, for whom responsibility acts as a brake on her natural sense of adventure.

The subordinate role of girls in adventure stories, which divided heroines into the passively domestic or the aggressively trousered, is meeting a strident challenge today in criticism and, in broader social terms, in new educational requirements. The search for equality, sometimes honest and sometimes political, suffers from an eternal obstacle. In the climate of today, girls can be boys but boys may not be girls. This is shown clearly in the following extract from a newspaper report concerning a discussion paper designed as a guide for new curriculum plans to be made by the Education Committee of the Devonshire County Council. The paper was modified after it was felt that the advice in it might lead to fears that 'little boys would find themselves cast as fairies'; the revised paper:

> . . . still stresses that teachers can help to avoid artificial sex stereotyping by giving young girls a chance to impersonate 'criminals, leaders of communities or pirate captains' in formal junior school drama sessions.

These are roles which history shows to be quite feasible for women, says the paper. But it is studiously vague about the kind of parts that could be tried by boys – except for urging teachers to 'engineer' opportunities of role reversal to help children to see the world from other people's eyes.[6]

The difficulty can be corrected in the classroom by common sense and in children's stories by the writer who is more deeply concerned with individual characters than with stock-in-trade boys and girls. It can also be by-passed in historical stories, when the roles of the sexes in the context of the past can be managed with less self-consciousness than if they belong to the society we live in. This is, of course, assuming that the heroes, and particularly the heroines, are considered properly in period and are not merely children of our own time suitably dressed for a charade. That most urbane and civilised of innovators, Geoffrey Trease, has shown the way with his adventuring girls. Their ultimate source might be none other than Shakespeare; they have the gallant gaiety of a Rosalind, the quick wit and flexible mind, the candour of speech and the forthright attitude to life. So that they may enter upon adventures on equal terms with boys, Geoffrey Trease has chosen periods and places where girls could expect to be educated as thoroughly as boys and where a literate society could allow him to give intellectual bite to his tales. The attitude implied towards girls is part of the wider theme of all his work. Whether he sets his story in Renaissance Italy, Tudor England, revolutionary Russia or the European theatre of Garibaldi's campaigns, he promotes a silent but forceful argument for the pursuit of freedom and a liberal outlook. His youthful characters enter upon adventure with a certain idealism added to their instinct for new, active and exciting events.

Trease's approach may be conveniently illustrated in two stories linked neatly though not formally in sequence, *The Hills of Varna*, published in 1948, and *The Crown of Violet*, which appeared four years later. A Yorkshire lad studying in Oxford early in the sixteenth century accepts a mission from Erasmus, who has received news of a lost Greek play, an Aristophanean piece called 'The Gadfly', which exists in a single copy in a monastery by Lake Varna in Dalmatia. At seventeen Alan is no firebrand, though he has been rebuked by his master for settling an argument by violence; as he says, he may love the new learning but he craves action as well as books. To journey through unknown, potentially dangerous lands is a tempting prospect and so is the incentive that unless the unique manuscript is put in the hands of somebody who will give it to the world, in the original and also in translation, the play could well vanish into the private and exclusive library of a wealthy Italian nobleman. The plot is as close to our own times as it is appropriate for the period of the Renaissance and the selection of characters (the lively, resourceful student, the arrogant Duke of Malfetta and his hired bravoes, the liberal-minded printer Aldus Manutius) suits the plot of the book as neatly and naturally as it suits its period.

Skilfully chosen for her role, the heroine Angela d'Asola, Aldus's niece, has grown up with books, languages and a free discussion of social and abstract ideas; she is well able to hold her own in argument with Alan when the disconcerted youth, set on the way from Venice in a trading ship, finds that the girl has stowed away and intends to accompany him. She argues for her rights:

> 'I don't know how girls behave in England – judging by the way you talk sometimes, I wonder if you keep 'em shut up, like the Turks . . . Well, Italy's different. Girls go to school like boys, they learn the same things, and when they grow up they're fit to *do* the same things. It isn't just that we can hold our own with you at Greek and Latin . . . Italian girls have done other things – they've led armies, they've governed provinces . . .'[7]

When Alan offers his own ignoble but characteristic counter-argument:

> 'It's not what God intended for women. They should stick to their proper job. All this is sure to make them unfit for it. It'll make them mannish – they'll be growing beards next . . .'[7]

she makes it clear that she has no intention of de-feminising herself, although she has suitably assumed masculine dress for the adventure. Her straight look at arranged marriages leaves the astonished Alan in no doubt that she will accept social convention, when the time comes, and will see to it that she has her own way when it is important that she should.

Matching her companion in courage, in physical endurance and in ingenuity, Angela gently corrects Alan's somewhat limited views of life when the opportunity arises; and when, after escaping more than once from the Duke's men and making a bargain for the play, they lose it at the last moment to the enemy, it is her practical wit that perceives how they can reverse their fortunes. Through their return journey they have read, acted and enjoyed 'The Gadfly' and are well able to dictate the whole work to Aldus's secretaries, and Angela boldly faces the Duke with the argument that as the play *will* be printed, he might as well allow them to borrow the original to correct any errors that might have crept in. All through the tale Angela has behaved not as a hoyden but as a capable, intelligent girl.

The imaginary Greek play was too good a subject to squander on one book, and Geoffrey Trease returned to it in *The Crown of Violet*, ingeniously explaining its provenance while creating another boy-girl partnership in a challenging enterprise. Set in Athens just before 400 BC, when Socrates was exposing social evils and the Theatre Festival was promoting magnificent plays, the story exploits unashamedly the familiar sequence of coincidence and luck, lurking and overhearing, with which the young in fiction expose villainy, in this case through a plot against the State initiated by a vicious, rich aristocrat and sundry foreign associates. A good deal is demanded of the reader in accepting that a boy of fourteen or so could write a comedy good enough to be entered for the annual competition, even though Alexis is given a suitable background – a good education provided by a well-to-do father and an artistic great-uncle willing to put the play forward in his name and find the necessary sponsor to pay for actors, costume and so on.

If Alexis is a peg to hang a story on, rather than an individual, the heroine amply makes up for this. Corinna enjoys a social freedom denied to those respectable girls of Alexis's class whom he would be expected to meet in his private life, because she has not had an enclosed Athenian upbringing. She has travelled widely with her mother, has lived in Syracuse and Massilia, and now has her home in an inn where she is accustomed to meet all kinds of people and to look after herself; although her mother insists on good behaviour, she allows her to wander alone outside the city, and Alexis's first meeting with her is on a hillside where she is playing a flute and is unperturbed at being accosted as a nymph by two schoolboys. When through plausible accidents she and Alexis become aware of the plot being directed by Hippias, she is ready to play her part and at one moment rescues Alexis from being caught by the enemy, but when in order to act the spy, she agrees to attend a crucial dinner-party as a flute-girl and dancer, she takes a naturally feminine view of the situation:

> Some of her self-confidence faded as the week went by. She hated the thought of showing herself off as a public entertainer. Sometimes she went hot and cold, imagining the crowd of guests, the way they would stare and pass personal comments without troubling to lower their voices. She had not spent her whole childhood in common taverns without learning something of life, and her whole nature revolted against the uglier side of it.

236

Only her pride stopped her from backing out. She would go through with the plan, she told herself, but, oh! how glad she would be when it was over.[8]

Without pressing emotion too far, Geoffrey Trease allows his heroine more than one side to her character and her good-natured, mature, humorous view of life enlivens the story. Placing Corinna in a section of society where she could reasonably engage in an adventurous move against villainy without sacrificing her honour or her charm as a girl, he puts the final touch to his portrait of her with a very Shakesperean dénouement when it is discovered that she is not after all the daughter of stout Gorgo but of none other than Conon, Alexis's reclusive sponsor, having been exchanged for a boy baby at birth to satisfy his desire for an heir. The rather melodramatic ending does not alter the fact that Corinna, as heroine of a junior adventure, has refreshed its fairly predictable course by her gaiety and her good sense.

Many more of Trease's tales owe their sparkle to heroines of spirited intelligence. In *Popinjay Stairs*, for example, Deborah Fane wins a reputation as a playwright in the early years of the Restoration (though prudently offering her work under the pseudonym Nicholas Arden, to suit the conventions of her day), while a young American travelling abroad with considerable independence expresses in emphatic terms her admiration for the prisoner on Elba and her scorn for British phlegm, in *Violet for Bonaparte*. Judicious compromise leaves Caterina Spinelli safely confirmed in her proper status as a marriageable girl, in *Horsemen on the Hills*, though her education with boys of her own age and the freedom of her kind in Italy in the 1440s help her to play her part in countering the plotting of a rival prince against her father; and Amoret Grisedale, the attractive young heroine of another disguise-adventure (*Mandeville*) ably justifies her claim that girls can endure hardship and outwit enemies as well as boys, when she slips neatly and uninvited into an Italian journey to buy pictures for Charles I. Moreover, her sympathy for Zorzi, a talented dwarf trapped in servitude to a degenerate Italian nobleman, is as emotional as it is practical; there is never any doubt that she is a true member of her sex, and when it comes to a fight for life against their enemies, her weapon is a cauldron of boiling stew where her fellow-adventurer, a lively lad from the London streets, relies on the more orthodox sword. In his unassertive, percipient way, Geoffrey Trease has effectively proved that when it comes to adventure, heroines have as much to contribute as heroes have – but in their own way.

The general assumption that the interests of girls and boys are entirely different has not been noticeably affected by changes in women's roles and ambitions in society. Moreover, adventure stories still to a large extent present domestic scenes dominated by male attitudes. In view of the publicity given to the women's liberation movement and the prevailing anti-sexist campaigns in the children's book world, it is surprising to find a chauvinist objection to allowing a girl into a new adventure gang launched in 1980 in A. D. Langholm's *The Clover Club and the House of Mystery*. The objection of the schoolboys who have commandeered a disused pigsty as headquarters for the Clover Club is very familiar, and so is Sarah's reaction to the place:

> She could see inside. Scattered about the flagstone floor were a few tattered old cushions, the only furnishings, and on one of them was sitting the third boy, arms round his knees, looking at her in a sort of solemn disbelief as if she couldn't be real. The walls were covered with pictures cut out from magazines, mostly of aeroplanes as far as she could see.
>
> The windows were too dirty to let much light through and Sarah longed to take a cloth to them. The floor was strewn with bits of chocolate wrappers, toffee papers and other litter. The whole atmosphere was, she thought, all in all and to put it mildly, masculine.
>
> 'It could be marvellous,' she said, and she meant it. She was thinking how nice it would be to clean it up and put curtains at the window and a carpet down.[9]

This houseproud young lady gets her way and is permitted to add various domestic touches, not all of them contributing positively to physical comfort, to the congenially scruffy club-room. The introduction remains the main line of Sarah's character and it is not surprising that she plays a fairly minor part in the adventures that follow, although she has clearly been given the part of token female in the book.

In theory at least, the device of the group-hero which is a natural part of the gang-story should make it easier for a writer to give his characters individuality within the conventions of the adventure story. The group-hero is a natural development from the dual-hero already discussed. Taking a number of boys and girls associated in a particular project or quest, an author can divide the traits he needs for his story between his characters and in this way can compensate for the limited opportunities for character-drawing in depth which pertain to the junior adventure story. He can also, in theory, make more room for girls to steer and

238

influence the action. This, at least, seems to be the intention: the result is astonishingly various. I offer the Lone Pine stories of Malcolm Saville as the type-specimen for several reasons. His close-knit group is a plausible gathering of young people from various backgrounds, giving him space for the agency of personality. Then, although he writes for a middlebrow readership, his style is lively and full of colour while being accessible to fairly unadventurous readers, especially because of his settings; predictable though his caves and tunnels, his floods and other accidents may be, they are always precisely localised, mainly in the West Country. Malcolm Saville had an eye for landscape and used it well.

A list of the Lone Pine adventures places him firmly in the long tradition of entertaining, light holiday-adventure. Many of his subjects could be duplicated in magazine tales of a century earlier than the mid-1940s, when his series began. A few of his plots are of a parochial kind – sheep-rustling, for instance, dog-stealing and the plundering of fir-nurseries at Christmas. The eager investigators are more often associated with such crimes as the traffic in fake jewellery, stolen documents or forgeries, the smuggling of watches and arms and the hijacking of lorries. Plots of a more romantic kind include the discovery of a Mithraic temple in a village near Rye and the locating of a valuable contemporary document describing Elizabeth I's visit to the same town, while a cipher in a family Bible and an ingenious riddle based on biblical references also attest to Malcolm Saville's inheritance of accepted motifs which, during the quarter of a century when the Lone Pine tales were appearing, became only too familiar in the profusion of adventure stories of this kind by other writers. The Janus-position of Malcolm Saville is perhaps most typically shown in the second book in the series, *Seven White Gates*, in which the children restore a long-lost son to his parents; he is not, however, an heir to a family estate but to a family farm.

If the Lone Pine adventures are, as I suggest, the type-specimen of their kind, this is not to claim any particular originality for either plots or character. All the same, the sheer professionalism of Malcolm Saville's writing is matched by his skill in choosing characters as well as subjects certain to appeal to a wide range of readers and in organising his tales in a masterly and consistent fashion. His handling of the gang theme is notably shrewd and entertaining.

The Lone Pine 'secret club' was formed in a cheerful holiday spirit in the first book in the series, *Mystery at Witchend*, published in 1943, when three children evacuated from London to Shropshire found companions in the locality at the conveniently right moment for investigating certain mysterious sounds and appearances in the neighbourhood; it is axiomatic in such stories that there is always more to find when exploring new surroundings than flora and fauna. Malcolm Saville defined his characters firmly at the outset, realising that the main attraction of a series is the fact that readers get to know them as friends, identifying with one or other of the group according to age or temperament.

David Morton, who becomes by common consent the captain of the Club, is fourteen in this first story, an intelligent but unbookish lad with a strong sense of responsibility for the nine-year-old twins, Dickie and Mary, who supply comic relief through all the books, regarding adventure as a joyous game where they can assume the roles of pirates, Red Indians, mountaineers or seafarers as events may suggest. Petronella Sterling, a fair-haired girl who rescues the Londoners from a bog on their first, incautious foray into the Long Mynd, represents the country as opposed to the town, well content with her isolated home at Hatchholt, where her father is in charge of an important reservoir; the convenient abbreviation of her name to 'Peter' is certainly not intended to suggest that she covets a boy's role, for Peter all through the series enters upon adventure as a perfectly contented member of her sex. The other new friend whom the Mortons are glad to include in the Club, Tom Ingles, has been evacuated to his uncle's farm, down the lane from Witchend; as the books proceed, he gradually comes to accept life in the country and indeed he appears, now and then, to be offered as something not far from a yokel, or at least an inarticulate country-man, in contrast to David Morton's social ease of manner.

The chance meeting of the Mortons with Peter Sterling satisfies a need on both sides for companionship and stimulus in adventure, starting with the simple desire for 'a real secret camp' where they can enjoy an ordinary routine of meals in an unordinary milieu. The plan develops after the two girls, Peter and Mary (happy to steal a march on the boys) find an irresistible secluded clearing surrounded by a gorse thicket and immediately named 'Lone Pine Camp' by Dickie from a mind fully stocked with the terms and practice of traditional adventure stories. The place becomes at once the headquarters of the 'Lone Pine Club' which, after an almost ceremonial meal of hard-boiled eggs, jam, sardines and tea, is given a set of rules recorded by David with the names of the first four members and subsequently buried (in the somewhat oily sardine tin).

The rules cover secrecy and discretion, obedience to authority (to David as captain and to Peter as vice-captain) and kindness to animals, but the most important from the point of view of the stories is Rule Five, which states that 'The Club is for exploring and watching birds and animals and tracking strangers'.[10] In fact, 'watching birds and animals' is entirely incidental to the requirement that strangers should always be investigated; binoculars and birdwatching become almost invariably a sign of impending villainy, although on one occasion (in *Stranger at Witchend*) Dickie's supposed villain, a birdwatcher lodging in the neighbourhood, proves to be a silver assayer on the track of a couple making and selling fake silver. It is typical, and indeed essential, in the holiday-adventure scheme of things, that strangers almost always prove to be villains of one kind or another, whether or not they are also identified by scars, beards, red hair or some other accepted mark of their kind.

The Lone Pine books are essentially holiday-adventures and in most (though not quite all) of them, danger is part of the game. There is, all the same, a more purposeful, moral theme in the stories, expressed in the oath worked out when the Club is founded:

> Every member of the Lone Pine Club signed below swears to keep the rules and to be true to each other whatever happens always. . . .[11]

and extended in the Foreword to *The Man with Three Fingers*:

> The Lone Piners have so often come to the rescue and helped to right a wrong, but this is the toughest job they have taken on for a long time.[12]

Firmly on the side of right, then, and bound in that group loyalty which lends a feeling of reassurance, and of vicarious comradeship, to young readers, the Lone Pine Club takes shape as an effective framework for a series of adventures in which, gradually, other members are added.

As the sequence of stories proceeds, the Lone Pine Club acquires four new members, three of them girls. Their contribution to the course of adventure proves to be somewhat disappointing. Jenny Harman, who lives with her father and stepmother in a Shropshire village, has a longing for romantic adventures of the kind which she reads about in the magazines she borrows from her father's shop; her naïveté makes her a natural victim of kidnapping and other deceptions. The gentle, unobtrusive Harriet Sparrow, whom the Lone Piners meet when they stumble on a mystery connected with stolen flower-prints, is useful chiefly in introducing investigative projects through the vicissitudes of her grandfather's antique business; in so far as she influences the stories it is because her vulnerable nature enforces the oath of loyalty and mutual help taken by the group. The third girl, Penny Warrender, lively and opinionated as she is, is something of a formal pair with her cousin Jon and both serve in the main to open up new areas of adventure in Rye and in London.

The brief definitions of his young characters offered by Malcolm Saville in the Preface to each of his books describe status rather than temperament; they are notes for new readers and no more. The Lone Pine children develop very little during seventeen adventures, which occupy in temporal terms the space of four or five years. Clearly in such a long sequence the author could not use a specific time-scheme of the kind which Ransome used in the 'Swallows and Amazons' tales and Peter Dawlish, with varying degrees of accuracy, in his 'Dauntless' series. After a time, however, it became necessary for the characters to grow a little older and to move with the times. In the Foreword to *Not Scarlet but Gold* Malcolm Saville explained:

> Now I must give a special explanation about this story to those boys and girls who have read some of the other Lone Pine books – particularly the first, called *Mystery at Witchend*. Over the years some readers have asked me never to let the Lone Piners get any older and others have felt, quite rightly I am sure, that it is now time for the David and Peter of the first story, published nearly twenty years ago, to behave as if they are sixteen today. So now, at last, you older, faithful friends of the Lone Piners may notice that these characters are facing their adventures – and indeed each other – as if they were living in the 1960s. . . .[13]

and in the final book of the series, *Home to Witchend*, he added that though he had not allowed the 'irrepressible twins' to grow up as quickly as the rest, 'older readers will soon realize that they could not forever converse in the childish manner which they used in the earlier stories'.[14] In fact this last modification was largely one of cutting. The revised editions that appeared in paperback during the 1970s, prepared under the author's direction, were brought into line with the demand for shorter, more concise stories which was at least partly due to the influence of television, and the long-winded recitals by the twins of events already adequately described in direct narrative were most readily, and usefully, curtailed.

As the adventures followed one another the Lone Piners fell naturally into pairs. A few sentimental exchanges were allowed to David and Peter as they approached their seventeenth year;

Jenny Harman's friendship with Tom Ingles, always a little possessive, became serious; the Warrender cousins found their relationship deepening. Suggested in the most respectable, not to say
tentative way, these youthful romances added little to the stories
(the official engagement of David and Peter served chiefly as a
device by which most of the characters in the books could be
collected at White Gates for a grand finale) nor did the deeper
feelings which Malcolm Saville promised to his readers in the
sophisticated sixties extend or develop the youthful characters
outlined in the mid-forties.

There were, though, occasional signs that adventure-games in
which the danger and villainy had been so lightly tackled did now
and then make a more serious impression on the Lone Piners.
The open moral standpoint which in the earlier books was a
matter of authorial statement rather than personal conviction
took on a new meaning in *The Elusive Grasshopper*, for example,
when the young people saw their old enemy Miss Ballinger
caught in a smuggling plot. Penny Warrender felt no triumph as
she looked at the woman:

> She had gone to pieces. Her dyed hair was awry and her clothes
> that once had been so smart now looked almost shapeless as she
> slumped forward with one hand on her niece's shoulder. Her eyes,
> behind her heavy spectacles, flicked from one to the other almost
> without recognition. Her mouth looked different too, and she was
> mouthing something which sounded like, 'All a ridiculous mistake'.
> Penny heard Jon say to Rawlings, 'Yes, that's Miss Ballinger . . .
> Can we go now? I think we've all had enough.' Then, most unex-
> pectedly, he put an arm round her shoulder.
> 'I know how you're feeling. I hate it too. Let's go.'[15]

There are signs also in *Not Scarlet but Gold* that the young
people *can* see beyond the immediate implications of action when
they argue about the hoard of money which Jenny has found and
which the so-called 'John Smith' had been trying to locate from
directions left by his father, a German who had been killed in
England during the war. Peter feels the Lone Piners have a right
to what they have found but Harriet, sickened by the sorrow and
hardship caused by the search, is sure that the money should go to
the innocent Mrs Clarke, who has suffered from the imposture.
For a moment at least the questionable morality of treasure-
hunting has been recognised.

On the whole, though, the Lone Piners do not develop as
individuals, though they are distinguished by age and background
and by the respective parts they play in the adventures. They

respond to challenge in a generalised way and remain, almost always, unchanged by their encounters with a surprising assortment of villains. The books take their colour and their particularity most of all from the settings which Malcolm Saville uses with such obvious affection. Never mind the Thomas Cook lecture with which he prefaces so many of the stories. Within the adventures, tourist advertisement gives place to sensitive, assured knowledge of locality which sustains and offsets the formulas of plot and character. Shropshire and the Welsh border, in many of the tales: London, in one particularly lively story: the Southwold part of Suffolk, in another, ravaged by the great flood of 1953: Rye and Romney Marsh, with the antique beauty of town buildings vividly contrasted with the rainswept acres of open country. These settings evoke curiosity and nostalgia and add richness to well-managed but relatively commonplace plots.

It is not, then, in this very popular series nor in most of its imitations that we should look for an enlightened, perceptive and tolerably realistic view of girls as actors in adventure-plots. It is broadly true that traditional adventure stories have been addressed specifically to boys, with the assumption that girls would read them as a relief from the domestic limitations imposed on them; the subordinate role of girls in such stories was confirmed even by such exceptions as the Trease books already discussed. It is not, though, for the sake of a contrived anti-sexist plot that I wish to see this balance altered but because, as I firmly believe, adventure stories are at their most compelling and enduring when character, plot, background and theme are all given their just due. I have already suggested that the emotional *effect* of action is an essential part of a story.

This element can compensate for cliché and romanticisation (as I believe it does in *The Prisoner of Zenda* and its sequel), for the hyperboles of plot (as I believe it does in Buchan's shockers), for the manipulation of battle-scenes in the Hornblower books. It is rarer in junior stories than one would wish and its presence accounts for the fundamental difference in range between, say, Malcolm Saville and Antonia Forest. It is possible that this emotional element rests more surely in the female than in the male characters.

There is a critical (and social) dogma which asserts that men and boys are mainly concerned with action, women and girls with relationships. Like all generalisations, it contains a certain proportion of truth behind the countless exceptions that could be brought to refute it. At least there could be, here, a way to track down that elusive emotional content which animates certain books for the young and makes them stand out from the mass of formula-writing, lying as they do on the borderline between the traditional adventure story and the problem novel.

Considering 'why women make good thriller writers', Janet Morgan threw out with journalistic abandon a number of reasons. Women 'work with hypotheses' rather than with views, she reasons; they are acutely interested in motive (and so, in character); they are 'skilled at understanding relationships between people working and living together . . . they note what is peculiar to certain places and how environment affects behaviour . . .'; above all:

> . . . there is one sphere in which women are supremely consistent and confident – in their awareness of good and evil, in their passion for fairness and justice (which are not the same thing) . . . even as they hypothesise, women have certain deep beliefs: in Order, Innocence and in a Day of Judgement.[16]

To this I would add one more attribute, an instinct for compromise, an intuition about the coexistence of good and evil which has often shaken a comatose formula into active life (in the work of P. D. James, for example). It might be in this sense that girls could, and sometimes do, claim a leading role in adventure stories.

10. The Villain

Aggression lies at the centre of the novel of adventure. The hero takes up a challenge from an adversary, a human or natural force; if the adversary is human, the struggle will represent in differing degrees of seriousness the conflict between good and evil. Hero and villain are representatives of a moral condition and each writer must decide on the balance he needs between generalised, even mythical figures and fallible, striving individuals. He must decide how far to relate the villain of his fiction to the society he lives in and particularly those types of villain which society currently fears. The adventure story has taken upon itself enough of the trappings of the world we know to move away from the vast anonymities of myth and folk-tale but the source is invoked in the largeness, the separate and isolated identity of the hero and, still more, of the villain.

Associations with figures larger than life provide authors with a way to alert their readers and force a recognition of evil beyond the immediate wrongdoing which the hero seeks to correct. In *No Other Tiger*, A. E. W. Mason introduced the infamous Archie Clutter in two impressive images in an unforgettable scene. Colonel Strickland is on a *machan* in the Indian jungle, waiting to shoot a man-eating tiger, when a man as lean, savage and shockingly majestic as a tiger leaps into the clearing. The eerie scene is brought to a conclusion in a still larger image: John Strickland reflects, 'Thus . . . must Lucifer have looked on the morrow of his fall.'[1] Similarly, the flawed, ambitious Paul, heading a gang of desperadoes in Buchan's *Huntingtower*, is likened to a lost angel, beautiful in features and wicked in intent.

Used again and again, the simile of Luciferian stature suggests that writers rely more on a general impression of evil than a particular line of misconduct through which to convince their readers that the hero has a real challenge to face. In his study of thrillers, Jerry Palmer noted that the hero reacts to '*prior* aggression' and that he acts to restore normality – in an ordered world 'disrupted by villainy'. He suggests that there is a difference in the way hero and villain need to be developed:

> The villain as a character is subordinate to the conspiracy as a function; we do not need to know anything about him. The hero,

246

on the other hand, is in no way subordinate to a narrative function – he *is* a narrative function, among the most important, and his personal qualities are an integral part of that function.[2]

This implies that while the hero must be conceived as an individual as well as a Defender of the Right in general terms, the villain is required only to provide the necessary 'conspiracy' while remaining an undefined, inorganic figure. This is to elevate action over character in a way which surely need not restrict the genre of thriller, let alone the broader reaches of the classic adventure story. We need to know something of the motives and the personal attributes of the villain if the acts of the hero are to be understood and appreciated. No story can achieve a proper balance if there is not some individualising on both sides.

This need not imply any intense, analytic probing of the nature of the villain but we do require something more than the kind of set piece which Dornford Yates, for example, offers to his readers, when he describes one of his many totally characterless villains as:

> . . . an awful blackguard. A very low forehead, and his ears stick out from his head. Very dark he is, and a scar runs down from the edge of his mouth to his chin.[3]

This kind of cliché, as persistent in adult thrillers as in their junior counterparts, diminishes the force of evil to domestic status without actually drawing a recognisable person. The villain who appears to be a hero, though equally susceptible to type-casting, can be a far more potent focus in an adventure story. Conan Doyle used the device light-heartedly but very effectively in *The Valley of Fear*, when he allowed Holmes to describe to Watson the cryptic coloration of his terrible adversary, insisting that technically he is libelling the man to call him a criminal:

> The greatest schemer of all time, the organizer of every delivery, the controlling brain of the underworld – a brain which might have made or marred the destiny of nations. That's the man. But so aloof is he from general suspicion – so immune from criticism – so admirable in his management and self-effacement, that for those very words that you have uttered he could take you to court and emerge with your year's pension as a solatium for his wounded character. Is he not the celebrated author of *The Dynamics of an Asteroid* – a book which ascends to such rarefied heights of pure mathematics that it is said that there was no man in the scientific press capable of criticizing it? Is this a man to traduce? Foul-mouthed doctor and slandered professor – such would be your respective roles.[4]

So successfully has Moriarty established his credentials in society that Scotland Yard thinks Holmes has a bee in his bonnet about him, thus usefully leaving the way open for Holmes to meet the challenge alone. The irony of Holmes's words, and the dramatic irony by which the reader enjoys the privilege of knowing better than the police, amply compensate for the fact that Moriarty remains a distant, looming, almost superhuman antagonist: we never get nearer to him than third-hand. The ambiguities of Moriarty the scholar and Moriarty the villain produce much of the tension in Conan Doyle's superlatively directed thrillers.

For Buchan there had to be something more, since he was writing novels rather than detective-stories (even if he did call them 'shockers'). He, too, presents villains in the lofty, grandiose style who aim at world domination rather than private harm. They represent not mythic evil but political evil, standing as personification of Buchan's grave concern for the state of society and politics in the post-war world of the 1920s. Beside the more conventional villains, like D'Ingraville or Mantel, who are sometimes defined through images of the larger carnivores, the cryptic villains stand out as individuals whose grandiose ambitions, decently concealed behind the demeanour of a gentleman, are tolerably well specified.

Buchan succeeds by gradual, subtle hints. The attractions of Medina, evil genius of *The Three Hostages*, disappear after he has failed to hypnotise Hannay, but at first that most practical of heroes sees only an arrogance and cynicism which seem to have no direction. It is only gradually, by chance and coincidence as much as by logic and perception, that he comes to see the depth of the man's lust for power, for dominion over men through knowledge and what would now be called brainwashing. The terms of Medina's ambition are boundless and necessarily left vague. We perceive Hannay's antagonist through his proud bearing, his ruthlessness, his dependence on his mother. He reveals himself less in his self-cherishing monologues than in scenes which suddenly become strongly concrete and visual, most of all the scene in the library where Hannay is ordered to act the retriever and fetch a paperknife in his mouth. The grotesque detail here, like the sharply observed details of the hostages in their disguises, catches the breath even at a tenth or twelfth reading.

Buchan was serious in the political evils which he attached to his villains but it is in the moments of immediate terror that he excels. The instant when evil becomes apparent behind the façade is a turning-point in *The Three Hostages*, as it is in the tales

in which the bland, nondescript features of Moxon Ivery change –
for example when he appears to Hannay with 'a jowl like a
Roman king on a coin, and scornful eyes that were used to
mastery'.[5] Again, Hannay recognises in the Pickwickian
archaeologist who befriends him the man who could hood his
eyes like a hawk; he identifies him again, when the enemy has
almost won the duel of *The Thirty-Nine Steps*, because 'his eyes
had the inhuman luminosity of a bird's'[6] though he remained
outwardly the pattern of a respectable householder. It may have
been the political concepts in Buchan's thrillers which induced his
public to take them seriously and to elevate them to the status of
literature, but his readers take most seriously his general proposition that evil is 'as old as human nature and as wide as the earth'.[7]
His villains are sinful citizens of the world as well as symbols of
evil.

The tradition which kept alive for a century of thrillers the
grandiose figure of the villain aiming at world domination similarly
prolonged the life of the deadly female who, working in a more
domestic sphere, was allowed a peculiarly nasty range of weapons
to compensate for a lack of brute strength. The long line of
deadly women, customarily raven-haired and glittering in costume,
seldom achieved any individuality beyond a well-defined personal
appearance. Buchan's Hilda von Einem, Sapper's Irma Peterson,
the vicious Rosa Klebb in *From Russia with Love*, are little more
than ventriloquist's dummies expressing a series of clichés uttered
by men against the deviousness of women.

The contrast between open-faced, blonde heroines and enigmatic, dark-browed villains is seen at its most obvious in *The Red
Axe*, an historical romance by S. R. Crockett set in a city-state of
north Germany in the sixteenth century. Hugo Gottfried's first
sight of the beautiful Ysolinde, who seduces him from his lifelong
love of his playmate and foster-sister Helene, is of a pale, passionate figure whose dress, 'sea-green silk of a rare loom' . . . with
'scales . . . of dull gold' upon it, enhances the impression of a
'spangled serpent of the Orient'.[8] The contrast of innocence and
ruthlessness on which much of the story turns is subtly expressed
for the author by the hero in a set speech:

> Helene, of a bodily beauty infinitely more full of temptation,
> bloomful with radiant health, the blush of youth and conscious
> loveliness upon her lips and looking out under the crisp entangle-
> ment of her hair, all simple purity and straightness of soul in the
> fearless innocence of her eyes – the lady Ysolinde, deeper taught in
> the mysteries of existence, more conscious of power, not so beauti-
> ful, perhaps, but often times giving the impression of beauty more

strongly than her fair rival, compact of swift delicate graces, half feline, half feminine (if these two be not the same) . . . Ysolinde was the more ready of speech, but her words were touched constantly with dainty malice and clawed with subtlest spite. She catspawed with men and things, often setting the hidden spur under the velvet foot deeply into the very cheek which she seemed to caress. Such as I read them then . . . appeared the two women who were to mould between them my life's history.[9]

The ultimate literary comment on this species of villain was made by Dodie Smith, when she created the comically sinister Cruella Deville, the ruthless dognapper of *A Hundred and One Dalmatians*. The artificiality of the female villain was too convenient to be often corrected. One exception deserves to be noted, confirming Stanley Weyman's often unacknowledged power to draw individuals rather than types.

The Abbess of Vlaye has its statutory villain, an opportunist soldier of doubtful parentage who has built up a stronghold and an outlaw army during the civil wars in France at the end of the sixteenth century. Odette de Villeneuve, elder daughter of an impoverished noble house, has thrown in her lot with the Captain of Vlaye, driven by a powerfully possessive love which overrides her position as head of a convent on which she has imposed her private morals no less than her official rule. Odette abets the captain in his attempts to stir up trouble in the province of Périgord but when he kidnaps a young countess and plans to marry her by force to add her soldiers to his own, jealousy drives his devoted ally to twists and turns in which the ingenuity of her planning is equalled by the confused feelings that sway her. To please the man whose will alone is equal to her own, she works subtly on a wounded duke, as a second, valuable hostage, by resuming the religious habit so often discarded and feigning an angelic purity which Weyman makes entirely convincing; even at the climax of the story, when Odette tricks the captain by putting on the marriage garments intended for the countess, the fairy-tale situation is turned into a scene of *particular* intensity because of the slow, logical steps by which the passion of a woman warring with family pride and family affections has been described.

Odette's ambition is powerful, her sphere of action large, but she is not inhumanly larger than life; she is a young woman who has consciously and uneasily moved out of her normal moral sphere and has suffered in consequence. The fact that her villainy is not rewarded is not just the expected moral ending but the natural result of the violence which she has done to her own nature. The super-villain does not readily translate into the terms of junior adventure stories but the kind of flawed character which Weyman drew in Odette de Villeneuve could be more easily understood by the young, simply because it is a more interesting and so a more absorbing study. The exaggerated, power-mad figure of Max Pemberton's Iron Pirate, offered to the young in a serial story as long ago as 1893, the mad scientists and obsessed dictators of Westerman, the sinister bald figure of The Master in T. H. White's yarn of that title (if not written 'for children', at least written for the child in T. H. White) – these and other villains could hardly be more than stereotypes, since the accepted limits of length and depth in children's stories would not allow even the degree of complexity which Buchan lent to Barralty, Medina and Ivery or Rider Haggard to his many arrogant and powerful villains.

Were children then to be left with generalised villainy in stories where sensational action diverted them from any desire for motivation, rather than individuals who themselves promoted that action? Did they – do they still – deserve no better than this? Stevenson certainly thought they did, when he added to the simple, bloodthirsty gang of pirates in *Treasure Island* (villains in traditional mode) the more complex character of Long John Silver, the sea-cook. Mystification is one of adventure's most valuable stocks-in-trade, mystification and misdirection by which the reader is teased into attention. Some may be alerted by the first reference to Silver because of the warm-hearted, ingenuous tone which sounds through the whole of the Squire's letter, as he reports on his success in finding a ship and a crew for the enterprise:

> 'I was standing on the deck, when, by the merest accident, I fell in talk with him. I found he was an old sailor, kept a public-house, knew all the seafaring men in Bristol, had lost his health ashore, and wanted a good berth as cook to get to sea again. He had hobbled down there that morning, he said, to get a smell of the salt.
>
> 'I was monstrously touched – so would you have been, and, out of pure pity, I engaged him on the spot to be ship's cook. Long John Silver, he is called, and has lost a leg; but that I regarded as a recommendation, since he lost it in his country's service under the immortal Hawke. He has no pension, Livesey. Imagine the abominable age we live in.'[10]

The theatrical cunning, the impudent servility of this more-than-story-book villain is there to be picked up by the discerning reader from his behaviour towards the adults – captain, squire

and doctor – whom he skilfully exploits for his own ends. His true
nature is suggested by the manner of his speech before it is
confirmed by his actions. But *Treasure Island* is told in the first
person and almost entirely by a lad whose lack of experience
makes him as gullible as the Squire's lack of sense renders that
benevolent but slow-witted gentleman. The revelation of Silver's
perfidy is, in relation to Jim Hawkins, very direct. Jim accepts
the man as honest at first sight in the inn because he differs from
a natural preconception. 'I thought I knew what a buccaneer was
like,' Jim tells us, 'a very different creature, according to me,
from this clean and pleasant-tempered landlord.'[11]

The simplicity of Jim's view is sustained all through the book,
from the crucial scene where, hidden in the apple-barrel, the
boy listens to a conversation in which rough idiom instead of
smooth diplomacy makes Silver's villainy shatteringly clear, to
the moment when he eavesdrops on the murder of one of the
few honest seamen and watches Silver ignoring the corpse as he
cleans his bloodstained knife on a wisp of grass. The twists and
turns with which Silver ensures Jim's safety, during the violent
clashes of pirates and treasure-seekers on the island, occasionally
confuse the boy, but he is never really deceived in spite of Silver's
occasional return to his impudent charm of manner. In the most
straightforward terms Stevenson shows that Jim has learnt his
lesson and has left his innocence behind:

> That was Flint's treasure that we had come so far to seek, and that
> had cost already the lives of seventeen men from the *Hispaniola*.
> How many it had cost in the amassing, what blood and sorrow,
> what good ships scuttled on the deep, what brave men walking the
> plank blindfold, what shot of cannon, what shame and lies and
> cruelty, perhaps no man alive could tell.[12]

The strength of the book lies in its directness, a fact sometimes
forgotten in the thesis-actuated analysis of critics in our time.
Stevenson was well aware that piracy was a nasty, brutish, unromantic business and that the morality of treasure-seeking was
usually dubious. He chose to include the truths in a straight
narrative delivered by a boy of ordinary shrewd intelligence and
his classic tale calls upon a similarly ordinary shrewdness and
intelligence in his readers. The duality of Silver, his good and bad
attributes, are there to be understood, as they contribute to the
wholeness, the broad, unobtrusive wisdom (and the excitement)
of the book.

Buchan's magnificent African adventure, *Prester John*, offers
a villain who wears the trappings of a hero, but the duality of

Laputa is not a matter of the kind of malicious deceit which activates Long John Silver. In place of the surreptitious humour of *Treasure Island*, which to a great extent is reflected from the tricks of the sea-cook, Buchan offers the portrait of a man of huge ambition. Laputa's dream of reviving the old empire of Prester John, as grandiose as the dreams of world-power in Medina or Ivery, has an element of nobility in it which colours the story and accords well with its buoyant, active tone.

Although the narrator, the young store-keeper David Crawford, is not a child like Jim Hawkins, he has something of the same innocence, the same taste for adventure. Buchan wrote the book for boys (it was serialised in *The Captain* between April and September 1910 as *The Black General*) and the dedication to Lionel Phillips confirms its position in the category of junior adventure:

> Time, they say, must the best of us capture,
> and travel and battle and gems and gold
> No more can kindle the ancient rapture,
> For even the youngest of hearts grows old.
> But in you, I think, the boy is not over;
> So take this medley of ways and wars
> As the gift of a friend and a fellow-lover
> Of the fairest country under the stars.

The lines define succinctly the colour and the youthful generosity of feeling which are everywhere in the book. Admirable as a school reader (there have been many editions published for this purpose), *Prester John* has a maturity of style and outlook which can extend the emotional horizons of the young as surely as the horizon of young Crawford was extended by his various, often alarming confrontations with the gigantic Laputa. The young man's experience of evil in greatness, dignity in obsession, gives moral substance to a story which relies equally on strong, dramatic descriptions to make the same point. Captain Arcoll, whose duty it is to check Laputa's bid for power, offers his opinion of him in general terms:

> 'He is a born leader of men, and as brave as a lion. There is no villainy he would not do if necessary, and yet I should hesitate to call him a blackguard . . . He would be a terrible enemy but a just one. He has the heart of a poet and a king . . . I hope to shoot him like a dog in a day or two, but I am glad to bear testimony to his greatness.'[13]

The contrast between Laputa and the rascally Portuguese Henriques, a character totally without honour, confirms Crawford's admiration for Laputa. Most of all this huge villain-hero is brought to life by concrete detail in every scene in which he is the centre, from the first unforgettable night-scene on the beach to the sudden, shocking manner of his death.

The word 'romantic' cannot be avoided in discussing *Prester John*. Buchan offers a large-scale example of duality without the complex analysis which another kind of novel would have made necessary. Because the story was distanced in time (it deals with an African rising of 1906) and in place (an Africa exotic to most of Buchan's readers), it could be simplistic in its theme and approach without raising uncomfortable doubts. There is a generosity of intent and style in the book which appeals to the mood with which the young react to tales of courage in adventure.

But this kind of romanticisation is somewhat out of key with the world of today, and writers who want to probe the nature of evil and the dichotomy of villains look for a rather different response from their readers. The dangerous, stultifying clichés of cops-and-robbers stories, where criminals are instantly recognised for what they are, are challenged very strongly by Emma Smith in a remarkable adventure story, *No Way of Telling*. The question implied in her title is asked not only in relation to Amy Bowen, the twelve-year-old heroine, but also as it touches the whole genre of adventure stories in which children and villains are seen in violent confrontation. Can the hackneyed situation work any longer? Even Emma Smith's familiar, Buchanistic plot of South American revolutionary intrigue, which at first glance seems to consort ill with the very domestic characters and setting, seems to have been chosen deliberately to stress the potential artificiality of this kind of junior adventure before we realise how flexible it has become in her hands.

The framework and machinery of *No Way of Telling* is another boldly chosen cliché. The innocent victims of evil, Amy and her grandmother, are cut off by a blizzard in their isolated cottage in the Radnor hills. Card-games, good health, a well-stocked store-room, are in their favour, but they are not equipped to deal with an invasion from outside which sets far more than a problem of physical survival. How can the two of them decide which of their unexpected visitors is the villain? Is it the huge, hairy, wordless giant, one arm 'held across his chest by some kind of tattered rag or scarf knotted round his neck',[14] who snatches blankets and a whole leg of lamb and bolts away? To Amy he is a frightening figure but at the same time one to be pitied for his speechless desperation, his obvious need for help.

Still more misleading is the appearance of the two figures on skis swooping across the empty snowbound space, as Amy watches, with an approach 'so rapid that it was like some kind of conjuring trick'.[15] The sudden descent on the cottage seems almost magical to the child and she sees one of the men at least as a fairy-tale apparition:

> It was not as though they were anything like that wild creature who had broken in on them the night before. The tall man talking to Mrs Bowen was polite and smiling. Everything about him seemed to Amy wonderful – his voice, his clothes, his eyes, her first sight of him swerving down the valley out of the setting sun as though he had been some sort of angel or hero, too good to be true. Yet he had been true after all. She had longed for them to cross the stream and her wish, like a wish in a fairy-story, had been granted: they were here. They were actually *here*, and Amy had an overwhelming desire to be allowed to keep them, to make friends with them – with this one anyway, the one with the soft pleasant voice and the dazzling eyes . . .[16]

Little by little the spell wears off. Old Mrs Bowen, shrewd enough to distrust the smooth-spoken strangers, puts doubt into Amy's mind. They had noticed the blond, beautiful traveller kicking their faithful dog Mick out of the way but Mick had *not* growled at the wild dark man. He seemed to Mrs Bowen to have appealed for help in the voiceless way of an animal: the skiers appearing so swiftly and suddenly seemed to her like hunters.

Keeping her counsel, warily observant, Mrs Bowen was proved right on one count when the hairy man reappeared and she was able to dress the jagged wound on his arm and give him food, while Amy accepts the letter which he presses on her and which she realises is in some way vital to his safety. By the time the two skiers reappear and introduce themselves as Scotland Yard officers in pursuit of a murderer, suspicion has deepened and is finally confirmed when Amy overhears a conversation in the night between 'Inspector Catcher' and his associate 'Nabb'. She sees the fairy-tale figure more clearly:

> Blue, pale, his eyes, intently focused, reminded Amy of the eyes of the Post Office cat, that huge fluffy creature whose time was spent dozing in the sunshine apparently unconscious but coming, at the faintest rustle or squeak, instantly alert. The Inspector looked at Mrs Bowen as though all at once she was of interest to him. One hand hung lax over the side of his chair, but Amy noticed that the tips of the fingers were crooked slightly inwards. Again she was reminded of the Post Office cat; and then, with a sense of shock,

realised why she had felt that the soft voice and easy manner were a disguise, and what it was they disguised: he was cruel.[17]

Eyes that had been dazzled by looking into the sun were now clear and the brilliant blue eyes that had seemed so fascinating now had no power to hide their evil thoughts from her. In contrast to traditional expectations, fair has been revealed as evil, dark as good. When Amy reaches the farm in the valley after a perilous journey by toboggan over mountain heights and hollows, she has to decide whether to give the letter to a man purporting to be an Ambassador, as unknown to her as Bartholomio the wounded sailor and the evil conspirator Vigers had been. But she is in no doubt, when she has looked into his face:

> 'For what are you looking, my child?' he asked her, smiling a little.
> 'You can tell by the eyes,' said Amy briefly; and then she gave him the letter.[18]

Now she can judge the worth of the two men; but she defends herself to her friend Ivor at the farm for her earlier mistake. There was no easy way to pierce a disguise: it was natural to judge by appearances: enlightenment had come slowly and surely to eyes sharpened by a sense of danger.

Emma Smith has made her point by choosing to contrast a contrived plot and a villain of storybook dimensions with a total, immediate reality in the characters of Welsh Amy and her grandmother and the homely, practical, companionable circumstances of their life. Through this contrast she has shown how Amy has been able to put aside the preconceptions of a child about the good and the bad in people, led by the natural impulse of pity and an unconscious recognition of honesty in their wild visitor. She has combined the external, accepted elements of the junior adventure story, the child faced with the challenge of villainy, and has extended the range of her story (as the best adventure stories are extended) by showing how the meeting of the challenge has altered the protagonist.

A large-scale hero of traditional kind can be an inspiration to the young but only within certain limits. There may come a time when children need something more than the absolute black-and-white of heroes and villains in the stories which are supposed to offer them in a sense a rehearsal for adult life. It is in the grey shades of everyday life that authors must look for characters and events capable of stretching the adventure story to its limits. The intricacies of personal relationships can be as dangerous and as stirring as the most exciting scenes of violent action.

The Villain

Few of us have escaped being excoriated, in childhood, by acts of insensitivity or injustice which, with a little understanding on both sides, could have been avoided. It is on this kind of situation that Emma Smith based a tale of good against evil as compelling as the brave stand made by Amy Bowen against the evil Vigers. *Out of Hand* at first sight seemed to belong to the genre of holiday-adventure popular in the two decades after the war. But the expectations of readers, the range itself of those readers, had been changing significantly during that time, and when *Out of Hand* appeared in 1963 it was in tune with the time in its unique contribution to those changes.

Nothing could be more evocative of the school of Ransome than the proposition which opens the book. William, Dicky, Rose and Harriet Armstrong arrive at a West Country station at the beginning of the long summer holiday which they are to spend with Cousin Polly, a frumpy, middle-aged, gloriously free-and-easy relation who can be relied on to aid and abet any holiday enterprises. The first chapter, entitled with misleading simplicity 'The Holiday Begins', includes every accessory needed for the successful, familiar adventure – a compact stone house, river and mountains, tents and freedom, and an attendant adult who will be an even more acceptable ally, since he is still a child at heart. Walter, like the Amazons' uncle, Captain Flint, has done everything in his power to escape from orthodox adult life. Once a pupil of Cousin Polly's at the village school, and her staunch friend, he owns a garage but does little to keep it going and his walkabout, casual existence troubles Cousin Polly a little, though she knows his worth better than anyone realises. By a twist of authorial perception, Emma Smith makes Walter her hero, in storybook terms; he is St George, opposing the dragon who has the distressed maiden, Cousin Polly, in its power. But the suggestion of any formal hero/villain encounter does not stand up to scrutiny. There are no heroes or villains in this book, only people forced into uncongenial, uneasy relationships.

An equally explicit chapter-heading, still seeming to promise one of those innocuous, customary setbacks of run-of-the-mill holiday adventure, announces 'Something Awful Happens'. Cousin Polly breaks her ankle. There seems no reason why this should interrupt the joys of timeless summer days. The family doctor accepts the children's assurances that they can look after their hostess and, with the old sofa hauled into the backyard, there seems no reason why she should miss the freedom of outdoors. But with 'Something Worse' there enters villainy, in the shape of two unexpected visitors, old acquaintances (Cousin

Polly is not ready to call them friends) from long ago who happen to be in the district.

Miss Hilda and Miss Eileen Collins, as they step out of their car into the sunshine, seem sinister enough to the politely assembled children:

> Their faces were similar, pale and bony, but one was taller than the other. The smaller of the two, who had been driving, looked round the yard at the flags and the bunting – more faded than ever after several days of sunshine – with the sharp, thorough look of someone inspecting something, and then writing it all down on a list in her head. She looked at the sofa with the broken springs, and Cousin Polly's bicycle lying on the ground; at the books and newspapers and rugs and cushions flung about all over the place. Her eyes flickered rapidly over the four children, and came at last to rest on Cousin Polly herself, propped rather high on her strange throne, with her plaster leg raised in the air.
>
> 'My dear Polly,' she said, frowning, 'whatever in the world is all this?'[19]

Far more dangerous than thieves or smugglers, the two middle-aged ladies have no difficulty in overriding the polite indignation of the young Armstrongs. Shut away indoors, officially an invalid, Cousin Polly may only be visited for a polite goodnight. This is bad enough to cloud the sun, even in the camp by the river – still permitted, for the two spinsters see the children as an encumbrance rather than as adversaries. But rebellion is being fomented, first because Cousin Polly is so obviously oppressed and enfeebled by the situation and later when it becomes clear that the Misses Collins are not content with temporary interference. The girl they had scorned for her absent-minded inefficiency in their schooldays now seems to them so lacking in common sense that their way is clear: they must arrange for Cousin Polly to sell her property and retire to a Home where she can be looked after in a respectable, orderly way.

From a real-life point of view Eileen Collins is merely a strong-minded, bossy female who has had things all her own way and who should not be too difficult to oppose, but Cousin Polly, physically weakened by her accident and mentally reverting to that long-ago self when she allowed herself to be bullied by the Collins sisters, is persuaded to accept their view of her future. If they are not villains to her, but disconcerting well-wishers, to the children they *are* villains, oppressors, gaolers: no amount of reason, no overtures of friendship will persuade them otherwise. This is something more than a curtailing of holiday fun. Dicky's definition of Eileen may seem melodramatic:

'I just thought of it, all at once – she's like Napoleon. I mean, she's got a power complex, like him. She just likes to have people in her power. That's what he liked – I know all about him. We're doing him at school. She's a power-mad maniac, like Napoleon.' . . .[20]

but it strikes to the heart of the problem. Eileen *is* power-mad, and her power is all the more dangerous because it can so easily be seen as wise and sensible in its application.

'Old Boney Collins' must be defeated by guile, and so she is. In a meticulously planned campaign the children rescue Cousin Polly from the prison of her sickbed and whisk her off to a secret camp in the hills, helped by Walter, who is perfectly prepared to see the interlopers as villains, for their treatment of him has been wickedly insensitive, snobbish and ungenerous.

This first rescue is in the best tradition of junior adventure – practical, hilarious and boldly simple. It can hardly be a final rescue, as the doctor is quick to point out, but there is more lasting help at hand. If Walter is not a child, he has a child's simple attitude to life. He sells his garage, takes over Aunt Polly's property and arranges a smallholding partnership with her, defeating more orthodox plans in one adroit stroke. But the children are not able to rejoice whole-heartedly in the defeat of an enemy, for they have been plagued by doubts about their conduct and by uncomfortable feelings of pity for the villainous Boney Collins; like the warm-hearted individuals they are, they are horrified when, after Eileen has been injured in a fire, the doctor tells them that she has had a nervous collapse and has been repeating again and again, 'They wouldn't call me Cousin Eileen.' 'Isn't it funny?' Dicky comments. 'You think you hate someone absolutely – and then you suddenly find you don't. It's very queer.'[21]

This has been an adventure enlightening in its contradictions; without pushing the point too far, Emma Smith has made it very clear that there were no villains or heroes here but fallible human beings making their own misguided and inexpert efforts to understand one another. Taken for the most part at a pace suitable to the young and narrated with young attitudes at its centre, the book ranges beyond its adventure framework as the author, presiding but invisible, adds her own ironies and perceptions to a spirited defence of freedom and fun.

Irony is at the heart of another seminal book from the same decade, John Rowe Townsend's *Gumble's Yard*. Like Emma Smith, he chooses for his story the familiar form of the Robinsonnade. When ineffectual Walter Thompson walks off in hopeless pursuit of his sleazy mistress Doris, after a more than usually bitter quarrel, his thirteen-year-old nephew Kevin and his sister Sandra, with their small cousins Harold and Jean, are left to fend for themselves. Their house in Orchid Grove is far from exotic; the names of the streets in this part of Cobchester (Mimosa, Japonica, Cyclamen and so on) are as misplaced in the slum as the contrast between the plight of the children, with the threat of the Welfare and separation looming and a shabby house whose rent is unpaid, and the various middle-class families who in cosier adventure stories, with eventual rescue by adults guaranteed, cope with accidental isolation by reason of flood, accident, sudden illness and the like.

That first night in Orchid Grove, Kevin and Sandra reckon up their assets – 'enough bacon and potatoes for a fry-up, firewood and a ten-shilling-note under the tea-jar that Doris must have forgotten'.[22] Warm and agreeably full of food, they settle down by the fire and call on Kevin's particular talent for entertainment:

> So I made up a story, all about children cast away on a desert island. And we imagined it was us, and that we could hear the waves beating all round us. And we pretended to be alone and in peril, instead of warm and comfortable in our home in Cobchester.[22]

The desert island they find, with the help of Kevin's tough, resourceful schoolfriend Dick Hedley, does in a sense have waves beating round it; their midnight flit, most capably organised, takes them to a row of empty, derelict, canalside cottages whose continuous attic seems to offer a perfectly good home, with a little contriving.

Unfortunately the isolation of Gumble's Yard is soon broken, for the cottages are being used as a temporary storehouse for stolen goods and a rendezvous for a dangerous jail-breaker who has planned to pick up a passport here and make his way by water to an arranged passage to South America. Flick Williams, journalistically nicknamed Baby-face, belongs to the most obvious species of story-book villain but there is room in this seemingly simple thriller for a different dimension. The irresponsible Walter, who has let himself drift into association with the thieves for the sake of ready cash, is definable as a villain in social as well as legal terms. But John Rowe Townsend does not see him as an example of social evils nor as a pathetic man destroyed by his own stupidity – he sees him as an individual whose virtues as a father are as real to eight-year-old Harold as his lack of sense is real, and pitiable, to the observant, philosophical Kevin.

With Kevin as narrator, the story achieves a fine balance

between the authorial irony which sharpens it and the congenial housewifery and tension of events which the children accept as adventure, uncomfortably real though it may become. Kevin is not used as an omniscient mouthpiece for the author; his shrewd appraisals go just as far as his age and experience allow, and no further:

> Doris was the only one who took no part in the proceedings. She sat looking dully at nothing in particular. On her flabby face there was no expression at all. More bitter thoughts came to me. But they were followed by a newer reflection still. The truth was, I realized suddenly, that Doris was simply not equal to things. She wasn't very bright or very energetic or very likeable. It was a further development in my understanding. Poor soul, I thought, life's pretty grim for her. We'll have to carry her along somehow.[23]

Technically it must be allowed that there are villains in *Gumble's Yard* and heroes as well – for if Kevin hardly presents himself as a hero, his admiration for his sister Sandra might be said to claim for her the status of heroine. Certainly her sense of responsibility, her certainty about domestic values and her sturdy common sense help to ensure that the deserted children escape real disaster. But the conventional idea of heroes and villains is irrelevant in a book which traces clearly and with economy the behaviour of a group of individuals.

Socially alert as the book is, it is not, as I have said, a social tract, and if the sequel, *Widdershins Crescent*, seems a little more weighted with a message for our times, it is perhaps only because the children-against-crooks theme, a matter of local government corruption, is less exciting and active than the desert-island theme of *Gumble's Yard*. The central point of the second book, the child's-eye-view of venal Councillor Widdowson and feckless Walter, remains true to the intention of a novelist interested in people and not in types.

The backsliding of Walter Thompson could, obviously, have been treated in a very different way; given children of more vulnerable personality or without the protection of their close loyalty to one another, we could have had a tragedy rather than a sharp but agreeable adventure. Equally, Nina Bawden could have made a psychological tragedy out of the circumstances of *Carrie's War*, making the character of the grocer Councillor Evans an evil and destructive one. But although Carrie and her younger brother Nick found him alarming when they were evacuated to his coldly ordered Welsh household (indeed, to Nick he did at first seem like an ogre) it was soon as clear to the children as it is to the reader that Samuel Evans was a petty tyrant but also a man to be pitied for the narrowness of his outlook and the unlovable, unloving limitations of his nature. Here once more we have a story which uses traditional devices (a family quarrel and a seemingly lost will, a mysterious invalid down in a dark valley) behind which individuals, brilliantly developed, work out their attitudes to one another. It is 'Carrie's War' not merely because she and Nick have been moved from the danger of enemy raids on London to the safety of rural Wales, but because she has to fight her preconceptions of good and bad people as she comes to know them better. The adventure in the book does not lie in the outward way two children find their way into new circumstances but in the inward progress of their investigation of new people and new relationships.

Walter Thompson and Samuel Evans are villains in a new kind of adventure – new at least to young readers, who are to be persuaded to look for more complex moves in the chess-games of good against bad. The stories which stand out from the average are those in which character matters as much as action, in which the *effect* of one person on another is far more than physical. This may be best illustrated with reference to a book which for its simplicity and subtlety, its emotional power, deserves to be included among classic adventure stories. *The Intruder* indicated the possibilities in a definite, restricted genre when it appeared in 1969 as surely as *Treasure Island* did when it appeared almost ninety years earlier. Comparison is not the best method of criticism, perhaps, but there will always be certain books against which others can legitimately be measured because they set a certain standard of technique, style and depth and also because they are pathfinders showing new ways to revive old formulas and to extend an accepted range of fiction.

John Rowe Townsend boldly chose an old, familiar formula for *The Intruder*, as he did in *Gumble's Yard*. In the village of Skirlston a lad of sixteen is moving gradually and easily towards maturity. In the small, isolated community he has his own status. He is Acting Sand Pilot, guiding visitors over the dangerous local sands in the immense bay when his mentor, the 'Admiral' Joe Hardwick, who has trained him, is too ill to perform his duties. Because the duty and responsibility are real and important, the sixteen-year-old has been able to accept the fact that his personal status is insecure and his parentage in doubt; the old man he lives with may be father, grandfather or even no relation at all. The future may seem limited but it is clear enough to Arnold until the intruder appears. At first he seems harmless, if a little odd, a bystander rather disconcertingly close as Arnold watches a boy and girl playing with a ball on the sands and assesses his responsibility to them:

> Colour was fading from the sky. It would soon be dusk. Arnold could just make out the stranger's appearance. He was thin, getting towards middle age, and he wore a shabby raincoat, and a black beret square on the head. His face was narrow, and even in this light you could see that there was something odd about his eyes. One moved, the other stayed still. His voice was sharp, northern, slightly abrasive.[24]

The regular reader of thrillers will recognise the villain at once by the attested clues of appearance and by the silent approach of the intruder, and it is also by orthodox methods of narration and description that the author deepens the menace of the man called Sonny and allows his designs to become apparent, more definitely at first to the reader than to Arnold. For at first it seems to the lad a joke, though an unpleasant one, that this insignificant man asserts his claim to the house where Arnold has always lived. It soon appears that he must take the claim seriously. Sonny introduces himself as Arnold Haithwaite, the true heir to old Ernest's property: the boy, he insists, is not a Haithwaite and will have to go. The terms of Sonny's enmity and his power are those of the conventional thriller. He is physically a match for the boy, as he proves in a simple but nasty conflict, and the bewildered youth becomes as it were a servant under notice in his own house.

There is worse. Old Ernest retires to his bed and his growing weakness may be due to something far worse than old age. Does the gruel contain a slow poison? The doubt adds to the menace of the intruder, in the orthodox terms of the adventure story, and equally orthodox are the means by which Sonny is defeated; he is drowned in a storm in spite of Arnold's efforts to rescue him, as though nature had come in on the side of the oppressed hero.

But Sonny's villainy does not lie in his thievish intentions nor in his spiteful mode of speech nor the manic manoeuvres of his grandiose plans to turn Skirlston into a major tourist resort. He is a poor figure of a villain. It is the insidious, invisible threat of taking Arnold's name and his identity which constitute his deepest evil, just as Arnold's slow realisation that he is not a name or a relative but an individual in his own right is his true triumph over his adversary, and this he owes, like so much more, to the admiral's common sense, which ties the sensations of the

past weeks into the realities of the present. Nothing is the same,
Arnold insists:

> 'You were at the inquest. They buried him as Arnold Haithwaite.
> As for me, I'll never know, but most likely my father was a
> Cardiff seaman. I'm nobody at all, that's the truth of it. Arnold
> Haithwaite's dead.'
>   'Dead?' said the Admiral. He downed the second glass of home-
> brew. 'You look pretty healthy to me. *You're* Arnold Haithwaite,
> always were and always will be. There's only room for one of them
> in Skirlston, and it's you. You might as well get used to it again.
> And now sup up like a man, don't moan like a lad.'[25]

John Rowe Townsend showed once and for all in *The Intruder*
that the archetypal conflict between good and bad can be translated into the most domestic and actual terms without losing any
of the force, but the deciding factor will be a psychological one.
Hero and villain must be individuals driven by particular emotional needs or deprivations, if the story is to work on any but the
most superficial level.

But supposing a time should come when the fictional villain
becomes unacceptable to public opinion, when aggression is out-
lawed in story as in reality? If this is an extreme and unlikely
situation, at least there seems a need to discover challenges for
the hero outside the routine conflict between good and evil.
Already writers have found a way to avoid the social confusions
and improbabilities of the crime-story by pushing action and
motivation back into the past or forward into the future and so
obscuring to some extent inconvenient questions of logic or social
pressure. There *are* challenges other than those of man-to-man
confrontation. There is a wide range of adventure-fiction in which
a hero, young or adult, is set against the forces of nature, challenged to find somewhat different kinds of courage, resource and
endurance from those required when the antagonist is human. In
this kind of story the balance between character and setting will
be altered. Character will, it must, still be paramount and active
within the story, but the implied personification of some natural
force – unknown wilderness, physical cataclysm or whatever it
may be – requires a fresh look at the powers of descriptive
narration and of atmosphere in a piece of fiction.

Places

11. Learning the Land

The polarities of the adventure story are people and places – that is, motive and circumstances. In those books where the plot depends on the interaction of people, the place or places concerned will either support it with a set background or will provide an impetus for human behaviour that depends ultimately on personality. In this kind of book, character seems to me to matter a great deal more than is usually allowed by critics: action alone will not do.

There is another large section of the genre where, although character needs to be defined, the antagonist and the challenge come from places rather than people. In such stories the dangers of civilisation give way to the dangers of natural forces, in tales of exploration and endurance. Paradoxically the challenge posed may be that of defending nature against man. The issue of conservation, which was the theme of recent novels by Hammond Innes and others, was used by Fenimore Cooper a century ago. Indeed, the development of communications and other forms of technology has gradually reduced the map of adventure until the actual protection of nature is now the most fruitful source of material for this group of adventure stories. The double role of exploration beyond the range of man, and of protection for a shrinking world, is hinted at in Buchan's *A Prince of the Captivity*, the tale of a man seeking an escape from the ills of civilisation:

> He [Adam Melfort] had wanted to get away from men and their littleness, but he found that the littleness was in nature. All his life he had dreamed of exploring the last undiscovered geographical secrets, and had thought of the world as a field of mystery of which only the edge had been lit up. Now he realised that the globe had suddenly gone small, and that man had put his impress upon the extremest wilds . . . Epidemics, germinated in the squalor of Europe, had destroyed whole tribes of savages in Africa. He remembered conversations he had heard that summer in England, when untrodden equatorial forests had been thought of only as reservoirs of wood alcohol, and plans were preparing for making a road by air to every corner of the inaccessible. The world had shrunk, but humanity was extended – that was the moral that he drew from his reflections. Many things had gone, but the spirit of man had enlarged its borders. The problem of the future was the proper ordering of that spirit.[1]

The challenge faced by the hero of an adventure story is likely nowadays to be not the dangers of the wild but the dangers inherent in man's own nature. Paul Zweig, in his study *The Adventurer*, offers this as a chronological point:

> . . . as the mysteries of geographical distance have been solved by camera safari, tourist cruises to the Antarctic, and the grim banalities of jungle warfare, the measure of distance has changed. Its horizon has come increasingly to exist in the emotional style of the adventurer, not in the 'white spaces' which the map no longer contains.[2]

Zweig quotes the works of Conrad and T. E. Lawrence as examples of this trend. But the 'emotional style of the adventurer' has always been fundamental in those tales which have more than an ephemeral value. Man in action can never gain credibility unless his attitudes and temperament are made clear.

Certainly it is true that writers for two centuries have been under increasing pressure to find new settings for adventure. Some have looked to the future, others to the past. Whatever their choice, they have had the task of conveying in words the feel of a particular place, a tract of land or sea in which the hero can be seen to operate. A century ago Fenimore Cooper, in his 'Leatherstocking' tales, made a huge, external metaphor out of the shrinking globe. He established the frontier tale as an important branch of the tale of man against nature. He found a way to extend the map by looking back into the past, stating the very problem of that shrinking map through the motives and philosophy of a particular individual. The conventions he established for the genre have never really been altered: his power to convey the atmosphere of place in a purposeful, directed way has perhaps never been matched except by his true descendant, William Faulkner.

The five 'Leatherstocking' novels, published between 1823 and 1841, look back to an earlier period in North American history, to New York State in the mid-eighteenth century and the Great Prairie at the end of that century. Fenimore Cooper drew his material partly from the records and reminiscences of his father, who had arrived in the wilderness of Otsego in 1785, and partly from encounters during his own childhood in the district with Indians, hunters and trappers. In the romantic picture he painted of a way of life made to vanish in the name of progress, character and landscape cannot be separated, nor can the adventure-plots of the books be divorced from the strong social theme which they carry.

Readers today, unused to waiting while action is interrupted by dense descriptive passages or lengthy disquisitions on principles of living, may turn to abridged editions. Children certainly do, if they read the books as their forebears did (probably only *The Last of the Mohicans*, at that), and from them the hero Leatherstocking and his Indian friend Chingachgook the 'Great Serpent', with their various adversaries, are no more than generalised figures in a redskin-paleface situation that has become little more than a playground game.

The character of Natty Bumppo was in fact carefully built up so that he could become the mouthpiece of the author's ideas about the fate of the Indian tribes and the settling of the wilderness; far more, he is an embodiment, an individual almost identified with the land. This symbolic aspect of the man is marked by the way his life impinges on the various groups of soldiers, pioneers and travellers whose fortunes he affects in many ways and in many places. The stories radiate outwards like the spokes of a wheel from Bumppo at the centre and he seems at times less like a human being than some mythological figure poised to save lives or turn disasters at some critical moment.

The breadth of vision in the books as regards Indian and white interests is achieved through the hunter's background. Young Oliver Effingham, whose grandfather had been one of the first people to take up land in Otsego County after agreement with the Indians, explains to his companions:

> 'He was reared in the family of my grandfather; served him for many years during their campaigns at the west, where he became attached to the woods; and he was left here as a kind of locum tenens on the lands that old Mohegan . . . induced the Delawares to grant to him, then they admitted him as an honorary member of their tribe.'[3]

The young Bumppo had become expert in woodcraft and tracking from his life with the Delawares, as he had become a crack shot and a strategist through experience with the army – experience that began very early, for he tells Mabel Dunham the sergeant's daughter (in *The Pathfinder*) that her father had taken him on his first scouting expedition, when the twelve-year-old Bumppo's rifle had in fact saved his life.

Natty Bumppo is seldom referred to by his baptismal name, for he has acquired several soubriquets, each of which marks a characteristic or an exploit. Apart from the descriptive name 'Leatherstocking', which became the title by which the series was to be known and which referred to his most typical hunting costume, his earliest title, 'Deerslayer', came from the Delawares, as he says 'not so much on account of a bold heart, as on account of a quick eye and an active foot'.[4] However, in the conversation that follows this remark the hunter explains enough of his philosophy to the listener, the gun-happy Harry March, to underline the implication that he does not want to make enemies but to employ his gun in shooting animals – and then only for essential food. The name 'Pathfinder' speaks plainly of the man's prowess as a scout during the colonial wars round the Great Lakes between French and English as well as of his success as a guide to the soldiers and civilians travelling the forests and waterways from one fort to another, while 'Hawkeye', the name by which the Indians most often designate him, was bestowed by an Indian of a hostile tribe whom he had fatally wounded in a contest not of his seeking.

All these names emphasise Bumppo's actions and skills, mark the stated points of his character by which we recognise him and relate him closely to the forests, lakes and prairies where he lives his determinedly self-sufficient life. He is recognised also by a blunt, unaffected mode of speech whose tones sound even in his most sententious and untimely harangues (untimely, as it seems to the reader, because they are often spoken, or even whispered, during moments of extreme peril). His closeness to nature leads him to a theological position nearer to the animism of his Indian friends than to the orthodox Christian views of the musician David Gamut, with whom he disputes energetically during a pause on a dangerous march:

> 'Do you take me for a whimpering boy at the apron string of one of your old gals; and this good rifle on my knee for the feather of a goose's wing, my ox's horn for a bottle of milk and my leather pouch for a crossbarred handkercher to carry my dinner? Book! What have such as I, who am a warrior of the wilderness, though a man without a cross . . . to do with books? I never read but in one, and the Words that are written there are too simple and too plain to need much schooling; though I may boast that of forty long and hard-working years . . . I have heard it said that there are men who read in books to convince themselves there is a God . . . If any such there be, and he will follow me from sun to sun, through the windings of the forest, he shall see enough to teach him that he is a fool, and that the greatest of his folly lies in striving to rise to the level of One he can never equal, be it in goodness, or be it in power.'[5]

Although, as Hawkeye says, he is 'a man without a cross' and has no Indian blood in him, he accepts the traditional customs of the Indians, notably their ritual boasting and the importance of taking the scalps of defeated enemies, as part of their way of life. His relations with the Mohican Chingachgook and his son Uncas are neither paternalistic nor self-consciously liberal. Chingachgook, the Great Serpent, commends his loyalty as a wilderness ally, sometimes to be helped (as in the search for the Indian maiden betrothed to the Mohican, in *The Deerslayer*) and sometimes to be relied upon completely (as in the twists and turns of danger in *The Pathfinder*). Their closeness is explained to the boat-dweller Hutter, when the hunter-scout has joined him on the lake:

> 'I'm a young man, and, as yet, have never been on a war-path; but no sooner did the news come among the Delawares that wampum and a hatchet were about to be sent in to the tribe, than they wished me to go out among the people of my own colour, and get the exact state of things for 'em. This I did; and after delivering my talk to the chiefs, on my return I met an officer of the Crown on the Schoharie, who had moneys to send to some of the friendly tribes who live farther west. This was thought a good occasion for Chingachgook, a young chief who has never struck a foe, and myself, to go on our first warpath in company; and an app'intment was made for us, by an old Delaware, to meet at the rock near the foot of this lake.'[6]

In spite of this understanding of the Indians and his respect for their place in the land, Bumppo is not at any stage of his life carrying on a solitary campaign for the restoration of their land to them by the Government. Rather, he regards the land as belonging to nobody, an attitude which he gradually has to realise is untenable.

As he approaches his seventies he comes into direct conflict with the civilisation previously represented mainly by military bodies or by trappers like himself. In *The Pioneers* he finds himself, as a solitary, dwelling by sufferance on the fringes of a new settlement, in passionate opposition to the law as it is administered by Judge Temple; he bitterly condemns also the 'wasty' ways in which passenger pigeons are being massacred by the thousand in an organised shoot for sport rather than for food and in which the local fishing is plundered with a similar disregard for the future. He sees the forests destroyed for fuel (though the Judge, indeed, has at least a theory that coal might be sought as an alternative) and the privacy which he has sought all his life is threatened by the malice of certain greedy, inquisitive local officials, who believe he is hiding secret knowledge of silver-bearing rocks.

He is threatened most of all by the prejudices and constraints which the small town, ever growing, has brought to the wilderness; most of all, white innovations have destroyed the simple dignity of Chingachgook, now baptised as 'Indian John', and much weakened by drink and enforced idleness. The hunter Bumppo stoutly defends his way of life to the people who are convinced that he should be made to conform to their laws and customs:

> 'I have lived in the woods for forty long years, and have spent five at a time without seeing the light of a clearing bigger than a wind-row in the trees; and I should like to know where you'll find a man, in his sixty-eighth year, who can get an easier living, for all your betterments, and your deer-laws: and, as for honesty, or doing what's right between man and man, I'll not turn my back to the longest winded deacon on your Patent.'[7]

More than twenty years later, when (in *The Prairie*) the gaunt old man leads less experienced travellers to the scanty shelter of hillocks or buffalo-hides, his honesty and sturdy independence are still untouched, and he dies, as Chingachgook had done earlier, with his dignity unimpaired. The consistency of the hunter's principles, necessary for the underpinning of the whole sequence, is demonstrated also as a matter of character-drawing by contrast with certain people holding less acceptable private codes of conduct – boastful Richard Jones and greedy Sheriff Doolittle in *The Pioneers*, for example, or callously deceitful Harry March in *The Deerslayer* and overbearing Ishmael in *The Prairie*. In the sense that he is an upright, honest, loyal and courageous man, Natty Bumppo is a hero of traditional mould: in the sense that he is an embodiment of a land and a way of life, he is a large, mythical, generalised figure.

However we choose to view this character, the books could not work as stories without him, nor could they work without the identification of character with setting. In terms of the plot, each book consists of a succession of chases, captures, escapes and shoot-outs, but in terms of imaginative force they hold the attention because of the immediacy of the telling. We forget the loquacity of the characters and the interpolated passages of historical explanation, the genteel courtships which not even the backwoods energy of some of the young ladies can animate, when we come to one of the incomparable passages where action and description fuse in the most precise, compelling, detailed narrative – the movements of canoes in the darkness between one wooded point at the lakeside and another, the skirmish between rival parties of Indians at a river-crossing, the hurling of axes and arrows at the captured Hawkeye in an Iroquois camp, the siege of the fort hidden among the Thousand Islands, a buffalo stampede on the prairie – these and scores of other scenes have a unity of purpose, of tempo and of atmosphere which is the mark of the classic, lasting adventure story.

Another frontier in the 1830s and 1840s was evoked by Mark Twain some forty years later than Cooper, when he recreated the small town of his boyhood, Hannibal on the Mississippi, under the name of St Petersburg. Like Fenimore Cooper, he viewed the past with nostalgia stiffened by a purpose, the purpose of criticising the changes made in the name of progress and encouraging the growth of materialism. Because *Tom Sawyer* was written for young readers, the comment is implied only, in the celebration of the freedom and enterprise of childhood. The Preface, superscribed from Hartford in 1876, expresses a genial intention:

> Although my book is intended mainly for the entertainment of boys and girls, I hope it will not be shunned by men and women on that account, for part of my plan has been to try pleasantly to remind adults of what they once were themselves, and of how they felt and thought and talked, and what queer enterprises they sometimes engaged in.[8]

Though Tom Sawyer and his friends delight in escaping to the woods, it is really only a partial freedom which they claim. Jackson's Island, where the gang proposes to set up as outlaws, is a refuge from the domestic demands and retributions of daily life; besides, it is coloured by the romantic tales of pirates or Robin Hood with which Tom directs his plans:

> About two o'clock in the morning the raft grounded on the bar two hundred yards above the head of the island, and they waded back and forth until they had landed their freight. Part of the little raft's belongings consisted of an old sail, and this they spread over a nook in the bushes for a tent to shelter their provisions; but they themselves would sleep in the open air in good weather, as became outlaws.
>
> They built a fire against the side of a great log twenty or thirty steps within the sombre depths of the forest, and then cooked some bacon in the frying-pan for supper, and used up half of the corn 'pone' stock they had brought. It seemed glorious sport to be feasting in that wild free way in the virgin forest of an unexplored and uninhabited island, far from the haunts of men, and they said they would never return to civilization.[9]

But it is not long before hunger, cold and the fearsome, un-expected pangs of homesickness drive them back to the security of grown-ups and discipline. There are no true loners here, no free spirits attuned to nature: for them, nature is only a stone's throw from Aunt Polly's whitewashed fence. The limits which Mark Twain had set himself are clearly indicated in the conclusion which, as omniscient author, he places unselfconsciously after a final sentence in which Tom's boon companion, Huckleberry Finn, seems to accept the romantic role-playing which hides the routine of everyday:

> So endeth this chronicle. It being strictly the history of a boy, it must stop here; the story could not go much further without becoming the history of a man.[10]

Enriched by the discovery of hidden treasure, Huckleberry Finn, who has lived rough in St Petersburg, abandoned by his profligate father and feared by sober citizens as a bad influence, is adopted by the Widow Douglas; he is persuaded to accept civilisation by Tom's promise that they will form a secret gang of robbers, 'more high-toned' than pirates and obliged to enter into strangely alluring forms of initiation. When Mark Twain left Huck here he was still 'a boy': when he returned to him, he still intended his character to be a boy, though planning a far more drastic escape than any which Tom Sawyer's romantic soul had envisaged.

When Huck Finn decamps from St Petersburg it is not primarily to escape from domestic constraints, however irksome these may seem to him, but to avoid a confrontation with his father, who has come to reclaim him on hearing of the money invested for him; although Huck has a shrewdness and resource beyond his years, he still lacks the experience to stand up to a determined and ruthless adult. Jackson's Island is not his goal, but the starting point for a journey downriver on a raft which takes him deep into the South and brings danger and problems far beyond most of the cliché-adventures which Tom contrives from books. All the same, *The Adventures of Huckleberry Finn* belongs in the same category as *The Adventures of Tom Sawyer*. Indeed, it seems a pity that the close scrutiny given to 'the greatest American novel' by so many critics has made it hard to read the book as a story, with the same expectations that one had as a child.

Psychiatric comment on Mark Twain's dislike of being labelled as a comic writer, 'a buffoon' as he put it, makes one almost embarrassed at enjoying the rich humour of the book, even when one takes in also the irony and melancholy, the lurking distaste, the farcical sordidness of some of the characters – the skull beneath the comic skin. As a story claimed by children, as well as by adults, the book has been read first of all as a sequel to *Tom Sawyer*; Mark Twain gave it the subtitle 'Tom Sawyer's Comrade' and it can be approached with the same anticipation of role-playing and retribution which are satisfied by the earlier book. The idea of a boy escaping the shackles of domestic propriety is immediately appealing to young readers and so is the method of escape. Whatever symbols an adult interpretation may attach to Huck's raft, to a child it is part of the dream of freedom and independence in which he can avoid the uncomfortable fact that home-made rafts tend to collapse.

None-the-less, the beguiling action and idiom of *Huckleberry Finn* contain layers of meaning, clusters of imagery, which work on the imagination even though young readers, held by incidents and scenes, are not consciously aware of the moral complexities and the trenchant social comment in Huck's adventures – indeed, they may be bored or puzzled by such parts of the story as the crazy obligations of the feud between the Grangerfords and the Shepherdsons or the tortuous schemes of the confidence tricksters self-styled the Duke of Bilgewater (sic) and the exiled King of France.

Accepting Huck Finn as a boy-hero, children are able to regard as perfectly natural the way he sees through the pretensions of villains while still remaining with them. They will understand in simple terms the difficult decision Huck has to make, whether to do his civic duty and betray Jim, the runaway slave who has joined him on his journey, or whether to keep his secret in loyalty to a friend.

They may well feel less ill at ease than adults do with the change towards the end of the book from a harsh, sardonic description of corrupt people to a farcical return to boyish fantasy, when Tom reappears to plan the elaborate, book-oriented and totally unnecessary rescue of Jim (who, as Tom knows perfectly well, has already been freed by his owner). They may sense that Huck, though he too is an escaper, keeps his lifeline to civilisation: the raft is his home, his point of reference on the river and his link with the town he is unwilling entirely to give up. The raft, in fact, is from the point of view of a young reader the significant centre of the book. For an adult it is the river, impersonal and outside civilisation but admitting to its banks a succession of imperfect, greedy and sordid men, which is the true centre, the concrete embodiment of Mark Twain's assertion of the creative, natural world which he has seen threatened in the name of progress. Huck Finn, layabout and free soul though he is, is not the mouthpiece of a philosophy of nature in the way that Natty Bumppo is. It is the author, speaking through description, through the innocent common sense and honesty of his central character, through the breadth of Huck's involuntary experience, who expresses his theme.

Fenimore Cooper and Mark Twain described certain frontier events from what might be called nowadays a conservation stand-point. Far more common is the tale of the migration of a family or a group of would-be settlers from the known to the unknown – the plot of *The Pioneers*, as it were, recast from the point of view of Judge Temple rather than of Natty Bumppo. The numerous stories of the opening up of North America or Australia are based on the assumption that the duty of man is to impose on the wilderness his own patterns of society. A pioneer's luggage will include the Bible, the gun and the frying-pan; his mental equipment will only rarely include a scientific spirit of enquiry. The migratory families will become attuned to the land and to its indigenous inhabitants mainly through conquest, through visibly *changing* nature for their own purposes. Adventure – that is, the meeting of unexpected challenges – is subordinate to husbandry.

The pioneer story is particularly well suited to young readers, especially when it has a dynastic theme – for example, in Elizabeth Coatsworth's Maine journey in *Away Goes Sally*, Hesba Brinsmead's *Longtime Passing* with its tale of a family establishing itself in unexplored Tasmania, Elsie Locke's tale of the Small family making a permanent home in Lyttelton, New Zealand, *The Runaway Settlers*, and the classic Little House sequence by Laura Ingalls Wilder. These are essentially family stories (based, in fact, on actual family records) and they can modify the dangers of pioneering days because of the interaction of young and adult characters and the guidance available to the children concerned. There will be an element of *rite de passage* in such books, explicit or implied, but the young will grow with the active help of their elders. The appalling sufferings and incredible endurance of the young Sagers, described by An Rutgers van der Loeff in *Children on the Oregon Trail* and vouched for in contemporary documents, are exceptions to a general rule that pioneer children will be protected as they grow through danger towards adulthood.

So when frontier tales for young readers are in question we would expect a certain sense of wonder and surprise in the characters and a courage and endurance leading to a personal growth of outlook, a growth more obvious than it would be after they have reached maturity. We would expect dangers and disasters to be presented honestly but without cynicism and with at least some mitigation of the sordidness of greed, political deceit and territorial aggression present in adult novels in the genre (although such elements are often smoothed out or omitted in stories of a more romantic kind for adults).

At the same time the earliest frontier tales for the young, many of them starting as serials in the family magazines of the Victorian period, reflected as a prime duty the increasingly imperialistic attitudes of the time and the abiding sense of British superiority to the races already in occupation in the lands chosen for settlement. If it is natural to the young people central in such stories to be surprised and delighted by novel sights and experiences, their response is usually modified by an air of rectitude which is mercifully absent when we come to the young explorers of the twentieth century.

This double attitude is particularly evident in the proliferation of frontier tales set in New South Wales and, more rarely, in other parts of Australia. This continent, newer to the public mind than Africa or North America, offered attractively unusual material with which well-used plots of danger and endeavour could be rejuvenated: yet strangeness is seldom a deep influence on the characters.

One of the earliest Australian emigrant-tales, Anne Bowman's *The Kangaroo Hunters*, introduced a middle-class family whose social preconceptions are little altered by the hazards of a long journey through New South Wales. Yet there is a genuine sense of wonder in their reaction to their first sight of a kangaroo, killed (rather oddly) by a boa constrictor; it must be added, though, that the title of the book reflects a far from conservationist point of view:

> The kangaroo, which was but a young one, not standing more than four feet in height, was extricated from the murderous grasp of the boa; but was almost flattened by the powerful pressure. The boys gathered round the strange animal with great curiosity, lost in admiration of its graceful form, powerful hind legs, and pretty small head. The long ears, divided upper lip, like that of the hare, long tapering tail, and remarkable pouch, in which a very young animal was found, were all remarked before it was skinned and turned over to the cooks. The skin was then washed, and spread to dry, to be converted into boots when those useful articles of clothing should be needed.[11]

The Mayburns are seeking a new life for the sake of Mr Mayburn, a country rector recently widowed and able to afford to

277

uproot his three children so as to indulge his interest in natural history. Physically weak and indolent by temperament, he leaves the way open for sixteen-year-old Margaret and her younger brother Arthur to give a lead to the younger Hugh, their orphaned friend Gerald and their two young servants. It is their courage and their appetite for exploring new places and facing new experiences which dominate the book, yet their characters are already fixed and they take for granted their father's behaviour towards two friendly Aborigines:

> . . . it was with deep concern that Mr Mayburn saw the perfect indifference with which Baldabella regarded the religious worship of the family. She looked at first much astonished to see men and women kneel down, and to hear the solemn prayers pronounced by Mr Mayburn; but she soon turned carelessly away to dig for worms, or to collect sticks for the fire.
>
> Not so the little Nakinna; for, after observing the devotions two or three times, she walked up to Margaret, knelt down by her, lifted up her little hands and seemed to listen with interest, though she could not yet understand. This act of docility and obedience was very gratifying to her kind instructress, who anxiously wished for the time when a mutual understanding might render it possible to communicate to these heathens a knowledge of the truth.[12]

Insensitive towards the Aborigines, firmly condemnatory towards bushrangers encountered on their travels, Mr Mayburn remains true to his class and his period through an exacting journey.

The middle-class, well-to-do Mayburns are not unlike the Swiss Robinsons in the way they maintain their own standards in a new country. The imperialistic attitude is somewhat less oppressive in the numerous magazine stories which describe the emigration (which may be assisted or illicit) of village or slum boys escaping the threats of the workhouse or the cruelty of step-parents, or the fortunes of lads transported for minor offences earning freedom and prosperity after serving their time. In most of the stories of this kind an initial authenticity soon gives place to the kind of adventure expected of serial stories; bushrangers, gold and hidden enemies abound and there is little time for the author to describe any truly individual response to the new land. These tales also show a strong element of social propaganda; it is clear that one purpose behind them is to encourage members of the artisan class to take their skills and their strength to the new settlements in Australia.

Whether as settlers or visitors, the characters in such stories, meeting new experience with interest and excitement, still seek to perpetuate their own social pattern. Whatever we might expect of the youths in their middle and late teens who are usually central to these tales, the terror and allurement of the unknown will be tamed to some extent, when younger children are in question, by an emphasis on housewifery, on the domestic details of making a home in a wilderness. A sod-house carved out of a bank, a covered wagon, a tent, a log hut, can all become home because of the presence of parents, and the world outside can be explored in a spirit of adventure but with help and safety close at hand. The child as a member of a pioneer party will not as a rule be required to act alone nor will more be demanded than he is capable of giving to the enterprise. On the other hand the presence of adults and the mature framework of the plot in this type of story aids credibility for the very reason that children do not act alone; events can be seen in many ways and with many degrees of danger and a certain breadth can be assured, something not easy to achieve if children face a wilderness alone.

The child in a pioneering family, or a family living beyond the frontier of so-called civilisation, may feel at home in his environment, may indeed acquire a special, detailed knowledge of it, as Badge Lorenny does, for instance, in Nan Chauncy's three stories set in a remote part of Tasmania in our own century. Even so, in *Tiger in the Bush, Devil's Hill* and *The Roaring '40* the land and the landscape remain backgrounds for enterprise and adventure, and the boy investigates the strange and unknown in order to add them to the familiar dimensions of home. Nan Chauncy uses her material with a double standard. The isolated district where Badge has his home, and the unfamiliar domestic contrivances like the rope-bridge over the river, are imbued with a romantic flavour for her readers while being entirely familiar and comforting to the boy himself. This deliberate contrast of attitudes gives the books their particular credibility; adventure has been domesticated without losing its bright colour.

The close attachment that Badge feels for his environment cannot be taken for granted while urbanisation increasingly affects Australia, as it affects every part of the world. Joan Phipson is clearly pointing to the danger of alienation from the land in *The Way Home*, a remarkable story part adventure and part speculative fiction. A brother, sister and cousin driving with an aunt from Sydney to Adelaide are separated from her after the car is overturned by a flash flood. A situation alarming enough to city children is intensified as time shifts to force them into a kind of ab-evolution. Lost in the past, viewing the making of their continent, two of them survive because they learn to trust a mysterious presence; cousin Richard, arrogant and unimaginative,

279

finds it unbearable that he is no longer in control of circumstances and scorns Prue's vision of their helper:

> 'I can see everything there is to see. I can see everything a rational person can be expected to see in this place. I hope I never see anything else.'[13]

He does see the female figure, once, and calls it a 'hater': because he can no longer relate to this being, who is nature herself, he dies, while his cousins survive. The depth of meaning here has stretched the adventure-story formula to its limits.

Every child is an explorer in his own world: every corner of it is a frontier to him. There are in fact many elements, often seeming to be contradictory, in a child's attitude to his surroundings – his reactions, if you like, to the natural world. He may, as we have seen, regard an exotic background as perfectly ordinary. Conversely, he may choose to change the ordinary and familiar into the exotic by a deliberate but playful exercise of imagination and, pre-eminently, imagination fed by books. The interrelation of literature and life is illustrated over and over again in the continuous traditions of the adventure story, and never more clearly than in the scores of junior stories which seem to stem from one source, Richard Jefferies' *Bevis*.

Jefferies could have made, with some justification, the claim familiar in our own time, that he wrote for himself first and for children afterwards, for Bevis is a rearrangement, a remembering of the days he and his brother spent in and around the 'lake', Coate Reservoir near Swindon. Like Bevis and his friend Mark in the story, the boy Richard and his brother Harry viewed the fields and waterways as places to be explored and made their own, as a kingdom where they could be at least relatively free from the claims of everyday life and where the store of exciting situations, of desert islands and ancient wars, amassed through the books they read, could be used in extended games. Looking back at the 1850s from thirty years on, Jefferies reconstructed the past in a book whose leisurely manner masks a careful organising of small events and scenes within two main centres of action, a mock 'war' on the model of the conflict between Caesar and Pompey and a brilliantly contrived sojourn on a 'desert island'.

Jefferies' own emotional bonds with nature are implicit everywhere in the book, in the devoted descriptive detail which keeps the *place* of the story precisely before the eyes of the reader. Ultimately it amounts to identification of boy with nature, but in its deepest form it is expressed *only* by the author. In the chapter

'Bevis's Zodiac' he gives us an extended vision of sky and stars as the boy sees them, wakeful at night. There is a deepening of style here which almost casts back to the fantasy-style of *Wood Magic* in which Bevis as a very small boy is able to communicate with trees, animals, wind, and to feel in direct relation to them. But *Bevis* is a tale of adventure and not a prose-poem of imagination, and Jefferies does not try to impose any mystical interpretations of the landscape on his young characters. Bevis, he remarks, 'did not think: we have done the thinking, the analysis for him. He felt and was lost in the larger consciousness of the heavens'.[14]

Landscape comes across in the book first as the author's emotional habitation and then as a world in which the boys exercise their practical skills and their imagination with equal joy and zest. It is first of all a real world, minutely observed as a part of the action. Here, for example, is Bevis trying out the raft made of part of a packing-case carefully caulked with moss, clay and a torn-up handkerchief:

> Round the bend the brook floated him gently, past the willow where the wood-pigeon built (he was afraid to come near his nest while they were about), past the thick hawthorn bushes white with may-bloom, under which the blackbirds love to stay in the hottest days in the cool shadow by the water. Where there were streaks of white sand sifted by the stream from the mud, he could see the bottom: under the high bank there was a swirl as if the water wrestled with something under the surface: a water-rat, which had watched him coming from a tiny terrace, dived with a sound like a stone dropped quietly in: the stalks of flags grazed the bottom of the raft, he could hear them as it drew on: a jack struck and rushed wildly up and down till he found a way to slip by . . .[15]

The immediacy of the description comes partly from the overseeing eye of the author who is rearranging details exactly remembered and partly from the unanalytic, practical eye of the boy assessing these details as they affect his particular aims – in this case, the challenge of making a raft which will be strong and watertight and will enable him to explore, with Mark, the superb unknown world of the 'New Sea'. The sea (that is, the reservoir) is new to them (they are only now able to explore it, because they have learned to swim at last) but it is also familiar in the sense that it is not far from their homes and the landscape has not altered.

Imagination comes in now, to extend both time and space. Quickly, in the elliptical dialogue possible between close companions, Bevis and Mark change a local reservoir into an ocean whose shores can be Africa or the ancient Aegean, whose flora and fauna must be renamed (rabbits become kangaroos, yellow-hammers are 'gold dust birds', bulrushes are bamboos). The translation is perfectly serious and perfectly conscious. So flexible are their fancies that they can play alternate roles without any bother. As they circumnavigate the New Sea they are sometimes explorers and sometimes 'savages'. Mark suggests: 'We ought to see ourselves on the shore with spears and things when we are sailing round' and Bevis agrees at once, 'So as not to be able to land for fear', and they enjoy the thought of 'seeing them dancing and shouting with bows and arrow-sticks, and yelling' while adding 'That's you and me'. 'Of course.'[16] There is obviously a special piquancy in manipulating their fancy in this way and while they are anxious to make their adventures as authentic (that is, as true to book-tradition) as they can, they do not allow their comfort to be impaired. When they are tired of living on the rabbits they have shot (with a matchlock elaborately constructed from bits and pieces) they arrange for a friendly farm-labourer to do some shopping for them:

> . . . potted meat, and tongues, and soups, that would save cooking, only it was not quite proper. But Mark got over that difficulty by supposing that they fetched them from the wreck before it went to pieces.[17]

The candid, comical ambiguities in which their adventures are worked out are seen most clearly in the 'shipwreck' in which ingenuity and the influence of books come close together. In their exploration of the New Sea the voyagers have discovered more than one island and they organise their own Robinsonnade on the one they call New Formosa. They are entirely practical in choosing a moment when the grown-ups are preoccupied with other affairs and easily arrange for a supposed visit to a friendly neighbour which is not likely to be checked for some days; wisely, they also persuade a small boy to signal from the 'mainland' every day that all is well at home, making sure that Charlie believes they are merely camping in the woods on the opposite side of the lake.

There are greater difficulties in making the shipwreck convenient, secret and authentic, all at the same time. They must first carry the necessary supplies and tools across to the island: then they must get their ship, the raft 'Pinta', back to the mainland, so that nobody will come looking for them: finally, they must be shipwrecked to their own satisfaction, and this they manage with the help of their 'catamarans', made of planks. Careful planning, inventive fancy and practical skills keep them on the island,

undiscovered, for eleven days, during which moods of bad conscience and boredom alternate with delight in escaping the
'stupid silliness' of everyday life and the satisfaction of taking
at least some of their supplies – fish, duck, rabbits – from the
land.

The shores of the Coate Reservoir were to the two boys a
frontier at once unknown and familiar – familiar in family conversation and proximity, unknown because they choose to make
it so through their fantasy. They are always in control of their
environment even as they pretend that it offers them a challenge.
Their power over it lies in that acute, close observation with
which the young, like hive bees or young birds, gradually learn
their surroundings by establishing and extending landmarks.
In a place where they are already settled by family residence,
the boys assert claims like any other settlers on a frontier by a
gradual process of domestication – finding water, food, shelter,
a routine.

Memory played its part, more than forty years later, in an
adventure-game closely related to *Bevis*, *Brendon Chase* by
'B. B.'. Like Jefferies, 'B.B.' (the pseudonym of the artist, Denys
Watkins-Pitchford) is a countryman whose view of a particular
landscape (in his case, north-west Northamptonshire) depends on
the accuracy of a naturalist and the intense vision of a craftsman-
artist. Like Jefferies, he has set most of his stories in the past of
his own boyhood, reflecting rural society and manners in the
1920s. Like Jefferies, he sends the young adventurers of *Brendon
Chase* to the frontier of their home: a mere eight miles takes them
from the constriction of their known world at Cherry Walden to
the unknown acres of the royal forest visited once on a family
occasion and, to them, illimitable.

The Hensman brothers (Robin fifteen, John thirteen and
Harold twelve) have a somewhat more cogent motive for
escaping the 'stupid silliness' of everyday life than the motive of
enlivening a long holiday which inspired Bevis and Mark. While
their parents are in India the Hensman boys live with a strict aunt
with whom understanding seems impossible: existence with her is
tolerable only because of their instinctive love of the countryside
and the freedom they can snatch within it. The original plan is in
fact to escape from the rigours of boarding school. At the end of
the Easter holidays, even as trunks are being packed, Robin in a
fit of boredom and disenchantment suggests, 'Why shouldn't we
live in the forest like Robin Hood and his merry men?'[18] Circumstances change when Harold develops measles. With a far worse
prospect than school in view – quarantine with Aunt Ellen and

lessons with the vicar – escape becomes essential. In the best traditions of adventure stories, a night-flight is safely accomplished and a base is set up in a huge hollow tree in the heart of the Chase, where Harold eventually joins his brothers.

As the exploits of Bevis and Mark were built round the legends of Odysseus and sundry desert-island tales, so the Hensmans model their actions, and their language, on the exploits of Robin Hood. They succeed in their plan to stay hidden until their parents come home on leave – in fact, from April until the New Year – by virtue of borrowing from civilisation as well as by making sensible use of natural resources. With the family gun lifted from the guardianship of Aunt Ellen's factotum, they shoot pigeons and rabbits and duck, while satisfying their romantic leanings by making bows and arrows, slings and spears. There are fish in a secluded lake which is one of the most satisfying discoveries in their territory. Early in their sojourn they are lucky enough to kill a young pig strayed from the secluded cottage of Smokoe Joe, and their later alliance with him, which they readily justify to themselves as a legitimate extension of outlaw life, is important both for their health (the produce from his vegetable garden is handy) and their emotional security.

The romantic/literary basis of the Hensmans' outlawry is confirmed by the books which they take with them to the Chase:

> Robin had brought back with him from the Dower House, his beloved Thoreau's *Life in the Woods, The Amateur Poacher* by Richard Jefferies, and *Bevis, the Story of a Boy* by the same author. Big John had chosen *Huckleberry Finn* and Little John, *Tom Sawyer*.[19]

The Chase is explored and realised in a practical spirit but with the associations of books converting such everyday chores as the collecting of wood or the patching of clothes into an attractive part of living like outlaws. In all this rearrangement of ordinary life the land, the country, the patterns of nature are accepted without any introspection. Because the adventure is shared, it never becomes alarming or even more than mildly uncomfortable. Little John suffers a moment of enlargement from which he quickly recoils:

> He shut his eyes for a moment and felt the warm breath of the fire and smelt the reek of wood smoke. Then he opened his eyes again and floated away among the stars. Some were larger than others and hung solemnly regarding him, others wavered and blinked, one small orange-coloured star seemed to jig up and down.
>   Little John began to think about the stars and planets, of how

many were worlds and others were worlds to be or which were dead, like the moon. A foolish thought passed through his mind. They were like people, he was a God, seeing them all at a glance in various stages of creation. Then he began to feel frightened at the immensity of it all and his own littleness and at last he was glad to roll over and come to earth and watch the cosy flame-light playing about the faces of his brother outlaws.[20]

Through Robin, solely, 'B.B.' suggests a close bond with nature which is implicit all through the book in the way he sets the scene in a panorama of weather and the changing seasons. Robin is presented as a loner, a boy for whom nature is a necessity: from time to time he wanders away from the others and moves out of the mood of adventure-games and the Robin Hood role to a quiet, receptive response to the place which is the true motive force and centre of the book. Here he meets and merges with the author and fulfils the author's intention. Like *Bevis*, the story of the Brendon Chase outlaws is a rousing, plausible and often comical adventure whose basic emotional power is all the stronger for being secret and almost totally unexpressed.

The descent of *Brendon Chase* from *Bevis* is very clear. *Bevis* may also be one source of inspiration for the group of holiday-adventures published during the thirties and forties which were themselves the inspiration of innumerable imitations, Arthur Ransome's 'Swallows and Amazons' books. In an Author's Note written in 1958 for a reprint edition Ransome explained that *Swallows and Amazons* 'almost wrote itself' out of enduring memories of his own childhood when he and his brother and sisters spent their holidays on a farm at the south end of Coniston Water. Here, once more, as with Jefferies and 'B.B.', an author is recreating and rearranging a childhood for the purposes of fiction – and of nostalgia. He is contriving, as it were, a postpone-ment of adulthood, not of the tortured, obsessive kind which lies behind *Peter Pan* nor with the moral complexity of *Huckleberry Finn* but with a desire thrown upon the characters, but satisfying the author in maturity, to enjoy the exhilaration of indepen-dence, of contriving, of an imitative housekeeping, which in its degrees of responsibility could be partly a game and partly a rehearsal for adult life. As Hugh Brogan showed in *The Life of Arthur Ransome*, he was also paying a friendly compliment to the Adounyan family who visited him often in his home in the Lake District; the four Adounyan children were to some extent at least the models for the Walkers, though it seems that in his later years Ransome was not prepared to acknowledge this.

The 'Swallows' – Susan, John, Titty and Roger Walker – are not extending the known frontiers of their homeground, as Bevis and the Hensmans were. They are on holiday in the Lake District for the first time, knowing the lake and its shores only through their mother's reminiscences of her own holidays there. The holidays are to be their own, not an escape from adult supervision but a campaign allowed and encouraged (but ultimately controlled) by Mother. The stories in the sequence, particularly the first two (*Swallows and Amazons* and *Swallowdale*) are dominated by protocol; the four children are constantly having to decide how much help to accept from the adult home base and how much they can find out for themselves. When the boat *Swallow* is wrecked in shallow water (in *Swallowdale*), John, whose sea-man's pride is deeply wounded, doggedly works out a salvage plan and gets the vessel to shore before he accepts, with his usual common sense, the advice and instruction of James Turner (the essential Omniscient Uncle of adventure-story tradition) so that *Swallow* can be repaired.

The camping adventure on Wild Cat Island is carefully organised, with boatloads of provisions and equipment; there is no pretence of being 'wrecked' but the harbour for landing and the campsite are their own choice. The famous telegram from their father, who is on active service in Malta, emphasises the adult intention behind the adventure – 'Better drowned than duffers if not duffers won't drown'. By custom and for practical reasons, parents must be removed at the outset of holiday-adventures, but they will only retire to the background under conditions. John and Susan have already done a great deal of sailing in Falmouth Harbour under their father's instruction, and all four children can swim (seven-year-old Roger with one foot on the bottom, though).

In fact, the adventures in the 'Swallows and Amazons' books seem remarkably sedate to readers nearly half a century later. Hailed as classics in the years immediately following the Second World War, they inevitably suffered a decline in popularity thereafter because of demands for greater realism in circumstance and a wider range of social classes, and demands also for shorter, more compact forms of narrative to meet the taste of generations brought up with television. Even a scant ten years after the publication of *Swallows and Amazons* and while its sequels were still appearing, Mary Treadgold in her uncompromisingly realistic wartime tale *We Couldn't Leave Dinah* threw oblique doubts on Ransome's attitudes. As the children who had rashly escaped the evacuation from the fictionalised Channel Island of Clerinel gloomily trudge the road in search of a hiding-place from the occupying German forces, Mick complains that they look ridiculous in fancy dress and their escapade is 'frightfuily *silly* . . . not exciting like real book-adventure . . .' and his sister Caroline remarks, 'Just think how the Arthur Ransome children would dote on it.'[21] This trick to suggest the authenticity of a piece of fiction is common enough, but there is also a point of literary fashion here to be noted.

Ransome's genius as a story-teller is not likely to be fully recognised until his books are read as period pieces (in the way that E. Nesbit, for instance, is read now) so that their social and emotional content are seen in proportion and not as awkward or incomprehensible *alternatives* to the world of today. Read with a sense of history, the tales can be seen as inspired examples of the way children learn to relate to the challenge of a new place. It does not matter that the challenge is relatively mild (even when Roger and Titty are lost in a sudden hill fog, in *Swallowdale*, the period of real danger is brief and help is near at hand). What matters is that the children set themselves to learn, to earn their independence by drawing on their own resources, by discussing and assessing possibilities, by practising skills (sailing, Morse code, sledging, digging a water supply, assaying for gold through charcoal-burning) and above all, by map-making.

If there is any basic activity which most clearly represents the purposive element of the 'Swallows and Amazons' books, it is the making of maps. It is true that the names that appear on the map of the lakeside, as it is constructed in the minds of the exploring Walkers, are romantic rather than authentic. The lake and its shores are explored, not traced through the purchase of Ordnance Survey sheets. The North and South Poles are established, logically, at either end of the lake: the town on the shore is Rio, the hill above Swallowdale is Kanchenjunga.

This is all part of the continuous recreating of circumstance by which, in dialogue and behaviour, the holiday environment is claimed through private associations. The Walkers are never merely themselves (they are mariners or explorers or castaways or Eskimos but not in exactly the same sense); while John and Susan (in the early teens when the adventures begin) are able to switch in and out of roles easily enough, and Susan indeed is always halfway to being an adult, the younger Titty and Roger are consistent in imagining themselves other than they are. Where John refers to the moor, as they walk overland, Titty speaks of 'desert uplands'. Events which in the hand of lesser writers would remain ordinary are irradiated with a humour that comes from the double view of sense and fancy. Exploring part of the mainland, following directions from their friends the Blacketts (the Amazons), the Walkers surround a long walk with the attractive embellishment of stalking and tracking, but not from a common angle of vision:

> He [John] crawled carefully out from among the trees, looking this way and that.
> 'All clear,' he said, and the four explorers rushed headlong towards the great tree with low wide-spreading branches that grew at the very edge of the river.
> 'The Amazon,' said Titty solemnly. 'We ought to lie full length beside it and dip water with our hands to cool our parching throats.'
> 'Why,' said Susan, 'it's no time since you had an apple.'[22]

By constant verbal alterations (spoken out, mumbled or simply voiced in her thoughts), Titty translates the landscape she sees into the countries of her reading. The most sensitive of the Walker children, she falls most deeply into pretence and is far more seriously frightened when pretence threatens to become reality. When she is alone on Wild Cat Island and has to decide whether an approaching boat, alarmingly near in the dark, means a pirate attack or the passing of actual thieves, she calls upon a courage impressive because it is won by reconciling the real and the imagined with a real effort of will. There is always a basis of practical sense in Titty but it is not always easy for her to find and use it. The moments of true emotional tension in the stories come most often through her (in *Pigeon Post* most strikingly, when she faces the fact that she is a natural dowser) and a good deal of the humour also comes from the two facets of her nature – for example, when she wishes for the solitary watch on the island which proves so unexpectedly unpleasant:

> . . . [she] longed to have Wild Cat Island all to herself, to be a lonely lighthouse keeper, to be Robinson Crusoe, and to feel just what a real desert island was like. A blanket would do for a goat-skin.[23]

The contrast between the landscape as it is and the landscape as the Walker children choose to see it provides an element of humour in the books and ensures that the didactic or instructive aspect never becomes oppressive. Ransome keeps control of time in his stories; as the Walkers grow older their adventures become correspondingly more exacting. Where exploration was considerably assisted (though surreptitiously and tactfully) in the two earliest holidays, in *Secret Water*, some time later, the children are set down on a salt marsh on the East Coast to explore for a set period entirely on their own. The challenge put forward perfectly seriously by their father is that they must work from a rough chart, noting details of tides and the covering and uncovering of sandbanks, confirming contours – in short, making a proper map from their own observations and without help. The Walkers decorate the duty laid on them in their own way and, as explorers, they soon find themselves threatened by hidden enemies, so that an elaborate game of tracking, 'native' attacks and battles, is erected on the simple basis of making friends with local children. Romantic needs ensure that the well-organised holiday counts as being 'marooned', but the map-making proceeds with more technical expertise than the exploring of the lake did in the earlier books.

The particularly reassuring balance between everyday reality and its extension through image and mood in the 'Swallows and Amazons' stories is a matter of craftsmanship as well as of temperament. Ransome was well aware that the tone of *We Didn't Mean to Go to Sea* was different from the other adventures of the Walkers. He wrote in a letter:

> The trouble is that one single incident fills the book, that reality presses so hard on the children that there is no room or need for romantic transfiguration of fact, and so on.[24]

It is this 'transfiguration of fact' which will keep his books alive; in spite of his comment, it *is* present in the sea-adventure, in a different way.

Ransome's major contribution to the genre of holiday-adventure is probably not the quiet reality of his characters, though this counts for much: in children's fiction, personality and the intereffects of personality and action have been strikingly developed as a result of the demands of a wider readership than Ransome's original one. The enduring value of Ransome is surely his power to communicate the feel and the influence of a place.

This is by no means the same thing as a power of description. His own memories of places, and of Coniston in particular, act as a continuous undersong in the books, but they are seldom expressed by the author intruding on the story, and when he does allow himself as it were an unallocated passage of description, it always has a practical basis rather than being a piece of nostalgic recollection. When Roger and Titty are following a trail or patteran to the camp in Swallowdale, we seem to hear author and Titty speaking together, in a picture at once incidental and purposive:

> The compass did not seem to help. This part of the moor was covered with short grass, with patches of bracken and rocks and

loose stones, and stones not quite so loose, bedded in the ground, with ants' nests under them, if you lifted them. Here and there were thin tufts of dark green rushes, the sort of green rushes that are white when peeled and can be made into rings and plaits and even baskets. There was no track that anyone could have seen even if there had been no fog. Here and there were the sheep runs, but they ran all ways, and most from side to side of the moor and not straight along the top. It was very puzzling.[25]

For the most part landscape and lakescape are integral and dramatically arranged parts of the narrative. The adventure belongs to the children and evolves entirely from their contact with a particular place at a particular time and for a particular purpose. Ransome, by skilfully diversifying seasons and places and by introducing new characters (the Blacketts, the Ds and the members of the Coot Club), allows himself variations on the main theme of the stories, the way children learn to adapt to natural surroundings and to acquire the technique peculiar to those surroundings.

There is nothing mystical about the response of the Walkers to their environment – a response skilfully differentiated for each of them – but occasionally we are permitted to see that the games, book-derived, with which the children as it were domesticate the wild are not so romantic and jolly that they entirely mask the realities of nature. The challenges offered to them by the land do change them; they grow older in the course of the sequence and as they grow older the places they visit become familiar and unalarming because of all they have learned in exploring them. In the way the Walkers reach out to conquer a new territory there is even an imperialist touch, and yet they can be sensitive to something they cannot make their own – Titty through unbidden feelings of fear and suspense, John now and then with an unexpected intuition. While the others pack up the camp in the enchantingly secret valley they have named Swallowdale, John (who has gone to fetch milk for their farewell breakfast) looks down at the place from the hillside:

> Tents make all the difference to a place. Now, once more, it was a wild, rocky valley as it had been when first they came there. It did not look like anybody's home, and John knew that when they had gone back to Wild Cat Island, Swallowdale would look as if they had never been there. The first real flood would wash the dam at the bathing-pool away for ever. Everything would be as it had been, and their own Swallowdale, with its neat tents and cheerful fire, would be no more than a memory or something he had read about in a book. It was a queer thought, not comfortable. Still, at

the moment the cheerful fire was still burning and all the signs showed that breakfast was waiting only for the milk.[26]

The transition is careful and important. The Walkers, and in other ways the friends they include in their adventures, take in more from the settings of their holidays than they give: while they are visitors they are, as it were, at school to nature.

The particular philosophy of Ransome's books, the atmosphere and the patterns of growth and feeling which make them more than holiday-games, have seldom if ever been equalled by the scores of imitators writing in the two decades after the Second World War. The difference is especially marked in a group of three stories by Roland Pertwee whose source is obvious. The first of these, *The Islanders*, begins with a challenge very much like the challenge offered to the Walkers by Wild Cat Island and the lake shores, though this time it is not self-imposed. An elderly landowner in Devon, minded to adopt a war-orphan in memory of his own dead son, invites Patrick Faraday, a lad of twelve or so, to choose a couple of friends and enjoy a summer holiday as a test: a mile of river and five hundred acres of wood and hillside will be made over to the boys, who must find their own way to live there. Mr Beckett explains:

> 'To begin with, there'll be no roof over your heads, except of your own building, and no soft beds to sleep in. There'll be no meals either, for it'll be up to you to catch'em and cook'em as best you can. If you get into trouble you must wriggle out of it, and not come whining to me for help. That's one side of the picture – here's the other. Our Swiss friends didn't start from scratch, and I won't expect you to. They brought ashore some very useful stuff from the wreck, and I'll guarantee that you'll find equally useful stuff has been washed ashore, if you're smart enough to spot it.'[27]

Besides the obvious back-reference to the desert-island Robinsons, the educational aspect of the story harks back to the carefully limited independence which Captain Walker and his wife allowed to their children, and the famous telegram about duffers was surely in Roland Pertwee's mind when he put a final comment in Mr Beckett's mouth:

> '. . . if you can't make a living out of five hundred acres and a mile of river, you're not the chaps I hope you are, and would be better employed digging sand-castles at Margate.'[28]

Certainly a generous pile of useful objects is 'washed ashore', including tools, saucepans, cartridges, food, a goat in milk and a bundle of tangled fishing-lines (and the river contains salmon).

291

Moreover, though neither Patrick nor his ebullient friend Nick knows much about country ways, the pedantic, bespectacled Toby is a keen amateur naturalist and his eye on the outside world accounts for all that is best in the book. While he is used to some extent for comic relief, his eager exploitation of Nick's invention of a 'seethebottomscope' made from stove-pipe, originally intended as a way of locating butter lost in the river, leads to descriptions of water-plants and aquatic animals which are lively and concerned enough to be more than mere educational padding.

In fact, although it is obvious that Roland Pertwee wrote *The Islanders* out of a wish to recreate some of the fishing and camping joys of his own boyhood, he does relate his young explorers to the land, and the land itself to the unity of his story, with some degree of success. The importance of landscape in giving a special dimension to it is confirmed by the descent into cliché and contrivance in two sequels, *Rough Water* and *Operation Wild Goose*, in which a quarrel over property with certain unsavoury relatives of Mr Beckett's, and a race with Russian powers for uranium rights in Iceland, provide plots in which the actions of the three boys are only too predictable.

12. Desert Islands

The holiday of *The Islanders* was, as I have suggested, organised in the spirit of the Swiss Family Robinson, as Bevis and the Walkers had projected on to an actual landscape the associations of Odysseus, Robin Hood, Robinson Crusoe and other legendary or literary heroes. It is ultimately the spirit of Crusoe which breathes through the books I have been discussing. Frontier tales in which a place is explored and brought under domestic rule are also castaway-tales in the sense that the characters must act on their own initiative and, at least partly, without the benefits of civilisation.

The huge genre of junior adventure stories which has justly been given the name of 'Robinsonnade' is eternally enlarged and refreshed by new motives, new circumstances, new settings, but in whatever latitude the particular desert island is located, whether it is an isolated inland valley or truly surrounded by water, some combination of sand, coconut palms and heat will usually be found. These elements are not wholly derived from the primal source, *Robinson Crusoe*. As the centuries passed and the salient points of Crusoe's adventure settled into the literary consciousness, they became almost like signals evoking in readers a Pavlovian response. In a popular Robinsonnade of seventy years ago, H. de Vere Stacpoole's *Bird Cay*, the boy of fifteen who tells the story asserts the influence of that marooned hero on him:

> I could have read that book upside down, I believe, if it had been given to me to read it in no other way; as it was I had read it through, and backwards and forwards, and here and there. It was a heavy old copy with a blue and gilt cover, and two pictures were missing; but little I wanted with pictures when I could see, as clearly as though I were looking through air, the island, and the goats, and the grapes, drying in the sun and turning into raisins, Friday's footprint, and Robinson's fur cap, his two guns, and the sea washing in on the beach – I who had never seen the sea.[1]

In fact this story of a stowaway's adventures in search of buried gold, his encounters with greedy rivals and venal sea-captains, offers little atmosphere to the reader, who is left to supply his own imagined setting from a predictable sequence of sand and skeletons, waves and wickedness.

As it has developed over two and a half centuries since *Robinson Crusoe* was published, the Robinsonnade has used settings varying from the strictly geographical to the frankly fantastic; to some extent at least these settings have been pre-dominantly decorative in the case of books for entertainment, less luxurious with more philosophical works. The usual mental picture of a coral island, fertile and hospitable (the picture reflected in its most stereotyped and suggestive form in the television advertise-ment for the Bounty chocolate bar), is very distant from Crusoe's island. Though Defoe based his sturdily matter-of-fact fiction on the true circumstances of Alexander Selkirk's ordeal on Juan Fernandez, off the west coast of South America, he landed his fictional hero on an island in the Gulf of the Orinoco within sight of Trinidad in a part of the world he called the Brazils. It was at first sight a barren place, where rocks predominated and available food consisted of wild goats and turtles. If Crusoe could be excused for his lack of response to this unpromising place, we may allow ourselves to be surprised that it was not until almost a year had passed that he ventured inland and discovered a green and fertile valley where he picked limes and was later able to harvest melon, sugar cane, wild tobacco, grapes and lemons.

Although he was refreshed by the contrast between the open savannah and close forest and the bleak shore on which he had landed, he never showed any kinship with the land or any desire to adapt himself to its atmosphere. He was a survivor, not an explorer. His first reactions to the pleasant valley are typical:

> . . . the country appeared so fresh, so green, so flourishing, every-thing being in a constant verdure, or flourish of spring, that it looked like a planted garden. I descended a little of the side of that delicious vale, surveying it with a secret kind of pleasure (though mixed with other afflicting thoughts), to think that this was all my own; that I was king and lord of all this country indefensibly, and had a right of possession; and if I could convey it, I might have it in inheritance as completely as any lord of a manor in England.[2]

The national and mercantile impulse to acquire the island (the legal term 'convey' is precisely chosen) is tempered by a modera-tion which is at the centre of Crusoe's character. It is also, presumably, at the centre of Defoe's irony, as he points to the stolid, unimaginative, tenacious middle-class readers to whom he is offering 'strange surprising adventures'. He has drawn the portrait of a man thrown entirely upon his own resources in unknown country, completely alone for fifteen years and then with a companion not judged to be his equal, who is not basically changed by his experience – that is, neither the strangeness nor the solitude affect him permanently. When there are storms, he flinches and repents of his misspent life; his desire for companions is intermittent and brief; he suffers no superstitious fears of unknown presences, no mystical experiences, but an entirely natural and practical access of alarm when Caribs from the mainland visit the island. He is concerned to survive and to build a life of routine, helped by the tools and stores he has been able to carry from the wrecked ship and by the comforting measurement of time on a tally-post.

Indeed, the affecting initial entry in his journal:

> September 30th, 1659 . . . I, poor miserable Robinson Crusoe, being shipwrecked, during a dreadful storm in the offing, came on shore on this dismal, unfortunate island, which I called the ISLAND OF DESPAIR; all the rest of the ship's company being drowned and myself almost dead. . . .[3]

has a contrived air about it, for by the time the passage has been indited (on paper and with ink recovered from the ship), Crusoe has already made a shelter, a table and chair and shelves for his possessions; he has, in short, established a bourgeois home in which to settle down in the kind of moderate, middle station of life which his father had recommended to him but which, in the wildness of youth, he had rejected for the anticipated freedom of the sea.

Robinson Crusoe is hardly a romantic book, with its sturdy recitation of domestic matters and its compact, controlled moments of emotion, but equally, it cannot be called realistic, as Walter de la Mare pointed out:

> . . . if Defoe had really faced, as he might have tried to face, the problem set in *Crusoe*, his solution could not have been in that book's precise terms. All praise and thanks that it is what it is, a triumph in its kind; and yet one may pine for what, given a more creative imagination and a different Crusoe, the book might have been if the attempt had been made to reveal what a prolonged unbroken solitude, an absolute exile from his fellow-creatures, and an incessant commerce with silence and the unknown, would mean at last to the spirit of man. A steadily debasing brutish simplicity? Hallucinations, extravagances, insanities, enravishment, strange guests?
>
> Selkirk after but four years' silence was scarcely articulate. Crusoe after his eight and twenty years addresses the three strangers whom he finds trussed up on the beach with the urbanity of a prince, the courtesy of an Oriental, and in faultless Spanish . . .[4]

'A triumph in its kind' – de la Mare clearly read *Robinson Crusoe* not as a study in religious regeneration (one modern interpretation) nor as a definition of a particular social class, but as the adventure story which children, and many adults, have taken it to be, establishing as fixed points of the plot the fur hat and umbrella, the tame parrot and submissive Friday. De la Mare commented:

> Defoe descends with limpid ease to the level of the boy latent in old men and active in his heroes, and so within this narrow range comes near to being the most imaginative author the world has ever seen.[5]

His speculation about the equilibrium which Defoe allowed his hero *was* just speculation about an approach which, as he realised, Defoe never intended. His remark about articulacy needs to be considered in a different light, since this is the kind of outward symptom of an inner condition which Defoe, given the factual cumulation of his fiction, could hardly ignore. Defoe did offer at least a partial explanation for Crusoe's hold on the power of speech. First, he could address the dog which had survived the wreck, in words a degree less unsatisfying than total monologue. Then, the parrot could be taught to repeat phrases and so an illusion of conversation could be maintained. We are to accept that when after fifteen years Crusoe acquired a human companion, his tongue was therefore sufficiently well exercised to be a proper means of communication with Friday who, within the conventions of fiction, is a quick learner.

Defoe makes us believe that Crusoe remained fully articulate on his island by the same trick of offering disarmingly concrete details which he used in his other stories: we need not be aware, unless we wish to be, that he has avoided any question of mental disintegration as a result of prolonged solitude. On the contrary, he makes it clear that when Crusoe does acquire companions – after Friday, Friday's father and a Spaniard, both rescued from Carib enemies – he does not welcome them for the sake of wider conversational opportunities but for quite different reasons:

> My island was now peopled, and I thought myself rich in subjects. And it was a merry reflection, which I frequently made, how like a King I looked. First of all, the whole country was my own mere property, so that I had an undoubted right of dominion. Secondly, my people were perfectly subjected; I was absolutely lord and law giver; they allowed their lives to me, and were ready to lay down their lives, if there had been occasion for it, for me. It was remarkable, too, I had but three subjects, and they were of three different religions: my man Friday was a Protestant, his father was a Pagan and a cannibal, and the Spaniard was a Papist: however, I allowed liberty of conscience throughout my dominions.[6]

Defoe did what he set out to do, no more and no less. De la Mare's speculations about what he might have done were answered by Michel Tournier's remarkable novel, *Friday*. Here is a recognisable Robinson given existential form. The Dutch captain of the brig *Virginia* describes his twenty-two-year-old passenger as pious, parsimonious and pure; in a session with a Tarot pack he predicts:

> 'The kingdom over which you will preside will be like one of those great tidy cupboards where the women of our country keep their piles of immaculate linen scented with lavender.'. . .[7]

but his view of Robinson is not immediately, nor indeed permanently, justified.

The despairing moments of Defoe's Crusoe are no longer robustly and directly expressed; they are Freudian and introspective. In an animal access of terror, Robinson sinks into a mud wallow, from which he emerges eventually with a frantic resolve to organise life on the island he calls Speranza. This resolve is carried out in architectural fantasies of palaces and assembly rooms, a pavilion of weights and measures, a water-clock and a penal code of punishments for any relapses into uncivilised behaviour. For this excessively anxious ordering of his kingdom is interrupted by lapses, in one of which he retreats for a time into a womb-like cavern, and by equally intense moments when he tries onanistically to possess the island, his seed producing a crop of mandrake-like plants which he calls his daughters.

It is through Friday that Robinson finds (as the enigmatic subtitle perhaps suggests) 'Les Limites du Pacifique', as he gradually learns to regard the irresponsible and wayward behaviour of his usually docile servant as the right and only course; he was:

> . . . becoming ever more conscious of the gap between the image of the island projected into his mind by his garbled recollections of human society, or his reading of the Bible, and the inhuman, primitive and uncompromising world whose truth he was timidly seeking.[8]

When Friday's carelessness with an illicit tobacco-pipe destroys the dwelling-house and its contents, Robinson abandons his set habits, treats time as circular and unmeasured, and learns to worship the sun. He is at first tempted by the captain of the schooner *Heron*, when it touches the island he has been 'learning' for twenty-eight years, to return to England to preach his new philosophy; but, disgusted by the crude, greedy attitude of captain and sailors, he elects to remain outside the civilisation he distrusts. His place on the ship is taken by Friday, deserting in search of fancied advantages: the Esthonian cabin-boy crosses his path, deserting to the island to escape the cruel treatment of the crew. We are left to guess how Robinson will treat the boy and whether a new disciple and servant will corrupt the purity he has seemingly achieved in surrendering habit, education and predisposition to the island. His own musings have an ironical edge to them:

> The truth was that he was younger today than the pious and self-seeking young man who had set sail in the *Virginia*, not young with a biological youth, corrupted and harbouring the seeds of its decrepitude, but with a mineral youth, solar and divine. Every day was for him a first beginning, an absolute beginning of the history of the world. Beneath the rays of the sun-god, Speranza trembled in an eternal present, without past or future. He could not forsake that everlasting instant poised at the needle-point of a perfect ecstasy, to sink back into a world of usury, dust and decay.[9]

The searching ironies of *Friday* are repeated in a shorter, simpler way in *Friday and Robinson*, designed for young people who know their *Robinson Crusoe* and are capable of recognising the implications of the way similarities of event and attitude become vital differences. Here, again, is the hero setting out to tame the island through husbandry and law-giving, aiming to construct a version of the world he has left behind (even to the extent of dressing for dinner). Here, as in *Friday*, Robinson is seen retreating from past, present and future by burying himself in mud and by curling up in the cavern: the momentary disintegration of his personality may be all the more distressing to the reader in this junior version because it is described so briefly and bluntly. Here, again, we see Robinson learning 'how to live on a desert island' by watching his servant Friday and accepting his values as well as his domestic customs. Master and servant play out a game of identities which presages the end of the master's assumed superiority:

> They never invented anything new but always played true scenes from their past life, scenes from the days when Friday was a terrified slave and Robinson a severe master . . . The scene which Friday liked to act out the best was the first one, the one in which Robinson saved him from the Indians who wanted to kill him.
> Robinson understood that Friday liked this game because it enabled him to come to terms with his past life as a slave. And Robinson was happy to play it because he felt sorry he had been a hard master to Friday and his conscience still troubled him.[10]

Young readers who follow with understanding the total reversal of Robinson's social and emotional attitudes will have to decide how far irony is intended in the final scene. They will speculate how Robinson is likely to treat the unhappy cabin-boy. Is the boy's hope of freedom an illusion? Will the whole pattern of domination begin again? The questions raised by these two acute Robinsonnades from France go further than the pleasant sting of parody.

Friday and Robinson, if it can be called an adventure story, stands at the outward edge of a type of junior fiction which has predictably avoided the emotional challenge of life on a desert island. Tournier's Robinson elected to stay on the island for the sake of a way of life which had moved away from the bourgeois model because of a mysterious natural influence. The father of the Swiss Family elected to stay on *his* island because he had successfully reconstructed the life he had formerly known, adapting the resources of the island to his preconceived plan rather than adapting himself to the new world. If Defoe's Crusoe was a survivor and Tournier's Robinson a philosopher, the Swiss Father Robinson was essentially a colonist. He simply transferred his energies from the intended landfall, deferred by shipwreck, to the island on which he and his wife and four sons were cast away. Tenacious of purpose, he seized the opportunities offered by an uninhabited island where he could build a New Switzerland answering to the wishes of his family with no interference from the outside world, guided by a cheerful piety which held any trace of fear or doubt at bay.

From the moment when the castaways, on their improvised rafts, found a small inlet in the rocky shore and a flat beach on which to land, the means of survival and prosperity were ready to hand, either from the ship or in the island itself: the generosity of provision for the comfort of the family makes the material help available to Defoe's Crusoe seem positively meagre. In a few days the Swiss family had collected tools and domestic animals from the ship, had made a substantial tent from sailcloth, discovered coconuts and sugar cane and turtle's eggs near at hand and had enjoyed an uncommonly civilised supper:

> The meal which awaited us was as unlike the first supper we had there enjoyed as possible. My wife had improvised a table of a board laid on two casks; on this was spread a white damask table-cloth, on which were placed knives, forks, spoons, and plates for each person. A tureen of good soup first appeared, followed by a capital omelet, then slices of the ham; and finally some Dutch cheese, butter, and biscuits, with a bottle of the captain's Canary wine, completed the repast.[11]

Robinson Crusoe, telling his own story in a combination of diary entries and recollection, makes it clear that he found comfort for his solitude in using or contriving the domestic objects which recalled his past. The Swiss Robinsons had no problem of solitude to contend with nor did they need to assert an aggrandised dominion over the island. They took possession of it like settlers continuing in the wilds their accustomed family life, the kind of life which Pastor Johann Wyss, working out his fiction for his own children, wished to offer them as a model. The dust-jacket of the Macdonald edition describes the book's conclusion like this:

> And one day, when a ship anchored off shore and they were offered a passage back to civilisation, they found they could not bear to leave. Their roots had penetrated too deep into the soil of this remote island home.[12]

In fact, the Robinsons had not really become rooted in the island as they found it: rather, they had converted it to their own use, altering their way of life in very few respects and those, superficial ones. They had founded a dynasty (conveniently, a young female castaway was found on the island just when Fritz, the eldest boy, was ready to carry on the line) and when father and mother discussed the future, both agreed that they wished to 'adopt New Switzerland' as their permanent home, while their sons, free to return to Europe, 'must endeavour to send out emigrants of a good class to join us, and form a prosperous colony'.

The fortunes of these happy, God-fearing castaways were planned to suit a book intended to instruct as well as to entertain young readers. The successive adventures, each as strange and beguiling as the heterogeneous character of the island, are linked by the theme of education, and the nurture of children by responsible parents is, as it were, an image of the growth of a well-managed colony. The open didacticism of the story may provoke an occasional smile:

> I explained, as well as I could in a hurry, the principle of the lever; and promised to have a long talk on the subject of mechanics, should we have a future opportunity.[13]

But Father Robinson's lectures on the properties of flax, rubber, beeswax, gypsum and turpentine, his instant identification of the island's fauna, have never interfered seriously with the enjoyment of young readers nor have those readers been unduly troubled by the wild inaccuracies of geography and natural history consequent on the idea of an island with the global resources of the Garden of Eden. A child reading the book can fancy himself in a zoo without bars where he can be towed by a turtle, can tame a young jackal or a flamingo and ride on steeds like onager, buffalo and ostrich. Given four boys of assorted ages to identify with (boys of varying temperaments but with no inconvenient tendancy to quarrel with one another or to rebel against their parents), the young reader can enjoy vicarious adventures in an ideal setting which hardly fits the traditional epithet of 'desert' island.

The immediate popularity of this absurd and endearing book is attested by the fact that some twenty years or so after it appeared in an English version Marryat's children, when the time came for him to keep his promise of writing a book for them, begged for a sequel to *The Swiss Family Robinson*. When he read it for himself, he found it was neither 'probable nor possible' and could not undertake a true sequel. Veracity being a vital element in all his work, his comment on Wyss's licence is not surprising:

> . . . what compelled me to abandon the task was, that much ignorance, or carelessness, had been displayed in describing the vegetable and animal productions of the island on which the family had been wrecked. The island is supposed to be far to the southward, near to Van Dieman's Land; yet, in these temperate latitudes, we have not only plants, but animals introduced which could only be found in the interior of Africa or the torrid zone, mixed up with those really indigenous to the climate. This was an error which I could not persuade myself to follow up. It is true that it is a child's book; but I consider, for that very reason, it is necessary that the author should be particular in what may appear to be trifles, but which really are not, when it is remembered how strong the impressions are upon the juvenile mind. Fiction, when written for young people, should, at all events, be *based* upon the truth . . .[14]

Planning *Masterman Ready* 'in the same style', Marryat chose to land his castaways on a South Pacific island and to order his details accordingly, while having in mind their needs. His characters were just as carefully chosen. Mr Seagrave, standing for the 'theoretical' man, is to some extent equipped for his ordeal by his moral and religious beliefs and by his status as a station-owner in New South Wales; the fact that he is returning to the colony after leave, with various tools and necessities for his property, is useful in providing many basic needs for survival on the island. The 'practical' man, the sailor Masterman Ready, has been at sea for fifty years; second mate on the *Pacific*, he alone stays with the Seagrave family when the captain refuses to find room for the passengers in the lifeboat, and is rewarded for his loyalty, since boat and crew are engulfed in the storm. Respectful and hardworking, Ready organises the means of survival, cheers Mr Seagrave in moments of despair and, in the end, gives his life to save the family from an attack by cannibals, holding them off until the ship, opportunely arrived, can put them to flight.

For his part, Mr Seagrave acquires a modicum of physical aptitude to reinforce his determination to make a life for his family such as they had expected to resume in Australia. His delicate wife and four children become the audience for his lectures and the children, with Juno, their African nurse, respond to his formal and informal lessons. The island, in a sense, becomes a school, its natural forms interpreted and used as a means of education. Unlike the Swiss Father Robinson, Mr Seagrave has no wish to take possession of the island and found a colony, but to survive, in the hope of rescue, preserving his own standards of conduct and custom. His instruction is concentrated most of all on his eldest son, William, an intelligent lad of twelve at the time of the wreck, and the younger Tommy, who at six years old is headstrong and mischievous.

Information and discipline are directed to each boy in proportion to his age and temperament, Ready offering instruction in carpentry and navigation while Mr Seagrave explains the nature of colonial enterprise or rehearses the Christian dictates with which the family is to be guided. At the outset of the voyage William enquires ingenuously of the sailor Ready, with whom he has quickly struck up a friendship, 'Were you ever shipwrecked on a desolate island like Robinson Crusoe?'[15] and receives a literal answer:

> 'Yes, Master William, I have been shipwrecked; but I never heard of Robinson Crusoe. So many have been wrecked and undergone great hardships, and so many more have never lived to tell what they have suffered, that it's not very likely that I should have known that one man you speak of, out of so many.'[16]

William promises to tell him the story, but in the event he lives out the year or two on the island under a regular and unromantic régime which makes him a suitable support to his father on the family property to which he eventually succeeds: meanwhile Tommy's ebullient temper, tamed but not wholly destroyed by the educational care of his father and the old sailor, finds an appropriate niche in the army. To each member of the Seagrave family the island has been a salutary and instructive rather than an alienating experience, nor have they been changed by its essential, unique atmosphere.

The presence of adults in a book for children and the way these adults are presented are decisive factors in the tone of the whole. The Swiss castaway children and the young Seagraves, with adults in attendance, are spared the extremes of physical toil and danger and – which is more fundamental – they need not suffer from intellectual deprivation with protectors to guide and illuminate their lives. With this balance of characters, Wyss and Marryat were able to combine the playfulness, humour and ingenious surprise congenial to young readers with a moderate, sober assessment of the realities of the situation. As castaways, the adults take a long view of their plight: the children can enjoy the adventure from day to day. The substantial feeling engendered in *The Swiss Family Robinson* and *Masterman Ready* is largely due to this careful blending of young and mature attitudes.

Barbara Hardy has pointed out that *Robinson Crusoe* contains both points of approach as well. Though no children are present in the story, it has understandably become a book for children to read because Crusoe's adventures can be read in one way as fantasy and game, with his accumulation of domestic objects and animals, his 'magazines, castles, town and country houses' and his pretence of kingship, while the 'economic meaning and moral ironies'[17] of his means of, and efforts for, survival take over for adults:

> His achievements are not only . . . steps in technological develop-
> ment, but are games, too, to be played painstakingly, clumsily,
> sufficiently, like the making of planks (one plank each tree); and by
> scientific observation and experiment, like the making of cooking
> pots. Crusoe is the one who learns, by trial and by error . . . The
> borderlines of skill and clumsiness, achievement and failure, make
> the environment game credible and exciting. The making of a
> thing, like the building of the card-castle or meccano bridge, is a
> feat, another kind of adventure.[18]

Considering the essential suitability of Defoe's novel for children to read, she suggests that Crusoe:

> . . . is simple enough to be Everyman, and simple enough to have
> an unmysterious emotional life which is accessible to the child, but
> sufficiently vivid and various for the adult.[19]

This dual appeal becomes a point to consider when we turn to Ballantyne's *The Coral Island*. Of his three castaways, one is a young adult – perhaps even two of them may be considered so – but we cannot expect them to provide the story with the experience and instruction offered by the two fathers in the earlier books. Moreover, because they have no adult mentors (their contact with the missionary on the island of Mango is superficial), their means of growth and apprehension are limited to what they can give to one another – comradeship in adventure rather than any stimulus to personal development. *The Coral Island* is a rousing, extrovert, active book: the shipwreck is aptly summed up by Peterkin as 'the most splendid prospect that ever lay between three jolly young tars'.[20]

The adventure of the jolly young tars is predicted and carried out in essentially romantic terms, each of the youths being ideally cast for his part. Ralph Rover, who tells the story, comes of a seafaring family and has preconceived ideas of adventure at sea, nourished by the tales of the men he meets while working on coastal tenders:

> . . . of all the places of which they told me, none captivated and charmed my imagination so much as the Coral Islands of the Southern Seas. They told me of thousands of beautiful fertile islands that had been formed by a small creature called the coral insect, where summer reigned nearly all the year round; where the trees were laden with a constant harvest of luxuriant fruit; where the climate was almost perpetually delightful; yet where, strange to say, men were wild, blood thirsty savages, excepting in those favoured isles to which the gospel of our Saviour had been conveyed. These exciting accounts had so great an effect upon my mind, that, when I reached the age of fifteen, I resolved to make a voyage to the South Seas.[21]

Taken on the *Arrow* by a merchant captain known to his father (whether as passenger, crewman or supercargo is not clear), Ralph chooses for his friends Jack Martin, 'a tall, strapping, broad-shouldered youth of eighteen' who was well-educated, 'lion-like in his actions; but mild and quiet in disposition, and Peterkin Gay, who was 'little, quick, funny, decidedly mischievous, and about fourteen years old'.[22]

The three of them respond cheerfully to shipwreck on an uninhabited island (the rest of the ship's company being, naturally, lost at sea). Ralph's surname (in fact, a nickname) suggests that he will readily work for survival and Jack has 'been a great reader of books of travel and adventure all his life', while Peterkin, relatively inexperienced, is quick to learn. Each recognises the beauty of the island but each turns quickly to practical matters, listing their assets (a ship's telescope, an oar tipped with iron and a penknife with a broken blade) and extending these by discovery or sensible experiment. For them, the island is new rather than strange, and their approach to it is that of tourists looking for temporary comfort.

From the introductory chapter one might almost expect character to weigh more heavily than event in the book. As narrator, Ralph Rover introduces himself as an old-fashioned boy and he exhibits a certain self-satisfied naïveté (especially when he accepts the visiting pirates' assurance that they are traders) which provides a second, more elusive kind of humour alongside the comic, irresponsible interpolations of Peterkin. But although he is the narrator, Ralph does not dictate the tone of the book. The author's overriding view is apparent everywhere, telling his readers how three young British boys meet the challenge of danger (and with pirates and cannibals, as well as hurricane and volcanic explosion, there are enough dangers to constitute a challenge). There is no suggestion that Ballantyne's trio were emotionally changed or charged by the island, though it is clear that they enjoyed, at least for a time, the quiet and undisturbed freedom it gave them. Such incidental descriptions as he allowed his narrator to give us are general in character and Ralph's last word on their experience is significant:

> That night, as we sat on the taffrail gazing out upon the wide sea and up into the starry firmament, a thrill of joy, strangely mixed with sadness, passed through our hearts; for we were at length 'homeward bound', and were gradually leaving far behind us the beautiful, bright green coral islands of the Pacific Ocean.[23]

Although it is hardly possible to ascribe the long-standing tradition of the desert-island adventure directly to any of the books I have been discussing, the package seems to be most complete and definable in *The Coral Island*.

Certainly both island and characters served William Golding as a suitable starting-point for *Lord of the Flies*, a bitter adult novel of the mid-fifties which, among other things, questions the assumptions of the Robinsonnade and perhaps of the traditional adventure story as a whole. The luscious, exotic fruits which had comforted so many castaways in literature induced chronic dysentery in his marooned schoolboys, while the sun was more of a menace than a comfort to them. Small details of this kind parodied the customary picture of a (largely) beneficent island and pointed to the wider implications of a book which, like *Pincher Martin* and *The Inheritors*, speculates on the remote beginnings of man as a sentient, articulate, reasoning being.

The opening of *Lord of the Flies* evokes Ballantyne's story in circumstance as well as in setting. A group of boys, their ages ranging from fourteen down to six, survive an air-crash while they are being evacuated from a war-zone: Ralph Rover and his friend had left behind them a secure imperialist Britain. Sharing, as they did, common national and social assumptions and a common religious belief, Ballantyne's heroes did not need to compete for leadership or to argue opposing views; life on the island brought them always closer in friendship. The differences in their temperaments made for harmony, as Ralph recognised. He learned to appreciate Peterkin's jokes and his casual approach to life, to understand that 'the things very opposite and dissimilar in themselves, when united, do make an agreeable whole' and that 'There was, indeed, no note of discord whatever in the symphony we played together on that sweet Coral Island . . .'[24] Given this harmony, which we must accept in romantic rather than realistic terms, the nineteenth-century trio could well afford to remain, entrenched in outlook and shielded by companionship.

Golding's Ralph, a twelve-year-old with a naval commander for father and model, would have been a familiar hero in a junior adventure story at least between the 1940s and 1960s. In this adult problem novel he is an acutely class-conscious product of prep-school education, assuming as of right his superiority to the fat boy whose nickname of Piggy has followed him to the island; because Piggy, as he ingenuously confides to Ralph, used to live with his auntie who kept a sweet-shop, the fact that he is a great deal more intelligent than clever Ralph can be exploited without being acknowledged. The moral struggle between the two is apparent to the reader, not to the boys. The predictable contest for actual leadership is not between Ralph and Piggy but between Ralph and his rival Jack, who turns up from another part of the island with a well-drilled band and declares he should be chief 'because I'm chapter chorister and head boy. I can sing C sharp.'[25] With their comparable education, Ralph and Jack agree at least in establishing enough of a routine in their alarming new life to give an illusion of security: in matters of time and habit, at least initially, they manage to reproduce something of the structure of school, in the way that Crusoe ordered his days and his successors likewise. The temptations of freedom soon destroy this remembered discipline and the substitute of Jack's insidious tyranny, the routine of the 'hunters' as opposed to the stay-at-home campfire and assembly rule of Ralph, soon turns to persecution of the dissenting minorities.

At the simplest level of Golding's fable, the slow, horrifying disintegration of the children is due to their youth and inexperience. But the boys are not just themselves. They stand for a nation and a species. Isolation, the spirit of the island, the menacing apparition of the dead pilot trailing his parachute, the temperamental differences which they are too young to resolve without help, lead them into a kind of ab-evolution in which superstitious idol-worship and ritual murder are, as it were, newly invented as expressions of inner selves they have never had to meet before.

The proposition of the probable course of a castaway existence is confirmed in broadly sociological terms. When a ship arrives at the island to hear from the filthy, disorganised survivors that there have been two deaths and that they are not sure how many boys there are on the island, the ship's officer comments:

> 'I should have thought that a pack of British boys – you're all British, aren't you? – would have been able to put up a better show than that . . .'[26]

and Ralph's halting apology that they had at least begun their sojourn in the right spirit is answered with 'Jolly good show, like the Coral Island'. Ralph sees at that moment an island that had seemed glamorous but which had become menacing, and he sees further than that: '. . . he wept for the end of innocence, the darkness of man's heart, and the fall through the air of the true, wise friend called Piggy'.

The ironic final paragraph relaxes the tension of terror and destructive aggression in the book: embarrassed by Ralph's sobs and the lack of control generally, the officer 'turned away to give them time to pull themselves together; and waited, allowing his eyes to rest on the trim cruiser in the distance'. So in an adroit literary curve Golding brings his tale of original sin back from the primal, intolerable paradise island to the actual world which the boys had lost for a second time with that lost 'innocence'.

A very different 'Ralph' and 'Jack', then, from Ballantyne's heroes, and an interpretation (if it can be so termed here) of the Robinsonnade which isolates and queries one of the main conventions of his genre, the 'happy ending'. Golding goes far beyond the questioning of social assumptions. It is worth remembering here (since *The Coral Island* was Golding's starting-point) that an adaptation of Ballantyne's romantic adventure for television (in nine instalments shown in the first three months of 1983) reconstructed a story-book island complete with wild (domestic) pigs, coconut palms and dazzling blue seas and at the same time introduced a social pattern relevant to our own times. Far from being already a 'Rover', Ralph was depicted as the somewhat effete son of a titled landowner of New South Wales, on his way home to finish his education at Eton. Blond, snobbish and arrogant, Ralph at once falls foul of the coarse, energetic cabin-boy Jack Martin, and their social antagonism persists after they have been thrown up on the island in company with Peterkin (here a twelve-year-old vagrant caught pilfering in the Rover mansion and escaping as a stowaway).

The social contrast was pressed heavily, presumably in order to give a certain point to the various contrivances – making fire, finding shelter, hunting for food – in which Ralph showed himself thoroughly useless. With the same wrenching of Ballantyne's fiction for the sake of topicality, the independent, sexy Jack established a tender relationship with the Princess Avatea, so that the involvement of the three heroes in the tribal wars of Mango Island became an amatory rather than a missionary enterprise. The whole production, with its emphasis on the clash of person-ality (the mere fact of visual presentation by actors made character prominent in spite of elaborate settings) contradicted to a great extent the original, active nature of Ballantyne's story.

In essence the Robinsonnade as a type of fiction turns on the sudden, unexpected juxtaposition of a person (or persons) and a place; the events that follow will depend in varying degrees on how the character or characters adapt to or make use of a particu-lar place, a desert island – that is, a place isolated from the rest of the world and presenting an unfamiliar aspect to the person thus unexpectedly thrown upon it. The desert island is a convenient literary device through which an author can control his fiction in a particularly neat and definable way. As in any other type of adventure story, he is free to decide on the emotional depth of his narrative; but because of the sharp, immediate and self-contained nature of this particular plot/setting combination, the reader is especially aware of the direction of individual examples of the genre. He will notice that in some tales the island is merely an excuse for a sequence of action, affecting the characters in a concrete way – as, for example, Wild Cat Island affects the behaviour of Ransome's Swallows and Amazons in their carefully arranged castaway state or as Ballantyne's island offers external situations for the three youths: in other books (and these the reader may find more satisfying) the *atmosphere* of the island, the strong sense of place, will be seen to be a vital, central part of the whole.

Among the brightly coloured tropical islands lavishly picked out of the Pacific for attention, Jules Verne's whale-shaped vol-canic landmass, located 'at least 1200 miles from Tahiti and more than 4500 from America'[27] dominates his massive three-part story, not in any romantic sense nor because the castaways in the case develop any mystical relation with it, but for the sheer size, impressive nature and prevailing mystery of the place. Even when the last caves have been explored, the last secret uncovered, the reader is left with a sense of strange experience that strikes a nerve untouched by most Robinsonnades. Part of the force of Verne's fantastic tale is also due to his unique mixture of dramatic tension and mature, ironical humour, the two elements which sustain its concentrated, circumstantial detail.

Above all, he had an easy mastery of his narrative, an almost casual way of mixing scraps of philosophy or scientific fact with straight reporting, a habit of leaping from a sober enumeration of domestic matters to an energetic moment of danger, which offered an exhilarating experience to readers in his day and could offer one still to our own time. There is an extra piquancy in the way the five castaways are manipulated through the narrative. Carefully chosen for useful attributes, they are as carefully placed in their period – and so, in their attitudes. Prisoners in Richmond when it was under siege by Grant's troops, they escape the rigours of the American Civil War in a stolen balloon which drops them summarily on the island in a storm. Captain Cyrus Harding, a Yankee engineer, at once becomes leader by virtue of his technical knowledge: Gideon Spilett, a reporter on the *New York Herald*, supplies a certain abrasive spur to endeavour: the sailor Pencroft, 'a bold, dashing fellow, ready to dare anything and . . . astonished at nothing', has with him an orphan of fifteen, Herbert Brown, son of his former captain: Herbert is a useful recipient of knowledge, with an interest in natural history, and a point of appeal for young readers, while Pencroft shares with the black Neb, Harding's freed and deeply loyal servant, a good deal of the physical labour attendant on making a home out of a wilderness. Harding's supreme confidence holds the group together, encouraged also by the sailor's determination to 'make a little America of this island' and to consider themselves not castaways 'but colonists, who have come here to settle'.[28] Encouragement is needed, for at first prospects seem bleak:

> The imaginary heroes of Daniel Defoe or of Wyss, as well as Selkirk and Raynal shipwrecked on Juan Fernandez and on the archipelago of the Aucklands, were never in such absolute destitution. Either they had abundant resources from their stranded vessels, in grain, cattle, tools, ammunition, or else some things were thrown up on the coast which supplied them with all the first necessities of life. But here, not any instrument whatever, not a utensil. From nothing they must supply themselves with everything.[29]

It is with 'instruments' and 'utensils' that Jules Verne is most concerned as he describes with the utmost plausibility the change on the aptly named Lincoln Island from bare rock to the elaborate construction 'Granite House' and the lookout on Prospect Heights. The scientific basis of the three linked books makes a welcome change from the familiar agriculture and furnishing of the Swiss castaways and their like. Harding is bent on a technological community and the raw materials on the island (iron, clay, lime, coal, wood) are expertly used. Iron-smelting is made possible with sealskin bellows and a brick furnace, nitro-glycerine (to blow a hole in the cliff and lower the water level) is made from the fat of a dugong and a small store of dynamite. Pencroft runs counter to desert-island tradition by failing to make fire by rubbing sticks together; he resorts to a single match in the journalist's pocket and then to a burning glass.

Jules Verne and his characters express less enthusiasm over the routine food-gathering (pigeons, turtles, rabbits and other animals are available, as well as various herbs and the statutory breadfruit) and there seems to be a surreptitious joke in the comment that they planted a single grain of wheat found in Herbert's pocket. Pencroft the sailor was of the opinion that 'they quite took the wind out of the Robinsons, for whom everything was done by a miracle'.[30] Herbert's intellectual growth was amply provided for; 'he found in the engineer for science, and the reporter for languages, masters who were delighted to complete his education'.[31] On the anniversary of their landing (in 1866) they could congratulate themselves on the successful founding of an American colony abroad and Jules Verne evidently relished describing their smug confidence:

> It was real enjoyment to the settlers in their room, well lighted with candles, well warmed with coal, after a good dinner, elderberry coffee smoking in the cups, the pipes giving forth an odoriferous smoke, they could hear the storm howling without. Their comfort would have been complete, if complete comfort could ever exist for those who are far from their fellow-creatures, and without any means of communication with them. They often talked of their country, of the friends whom they had left, the grandeur of the American Republic, whose influence could not but increase; and Cyrus Harding, who had been much mixed up with the affairs of the Union, greatly interested his auditors by his recitals, his views, and his prognostics.[32]

The clubbable tone of the books, and their pervasive irony, gives them a character quite unlike that of any other junior Robinsonnade, while in the profusion of exciting incident they outdo their rivals with an equally generous margin. The second book, *Abandoned*, ends with the discovery of a bottle containing a message from a castaway on neighbouring Tibor Island and a cruise there, in their scientifically-built boat, brings them in touch with an 'ape' who proves to be one Ayrton, one-time bosun marooned as a punishment for putting his captain's life in danger;

after twelve years on the island, he has become brutish but recovers his memory and becomes a member of the Lincoln Island community. Danger threatens in the third year of the adventure, in *The Secret of the Island*, when a ship flying a black flag, manned by convicts escaped from Norfolk Island, besieges Granite House, but it is averted by the timely but unexplained explosion of a torpedo. Mystery deepens when a message 'Follow the new wire' leads the colonists to a huge cave:

> An immense saloon – a sort of museum, in which were heaped up, with all the treasures of the mineral world, works of art, marvels of industry – appeared before the eyes of the colonists, who almost thought themselves suddenly transported into a land of enchantment.
>
> Stretched on a rich sofa they saw a man, who did not appear to notice their presence.
>
> Then Harding raised his voice, and to the extreme surprise of his companions, he uttered these words –
>
> 'Captain Nemo, you asked for us! We are here.'[33]

A surprise for the reader, no less. The bold backward glance at Verne's masterpiece is amply justified. The captain, who is dying, reveals his identity and hands over his wealth, together with a warning that the volcanic island is liable to explode at any moment. The astonished comrades, grateful for his secret protection against the convicts, give him the burial he had asked for, sinking his body in the *Nautilus* before they leave Lincoln Island – dramatically; they are hurled into the sea on a rock and neatly fielded by a yacht sent to pick up the marooned seaman. By a series of astonishing and plausible events, Jules Verne was able to bring his story to a quietly ironic and satisfying conclusion, with his castaways prosperously established on land in Iowa purchased with the enigmatic captain's gift:

> There, to conclude, all were happy, united in the present as they had been in the past; but never could they forget that island upon which they had arrived poor and friendless, that island which, during four years, had supplied all their wants, and of which there remained but a fragment of granite washed by the waves of the Pacific, the tomb of him who had borne the name of Captain Nemo.[34]

Well might Verne place the island as his final focal point, for it is the island, described in tantalising glimpses, which touches the imagination most powerfully in these most compelling narratives.

Jules Verne's fantasy-adventures are educational rather than didactic – that is, the reader may pick up along the way, if he will, sundry technological and geographical facts, but he is under no compulsion to do so, and any moral or social recommendation is offered in a casual, urbane manner. If his books have always been accepted in the juvenile category, their style and interest in fact invite a far wider readership. The Robinsonnade as addressed specifically and solely to children reflects far more directly the didactic element of Marryat and Wyss; the most light-hearted tale of children thrown on their own resources, whether on a true uninhabited island or a piece of land cut off by flood, has somewhere at its heart the idea of a test, a kind of O-level in intelligent survival. Alike in this, most junior Robinsonnades of our own century depart from their predecessors in that convenient separation of children from adults which is one of the hallmarks of the period.

One early example shows clearly how the conventions of the adult castaway tale have been modified to suit a readership which required (or was perhaps taught to require) the flattering kind of adventure in which the young accepted risks and rewards entirely on their own. The moral basis of Herbert Strang's *Palm Tree Island* is implicit in the subtitle, 'A Story of Perseverance under Difficulties', a prospectus which links this tale of 1934 with its nineteenth-century ancestors. On the other hand, it reflects also a choice of characters steadily increasing in popularity in the years after the First World War. T. C. Bridges, offering advice to aspiring writers for boys, contrasted the plethora of characters in a school serial with the two boys more suitable for 'the ordinary adventure story'. 'It is best to have two boys,' he says, 'for then they can talk, and it is a great deal easier to let a story tell itself in this way than to describe the doings of one boy.'[35] The separation from adults is taken for granted.

Herbert Strang's use of this device gave him far more than the advantage of dialogue. His shrewd choice of his heroes allowed him opportunities for humour and for the dramatic tension of opposite personalities, besides compensating plausibly for the absence of adults by allowing his two boys a reasonable amount of practical skills and intellectual stability. Orphan Harry accompanies his uncle on a voyage to look for the 'Southern Continent' but is wrecked on a volcanic Pacific island together with a mutinous crew which, alarmed by an earthquake and partial eruption, clears off in the ship's boat, leaving Harry marooned with a younger stowaway, humbly-born William Bobbin, as his only companion.

The opening chapters of the story have a playful flavour, with an attractive enumeration of the stock activities of castaways (making fire with flint, collecting seabirds' eggs, contriving a variety of weapons with plaited creeper, stone, flints and wood, building hut, pigsty and fowl-house). But if this is all familiar stuff, there is a fresh, lively note that comes from a light but decided attention to character. As narrator, Harry preserves indomitably his own values. He disapproves of Billy's suggestion of 'Smoky' or 'Lonely' as names for the island which they are rapidly turning into a home and offers 'Perseverance' as an alternative – unsuccessfully, for Billy comments that 'it looked like bragging, and besides he hated the word perseverance, because he had to write it so many times on his slate at school, and it made him think of raps on his knuckles'.[36]

Far from being disconcerted by Harry's intellectual superiority, Billy accepts it in his own way. Listening to Harry's tales of Robinson Crusoe, he scoffs at the mariner's activities, asserting that he could do as well 'especially if he had a forge and black-smith's tools',[37] and his literal mind neatly separates Defoe's fantasy from his fact:

> . . . in particular, when I told him of Crusoe's horror when he saw a footprint in the sand, he burst into a laugh, and asked why there was only one footprint, and made me go down to our little bit of sandy beach there and then, and showed me the prints he had made with his own feet, and asked me triumphantly whether the man whose mark Crusoe saw was a one-legged man, or what.[38]

He is equally scornful of what he is told about the prowess of Robin Hood, when after successfully making bows and arrows the boys embellish their regular hunt for food with greenwood lore; as he becomes adept with his bow, Billy boasts that he could outdo Robin Hood, and although he agrees to accept the role of Little John, he regrets the part of Friar Tuck, whose taste for venison was as keen as his own for roast pork.

The gamesome atmosphere of the story soon changes, and Harry is forced to forget Crusoe and Robin Hood and to assume a wholly adult leadership. The agreeable details of island house-keeping give place to violence when the mutineers reappear and take over the food and shelter won by the boys' own efforts. The genuine reality of action and character in the earlier part of the book is overtaken by melodrama, as the two boys, when concilia-tion fails, manage by a trick to maroon the villains on a rock in the sea and starve most of them into submission. The conclusion of the adventure veers uneasily between a young man's sense and a boy's fantasies:

> Thus I found myself at the head of a very thriving community. Our active and open-air life kept us in good health, and the little

313

diversions which we mingled with our work – shooting and fishing, quoits and skittles and Aunt Sally, performed with rough things of our own making – these helped to keep us cheerful, and we had no troubles beyond the storms and cyclones, no savages appearing to molest us, and Old Smoker never showing more than a light crown of vapour, and sometimes not even that. Billy and I lived alone in our hut, with Little John [their dog], and we were, I am sure, happier than we were before the men came, for we had more to think about and a great deal more to do. Billy said once that I was now a king indeed, and asked whether I wouldn't like a crown, though it would be made of leaves, there being no metal to be had. I told him that I was quite content as I was, and besides, if I was to be a king I must have a title, and I thought Harry must be an ill-starred name, for Harry the First was the king that never smiled again, and Harry the last (that is, the Eighth) was not a very estimable character.[39]

When after eight years and seven months (on 2 April 1783) the boys reach London in a rebuilt boat, they have not changed a great deal as a result of their adventure, though their friendship has brought about a certain tolerance of their differing backgrounds and attitudes. Certainly the island as such has had little effect on two boys basically sensible and notably unimaginative. The emphasis in the book has been on the external means of survival and on an undemanding, unprobed junior relationship, and this limited exploration of the castaway theme has persisted over the past half-century, with one exception. This exception (like Tournier's two novels and Golding's *Lord of the Flies*) sets in strong relief the established conventions of the Robinsonnade.

At first Ivan Southall's *To the Wild Sky* seems to be a direct companion to his earlier disaster-stories – *Hills End*, for instance, and *Ash Road* – in which a group of children stretch their capacities and their powers of endurance in times of crisis, in a freak hurricane and a bush fire respectively. The comparison seems most obvious with *Hills End*, with its version of a castaway plot, as children are cut off from adult help, marooned by landslides and responsible for the remaining adult, their schoolteacher, who is in great physical and emotional stress. *To the Wild Sky* is more definably a Robinsonnade, with the children placed in a double isolation. First, the aeroplane carrying them from the city to a sheep-station in the north-west of New South Wales becomes, as it were, a desert island, when the pilot dies of a heart attack: then, they are ditched for the second stage of their ordeal on a true 'desert island' in the Gulf of Carpentaria. The response of children to stress and the abrasive effect of individuals on one another, the main themes of all Southall's work, account for the deliberate realism, the denial of any attractive Crusonian detail in the book: the nature of the island and its influence on the children is more subtle and original.

Class differences, as well as personal traits, activate the plot. Gerald Hennessy has invited five of his schoolfellows to his home for a spectacular weekend, where his birthday is to be celebrated with barbecues, a trip to an opal mine and other pleasures. There will be neighbours of his own age with similar wealthy pastoralist backgrounds, but Gerald does not, like them, attend an exclusive private boarding school and the friends he has chosen to join him on the flight home are city high school pupils, used to a less sheltered life. Of the five, Gerald is most at his ease with hearty, extrovert Bruce Martin and most attracted to Carol Bancroft, who has 'poise and polish and maturity way ahead of her thirteen years'.[40] He is less happy that the invitation has been extended to Bruce's twin sister Janet, who is clumsy and unpredictable, and though he can get on well enough with clever Colin Kerr, a boy who has been described by one astute parent as having an accountant's face, he feels sure that Colin's tiresome brother Mark, just eleven and not his choice in the first place, will disrupt the party. Indeed, Colin has been instructed by his mother to keep an eye on Mark – 'He's to keep his hands clean and his hair tidy and he's *not* to belch after meals.'[41]

Each of Gerald's guests has a private opinion of the rich only child. Carol admires him and covets his friendship; Janet resents his air of privilege; Mark foresees he will nag as much as the grown-ups always do; Colin and Bruce both expect him to be less approachable at home than in the notional democracy of school. And for each there is a change of attitude when Gerald unwillingly takes over the controls of the aircraft and flies it despairingly through sun, dust-clouds and eventual darkness to a dangerous descent into the edge of the sea. These changing attitudes, and the equally varied states of mind in which Gerald calls on his scanty experience with the family plane and his latent courage, fill the time and space during which the children endure the first stage of their castaway adventure.

Gerald is the centre of the author's panoramic view of his characters and their behaviour in this first stage. Once they are on the island, the narrative becomes more diffused, with short scenes focused on each child in turn – on Mark cowed by fear, on Bruce asserting himself by exaggerating a minor injury, on Janet and Carol, each beset by emotional stress and by an unrealised sexual rivalry, on Colin in misery for a social disadvantage (he has stripped to his underpants during the struggle to land and hides until Carol persuades him to forget his correctness and wear a pair of pink trousers from her rescued suitcase), on Gerald suffering a temporary breakdown after his ordeal and trying to regain his authority over the others.

But the true centre of this second part of the story is Carol, since her contribution to the party's survival is more crucial, to them and to the basic nature of the Robinsonnade, than that of any other child. Janet succeeds in making fire: Gerald sensibly withstands a proposal to make a raft and venture into the unknown sea: it is Carol who reacts to the island most surely and most usefully.

This is no hospitable South Sea island. There are no bananas or coconuts and the straggling bush is thorny and coarse; apparently, there is no water; the ruins of a jetty and stone huts offer little shelter. In fact, they seem sinister after the date 1874 over one lintel, a discussion about the coastline and the course of their flight, and Janet's memories of a history lesson, have enabled them to identify their landfall as Molineaux Island, deserted by its settlers, a religious sect, after a disastrous epidemic. Only Carol has any chance of finding a practical way to live until the hoped-for rescue. And Carol, wandering off alone in a sudden distaste for her companions, faces the secret which she has guarded all her life, the aboriginal blood inherited from a great-grandmother. When Gerald tracks her to the sandhills on the edge of the bush he sees 'on the ground not far from where she had been digging a heap of little fruits, nuts, and the roots of plants swollen with juices, and a dead lizard'.[42] When he comments on the 'blackman's food' she bitterly accuses him of prejudice, but keeps her secret, as she keeps to herself the struggle she has had with herself; the instinct to get close to the earth has conflicted painfully with the acquired social pattern of her class.

Ivan Southall does not press the point too far but does make it emphatically a part of his interpretation of the castaway theme. Always a purposive, not to say a didactic novelist, he exercises an almost Victorian control over his fiction, *telling* us directly what one or other of his characters is feeling and laying down hints and clues to the reader which often amount to dramatic irony. His particular method of piecemeal narrative has never been more probing and alert than in *To the Wild Sky*. Lying between the extremes of romantic adventure-game and bitter realism, his version of the Robinsonnade asserts more powerfully than any other the special importance, so often unexploited by authors, of the 'desert island' itself.

Seventeen years after *To the Wild Sky* was published Ivan Southall was persuaded to satisfy public demand with a sequel. In an Author's Note to *A City Out of Sight* he explained:

> I have always held the view that readers might have their own expectations and might enjoy living them out in their imagination. At heart, I have not changed my position, but I have agreed to go on with the story.[43]

Those who prefer a traditional outcome of the castaway theme will find their expectations satisfied. After the first desperate day or two on the desolate island without the aids of civilisation, during which Carol's hunting becomes more ambitious and Janet succeeds in making fire without matches, Gerald stumbles on evidences of the abortive settlement (a flourishing plantation of sunflowers, chickens, a good well) which change the situation completely and turn the book in the direction of the Crusonian kind of story. An enigmatic coda to this second book suggests that the children will work to create a world much like the one they have lost. Adept and logical as the sequel is, it leaves me disappointed that, after all, Ivan Southall has not followed Tournier and Golding in probing the depth of the relation between civilised beings and a totally lonely place with an atmosphere of its own.

13. Techniques of Description

I chose the Robinsonnade as a particular example of the disaster-adventure (man against nature, in its broadest aspect) because it can be isolated easily by its traditional characteristics and its setting. The special implications of solitude and its effect on human behaviour do not necessarily disappear from other kinds of disaster-stories but they may be more easily ignored or masked by different considerations. We may still look for the effect of place and natural phenomena on character, for example, in a piece of popular adult adventure-writing like Desmond Bagley's *The Snow Tiger* which describes the behaviour of a small community in a New Zealand valley isolated by an avalanche, but we shall look in vain, for the attention is almost wholly concentrated on the way the characters face the situation; they face it in terms of their personal relationships or desires rather than in any emotional reaction to the lowering mountains and darkened windows, the natural menace which shows up the limits of their tenure of the land.

It is not in popular adventures like this that we shall find *place* as a truly active factor in a story: rather, description and localising work to provide a background for action, no more, and a means of producing an artificial isolation which is likely to cause unusual behaviour. In this type of book, character-drawing consists of little more than the attaching of labels to each individual. In adult novels we recognise instantly the prostitute with the heart of gold, the doctor or airman inhibited by age or failure, the spoilt rich heroine, the incisive psychiatrist: in children's books the same kind of encapsulated character (the bully, the loner, the plain or diffident girl and the pretty, self-centred one) can carry the story with a token background. Even the marked realities of Ivan Southall's stories depend on the instant recognition of certain types of boy and girl with an equally obvious, uncomplicated background (with *To the Wild Sky* as an exception, as I have suggested).

The sting of danger and the possibility of real emotional change are limited in the average disaster-adventure. This limitation is perhaps more surprising in books where the sensitive areas of personality are still relatively uncomplicated by experience and should therefore be more accessible to the author's scrutiny.

318

Most often a boy or girl will emerge from a period of stress or endurance, whether with cold or heat, flood or fire, very much the same as before, springing back easily like new elastic to a former shape, and a sense of experience, if it is present, is more likely to come from the interaction of personality than from the influence of natural forces in a particular place.

It is rarely that we find a situation like the one described by Farley Mowat in *Lost in the Barrens*, where two boys lost in the Canadian Arctic have to find a way to survive the winter *in relation to* the land itself. Jamie Macnair, at sixteen, has a certain knowledge of the country, for he has already been trapping with his uncle for a year: his friend Awasin, a Cree Indian, has a deeper knowledge with which he can correct the Canadian boy's impetuosity and self-confidence. While they usefully complement each other's skills in camping and hunting, they are not truly equal until Jamie has realised for himself that their attempt at a winter journey was ill-advised:

> '. . . we'll go back, Awasin . . . and we'll stay at Hidden Valley. Stay there as long as we have to. I've learned my lesson. As long as we went along with things the way they were, and never tried to fight against this country, we were all right. But when we set out on this trip we were standing up to the Barrens and sort of daring them. We were going to bulldoze our way through. And we're lucky to be still alive!'
>
> Awasin looked long into his friend's face.
>
> 'I never thought you'd understand about that, Jamie,' he said at last. 'White men don't as a rule. Most of them think they can beat the northland in any fight. A lot of them have found out differently, and didn't live to talk about it. My people *know* differently. It's hard to put into words, but I think you understand. If you fight against the Spirits of the north you will always lose, obey their laws and they'll look after you.'[1]

Farley Mowat does not press the point but the book, as an active and exciting adventure, is expanded by the hint that Jamie has had an experience beyond the physical challenge.

Adventure stories thrive on concentration – precision and compactness of style demanding attention, a single area of interest. The ardent particularisation of subject-matter is one of the main reasons (perhaps the chief reason) for the popularity of novels by Nevil Shute and Dick Francis: the combination of technique and enthusiasm offers a special unity and shape which gives the reader an almost physical pleasure, akin perhaps to the pleasure of counterpoint in music. Description as an organic rather than an incidental part of the whole is one of the glories of the adventure

319

story. The close alliance, even integration, of *place* and *procedure* is notable in Masefield's novels of action and especially in a master-piece of expandable compression, *The Taking of the Gry*.

The 'Odtaa' narrative method, expanded and exalted in the two great Central American romances (see p. 74), is used in a briefer form in this novel. The 'and then' so typical of Masefield is shaped by alternate stages of verbal or mental planning and the actual concrete procedure of the plan: the place, the harbour of Santa Barbara and its outlets, provide plot, setting, theme and motive power of the story, all at once. *The Taking of the Gry* is one of the most skilful and the most casual-seeming of all Masefield's tales of adventure.

Charles Tarlton, a young officer in the merchant navy, describes from the distance of a year or so the critical days when he associated himself with rebels in a bid to win back a ship carrying armaments and impounded by the totalitarian government. Tarlton tells the story as though to an invisible listener, reliving the headlong adventure when thought and action were crammed together in an immensely concentrated area of time and place. Framed within the beginning and end of one episode of continued political unrest in the author's imaginary 'Sugar States' countries lies the account of how Tarlton, taking the place of the hired tug-master at the last moment and supported by the nonchalant, skilled mate Harry, pilots tug and tow through Drake's Channel, a winding waterway impeded by rocks and sandbanks, long forgotten, which leads from the inner harbour where the *Gry* has been moored, shut in by a boom and guarded by a naval crew.

The map supplied on the endpapers of the first edition is useful to an understanding of at least the external part of the adventure. Besides, its fanciful style recalls the romantic nature of this parti-cular area of Masefield's invention (a romantic note touched lightly in *The Midnight Folk* no less than in *Sard Harker* and *Odtaa*). Romantic, too, is the constant invocation of the spirit of Drake in Tarlton's mind as he squares up to his enterprise: he feels Drake's presence in the channel, not only mystically but also as an encouraging thought, and sees the Elizabethan sailor in Harry's 'short, compact figure, all readiness and force and humorous courage'.[2]

But Masefield is not concerned to make this brief, difficult sea-journey wholly romantic, as the journeys of Sard Harker and Hi Ridden were; the atmosphere, the total effect of the book lies in the way this decorative, fanciful aspect of it meshes with the meticulous, concrete, practical description, as the tug and the *Gry* edge their way through the channel to freedom in the open sea. In the fusing of thought, action and setting Masefield had no equal. In *The Taking of the Gry* he marks the interplay of place and procedure by offering two transits of the channel. The first is exploratory – Tarlton and the captain of the tug, purporting to be harmlessly fishing, make a preliminary survey of hazards which Tarlton has observed on his chart. At this stage there is time for personal private fancy:

> We went slowly on towards the East Roarer, on a course of east by north. The water is exquisitely clear there, so clear that I could see on both sides of me the rocky walls of the channel, almost like the banks of a gorge, all beautiful with scarlet coral, and dazzling white shells. I could see fish floating and gulping or flashing away with a quick fin; and I thought to myself: 'Charles Tarlton, if you don't watch your tip, those fish may be nibbling you before to-morrow morning.'[3]

When the escape is attempted, and achieved, the prose quickens and becomes more technical, more practical and more urgent, and there is a strong illusion of speed as the two vessels pass each of the hazards earlier noted at more leisure:

> I remembered that in the earlier flood that afternoon the jobble had ceased to be a race about midway down the Boneyard. I prayed that that might be so at that state of the tide, for if not we should smash. We went down that reach in double-quick time under the shove of the current; and I suppose at each second of the run we risked losing our tow, for we had no real hold of her. She seemed inclined to take charge, and get across the stream: she very nearly did: but just didn't until the end of the rush, when the jobble checked against the incoming flood, and gave us a chance to straighten her. We regained control, and made that last turn round a bend in a clear moment when we got good bearings of the lights that would guide us to open water. Never was such luck.[4]

No map could give one the feeling of immediacy conveyed by the progression teased out in meticulously selected words: no filmic representation could arouse in the reader at once a mental image of place and action and an emotional response to the narrator's remembered feelings. Words – the best words for the occasion – have the power to induce a vital, if temporary, conjunction of author and reader.

Procedure – exactly what happens to what objects in what circumstances – has always been of paramount interest to children, who as readers like to know just where they are and what they are to contemplate. But mere lists, accumulations of practical detail, are not enough in themselves; like endpaper maps, they are auxiliary to the integrating power of the author in selecting, placing and relating the words in his lists that will make up his picture of a place and his recital of a certain procedure related to that place. And to make the most of the author's selectiveness the reader must work for him, must record and notice and relate his details, unconsciously but actively.

Because of his extremely terse, subtle, elusive and allusive selection of words, William Mayne will always be a minority writer, in the sense that not all young readers are willing to match his uniquely observant, elliptical style with an awareness of their own. Yet his own particular merging of place and procedure have made some of his mystery-adventures experiences in reading beyond any other.

Mystery is the key to the continuity of his books, a puzzle whose solving the reader is invited to follow (but not to anticipate) in sympathy with the characters. Many of the objects sought and found belong to the long tradition of mystery-adventure, with tunnels, buried treasure, lost documents as the common coin. Mayne mints his coin afresh by conditioning each central object, scrupulously and with unique force, in a particular environment and with his camera-eye observing that environment at both close and distant range. This continual change of focus means that the place he has chosen is not only the *cause* of the puzzle but is also a peopled background, a place in which behind the active, foreground figures whose actions make up the story we can glimpse a more distant world going about its business. This invaluable device of populousness, of thrusting sharply, momentarily, beyond the bounds of the story, is especially telling in *The Member for the Marsh*.

On a cold March morning a schoolboy in his first year at the local grammar school misses his bus and has to accept his father's suggestion of an alternative route. David Rosley is unwilling to do this, not from laziness (although he will now have a longish walk to a different bus-stop) but because he will have to walk across a Somerset marsh, crossed by rhines and hiding who knows what creatures and hazards in the sedges and thickets. The first mysteries the marsh provides are created by David's imagination and are quickly, if fearfully, reduced to commonplace facts. The monster approaching him turns out to be Fred Tuckee, farmer-owner of the marshland, keeping off the rain with a sack over his head. The mysterious clankings and slurpings coming out of the mist eventually prove to be caused by a pumping-engine working in the drainage ditches and not by the Chinese dragons

which David almost makes himself believe in as fancy takes hold
of him.

The third mystery belongs to the Harmonious Mud Stickers
whose bus-travelling group David is allowed to join as the necessary, and only member – for sixth-form Clipper is already constituted President, moody, musical Kitson of the fifth form is
Treasurer and Victor Starr, fourth-former and farmer's son, Secre-
tary. To confirm his membership and mark the fact that he is now
committed to the alternative route to school, David has to introduce
the gang to the marsh which, with the offhand verbal pyrotechnics
typical of their kind, they have named the Chorasmian Waste. Here
the 'Chinese dragons' are to be placated with fire-crackers, by
permission of the farmer, and here as they ramble and comment
they find an unexplained piece of high, open ground:

> The ridge continued to the left, and all at once opened out into a
> clearing of brown grass, with the sedge all round. The ground was
> not quite level: there were small tumps all over it, bigger than
> ant-hills, and flatter: not the same shape at all. The whole was
> round, and about the size of two tennis courts.[5]

The suggestion of a dancing-floor offered by David's small sister
(who has been allowed to join the party, for fear of tantrums) is
taken up by Clipper: Kitson offers a jocular 'Tableland . . . Table
has broken leg': David suggests 'camping place for Romans'.[5]

Clipper's afterthought proves correct and on a later visit he is
able to convince his sceptical schoolfellows, when a handful of
earth from one 'molehill' produces five objects – a gravel pebble,
a fragment of 'grey brick-like stuff', a beetle, a second stone, and
what feels to Clipper like a 'fossil haricot bean',[6] looks to David
like a bit of old bottle but is, in fact, a bead from an Iron Age lake
village. As always, Mayne enjoys and communicates his enjoyment of precise details but there is a point beyond the mystification. Fred Tuckee is in fact not redraining the marsh but flooding
it to protect his adjacent arable fields. He has allowed the boys to
range his land on the casually, indirectly expressed condition that
nothing is to be discovered that might hold up the operation
(the financial frustration and legal protestations of a certain Mr
Harcombe of Semplet are frequently quoted). Clipper is well aware
of the dilemma, as a boy of academic leanings who would enjoy
excavating the area, though not obsessively; Starr, whose father's
land marches with Tuckee's, thinks, as a farmer, that present land
use is more important than the rescuing of historical evidence.
The problem is resolved by a compromise – one day of exploration and more small objects retrieved, but guaranteed silence.

It is a conclusion that might be difficult to sustain nowadays; twenty-seven years later, the conservation theme is aired in junior holiday-adventure stories more conscientiously and with a strong social message. But Mayne is not concerned with a moral issue. Rather, he is creating a small, significant world, inhabited by people with diverging points of view, some reconcilable and others not.

In this world, lines radiate from the four boys at the centre who are incorporating a mystery light-heartedly into the free play of their energy and imagination. The lines go from the centre out to Tuckee's home and holding (the distinction between Starr's neighbourly 'Fred' and David's respectful 'Mr Tuckee' separating farmer from owner); to David's home, where his father, who works for a firm making agricultural machinery, has his own professional view of the matter; more distantly, to the sweet-shop where, in silence, a fresh supply of pink, clove-flavoured sweets is laid in for a week of bus journeys; further still to barely mentioned, peripherally important connections at school. The homes of the four boys sort themselves out on a mental map as the reader picks up hints from nicknames. Clipper lives in the 'Barbary Coast', Kitson in 'the Pool' (with mermaids, Clipper says), Starr 'in a milky way on the Milky Way, with a lot of cows'.[7] Occupations make their contribution to the map – ditching, butter-making, cooking, homework, pipe-laying. Identities change with each situation. David is Governor of a Province, the latest recruit to an organisation, bossy brother, docile schoolboy, as the occasion demands. A cumulation of small, selected details merges into the broad picture of a community, frozen in time *and place* for our examination. Descriptive detail is essential and integral to the whole work.

A tighter frame and a more complex procedure promote the special immediacy of *A Parcel of Trees*, while the theme of a search for privacy is more emphatically pursued than the opposite theme, the need to be gregarious, as it runs below the course of David's initiation into the daily renewed association on the back seat of the country bus. The emotional direction of *A Parcel of Trees*, more urgent and explicit than the theme of belonging in *The Member for the Marsh*, arises from the situation of Susan who, at fourteen, still has to share a bedroom with her silently inimical seven-year-old sister Rosemary; never unduly underlined as a message (this is never Mayne's way), Susan's need is summed up at the end of the book, when she has discovered a special freedom of her own in a place and in a state of mind:

> 'I can stand you all being a lot worse now, because I can always go there. It's when I haven't anywhere to go that I get mad straight away. But if I go there for half an hour it's beautiful to come back.

I can eat the apples and think of the dogs, and then go back. Then, when I've got back I can come home.'

'Give us time to get back ourselves,' said Mum. 'We haven't all got Parcels of Trees to ruminate in.'[8]

The freedom in question, designated as a truly private freedom, is found in a small piece of land, once an outlying orchard and paddock extending the garden of Susan's home, the village bakery, but now cut off by the branch line of the railway. Because the legal position had been left in abeyance at the time when the land was taken over, Susan is able to lay claim to the 'parcel of trees', if not in ownership, at least with a right to access. This she does with the help of a lazily astute lawyer in the same village who, taking up a hint from a visiting assessor, explains to the girl that she must prove continuous use by village residents over twelve years.

This typical Mayne situation allows him to depict a Wiltshire village in a double perspective, in the arrangement of characters in their degrees of importance and in the shifting view, both distant and close-up, of the piece of land in its various parts – orchard, shed foundations, walls and fences, nettle patches, over- grown tracks, encircling wheat-field. It is inherent in his narrative method that the reader is gradually put in possession of a mental map which far transcends any ancillary, labelled picture. The effect of this story, in particular, is something like the effect of those pre-Renaissance Nativities or portraits of saints where our eyes are led from vital foreground events to subsidiary groups and scenes in the far distance.

The puzzle in *A Parcel of Trees* is gradually resolved as Susan asks questions and provokes reminiscences from one person and another and establishes the facts and dates of Tom Royal's caper with a stolen racehorse whose skeleton still lies in the grass which Susan tries to subdue with an inadequate sickle; of the disastrous manufacture of rockets by David and Neddy, now respectable young wage-earners but still Susan's heroes from primary school days; of the dates when old Mr Monsey had buried the dogs whose temperaments he describes to Susan as she prompts him from the names of the memorial stones she has uncovered. Each successive piece of evidence brings into sharp focus the person concerned, his status and individual part in village life and the area of the piece of land with which he was concerned. The various threads of the story are as intricately woven together as a cat's cradle, each at once separate and entwined: there is no moment in which it is possible to say that feeling is more important than setting or personal idiom more telling than the strong identity of a plant, an apple tree, a piece of stone. Place and people are integrated and the reader has to hold the threads together in his mind. With Mayne's acute, selective use of words, his absolute possession of detail, this activity on the part of the reader, if not easy, is pleasurable in a very special way.

It is in the unity of sense-impressions and character-perception that Mayne has pushed the adventure story to its limits, as Peter Dickinson or Emma Smith have done in other ways. His special selectiveness in detail, operating powerfully in his use of dialogue, affects the settings of his stories towards the creation of secondary worlds – that is, of clusters of places and people assembled from reality (we always know which county we are in, though the actual places may be fictional) and extended and confirmed by imagination. The basic, familiar treasure-hunt plot which is his staple – the search for a well, a document, a lost house or a tunnel, a boat – is defined by its position and its importance in a particular place. In *Ravensgill* a family feud is composed after twenty years through the exploration of an underground watercourse; in *The Rolling Season* a Wiltshire village is saved from the effects of drought by the discovery of a well at the foot of a certain hill; his first book, *Follow the Footprints*, depends on a close scrutiny of minute changes in a path and a rock, due to light and damp. Always the reader is left with an impression, an almost physical recognition of a place, which has a compelling power far beyond the scope of any form of illustration. Mayne's books have been punctuated agreeably by many illustrators but none has even tried to assume the prime duty of words.

For this aspect of the reading experience the critic has to use the unsatisfactory phrase 'mental picture' – unsatisfactory because it has to stand for a considerable range of reactions from intellectual apprehension to an illusion of 'seeing' akin to but less definable than the vision of a dream, from the most subliminal response of the unconscious mind to the working of rapid associative memory, assembling previous experience from reading or from actuality. This unique and complicated reading experience lies behind the enduring appeal of the adventure story. Being far more important and lasting than the pleasure of escape usually claimed for this kind of fiction (and, as I have suggested, responsible for the undervaluing of the genre), it is an experience which depends on a tacit agreement between author and reader, an expectation on the one hand of quality, on the other of active participation. The reader's response will depend on the writer's clarity, his selectiveness and the power of the clues and signposts which he offers.

One of the most valuable keys to the fullness of an adventure story lies in the use of potent images. If it were possible to make an exact analysis, in neurological and emotional terms, of the effect of the word 'tunnel' on each individual reader, it would be easier to describe the special experience which is indicated by the phrase 'mental picture' and to justify, by something more than personal preference, one's reason for claiming a full significant pleasure for *King Solomon's Mines* and not for formula-tales with perfunctory settings. Certain literary points can of course be elicited. For instance, Rider Haggard uses variations in pace to arouse suspense and to create a feeling of claustrophobic terror, moving between fairly elaborate descriptive passages and quick statements of movement and interweaving his establishment of the *place*, the treasure-tunnel, with richly explicit indications of the changing reactions of Quatermain, Curtis and Good. Mayne's description of the underground waterway in *Ravensgill* affects the reader through the meticulous way he tracks the physical ordeal of Bob Chapman as he is bashed and cut about on his perplexing exploration, noting details of rock and water through the eyes of a boy afraid, hurt but intensely aware. Richard Church in *The Cave* energises an almost computerised catalogue of geological features in a limestone complex by coordinating concrete detail with the changes in the hierarchy of the five boys struggling to escape from danger. The elements of response to the idea of a tunnel – surprise, speculation, claustrophobic fear, bodily pain, wonder – vary in each case, but in each case the response of the reader will depend partly on his own experience and his own expectation.

Those who look for a brisk gallop through a cosy, unsmelly, safe tunnel will find just that, whatever further experience is offered by the writer. Readers 'see' what they are ready to see, what they are willing to see. Even then, they may not see all that the writer wishes them to see. Peter Dickinson probed deeply into the significances of a tunnel in *Annerton Pit*, luring his readers from the explicit and understandable to the near-mystical. In a topical plot he described how two boys looking for their over-adventurous grandfather, who had disappeared on one of his ghost-hunting journeys, were involved dangerously with a revolutionary ecological group working from deserted mine-workings in a northern county.

The stretch of mine-galleries is at first a simple hiding-place for the boys after they have rescued the old man from his captors, and for seventeen-year-old Martin it remains a refuge, cold and uncomfortable but unalarming. The reader 'sees' through the eyes of Jake, blind eyes helped by the compensation of acute senses and intuitions beyond his thirteen years. Smells and

textures build up the underground world for us and then, gradually and intermittently, intensify the whole picture intellectually
as Jake recalls random facts about children in Victorian mines.
Recollections of history lessons help him identify aspects of the
mines in which he has lost his way but they also sharpen his
feelings so that fear becomes urgent and, together with physical
pain, it induces an ultimate experience. At first he has an illusion
of seeing colours and shapes; then he seems to detect a presence
other than his own; finally he senses that the presence is somehow
a hidden part of himself. In the simple language of a boy in trouble,
believing anything is possible, he asks 'What are you?':

> The answer came strongly, but not in that first impossible blast.
> There was very little in it Jake could grasp. It was like hearing
> music, so strange that you can't even recognize that it's music at all.
> Pressure of rocks. Growth like roots along the shifting pressure-
> lines. Waiting that wasn't waiting, because time wasn't the time
> Jake knew. A curious caution and wariness, as if the life that was
> fulfilling its nature in this way was somehow a frontier life. Other
> lives – not the scurrying crowds of Jake's experience, but few,
> remote, deeper, safer, known along fine tendrils of contact, all
> waiting through the time that wasn't time. Not simply waiting.
> Waiting *for* . . .[9]

The slow, elaborate yet simply planned winding into the inmost
possibility of the potent image is here to work on the reader
through the sound, the arrangement, the meaning and the
mystery of words. The purpose is not to establish a setting but to
convert that setting into an experience. The intensity of this
moment in a very varied experience for a blind boy goes far
beyond the expectation which the average reader would be likely
to hold of an adventure in a tunnel.

Perhaps the persistence of a more romantic, more superficial
expectation, surviving in adults from childhood enjoyment of
easy-going fictional tunnel-adventures, is demonstrated in an
advertisement for a group of sixteen caves in rural Worcestershire
which were put up for sale in the spring of 1983. A multi-storey
complex of caves and tunnels in a country park, recommended as
'dry in winter and cool in the summer', could be, as the estate
agent put it, 'the ideal place for someone who is looking for a
really different holiday home':

> Most of the caves measure 20 ft. square. That's bigger than the
> rooms in many modern houses. They have about seven or eight feet
> headroom inside, and one even has a built-in fireplace.
> It may be possible to convert them into holiday homes or to use
> them as a base for camping expeditions.[10]

Beyond the practical uses suggested for these eligible dwellings, beyond the implication of a refuge in time of war, there is surely a secret, nostalgic suggestion: the buyers might well be tempted because of associations, barely realised but still potent, with adventures enjoyed vicariously in their youthful reading.

Powerful perhaps for more specific reasons, the effect of the picture conveyed in a story of a narrow, defensible mountain pass defended by a doomed hero may be as explainable in Freudian terms as the subliminal effect of a cave or tunnel as a vital background to action, but its reverberations in adventure-story act most of all because of their literary associations. The legend of Roncesvalles in particular has cast an image forward in European literature for many centuries, identifying a geographical feature, both particular and general, by evoking the deeply emotional concepts of honour and beleaguered despair at the climax of a military campaign. Arguments against war have so far failed to suppress the instinctive reactions of social man to the subtly desirable concept of glory in defeat.

For readers of our century the image has come most notably from novels about British exploits on the North-West Frontier of India – from *The Broken Road* by A. E. W. Mason and Buchan's *The Half-Hearted* among others. In later novels like John Masters' *The Lotus and the Wind*, published in 1953, and the frontier tales of Duncan MacNeil, belonging to the sixties and seventies, the gut-reaction induced by the spectacle of a trapped hero fighting to the death to save the world he subscribes to far outweighs the change in political and social attitudes influencing these two contemporary writers. While to some extent they view the history of the British Raj with hindsight, they are principally concerned to imbue the image of the mountain-pass beset by tribal and national enemies with all its historical overtones; they are as concerned to evoke the spirit of heroic honour in defeat as their predecessors who were not yet pressured by doubts about the validity of national pride.

None-the-less, the adventure story (like any other branch of fiction) reflects, if belatedly, the attitudes of the society for which it is written, and this particular image of place may well be replaced by something closer to our preoccupations. Certainly the mushroom cloud is already becoming a dominant image in fantasy-adventures. There is another analogous pictorial concept, a setting-turned-image if you like, which is likely to endure, for a number of reasons – aesthetic, emotional, literary, physical. The focal point of a citadel rising centrally and in isolation from a vast plain was used over and over again by Rider Haggard in his African romance-adventures. It was convenient as a narrative tool, obviously, as a place towards which his explorers and adventurers could be seen journeying. When he describes Allan Quatermain and his comrades seeing for the first time the citadel of the sister-queens, when he offers the first sight of the fastness which contains the fabled Ayesha or the honeycombed stronghold in *The People of the Mist*, he pricks the reader into a binocular view of a place vital to the story but powerfully resonant also of ideas and feeling – of apprehension, of excitement, of the lure of a distant object, of isolation and even imprisonment. It is in its simplest form a place where action is to take place, but a place also whose aura and atmosphere will extend through the book and affect the reader for longer than the time of reading.

It may be that it was partly through reading Rider Haggard in his youth that Masefield was to use the beleaguered citadel with special meaning, but there was a more powerful literary association as well. In all his writings, whether prose or poetry, the image of Troy besieged is paramount. It may be expressed in a direct evocation of legend. It is always a medium for expressing sympathy for the honourably defeated, the victim of aggression, even a civilised community overcome by barbarians.

In many instances Masefield's picture of a citadel on a hill is very direct, expressed in a very concrete definition of stone, water and space which powerfully reflects special emotions of pity and terror. In two instances the association with Troy is touched on through an African setting, with startling effect. The 'Zimbabwe' or ruined stone fort where Roger Naldrett takes refuge, where he tends his dying companion and desperately experiments with scanty supplies in the search for an antidote for sleeping sickness, is a refuge for him, from disappointed love and personal dissatisfaction, and a place where he must decide between despair or a determination to survive. In this central part of *Multitude and Solitude* – central in emotional as well as narrative terms – Troy is evoked directly and is present by association in the tumbled stones, the isolation and the vastness of the place.

Live and Kicking Ned, written thirty years later, is (like the earlier novel) a tale of rebirth. Where Roger Naldrett had made his soul, as it were, had burned out of himself the superficially social and, in solitude, had become fit for the multitude, the situation of Edward Mansell was at once simpler and less artificially described. This magnificently active, buoyant novel is a sequel to *Dead Ned*, a tight, tense account of a young man,

330

wrongly accused of the murder of his patron, Admiral Cringle, who was hanged at Tyburn but cut down and revived by friends. Ned escaped from England with the admiral's tales in his mind of a white nation isolated in Central Africa and, after a perilous journey on a slave-ship, escaped marauding tribesmen and found his way to the Kranish citadel.

The race he encountered there had, to him, features of many Mediterranean peoples, Greek and Trojan among them; similarly, the citadel, besieged by M'gai warriors in great strength and torn inwardly with dissension and bureaucratic lethargy, constantly reminds Ned, an educated young doctor, of fabled Troy. Travelling towards the stronghold with comrades of liberal stamp, opposed by the elders of the city, he wonders whether they will find it 'smoking like a fallen Troy, with the M'gai dancing in the embers';[11] later, observing a dangerously weak section of the walls, he reflects that he had been told 'Troy could only have been taken by a stratagem . . . since no primitive race had siege equipment'[12] and speculates how far the M'gai will be able to exploit the weakness: later still, having been either ignored or harassed by the weakly obstinate rulers in the city, he thinks of himself 'in a kind of Troy, in the heart of Africa, shut up, and to be killed, perhaps, before daylight . . .'[13] and when he and the determined rebels have escaped to win help for the citadel, he looks back at the watchers on the battlements, scantily equipped to hold off scaling ladders and firearms, and thinks of 'Troy watching for the heroes returning from the field'.[14] Intermittent clues to the importance of the Kranish citadel in the total atmosphere of the story cumulate in the idea of Troy which is at once confirmed and enlarged in typically nervous, misleadingly simple description. The Homeric walls and threatened strength of the place affect Ned, the narrator, from his first sight of the place:

> It stood upon a gentle rising of the plain; you could not call it a hill; and yet when you were at a distance, and when you were near it, or in it, the city dominated the plain; there was the queen, enthroned.
>
> Between us and the city was a small water-course, marked with shrubs and weeds. Beyond the city was a second, much larger, water-course. I saw that these two waters joined about a mile to the west of the town, and ran on into the west as one.
>
> The city herself rose before us with a style that took my breath away. I had been in untamed savagery for some weeks; I had seen nothing in Africa that was not savage; now here was a city, walled and builded, the sort of place from which we take our word 'civilisation'. The walls were a full eighteen or twenty feet high, ranged and

331

battered back for two-thirds of their height and perpendicular at
the top. Who had built such walls? Who were these Kranois? The
walls were of well-laid, hewn stones of hard, white-gray. There was
a gate in the wall in the side of the city nearest to us; we were on a
track which led to it.

There were some biggish buildings within the walls; some of the
lesser buildings had been lime-washed white; and the walls and the
seven tall watch-towers were crowded with people, among whom
weapons flashed in the light.[15]

Rocks, size and space, the unseen presence of Troy, the narrator's
nervous anticipation of action – these elements together form an
image which assaults and possesses the imagination as it holds in
suspension the selected items of description that make it up.

Rock and stone are enduring, rock and stone can be broken down.
This ambiguity in the image of a citadel, a city, a stone complex of
some kind, is especially fruitful in the space-adventures of André
Norton. Like other forms of fantasy, space-fiction has to throw
out its boundaries from our known world and still preserve a tight
relation with the familiar. The describing of alien star-worlds and
distant galaxies allows space for the imagination to translate
associations of everyday into scenes impressively different and
emotionally disturbing.

The new directions André Norton has given to adventure
through futurist speculations develop from preoccupations vital
to American society in the present – the threat of war and the
effects of Korea and Vietnam on the young, racism and other
forms of discrimination, genetic engineering and its dangers, the
control of technology. The immediate links between present and
future are forged from change and continuity in the nature of
man; André Norton's heroes may be Terran in origin but they
have to learn to adapt to new conditions, to communicate with
and accept mutants, to mind-read with animals, to overcome
predispositions and prejudices for the sake of the future. The
passionate wish for survival, no longer automatically catered for
in Christian and other beliefs in immortality, is satisfied, at least
temporarily, by the theory of successful emigration from Earth to
other parts of the universe. Space-fiction moves a step ahead of
actual research and exploration in technical matters and also in
philosophy. One of André Norton's abiding questions is, 'What
will man become in those future worlds?'

Relating present to future, she implies comfort, as well as
warning, in her tales of adventure in space. Besides the speculations about character-change and adaptation, she binds her

fantasy to our known world through the places she creates. The elements are those we know already but wind and water, rock and grass, earth and sky are subtly altered, in shape or in colour, in chemical substance or in unexpected powers of metamorphosis. The pattern of description in her books is dominated by her use of rock and stone as varying symbols. They may stand for man's long-lasting predisposition to contention and the desire for power. The stone-built underground tunnels and storerooms of Ruhkarv, a ruined city declared out of bounds on the planet Korwar, affect the hero, Troy Horan (and, through him, the reader) with an apprehension of evil still existing, a feeling induced by physical assaults on the senses which are the outward signs of a deeper danger:

> . . . he stepped into what might have once been some vast underground cavern adapted by the unknown builders of Ruhkarv to their own peculiar uses. His torch beam was swallowed up by the vastness of the open expanse and he halted, a little daunted by what faced him. Here was a city in miniature, open ways running between walls of separate, roofless enclosures. And yet the substance of those walls –! It was from here that the fetid odor had come. He could not be sure, yet somehow he shrank from putting his guess to the test of actually laying his hand upon one of those slimily moist surfaces but it looked at first, and even after a more careful examination, as if those walls grew out of the ground, that they were giant slabs of an unknown fungus.[16]

Always a sign of evil in André Norton's stories, the disintegration of rock and stone (by inference, the basic rearrangement of molecular order) is used powerfully in *Forerunner Foray* where a 'sensitive', the highly trained Ziantha, through hypnosis, telekinesis and psychometry uncovers layer after layer of the past in an island ruin whose stones have been maintained by the work of creatures not unlike coral-insects. The combination of material, actual reconstructed conflicts of ambition and an aura of antiquity reached by the efforts of the human mind – this combination, the essential driving force of the story, is communicated partly through the symbol of rock, preserving through millions of years of evolution, and carrying forward, the invisible evidence of human error, ambition, aggression.

Again, in *Star Born* a stronghold and storehouse, stone-built and suggesting in its shattered form a devastating conflict, is the central, physical point round which André Norton builds the account of a non-human race, once powerfully controlling a slave-state and now trying to regain its former power against the enlightened principles of a new galactic world. The enduring properties of rock and stone in the books culminate in references to the Forerunners which can be found everywhere. Her most emphatic, if indirect statement about the human race, at once an optimistic and a minatory one, turns on the concept of layers of ancient civilisations whose buildings and artefacts are found here and there on newly discovered or rediscovered planets or star-worlds. From what survives of the Forerunners can be deduced civilisations often infinitely more advanced than that of Terra and its associated colonies. Evidence of the persistence of intelligent life in the universe, at once a consolation and a warning, is built up mainly by the research and exploration of the lizard-type Zacathans, a race with a written history covering two million planet years, an alien race of long-lived archaeologists and recorders whose traditional dignity adds its own reassurance. To the Zacathans the Forerunners are a sign of what man might become in the future: to the Terran races the relics in stone which they are now and then privileged to see are wonders and portents, regarded in something of the way that we regard the myths of antiquity, always associated with the grandeur and impermeable nature of rock.

Poetry and history come together in *The X Factor*, where a search for the fabled city of Xcothal involves the mutant Fentriss, son of a space-explorer, with a Zacathan archivist explorer and with furred animals to whom Fentriss speaks with mind-talk. Alerted by the persistent legends of Xcothal, the explorers see the city in more than one dimension. The discovery of a paved road beneath marshland leads in a concrete but also an illusory way to their goal:

> It was late afternoon, but the shadows were not thick enough to veil what stood out in the embrace of the water and mud – square cubes, rectangular blocks of dull black, spaced in a definite design, as if the roofs of some long-drowned city protruded from the grove that engulfed it.
>
> Yet no matter how hard Diskan stared at a building, how he tried to concentrate on its size, its general shape, its position among the rest, there was a queer sensation of not seeing – of an intangible haze between him and the ruins, an unsubstantial aura about it.
>
> Those lines of blocks went on and on, fanning out from the foot of the giant square on which he stood, to vanish well out in the bog. He could not sight the other edge of what must have been an ancient metropolis.[17]

It is the property of imagery to be at once concrete and abstract, explicit and allusive. These opposites could also be claimed as basic to the adventure story at its best, a type of fiction to be read, concurrently, in many different ways and inspiring many differing reactions. To achieve this result with her stories, André Norton has used many kinds of images, notably of rock and stone, with striking effect.

Inevitably the force of certain images changes with the changing literary associations of different generations. Mary Lascelles has offered a striking example of this constraint on the writer when he relies on images to arouse associations in his readers. She comments on the change in the present century:

> I am bound to wonder how much of our older literature will be intelligible a generation hence. What will become of that potent image of desolation, *the cold hearth-stone*? Will it mean anything to town-dwellers? Will it mean much even to country-dwellers? Will it carry its whole burden of meaning except to those who have seen a deserted village? Perhaps the story-teller, less regarded but more approachable than the poet, may keep such symbols as this alive in the imagination.[18]

'Alive in the imagination'. We read adventure stories in search of emotional and aesthetic pleasure and perhaps it is the last of these expectations, the indescribable enlarging of one's apprehensions, which is helped by the working of potent images through a story. In Masefield and Rider Haggard, the places where events happen are far more than simple backgrounds for the movements of characters: through the images by which they are confirmed as description they can be made to communicate a larger theme, a philosophy, a statement of intent and purpose. One image that will survive social and geographical change, the road, stands for the most familiar plot and the most important theme of adventure-story – the journey. The properties of this abiding image were laid down in the simplest and most romantic form by Jeffery Farnol in the novel above all his others which best illustrates the point, *The Broad Highway*:

> As this life is a Broad Highway along which we must all of us pass whether we will or no; as it is a thoroughfare sometimes very hard and cruel in the going, and beset by many hardships, sometimes desolate and hatefully monotonous, so, also, must its aspect, sooner or later, change for the better, and the stony track overpassed, the choking heat and dust left behind, we may reach some green, refreshing haven shady with trees, and full of the cool, sweet sound of running waters. Then who shall blame us if we pause unduly in this grateful shade, and, lying upon our backs, gaze up through the swaying green of the trees to the infinite blue beyond, ere we journey on once more, as soon we must, to front whatsoever of good or evil lies waiting for us in the hazy distance.[19]

Farnol's peculiarly clotted prose, with its mixture of syntactic inversions and archaisms and a manufactured 'Regency' idiom suggests that Bunyan may have been one, distant source of inspiration, but the picaresque novel which passed on from Fielding to Marryat and others is a more obvious model for Farnol's plots, which often begin with a hero setting foot on the 'open road' in an uncomplicated search for adventure. For Farnol the image of the road was neither moralistic nor truly philosophical, in spite of the occasional apostrophes to life which break up his dashing action and garrulous dialogue; it was a very concrete and often an actual thoroughfare which could be used to give readers the special pleasure of recognition. They could travel in imagination along the London to Brighton road (inevitably Farnol's main thoroughfare, given the Regency plots of many of his novels), willingly forgetting modern Reigate or Sevenoaks because of persuasive details of coaching-inns, smithies and fords along the way.

Once this function of the road was discharged, its second purpose was just as simple. It allowed Jeffery Farnol to introduce events and characters in profusion and almost at random, in a lateral narrative scheme where the main plot (hero defeats villain and gets girl) can be stretched out over chapter after chapter by means of subplots, casual encounters, diversions and interruptions. The road offered two invaluable elements – familiarity and surprise, order and change. For author and reader there could be the constant refreshment of new characters, new settings in a narrative kept in order as it moved logically from one point of the road to another.

If the emotional content of Jeffery Farnol's novels seems today almost absurdly simplified, his manipulation of narrative is extremely skilful. The immediate impulse of his hero's journey is as a rule elementary. *The Broad Highway*, for example, introduces Peter Vibart, returned from Oxford with vague literary aspirations, mildly revolutionary social views and no prospects in life. When he learns that his wealthy uncle has left him a mere ten pounds and a fortune to his notorious cousin Maurice, Peter is inspired by the view from a window of 'that famous highway, built and paved for the march of Roman Legions, winding away to where it vanished over distant Shooter's Hill', and announces to his discomfited guardian, 'I shall go, Sir, on a walking tour through Kent and Surrey into Devonshire and thence probably to Cornwall'.[20] Fate decrees that the 'tour' shall be diverted almost at once. The residue of Uncle George's considerable property is to be inherited under certain conditions: 'the sum of five hundred thousand pounds, now vested in the funds, shall be paid to either Maurice or Peter Vibart aforesaid, if either shall, within one calendar year, become the husband of the Lady Sophia Sefton of Camborne'. The journey through which Peter intended to escape such a degrading competition leads to this very marriage, but under the kind of tantalising and suggestively romantic conditions typical of Farnol and his successor, Georgette Heyer. The reader's guesses are by turns encouraged and checked as the hero marches along the highway from one encounter to another.

A plot-structure so permittedly episodic, offering such chances for variety of setting, event and character, was to be immensely popular in children's fiction, for more than one reason. One favourite author of the late thirties and the immediate post-war years, M. E. Atkinson, composed many variations on the theme of an extended journey over a set route, over actual country which might be known to some readers and could be at least partly followed on a map. The most ingenious of these variations added an element of competition to the simple journey-with-accidents. In one of her earliest holiday-adventures, *Horseshoes and Handlebars*, she described a familiar situation, a group of children ranging in age from ten to sixteen spending the summer holiday in a manor guest-house in the Quantocks (with parents by custom temporarily absent) and facing disconcerting differences of outlook in their temperaments.

The Trenchard sisters, Meg and Guin, are horsy and outdoor in somewhat different ways (Meg at fifteen enjoys riding but is apt to comb her hair and sit down with a book rather too often for tomboyish, impetuous Guin): the Slater brothers are townies, though Richard at thirteen is only held back by his wary respect for his supercilious older brother Fabian from acknowledging a secret wish to ride. Their hostess, Miss Shepperson, hoping to persuade the silently polite couples to make friends, decrees an evening of games which includes the favourite board-game Michael is ashamed of enjoying so much, 'Willy's Walk to Grandmamma', played with ivory counters and 'a little ivory totem with numbers up to eight on it indicating movements along numbered squares':

> Willy, on his journey, had many adventures – although they were all somewhat commonplace. For instance, looking up your fate when your counter arrived at square eight, you would read: 'Gets a ride on a baker's cart to number twenty-two'. For square eighteen you found: 'Discovers he has lost his penny and must return to the start'. Indeed, from start to finish, Willy's walk was fraught with incident. He 'lost a turn' by having a fight – hard luck, this, Michael always thought, for in that same neat copper-plate it went on to explain that the fight came from Willy's endeavour to save a dog that another boy was teasing.[21]

337

The ill-assorted children are inspired by this artless game to plan a competitive hike along a stated route, with elaborate rules including visits to certain villages, to prove the superior virtues of their respective steeds – horses for Guin and Meg and the younger holiday guest, ten-year-old Michael, and bicycles for scornful Fabian and his loyal brother Richard. The four-day journey is in fact not much less 'commonplace' and safe than the journey of Victorian Willy, with his 'pantaloons, button boots, and queer little jacket', while at least one square on Willy's board is imitated when Fabian decides, deceitfully, that he and Richard are justified in accepting a lift, as they are toiling up a steep hill, in a lorry half full of bricks. Besides this, Willy's ride on a donkey which helps him over several squares is distantly echoed when the children arrive at the most desirable point of the journey, the scene of a point-to-point where Guin's cousin is competing and where the impetuous Guin, after her cousin has a fall, takes her place against the entreaties of the more cautious Meg and rides to the finish – not as the winner, in fact, but after rescuing a small bystander and covering herself with momentary glory.

This car-rally-type plot offers a single line of tension and anti-cipation on which ancillary events can be strung: 'Who will get there first?' often becomes less interesting to the reader than 'What will happen to them on the way?' In one especially well constructed 'Willy's Walk' tale, *The Stolen Seasons* by David Divine, an argument about how easily the barbarians might have slipped over the Wall without being seen by Roman sentinels leads to a challenge: Peter and his sister Meg and a visiting American friend take on a bet with the rather patronising grown-ups that they will work up to the Wall from fourteen miles away and cross it unseen. Their enterprise is side-tracked when they stumble on crooks stealing a treasure from an excavation in progress, a development that turns a game into a dangerous exploit.

M. E. Atkinson uses 'Willy's Walk' to shape some of the enterprises of her series-family, the three Locketts. In *The Nest of the Scarecrow*, they are invited by a brother and sister to join a trek from the New Forest to a certain point on the Dorset coast: the invitation comes because the Dwights have read earlier books about (and by) the Locketts and hope their obvious propensity for stumbling on odd people and events will enliven the normally tame course of Dwight holidays. The road between two West Country villages provides another games-board for a blind journey in *August Adventure*, the first Lockett adventure, in which they rush off in search of a missing aunt, their intended holiday

338

hostess: their movements are so carefully plotted and integrated with the movements of absent-minded Aunt Lavinia (an artist, as one might guess) in the opposite direction, that the illusion of a board-game is particularly strong.

'Willy's Walk to Grandmamma' seems in fact an appropriate name for the kind of junior adventure which gathered momentum before the Second World War and continued its innocuous course for at least two decades when peace had brought an acceleration of this and other safe, sensible and mildly exciting tales. One aspect of this kind of adventure-game did at least potentially act as a counterpoise to its rather bland and socially restrictive course. Given a plot centred on a specific journey by road, there was an opportunity to use the fact that other people were travelling at the same time to introduce a few adults into the story.

The type of people which the Locketts and other children like them were likely to meet were predictable. Where Jeffery Farnol's wayfarers found help or hindrance from innkeepers and postilions, fist-fighters and blacksmiths, children might be helped by undergraduates on walking tours, kindly farmers with useful carts (or, later, Land-Rovers), friendly cottage folk ready to provide anything from a drink of water to a night in a feather bed, or local children who were usually tormenting puppies and kittens or throwing mud at their social superiors. The journeys in this kind of story might be, and usually were, artificial and contrived, but the presence of adults did act as a stiffener and prevent, to some extent, that uncomfortable feeling of being isolated in a bubble of juvenile behaviour which makes so many of the stories published in the thirties and forties easy to criticise from the standpoint of today.

Such criticism has been inevitable as the changes in society in the years after the Second World War were slowly but surely reflected in children's fiction. Attitudes overlap to such an extent that it is not easy to point to a specific time when this type of fiction found room for a broader social scene and a greater maturity of outlook, but there are often single books which point the way forward. Such a book was Anne Barrett's *The Journey of Johnny Rew* which when it appeared in 1954 looked back to the comfortable 'Willy's Walk' type of story but presaged the richer mixtures of writers like Nina Bawden and Emma Smith.

The plot of Anne Barrett's story (her first, incidentally) is a familiar lateral one, an episodic board-game development. A boy of thirteen, Johnny had been taken in as a small child by a hospitable Cockney family after his mother was killed in the Blitz and his sailor-father was posted missing, presumed dead.

Discovering a clue to his origins and driven by the restlessness of his years, the boy accepts the challenging advice of a retired admiral met in Kensington Gardens, inspired by the old man's account of how he had to walk a hundred and twenty miles, as a lad, to join his first ship. Johnny's journey from London down to the southern coast, partly on foot and partly with lifts from friendly motorists, brings him into contact with adults whose problems delay and divert him. After witnessing a burglary, in which he is supposedly implicated, he pursues a zigzag course to escape the police and in the latter part of his journey he is traced from place to place by a mysterious pursuer who, in the way of the traditional adventure-journey, proves to be his own father.

So much is familiar enough. So, too, is the social stability with which each of the people he meets fits tidily into a particular slot – Sam Bridle the philosophical roadman, the forthright lady of the manor, the stout countrywoman met on a bus, the vague, scholarly parson. But there are differences to suggest that this is not quite the same story as before. First, Anne Barrett writes maturely, describing settings and characters in a particularised way that colours and enriches a seemingly familiar choice of landscape and figures. This is at once a new and an old style, reminiscent as it is of the amplitude of Stanley Weyman or Rider Haggard and yet novel in that there is nothing of the 'told to the children' tone which sounds in almost all the similar journey-tales of the period. She seems to be writing as she wants to, not finding it necessary to reduce or dilute for young readers her appreciation of the men and women who complicate Johnny's plans with map and compass. Here is a set piece offering the boy's view of Sam the roadman, as the two sit by a fire in one of Sam's hideouts, enjoying a well-roasted rabbit:

> The big man was chewing up and down a drumstick as though it were a flute, an expression of amiable contentment in his deep-lidded brown eyes. His largeness was more of height and big bones than of breadth; the legs that were stretched out in front of him and the arms that were supported on his knees as he chewed, were almost as long in themselves as Johnny's whole body. Where his shirt-sleeves were turned back, there was a tangle of grizzled hair on the spare brown forearms; Johnny looked up at his head in surprise, having thought him a younger man. Originally dark, his hair was now greying too, close cut and scrubby as a terrier's, growing forward into two short tufts on his prominent cheek bones.
>
> Everything about him was large, nose, chin and hands, and they were as brown and hard as though he had been carved, all to scale,

from the wood of some mighty oak tree. Even his voice came booming up from inside him, like the echoes of a rock thrown down into some vast cavern, and, as Johnny listened to it, he felt that nothing but large thoughts and feelings could ever come up out of that great body either.[22]

This amalgam of a boy's reactions and an author's experience was far from usual at the time when the book was published, as also was the effect of this and other encounters on Johnny. A journey started in a spirit of bravado and in reaction to a life of routine becomes a series of lessons which help to turn his boyish impatience into something like true independence. Anne Barrett sketches just enough of the situations and preoccupations of her adult characters to push her young traveller out of his known world and his known self. The journey changes Johnny, not only in the most obvious way, by giving him a father and a new sphere of action for the future, but also in giving him a better judgement of the world than he had before.

In a modest, unassuming way, *The Journey of Johnny Rew* has something of the *rite de passage* in it. In form, content and style a proper adventure story, it also has in it certain elements of the problem novel which has dominated at least the last two decades of children's fiction. And it raises a question which may lead to the most basic definition of the distinction between adult and junior adventure stories. How far are children's stories educational?

Attitudes

14. Who is the Enemy?

The story-teller's role in society is, by tradition, to record events and celebrate people in such a way as to confirm and perpetuate codes of conduct which will benefit that society: conversely, the story-teller may be said to exist in order to prepare the way for change by criticising, deriding or contradicting currently established views. The dual functions of entertainment and instruction are built into story-telling. Is there a difference in its operation in the case of stories told specifically for children? If so, is this a difference in degree and technique or something more?

Here, more than at any other stage of my argument, it is necessary to separate, or to acknowledge a difference between, characters and reader. We have to ask not only whether young readers are expected to learn from the stories they read but also whether the characters in the story are learning from the adventures into which the author precipitates them. A broad distinction could be drawn here between adult adventure stories and those written for children. In a junior adventure story there is something for the hero or heroine (or for the villain, for that matter) to learn from events and this lesson is part of the direction of the story. Children reading *The Swiss Family Robinson* or *Swallows and Amazons* join the children in the story at the school of active experience and, often, of straight didactic teaching as well.

Much depends on the identity of the 'teacher' if a particular adventure story is to become a true documentary or a classroom exercise. Ransome may serve as an example here. Because his tales are true extensions of everyday and not flights of fancy, there must be some control by adults of children. The mother of the Swallows has a sense of humour and of enterprise but Ransome vested in her (and, more remotely, in Captain Walker) the necessary discipline from above. Jim Flint, the Amazons' (Blacketts') uncle, takes on the role of that useful character of junior fiction, the Omniscient Uncle, but with a difference. He is allowed to behave for much of the time like an overgrown schoolboy, playing pirates and rigging elaborate practical jokes, easily rebutting the affectionate, half-joking criticism of his sister. This side of his nature never becomes foolish or exhibitionist. He carries on an efficient adult life at a distance and relaxes from it in

345

games with the young. In Jim Flint, also, is vested the duty of instruction. Behind the fun and the complicity in adventure, his practical skills and experience are available in matters of weather-lore, sailing techniques, camp organisation and so on, and his nephews and nieces and their friends will accept such lessons more readily from him than from parents whose status is more sharply defined and whose ambitions for their children cannot be entirely concealed. The cheerfulness and resource of this admirable uncle, diffused through the books, carry perfectly serious principles of conduct to readers who need only be aware of enjoying entertaining stories.

In making the right space in a book for this element of learning and teaching, an author is recognising a duty to his readers which he must reconcile with his duty to his characters. He is writing for unformed, inexperienced, *young* readers. It follows that his dialogue with them, however maturely he may express his point of view, is not the same as the dialogue he will hold with adult readers, in whom he can assume at least a certain experience of life and a personal standard from which they can assess the motives and actions in a story.

In the widest sense any adventure story is educational. Whatever the relative importance of action and character, there will be some direction towards an implied statement about human behaviour. The adult reader has the choice of enjoying the action and ignoring a moral or psychological point or of meeting the author halfway and using imagination to appreciate what he implies in the plain course of his narrative. A young reader does not have the same choice – or, at least, the author makes it clear that he *does* intend that reader to profit by his story. The fact that many children ignore this aspect of it does not alter the writer's intention or his duty. Apart from the moral need to make some kind of clear statement about the theme and purpose of his fiction, he has the literary need to integrate his lesson with his narrative, which will be either didactic or truly, broadly educational, according to his presentation of people and events.

Here some distinction must be made between education and information. This may be best pursued by comparing two books for children whose plots and characters are not dissimilar but whose purpose and effect are very different. Patrick O'Brian's *The Road to Samarcand*, published in 1954, is based on an almost formal thesis. A boy in the early teens, orphan son of missionaries, has been given a temporary home on the *Wanderer*, in which his uncle trades in the China Seas, but in time Captain Sullivan realises Derrick must go to England and become a schoolboy again. The purpose and use of education is tossed about between the captain (who sees the need for training towards a Master's ticket), his chief engineer Ross (who had run away to sea at an early age but who still pays lip service to higher education), the mate Olaf who believes in learning by doing, and the Chinese cook, Li Han, who points out the advantages of a pensionable job in the civil service over the perils of seafaring life. The final decision is made by Derrick's cousin, Professor Ayrton, an archaeologist who neatly solves the problem and satisfies his own research needs at the same time. His support for a conventional education is expressed in terms very congenial to the boy: he announces:

> 'I intend, with your uncle's consent, to gild the pill of education by a suggestion that may be new to you. How would you like to go to the school by way of Samarcand?'[1]

Formal learning and personal experience are to go hand in hand in this compromise. The professor is to give the boy Greek lessons and Mr Ross will continue instruction in trigonometry and navigation already begun on the ship. Everything else, from the right way to ride a camel to the technique of identifying types of jade, will come by chance along the way: the lessons in fortitude and self-reliance which a boy of Derrick's class and date would learn in the tough atmosphere of boarding school come, in this case, from encounters with Chinese warlords and hostile Kazaks and a gruelling mountain journey on the Tibetan border. When the adventure is over, it is evident to the reader that while fear and physical deprivation have to some extent tested Derrick, he has not really changed as a result of this exciting, varied and exacting journey. He has acquired information rather than growing in stature as a result of education.

In my second example, information is secondary in the experience of a boy travelling in the East at the turn of the century and meeting similar hazards. Peter Dickinson's historical adventure *Tulku* was written almost a quarter of a century later than Patrick O'Brian's spanking yarn and though I would not claim that any specific chronological change could be traced here, it does seem to me that the emotional, even philosophical tone of Dickinson's book has something to do with the present-day view of the moral development of the young and the way writers are responding to this in the tone of their fiction. Certainly *Tulku* should serve to show what I mean by education as opposed to instruction.

The central character of the book is a boy of ten, Theodore Tewker, who alone survives a raid of Boxer rebels on the mission station run by his American father. In terms of actual physical danger Theo is as adequately protected by his elders as Derrick was in *The Road to Samarcand*. In place of the ministrations of the traditional Omniscient Uncle figure in that book (a role shared between several characters, in fact, each one focusing his attention on the boy) Peter Dickinson has drawn as Theo's protector the magnificently individual figure of Mrs Jones, a strident Cockney travelling as a flower-collector, a woman of bold integrity who has no intention of subordinating her own journey through life to the needs of a small boy.

Although she acts with tact and delicacy towards Theo after she has accepted and returned the love of her servant and fellow-traveller, the Chinese poet Lung, she leaves it to the boy to find his own way out of the misery and loss he has suffered and to adjust to the behaviour of his elders. Instead of setting her up as a mother-figure to fill the place of Theo's dead father, Peter Dickinson has made her the means by which the boy gradually comes to look, again and honestly, at the strict, theological education which he has taken for granted. Father would have disliked Mrs Jones for her brazen speech and sexual manners, Theo realises very early in their escape, but he need not necessarily feel the same:

> It was strange to be thinking of Father like this, as it were from the outside. Father had been a wonderful man, good and clever and kind, but his personality had been so strong that it filled the settlement. You breathed and ate and drank Father. Sometimes he was a cliff towering above you; at other times you swam in the lake of his love. But all the time you were somehow inside him, as the unhatched bird is in its shell; and now Theodore was outside, looking back down the vista of travelled days to where Father was dwindling, just as the limestone pillars of the plateau had dwindled with the miles.[2]

Guilty but delighted at his feeling of freedom, Theo grows into his independence, at first learning to accept Mrs Jones for what she is; then in the Lamasery where they wait for the birth of her child, by divination believed to be the Tulku, the new lama, Theo moves out of received dogma and realises that he is an individual, solely responsible for himself. In keeping with his age and experience, he does not arrive at this vital point in his moral education by reason but through an inrush of feeling, a sharpening of the senses, partly due to the alarming and unfamiliar procedures of the oracle-priest and partly through the influence of the remote community where he has time to grow into his experiences:

348

> . . . and now, here, he was fiercely conscious of himself as Theodore, of the central numbness flooding with life, the broken roof rebuilt and the cold hearth glowing. He had heard Lama Amchi talk of those moments on the path to enlightenment when the soul seems to leave the body and soar free, and of the agony of its return to clogging flesh. Theodore felt the exact opposite. The return was the ecstasy. He was whole, and body and mind and soul sang at their healing.[3]

The whole course of this travel-adventure is built on the theme of education in the basic sense of the difficult search for identity. Supported as it is on recurring images of plants, growth and gardening, the book is educational but in no way didactic. Most readers have a robust protective instinct which operates against obvious didacticism in fiction and in this children tend to be more uncompromising than adults. They will either ignore a lesson too directly stated or they will discard the book in question. In his recollections of 'The Youth of a Children's Magazine', published in the *Cornhill Magazine* for May 1932, Harvey Darton commented that as a child he 'adored' *The Swiss Family Robinson* and that he only realised 'that it was stiff with prayers and piety'[4] when he looked at it professionally years later.

There is a greater danger for the reader here than the possibility of being bored. Every writer expresses his attitudes – moral, political, emotional – in his books, and propaganda is at its most subtle and persuasive when it is contained within a story. Yet the sense of responsibility which we must concede to any writer (combined as it will be with practical interests of fashion and markets) convinces him that he has a duty to children to recommend certain lines of thought and modes of behaviour accepted in the society and culture in which he works. Since attitudes change from one period to another, an over-emphatic note of propaganda in books written in the past causes them to be neglected or censored later; this is a particular danger in the sphere of children's books, where the protective impulses of parents and other guardians come into operation.

The type of adventure story where the educational desires of author and critic are most likely to come into collision is the story of war, where a natural patriotism is liable to lead to a glorification of violence. Two writers whose reputation has suffered from a change in attitude – G. A. Henty and Captain W. E. Johns – both made in their lifetime strong assertions of a mission to educate the young. In an article published in the *Boys' Own Paper* after his death, Henty wrote:

349

To endeavour to inculcate patriotism in my books has been one of my main objects, and so far as it is possible to know, I have not been unsuccessful in that respect. I know that very many boys have joined the cadets and afterwards gone into the Army through reading my stories, and at many of the meetings at which I have spoken officers of the Army and Volunteers have assured me that my books have been effectual in bringing young fellows into the Army – not so much into the rank and file as among the officers. . . .[5]

and Captain Johns, talking to Geoffrey Trease, made his sense of educational responsibility very clear:

. . . I give boys what they want, not what their elders and betters think they ought to read. I teach at the same time, under a camouflage. Juveniles are keen to learn, but the educational aspect must not be too obvious or they become suspicious of its intention. I teach a boy to be a man, for without that essential qualification he will never be anything. I teach sportsmanship according to the British idea. One doesn't need blood and thunder to do this. In more than forty novels about my hero Biggles he has only once struck a man, and that was a matter of life and death. I teach the spirit of team-work, loyalty to the Crown, the Empire, and to rightful authority. . . .[6]

emphasising that a boy is a born hero-worshipper and 'upon the actions of his heroes will his own character be formed'.

It is not always wise for authors to be categorical about their aims in such general terms. The blatant patriotism, not to say flag-wagging, of these two statements of intent was bound to mask the basic respect for courage and endeavour which both authors celebrated, like any other responsible writer of adventure stories. Captain Johns seems in fact to have been inflating the more moderate aim which he put forward in a prefatory statement 'About Pioneer Air Combat' in the collection of his magazine stories, *The Camels are Coming*, expressing his practical anxiety about the impending war and Britain's lack of preparation:

Finally, I hope that from a perusal of these pages a younger generation of air fighters may learn something of the tricks of the trade, of the traps and pitfalls that beset the unwary, for I fear that many of the lessons which we learned in the hard school of war are being rapidly obscured by the mists of peace-time theory.[7]

Henty's enormous output and the fact that he reflected the attitudes of the late Victorian period with special clarity meant that his influence was bound to be attacked as well as valued. His imperialist views were no more exaggeratedly expressed than those of Ballantyne for earlier generations, but because his material was history, and British history most of all, these views were likely to make more impression – favourably, on the parents of the boys he sought to influence, unfavourably, on later generations for whom Britain's future lay (ostensibly, at least) in other than imperialist aims.

His attitudes were not the only available source of influence for Britain's youth, in fact. If his books appeared on the shelves of preparatory schools in his own time and for generations to come, so did the stories of Conan Doyle in which boys eager to absorb themselves in active adventure could meet such varied points of view as the Gallic frivolity and cynicism about war filtered through the satirical stories about Brigadier Gerard's exploits in the Napoleonic Wars or the political prudence of civil servant Cyril Brown in *The Tragedy of the Korosko*, as well as the open patriotic élan of Micah Clarke and Rodney Stone. Henty's heroes, though, were all mouthpieces of the same nationalist view, not independent characters offering ideas appropriate to varying social situations, and conviction, endlessly repeated, was bound to have its effect.

Reactions against the political attitudes in Henty's books did not, as is sometimes supposed, begin as one of many effects of the Second World War on trends in children's reading. As long ago as 1908 a critic calling himself 'R. van Eeghen' (supposedly, but not necessarily, non-British) offered striking evidence of Henty's influence in hostile terms:

> There is no doubt that the immortal Henty and his hosts of imitators have made the British nation the most conceited people on this earth. It is the plotless trash of authors who shelter themselves behind the section in the library catalogue entitled 'Books for Boys', which has given the average young Englishman that very excellent opinion of himself which he now enjoys. Putting aside the question of the utter impossibilities of the usual boys' book, it is quite easy to see the harm the authors of these volumes cause by the exaggeration of the deeds and opinions of their *invraisemblable* heroes. After fourteen or fifteen years' perusal of 'piffle' written apparently for his edification, the young Englishman leaves home and country with the very firm idea in his head that he, personally, is equal to two or more Frenchmen, about four Germans, an indefinite number of Russians, and any quantity you care to mention of the remaining scum of the earth.[8]

The expertly judged exactness of the last sentence has been picked up and used by more than one critic in later years, as a more picturesque way of indicating disapproval than the all too familiar general comment – for example, Guy Arnold's somewhat stately accusation eighty years later that Henty must be held responsible for 'the racial arrogance which, unhappily, has been so marked a characteristic of British behaviour in what is now termed "The Third World . . ."'[9] Certainly Henty's books supported the advice and direction offered to the young in their day and for many decades later by teachers and parents, and a reaction against them was inevitable. But it was a reaction against the content of the stories rather than, or more strongly than, a judgement on their value as fiction, as stories; attention was focused on that content, with examples taken out of context (if indeed examples were quoted at all).

In fact, the propaganda element in many of Henty's tales is surprisingly slight in comparison with the one dominant element of *instruction* in them – namely, military history. Henty's abiding interest in the tactics and strategies of war often overloaded his books to the detriment of his fiction. In *The Bravest of the Brave*, for instance, the young hero is entirely eclipsed by the prominence given to Lord Peterborough and the part he played in the War of Succession, and the better balance of personal and professional action in *The Cornet of Horse*, which describes a youth's involvement in Marlborough's wars, still allowed Henty plenty of space to describe the battles of Blenheim and Ramillies in clear, telling detail. One can claim for Henty, in fact, a measure of an historian's accuracy, if not an extreme realism, in describing scenes of war. If he does not arouse anti-war sentiments, he does not glorify war either in the way that some of his successors were apt to do. Moreover, although the British point of view is paramount, he is well aware that there could be other sides to the question. The Boer claims are recognised, though not accepted, by the brothers who act as scouts and transport officers in *The Young Colonists*; and in *Maori and Settler*, a tale particularly rich in humour and incident, Henty distinguishes firmly between the first period in the Maori wars, in which the Maoris were fighting for independence, their own laws and their own ruler, and the second epoch dominated by the fanatic Hau Haus and the massacre at Poverty Bay.

Van Eeghen's phrase 'plotless trash' hardly applies to Henty, who satisfied his eager readers with an endless supply of sharply described and vigorous scenes of action arranged in a clear progression showing the success or failure of a hero just within their terms of reference. The definition of '*invraisemblable* heroes' is better justified, for the lads of fifteen or so in the books who precipitate themselves for one reason or another into national conflicts from Roman times to the nineteenth century are indistinguishable from one another as individuals, however properly labelled by appearance, class background and circumstance. Guy Arnold's label of anachronistic, in that they are always 'Victorian public-school prefects' even when they speak and act as 'fourteenth or fifteenth-century characters',[10] is certainly justified. What critics do not mention is Henty's attention to his minor characters. His heroes are, by choice and appropriately, representative, but the people they are involved with are by no means stereotypes. Indeed, now and then they seem to cast a reflection of their own energies on to the predictable hero or afford an opportunity for us to see that hero momentarily in an unexpected way.

In *A Jacobite Exile*, one of Henty's richest and least didactic tales, set at the end of the seventeenth century, young Charlie Lynnwood, an ardent supporter of the Stuart cause like his father, is forced to leave England because of the false witness against the family of a Whig cousin with eyes on the estate. He joins King Charles of Sweden and serves with the expected prowess in the army, so that before he is seventeen he is already heading a British contingent. After an exciting year or so with outlaws and aristocrats in Poland, he is taken prisoner while serving on a campaign against Russia, and meets more than once a sympathetic and congenial doctor, 'Peter Michaeloff', who arouses his (rather slow-witted) interest:

> I should think [reflects Charlie] the doctor must be a man of large property, and most likely of noble family, who has taken up his profession from pure love of it. He is evidently full of energy, and has an intense desire to see Russia greater and higher in the rank of nations. I suppose that, like Kelly, he is one of the principal medical officers in the army. Certainly he must be a man of considerable influence to obtain my transfer here so easily, and to see that I travelled so comfortably.[11]

By the time Charlie has realised that his captivity has been eased by none other than the Czar, the reader has recognised in the young man a fallible, even an interesting, human being and not a mere coat hanger for noble deeds to hang on.

This is not the only time that Henty allows himself a little relaxation with his heroes nor the only time he permits the colour of humour in his spectrum of red, white and blue. The stout emigrant and botanist, Atherton, who joins the Renshaw family in making a new home in the Taranaki district of New Zealand (in

353

Maori and Settler) is a man of shrewd intelligence who forestalls any comment on his girth by his own rueful remarks:

> Nature altogether made a mistake in my case. I ought to have been a thin wiry sort of man, and in that case I have no doubt I should have distinguished myself as an African explorer or something of that sort. Unfortunately she placed my restless spirit in an almost immovable frame of flesh, and the consequence is the circle of my wandering is to a certain extent limited.[12]

Superfluous fat does not prevent Atherton from playing an effective part in the resistance of the settlers to Hau Hau raiders and by the time he has diffidently confessed his love for Marion Renshaw he has certainly lost some weight; but he remains, not a figure of fun, but a recognisable individual whose behaviour and idiom add welcome variety to the familiar course of the growing up and testing of his young brother-in-law-to-be, Wilfred.

The undoubted virtues of Henty as a story-teller, a deviser of exciting action in a variety of times and places, a shrewd rearranger of the tedium of war, have been to some extent obscured by the natural but often critically unbalanced attention given to the attitudes implied or expressed in his books. The line of inheritance from Ballantyne and Henty to Kingston and Westerman and on to Captain Johns is so easily traced that it has almost come to be taken as representative of the entire genre of the adventure story. The kind of critical generalisation which separates content from style and results often in a blurring of literary standards may be seen in Martin Green's *Dreams of Adventure, Deeds of Empire*, in which he suggests that the traditional adventure story could be used as a foundation for 'British Studies' as a way of helping immigrants and citizens to a better understanding of one another. Implicit in his argument is the suggestion of a single, overriding influence of books on the young which is not necessarily the whole truth but which is easy to accept as such. He announces:

> My argument will be that the adventure tales that formed the light reading of Englishmen for two hundred years and more after *Robinson Crusoe* were, in fact, the energizing myth of English imperialism. They were, collectively, the story England told itself as it went to sleep at night; and, in the form of its dreams, they charged England's will with the energy to go out into the world and explore, conquer, and rule.[13]

The rigid nature of this comment may be contrasted with Henty's recognition of the way books helped to develop the active, unprejudiced heroism of one of his heroes. William Gale moves into the world from an orphanage school at Ely with a well-used library:

> Among the books were 'Robinson Crusoe', 'Midshipman Easy', 'Peter Simple', three or four of Cooper's Indian tales, Dana's 'Life before the Mast', and several of Kingston's and Ballantyne's books. These opened a wonderland of life and adventure to the boys. The schoolmaster used to give them out at twelve o'clock, and they were returned at two when school recommenced; and only such boys as obtained full marks for their lessons were allowed to have them. In this way, instead of the 'library' being a cause of idleness, as some of the guardians predicted, when they heard of its presentation, it was an incentive to work. Certainly its perusal filled the minds of most of the boys with an intense longing to go to sea . . .[14]

Implicit also in Martin Green's necessarily generalised view of a huge genre of writing is the assumption that this is entirely 'light reading'. This seems to have a deeper meaning than the very proper comment that books of this kind were written for enjoyment and that 'pleasantness is one of their strengths in the educational situation'. In legitimately proposing that stories could be a useful tool in bringing people of different races together, by discussing the particular attitudes and plot lines of certain writers, the critic has made it clear that he is going to discuss these writers almost entirely from the point of view of the content of their books. The attention to attitudes has dominated the criticism of at least the past two decades, so much so that a list of books in order of merit (if such a list would ever be worth making) might show some odd judgements. In the scales of assessment, however, the long series of tales which Captain Johns wove round Captain James Bigglesworth has been censured (and sometimes censored) by critics, librarians and teachers as much for a limitation in style and narrative quality as for attitudes no longer acceptable in our society.

As in the case of Henty, the accusations of excessive nationalism and of racism have been supported by quotations often made out of context or isolated from the whole tenor and the period setting of the book in question. Some of the virulence that has been exercised against the Biggles books has no doubt been due to the understandable annoyance of librarians and teachers who see a particular author taking up a disproportionate amount of space on bookshelves: besides this, there is the curious sub-jealousy that operates between adults and children which may be expressed in the old family joke, 'Go and see what little Willie is doing and tell him not to.' Apart from this distrust of a genuine, enormous, spontaneous enjoyment (the least admirable element in the desire of adults to educate the young), the resistance to the glorification of violence and the stereotyping of 'the enemy', whoever he might be, was bound to focus on a writer as accessible and as open in his attitudes as Captain Johns.

The lofty aims which he expressed to Geoffrey Trease in the sixties seem a good deal less telling than those included among the objects of the magazine *Popular Flying*, which was founded in 1932 to a large extent because of Johns's determination and his guidance as the first editor. The aims he had expressed in May 1932 had been fulfilled in a short story, 'The White Fokker' by 'William Earle', which appeared in the first number:

> To the younger male generation these stories satisfy the healthy natural craving for the thrills which were once supplied by stories of redskins, pirates and man versus beast. They know that the redskin and pirate have gone for ever, and the wild beast nearly so; but the aeroplane lives. So hero-worshipping youth turns his eyes upwards and visualises himself in the cockpit of the fighting plane that wings its way across the sky. The glorious romance of air fighting probably stands out far more clearly on the printed page than ever it did in actual practice.[15]

Whatever Johns meant by the last sentence (other than an obvious acknowledgement that fiction colours fact simply by its power to rearrange the ordinary), he intended the magazine to be an answer to the melodramatic view of air battles in imported American pulp-magazines. His own experience in the trenches in the Norfolk Yeomanry at the beginning of the First World War and his subsequent career as a second lieutenant in the Royal Air Corps from 1917 (and a prisoner-of-war after a crash, from the autumn of 1917 until the Armistice) qualified him as a recorder of that period of wild improvisation with inadequate machines.

A true recorder, though? The attitudes to war which are accurately reflected from their period in those Biggles tales set in the First World War are undoubtedly out of key with the present day. Perhaps the unquestioning patriotism, Britain-in-the-right, while it conflicts with today's question 'Who is the enemy?', is found less distasteful than the blithe, insouciant manner of Biggles and his fellow flyers which, though it was a legitimate and obvious defence mechanism, could be more insidious in its subliminal effect on young readers if we demand for them, now, an anti-war attitude. Dashing exploits and light-hearted chat, dominating the tales and obviating any sense of fear, boredom or pacifist doubts, inevitably turned stories firmly based on fact into adventure-games of an exhilarating kind.

Those who read the books now in their historical context can adjust to the attitudes of their time of writing and see these attitudes in proportion to the accurate and forceful accounts of dogfights, the development of air-weaponry and the tactics of reconnaissance at the Front. The books in which Johns's early magazine stories were collected, beginning with *The Camels are Coming* in August 1932, did not need to exaggerate but simply to reflect in retrospect the way flyers felt and thought. The trouble was that by the time Johns had prolonged his fictions into the 1950s he had as it were fossilised his attitudes so that they began to seem contrived and artificial and increasingly unattractive. To a great extent this was due to the development (or non-development) of the hero he chose to reflect his own views.

It is hard to recognise the poker-faced hero of later books, sure of his position as right against wrong, in the youth of seventeen who turns up at the Flying Training School in Norfolk in 1916, having given himself an extra year of age on paper:

> There was nothing remarkable, or even martial about his physique; on the contrast, he was slim, rather below average height, and delicate-looking. A wisp of fair hair protruded from one side of his rakishly tilted R.F.C. cap; his eyes, now sparkling with pleasurable anticipation, were what is usually called hazel. His features were finely cut, but the squareness of his chin and the firm line of his mouth revealed a certain doggedness, a tenacity of purpose, that denied any suggestion of weakness. Only his hands were small and white, and might have been those of a girl.[16]

While the creator of Biggles may be said to have left a hint or two here of the invincible resource which was needed to carry the hero through some of his subsequent adventures, he never in fact adopted the sensitive attitude to war that had been forced on the young men of the time; a certain revulsion against war *was* present, infrequently, in early stories written 'in answer to those who have asked when and where Biggles learned to fly'.[17]

In this early collection of episodes, published only three years after the first Biggles yarn, the youth meets reality very soon after his arrival at his first posting, to a squadron near St Omer, as a second lieutenant (after less than fifteen hours' flying, dual and solo). Two planes return, badly shot up, with a dead pilot and a gunner severely wounded:

> The events of the next few minutes were to live in Biggles' mind for ever. His whole system received a shock which sent his nerves leaping like a piece of taut elastic that had been severed with scissors. He was hardly conscious of it at the time, however, when, with the others, he reached the leading machine.[18]

357

Later he listens to his commanding officer arguing that spies are to be admired for their cold nerve and courage rather than scorned for devious activities: he is appalled to learn that a German fighter has machine-gunned a British plane shot down behind the enemy lines and sets out to get his revenge on the unsportsmanlike pilot: he is involved in what seems to him 'just a welter of death and destruction' in a dogfight which is 'not his idea of flying':[19] and he is finally sent on leave to avoid a break-down.

The Biggles of the early flying tales, particularly those describing days at the Front, reflects the honest patriotism and the concern for comrades which belongs to the period. The transition to a more insensitive, bang-bang hero was to come all too soon. It almost seems as though Johns had decided to concentrate on action in order to achieve the kind of adventure story which the young reader could assimilate without any undue exercise of imagination or any real emotional response. For a short time, though, he continued to allow certain reservations and human reactions in the increasingly 'heroic' Biggles.

In *Biggles Flies East*, for example, there still seems to be a real person behind the blood and thunder of the plot. When by a twist of circumstance Biggles becomes a double agent in the Sudan, ostensibly a spy for the German forces against the British but in fact secretly seeking the identity of El Shereef whose activities seriously threaten the British front, he is ill at ease and at times desperate in the need to dissemble and hide his straightforward, aggressive patriotism. At the end of this unusually exacting mission he assures the General who has made use of him that 'A Camel, blue skies, and plenty of Huns is the height of my ambition, and I hope to find them all in France'.[20] In a Foreword to this unusually emotional tale the author indicated to his readers what they were to feel about his hero:

> When he went there he was, like many another air warrior, still a boy; when he came back he was still a boy, but old beyond his years. Into his deep-set hazel eyes, which less than eighteen months before had pondered arithmetic with doubt and algebra with despair, had come a new light; and into his hands, small and delicate – hands that at school had launched paper darts with unerring delicacy – had come a new grip as they closed over joystick and firing lever. When you have read the story perhaps you will understand the reason.[21]

In one of the most difficult moments of Biggles's spy mission he finds himself shot down by British planes while he is on duty with a German supposed colleague. Mayer's leg is broken and he urges Biggles to leave him and make his escape. Biggles obstinately sets out to carry the wounded airman to safety through the desert – not, as might be cynically supposed, as a useful way of allaying the suspicions about his true identity which certain of the Germans at the base entertain by now, but for a more creditable (and believable) motive:

> The idea of leaving Mayer to perish did not occur to him. In the desperate straits in which they found themselves, he no longer regarded him as an enemy, but as a brother pilot who must be supported while a vestige of hope remained.[22]

The hackneyed expression of feeling in the passage need not denote insincerity, any more than we need distrust the sadness behind the sentimentality of Biggles's reaction after he has shot down a German decoy plane:

> Where was the Rumpler? He looked downwards. Ah! He was just in time to see it crash behind the British front-line trench. Tiny ant-like figures were already crawling towards it, some looking upwards, waving to him.
>
> Biggles smiled. 'Given the boys a treat, anyway,' he thought, as he pushed up his goggles and passed his hand wearily over his face. A sound like a sob was drowned in the drone of the engine. 'Well, that's that,' he said to himself, and turned his nose for home.[23]

Perhaps we should logically accept also as genuine the hangover from the simplistic attitudes of the First World War which enabled Johns to define the plot of *Biggles Goes to War* (a story published the year before the outbreak of the Second World War) in a phrase suggesting Ruritanian adventure, 'Greedy eyes are upon little Maltovia'. This small monarchy with its beautiful, golden-haired princess, north-east from the Black Sea, is threatened by invasion from its neighbour and hereditary enemy Lovitznia (aided by a Great Power). Contrary to its date of publication, the story appears to be set not long after the First World War, with Biggles and his friends at a loose end and upset by bad films of the air battles they had engaged in, and only too willing to respond to a request for help from the urbane Maltovian ambassador, even after his Lovitznian counterpart in London, the crudely violent Zanovitch, has warned the airmen against interference. Biggles's motivation sounds familiar:

> 'We are not doing this for money, Count Stanhauser. If you want the truth, we are doing it because there is in us, as there is in most Englishmen, a love of justice, a sense of right and wrong, and sympathy for the under-dog. That is why we shall be proud to wear our Maltovian uniforms.'[24]

These high-sounding sentiments, the final intervention of the League of Nations in the contest between the two small countries, and the reiteration of Maltovia's need for a viable air force and adequate machines, all suggest that Johns was using his hero as a way of facing for himself the change in the climate of politics and nationalism and the consequent moral complexities of the late 1930s. At any rate, by the time he has arranged once again for his demoted airmen to find suitable employment after their second war in the air, he has set the formula for involving them in a series of missions against the post-war crime wave anticipated by their erstwhile commander, Air Commodore Raymond, now back at Scotland Yard. The formation of a special Air Police branch described in *Sergeant Bigglesworth C.I.D.* confirmed Biggles finally as a stereotyped, and best-selling, hero.

The mixture of flippancy and idealism which does come over strongly in the earlier Biggles books is in a sense a diluted survival of the ideals of chivalry which lie behind any adventure story in some measure. The concept of honour which modern attitudes are unable to explain away, however dangerous this may be to the future of the world, is especially clear in the recurring contest between Biggles and his arch-enemy, Colonel Erich von Stalhein, which began in *Biggles Flies East*, continued in one or two fairly artificial treasure-hunt thrillers and ended in unexpected amity in *Biggles Buries the Hatchet* and *Biggles Looks Back*. This antagonist was introduced in one of Johns's rare set pieces:

> In appearance he was tall, slim, and good-looking in a rather foppish way, but he had been a soldier for many years, and there was a grim relentlessness about his manner that quickly told Biggles that he was a man to be feared. He had been wounded early in the war, and walked with a permanent limp with the aid of two sticks, and this physical defect added something to his sinister bearing. Unlike most of his countrymen, he was dark, with cold brooding eyes that were hard to meet and held a steel-like quality that the monocle he habitually wore could not dispel.[25]

The stock attributes of the villain, dark complexion and cold eyes, belong to the hackneyed mode of the portrait and to some extent the addition of a rigid Prussian code of honour is also a literary device, useful in affecting von Stalhein's actions at various moments in the stories where he is Biggles's chief adversary. In *Biggles and Co.*, for instance, the arch-enemy supposedly shot down and killed in the desert reappears as a member of a post-war gang stealing bullion to boost Germany's economy. When he threatens to shoot Biggles's ally Ginger Hebblethwaite, captured in a Dornford Yates sequence of chase and capture in a medieval castle, Biggles reminds him of his code:

> 'Whether you are acting for your government or whether you are simply out for personal gain, is of no importance. You cannot commit murder, for that is what the shooting of an unarmed man amounts to. We are not at war now, remember. If that boy has broken any of the laws of your country, send him up for trial; send us all up for trial. We'll stand or fall by a German jury; but your countrymen would never stand for what you're doing. We've fought in the past, you and I, but we fought fair. Even in that branch of service in which we were once engaged, there were certain rules. Kill your man in a fight, yes, but even at war we didn't murder unarmed men.'. . .[26]

and he comments to Algy (whose opportune arrival down the chimney has usefully reinforced Biggles's moral outburst), 'There is only one way of dealing with a Prussian of the old military school like von Stalhein.'[27]

If this Prussian seems unmindful of his code of honour when he appears as leader of a spy-ring in *Biggles in Australia* or as an agent for Iron Curtain activities in *Biggles in the Blue*, he has clearly remembered it during his years working for the Russian spy system, for he ultimately rebels against the ideology he has been serving and is imprisoned on the Siberian island of Sakhalin. Appealed to by von Stalhein's young nephew, who has escaped from East Germany for the purpose, Biggles discusses the matter with his colleagues in crime-prevention, Ginger and Algy, and recalls the occasions when the Prussian could have killed him out of hand:

> 'His weakness, if we can call it that, lay in the fact that he was what he was – a Prussian professional soldier of the old school, a rigid disciplinarian and a gentleman in the sense that by upbringing and training he had a certain code of behaviour from which he was unable to break away. Actually, I suspect that has been his trouble all along. As a monarchist born and bred he had no business on the other side of the Iron Curtain, and in his heart knew it. Like a square peg in a round hole he just didn't fit, which was why it was inevitable that sooner or later he would fall foul of the people for whom he has been working. They aren't hampered by scruples. He is, and always has been. I know that. I told him so more than once.'[28]

The piquancy of setting Biggles to rescue his enemy, together with an exceptionally well devised and exciting plot line, are technical virtues in *Biggles Buries the Hatchet*. The reader must decide how far the book really uses the code of honour in the deepest emotional sense. The rescue of von Stalhein and his settling in England as a friend may be little more than ingenious twists made by an experienced story-teller. There may be a hint, in the relations between Biggles and von Stalhein, of a less dogmatic attitude than usual towards the causes and motives of war and hostility between nations. A hint only, though. To use the same hero for more than eighty stories has its advantages but it rules out any real probing into moods and motives. To be recognised, to be centrally active in thriller after thriller, Biggles had to be fixed in character and attitudes.

It is significant that his experience with the beautiful German spy Marie Janis (described in the story 'Affaire de Coeur' in *The Camels are Coming*) left him impervious to female charms – an essential in a series of stories written for the young, where any James Bond frolics would have been out of place. A romantic memory could be alluded to delicately, now and then, to give colour to Biggles's predictable detective forays, and could be usefully developed in the hazardous rescue described in *Biggles Looks Back*. Here, von Stalhein and Biggles are allies in a daring enterprise in Czechoslovakia, where Marie, frail and middle-aged, is under pressure from the Communist government to give up her family jewels, including an ancient crown of Bohemia. The author can hardly have intended to introduce humour into such a formally romantic situation in which two men revive a love twenty years old (von Stalhein, we are told, had trained with Marie at the spy-school and wanted to marry her); but it is impossible not to smile at the dénouement, with Marie settled in a cottage in a Hampshire village on the proceeds of her jewels and 'Biggles and von Stalhein often running down for the weekend to talk of their many adventures'.[29]

Sanctions operating on children's books in the 1960s are certainly in question here. More important, the deadpan non-committal behaviour of Biggles is part of the way Johns saw him as the pivot of a series of adventures. If we are to assess the books honestly we need to distinguish between the early flying stories and the later thrillers. In neither group is there any literary finesse. Descriptions are generalised and often conceived in clichés, even when the countries in question were known to the author. The narrative style gains by its plainness in scenes of action but pace is often impeded by increasingly banal and repetitive dialogue as the attention to personality becomes perfunctory. But the earlier books have an honesty of attitude and an authenticity in the accounts of air combat which are sorely missed when Biggles is faced with the enemies of his later combats, the sinister dagoes and half-breeds and rancorous exiles drawn from a pool of stereotypes which has always been only too available to the writers of adventure stories. Biggles as the enemy of the Hun can be accepted in historical perspective: as the bloodthirsty, self-righteous opponent of thriller-villains, he deserves no critical charity.

As I have suggested, the attitudes to war which Johns communicated from his experiences in the First World War were genuine, but not totally representative: they were the attitudes he chose to reflect out of a sense of mission towards his young readers. The limitations of his point of view are very clear when we compare his books with the series of historical adventures about the First World War and its aftermath written in the seventies by John Harris. Where Johns's stories expressed a single point of view through a consistent, undeviating hero, John Harris used his central character, Martin Falconer, as a medium through which to point to the changes that took place in the reactions of men to war over five years. Martin Falconer is not in fact any more of a true fictional individual than Biggles is. He is a glorified test-pilot, through which his creator can offer, among other things, a clear progression of air tactics and planes.

Young Martin allows the author to take an overview of the war from the point of view of the Royal Flying Corps. Through him we become aware of the defects of the planes used in the early years of the war and get to know the virtues and eccentricities of the Camels introduced in 1917; we look at Fokker, Albatros and Gothas, we see Zeppelins over London, we are introduced to Richthofen and his group of fighters. This is material used in textbook style, with the direct educational purpose of a certain type of historical fiction. There is a more important line of argument in the books, though, depending on the climate of our times and the generation of young readers for whom the books were framed. From hindsight, here are the insouciance, the practical jokes, the unquestioning patriotism of the Biggles books but within accepted attitudes there is perceptible change.

Martin Falconer rushes into the war at the age of sixteen, ardently and with a romantic idea of warfare. He is strongly influenced by his first flight commander in France, 'Bill' Sykes, who becomes his closest friend:

> He seemed just too vague to be true but I noticed he had an M.C. beneath his wings and assumed that his airy indifference was all put on – the old cavalry attitude, that the war was just a vulgar brawl and that the cavalry were there merely to add a little tone. The war

had to seem a bit of a bore, because the boredom saved talking about it too much.

'See that you give the usual cheer-me-up particulars to the office,' he advised. 'Religion. Next of kin. Favourite Flowers. Nature of grandmother's rheumatism. All helps.' He seemed an amiable young man not prepared to take life very seriously, a thing I'd already noticed about most experienced people in the Flying Corps. They flew their unstable, inflammable machines with an air of indifference, and most of them seemed to set off for the war as though they were going to a football match. It was an attitude Frank and I had begun to cultivate ourselves.[30]

It is clear from the tone of this passage that Falconer is not a romantic hero of the Biggles kind but a mouthpiece for the author, in a series of five novels tracing the youth's exploits (*The Fledglings, The Professionals, The Victors, The Interceptors* and *The Revolutionaries*) which are really historical fiction rather than historical adventure. *Looking back* at certain attitudes governing the behaviour of men in the First World War, rather than *remembering* them as Johns did, John Harris reflects these attitudes as a matter of history, not of propaganda. He is not writing in a recruiting spirit but as a recorder of change.

Through Martin Falconer he emphasises the contrast between the views of civilians and of combatants. On leave in London after almost two years as a fighter-pilot, Martin finds himself ill at ease with the 'nauseating' talk of the people at home:

In France in 1916, you never heard much about patriotism and the sort of 'Scrag the Hun' talk that the sporting parsons in England liked to offer. After eighteen months in uniform, I had found my own attitude had become a sort of sheepish cynicism at having let myself be deluded into thinking it was a romantic adventure and rushing into it headlong when so many others had stayed at home. It was a strange attitude for someone not yet nineteen but there was never the same hilarious keenness for battle in France that there was in London, and never the same outcry when a night's sleep was disturbed.[31]

The almost chivalric, jousting atmosphere of Biggles's exploits in the air are a long way from Martin's mood when a few weeks later he is once more involved in a dogfight:

The war had suddenly become dangerous, I found myself thinking wildly. It had seemed bad enough in the days of the Fokker menace the year before but now it wasn't such a hit-and-miss affair as it had been then, with a touch of heroism about it and romantic with old-fashioned ideas about nobility and honour. It had suddenly become nasty and messy and dangerous.[32]

Though he was filled with a brief access of emotional patriotism when he was decorated by the King in the spring of 1918, he reflected as a rule the utter weariness, the distrust of official direction in the war, which has no place in Biggles's view of events (though Johns himself was by no means uncritical of governments and policies). The sentimental patriotism with which civilians, as Martin saw it, tried to prolong that early period of almost chivalric endeavour, was less to his taste than the robust belief of his tough observer Munro:

> 'If it's a case o' playin' dairty or not survivin',' he always insisted, 'then Ah reckon we should hit him as quick as we can, as hard as we can, where it hurts most, and when he isnae lookin'. An', if we get a chance, boil him in oil too, so that next time he'll keep clear of us. It might shorten the war.'[33]

In short, Martin is no romantic hero. Far from cherishing a life-long passion for a lost love, his mildly sentimental attraction for the Belgian girl Marie-Ange who helped him, with Sykes, to escape after being captured in 1916, fades in relief when he visits her in hospital two years later and finds she has set her sights not on an English hero but on her childhood sweetheart, a farm labourer.

In using Martin Falconer as a way to recreate the atmosphere of the First World War John Harris was fulfilling a duty to inform his readers, as honestly as research and his own detached view of the past could manage, and with an approach proper to the view of patriotism which writers are anxious to pass on to the present generation (not universally, and not easily, as the behaviour of the British at the time of the Falklands war clearly showed).

Reading these adventure stories as period pieces, we can accept the simple answer to the question 'Who is the enemy?' The simple answer provided by Johns in the later Biggles stories, when he has become an air-detective closely connected with Interpol, will not do as well. In an essay written more than twenty years ago T. R. Barnes analysed the elements in the Biggles tales that made them popular with boys and, in doing so, implied that the years had brought a need for a different answer to that vital question. He enquired:

> What would someone who knew nothing of life on this planet learn about it from these stories? He would deduce that nearly all the world's surface was jungle and desert, inhabited only by bestial savages; that civilization was only to be found in a place called variously 'Home' or 'England', whence men came by private

aeroplane to solve the problems of the dark places of the world; that these problems consisted always of evil men plotting the world's destruction for their own not-very-clearly-defined purposes; that these evil men could easily be recognized – big, black Negroes, harsh Prussian officers, fat, suave Eurasians; and that the only cure for these problems was to fight these evil men with their own weapons. . . .[34]

and he suggests that Captain Johns's socio-political attitudes were 'those one would associate with a not unduly intelligent Empire-builder of the late Victorian "white man's burden" period'.[35]

Peter Berrisford Ellis and Piers Williams have made a gallant attempt in their biography of Johns, *By Jove, Biggles!*, to prove that racism in the Biggles books is not consistent. The exceptions, however, are rare and are in fact rendered necessary by the course of a plot and by the need to show the hero as an undeviatingly 'good' character. *Biggles and the Leopards of Zinn* is prefaced by an oddly apologetic, evasive Foreword in which the author comments on imperialism and the time 'not very long ago' when:

> . . . small parties of men, dissatisfied with conditions in their own country, or perhaps seeking wealth, would set out for some new land that took their fancy and establish themselves there regardless of how the native inhabitants might feel about it . . . Let us admit it. The conquerors generally came from Europe, and their victims were the coloured races that occupied most of the great land masses of the earth. This has sometimes been called The Age of Discovery.
>
> This sort of thing, this casual seizure of other people's property, came to an end less than a century ago, and the coloured races, those that have managed to survive the disastrous habits and diseases introduced by the white men, are now reminding us of certain sinister facts that cannot be denied.[36]

With the customary suggestion that 'If the black man lost his right to govern himself there were compensations, for he gained many things he would otherwise not have had', Johns goes on to explain that the Colonial Office had chosen Biggles to investigate the reported exploitation of the Zinn, a small lakeside tribe, by unknown villains (in fact, criminals of South African extraction operating from the borders of the Belgian Congo with tribesmen whom they have corrupted; this could be called having your cake and eating it too). Biggles identifies the enemy and their motive, which is to work, secretly, a valuable source of bauxite. He decides for the sake of the Zinns to conceal the motive while handing over the criminals:

366

'Do you realize what would happen if one of the big metal operating companies knew what we know? Armies of workmen and engineers would arrive at Lake Jumu. The place would became a maze of factories and chimneys covered in red dust. The Zinns, instead of living quiet, peaceful lives in a little world of their own, far from the scares of hydrogen bombs and other horrors civilization is producing, would be wiped out, or what would be even worse, find themselves slaves, digging holes in the ground for stuff that's no use to them for purposes they couldn't begin to understand. Why should we inflict that on them? I say let's leave them alone, happy and content with their fishing.'[37]

Estimable as Biggles's view may be, it shows no real understanding of the nature of the Zinn and no deviation from the automatic assumption of the white man's superiority over races of another colour, with the corollary of Britain's superiority to any other white nation. Liberal proclamations dictated by the terms of the story do not wipe out the impression conveyed by numerous references to 'sinister dago types', by the pidgin English of *Biggles in Australia*, by Johns's own version of the phrase, so often adapted, about the 'four Germans, an indefinite number of Russians, and any quantity you care to mention of the remaining scum of the earth' which I have already quoted (see p. 351).

Captain Johns could not afford to let his hero ask himself 'Who is the enemy?' Professionally and personally, Biggles accepts the answer of the Establishment of the time. The question can only be answered, in terms of present-day attitudes, if the motives of *both* antagonists are explored in some measure. This will stretch the limits of the adventure story and may even provoke fresh definitions of the genre.

It will also alter the educational methods so far accepted. An author who intends to present more than one point of view cannot be as openly didactic as the author who takes his stand on one accepted attitude in a hero whose convictions implicitly condemn those of his enemy. Rather than asserting, as Johns and Henty did, that the attitudes they maintain are to be received by the reader without question, the writer in our own times has to invite his readers to consider, to realise the existence of varying points of view, to make up their own minds. Still permitted to indicate the attitudes acceptable to their time, the writer is obliged to admit to ambiguities – most of all, in the context of war, and particularly of the war still within living memory.

Robert Westall's *The Machine-Gunners* is built on a well-tried, orthodox adventure-plot, in which children irrupt into the adult world with the boldness of inexperience. The date is the winter of 1940 and thereafter; the abiding fear, of threatened invasion; the place, vulnerable Tyneside ringed with barrage balloons and anti-aircraft guns which provide unending interest to thirteen-year-old Chas McGill and his cronies. Uppermost in their minds, though, is the search for war souvenirs, the grislier the better, and at first it is his intense desire to equal the collection of bully Bodser Brown that supports Chas through the task of cutting the rear machine-gun free from a German bomber crashed in a wood near his town and finding a suitable hiding-place for it. It does not take long for the police and local wardens to discover this particular piece of looting and to anticipate its dangers – even to identify the culprits to their satisfaction. But not to catch them. Chas's determination and resource drive his weary allies to fresh efforts, until the gun is set up, bedded in concrete, in a dugout in the garden of an empty house which has become far more than the usual entrancing hideout of adventure stories. For the gun is more than an impressive, if secret, item in a private museum. Working out their own version of civilian proceedings, the oddly assorted but united group – loyal Cemetery Jones, tough Clogger from Glasgow, tomboy Audrey Parton, timid Nicky – has become to its own satisfaction the spearhead of local resistance to the threatened invasion.

Anyone who is in any doubt about the radical changes in children's adventure stories over the past quarter of a century may be interested to compare the rules drawn up by Chas with the table of aims and objects prepared after discussion by Malcolm Saville's Lone Pine adventurers. Chas's first item neatly fixes the group as far as age and attitudes are concerned. It reads:

> Anyone who steals food from the Fortress, if found guilty by Court Martial, shall be thrown into the goldfish pond. They may take off any clothes they want to first, but Keep It Decent.[38]

One of the many virtues of this seminal book is the precise, accurate balance between the received domestic discipline and customs in which the children have been brought up and the extent of their rebellion against them. There is an abiding reality in the fact that they are still bound, and feel themselves bound, by school and home rules, while at the same time they are hiding and proposing to use a weapon whose dangers they soon begin to suspect. The practical sense of Rule Four, which orders 'No peeing within fifty yards, or Anything Else' is balanced by the penalty for 'splitting to parents, teachers etc.' which is 'DEATH'.[39]

Who is the Enemy?

Malcolm Saville's children were no less loyal to one another than the squabbling, raucous Chas McGill and his friends, but their more polite set of rules belongs to a type of story slowly but surely superseded. This is not to suggest, though, that Westall's story belongs to its period of writing simply by virtue of a greater candour in the representation of the young. He is aiming at a more basic reality, in offering to his readers a chance to realise the complexities in war aims and the inherent contradictions in human beings. The challenge to the attitude in which children's fiction had been written for so long, the assumption that good and evil were absolutes (a challenge that goes back some way before Westall, of course) has changed the adventure story fundamentally. I have already suggested that one of the ways in which its scope has been broadened is in the change in the role of adults in adventures fostered and organised by children. Robert Westall does not claim any special sophistication for his young characters of forty years ago: indeed, he maps out their dependences and acceptances unerringly. They are bewildered and confused, as children always are, by adult problems.

The youngest and seemingly least useful member of Chas's group (co-opted for practical reasons), known crudely as Sicky Nicky, is a timid, unhappy child whose background of big house and naval family is far from the home settings of his school-fellows. When his father is killed in action, Nicky's misery is endured with a courage which Chas dimly recognises. Nicky's mother, consoled with food by the sailors billeted on her and in a more personal way by the officer in charge, has no comfort to offer him, nor is Nicky conscious of missing her as a person when, driven by fear and loneliness, he wanders out of the house at night just before it suffers a direct hit from a bomb. The reaction of the neighbours is natural enough:

> 'Dead in their bed of sin they was,' said Mrs Spalding dramatically, waggling the curling pins under her head-scarf. 'And a Judgment I call it. Lying there without a stitch on, nor a mark on their bodies. It was the Blast what done it. Or the Hand of God. God is not mocked!'[40]

Supposedly destroyed in the blast, Nicky takes refuge in the machine-gun emplacement which Chas has achieved partly by demolishing the air-raid shelter in Nicky's garden and rebuilding it further from the house. Here the little boy, together with Clogger who has pretended to go home to Glasgow, become the guards during school hours of a German air-gunner who has also found his way to the refuge after parachuting from a fighter.

369

Sergeant Rudi Gerlath presents no problems. With a badly injured ankle and then a fever, he finds this strangely efficient amateur imprisonment almost a comfort. Tired of war, almost soothed by the youth and spirit of the children, he is in no mood to play the enemy. As for the gang, they find it possible to see him in two ways – as someone to be guarded and finally handed over to authority, and as someone older than themselves who can be talked to openly and consulted, on a basis of entirely friendly bargaining, about the fault in the machine-gun.

To Nicky, most of all, Rudi changes from being 'the enemy' to being a father-figure, someone who seems to offer affection and support to the boy who holds in a wavering hand the captured Luger, cocked in case Rudi tries to escape. The German's feelings towards the children are canvassed, lightly but honestly, as one way of emphasising Nicky's state of mind and of underlining the theme of the book:

> They didn't feel like a guard with a prisoner now. More like a class with a teacher, even a family. Especially the little dark one. Every day he was nearer and nearer to Rudi. Now he was actually leaning against him. There was something wrong with that boy; a terrible need. He moaned in his sleep, and awakened crying. The others were very protective towards him. Where were his parents? Killed in the bombing?
>
> 'Give us a song, Rudi,' they chorused. '*Ich hatt einen Kameraden*!'
>
> Rudi obliged. He had a creaky voice, but the confined metal space of the shelter helped, like singing in the bath. How long since he'd had a bath.[41]

Fulfilling the bargain Chas had made with Rudi in order to get the machine-gun working, Nicky takes the airman by night to his family's boat-house and miserably hears his friend refuse to take him on his bid to row back to Europe. The night is further complicated by a false alarm, a peal of bells which rouses Chas to action. The coincidence of a Polish contingent newly sent to the district gives the boy his long-desired reason for firing the gun, and the story ends in a confusion of farce and near-tragedy with, as it were, a comic restatement of the question, 'Who is the enemy?' A story as rich in humour, wit and common sense as this can hardly be described as didactic, but educational it certainly is.

Imperialist attitudes are far from being extinct but in children's stories at least they have been slowly set aside for a more deliberate, impartial scrutiny of the motives behind war and its less romantic effects on families and countries. Indeed, it has been suggested that the Second World War and its aftermath have rendered the traditional adventure story obsolete. Certainly the trend in junior fiction has made it difficult, if not entirely impossible, for fictional children to remain entirely irresponsible and unaffected by their involvement in war. Susan Cooper illustrated this clearly in *Dawn of Fear*, a tale of domestic adventure published in 1972, in which the congenial and exciting gang-warfare on a suburban housing estate, with trenches and ambushes and mud-balls for ammunition, abruptly ceases to be amusing when the bombs of the Second World War bring tragedy to the homes of three cheerful boys of eleven or so. Like Westall's Chas McGill, Susan Cooper's lads have been shocked out of playing war by having to face it.

Books of this kind come near to being problem novels by definition rather than adventure stories. Bette Green's much-praised story published in 1974, *Summer of my German Soldier*, is indeed as much about a girl's family relationships as it is about her unwise but very natural attempts to help a German prisoner to escape. To the twelve-year-old Jewish girl, Anton offers an acceptable alternative to her brutal, unloving father; this powerful narrative, set in a small town in a Southern state of the United States, turns on a paradox by which the German 'enemy', a humane and civilised man, is deliberately and dramatically contrasted with Patty's father, whose violent cruelty has subtly suggested incestuous origins. Similarly, it is the emotional implications of anti-war feelings and the social problems of being a conscientious objector which dominate Dennis Hamley's *Landings* and Alison Leonard's *An Inch of Candle*, in which the dawn of maturity in young people is analysed through the impact of war. Even in the more obviously adventure-story approach of two of the more influential books of their time – Ian Serraillier's *The Silver Sword* of 1956 and Anne Holm's *I Am David*, a Danish story published in England in 1965 – the *effect* of war on refugee children pervades and dominates stories which follow patterns of journey and mystery congenial to young readers. One could conveniently signalise the change in attitudes between the 1950s and the present, in fact, by contrasting *The Silver Sword* with Serraillier's earlier, cheerfully active Ruritanian thriller, *Flight into Adventure*, in which a lad accompanies his uncle into safely distanced, romanticised, exuberant encounters with spies and shotguns.

Sober, exploratory, moralistic – any of these adjectives might be applied to the stories of past wars offered currently to the young and exemplifying the sense of responsibility fostered in writers by the prolonged scrutiny of psychologists and social theorists of the moral and emotional development of children. The immediate and the distant past have become subject to re-examination in the light of today's attitudes both to war and to young people. Yet there are universal, transhistorical values which can still enliven the old-style adventure story and ensure that it does still exist as an undidactic literary form. As Fred Ingles has suggested, 'it makes sense to speak of courage, candour, trustworthiness, and truth as meaning something in all historical circumstances – in the Trojan ditch, outside Harfleur, at Bloemfontein, or on the picket lines'.[42]

Nobody has spoken out more strongly for these values than Rosemary Sutcliff in novels offering many examples of man as warrior. Although none of her books comes nearer to our times than the late seventeenth century, her approach to the facts of war and destruction in the past has an emotional honesty and force and an underlying philosophy of race and nationalism which offer something like advice to young readers of today if they are responsive enough to her words. The least didactic of authors, she places in the context of war the virtues of courage and loyalty, demonstrated through the fortunes of a young hero or heroes. Rosemary Sutcliff's books are historical adventures as much as they are historical novels, to the extent that she is not seeking to reinterpret received history but to show the effects of past conflict on certain individuals. The great historical personages do not play central parts in her stories. She gives herself freedom to imagine private people caught up in major battles, conspiracies or mass movements in plausible circumstances. While she does not announce any particular attitude to war, as Henty and Captain Johns felt obliged to do, certain points of view are filtered through these chosen main characters – chosen to represent the views of their family, race or period but also to show how these views could change, and for what reasons.

The trumpets and banners of war are present in her books alongside the onrush of fear, the treachery, the wounds and the deaths. Loyalty in arms is demonstrated most clearly in the long linked sequence of books set in Roman Britain (*The Eagle of the Ninth, The Silver Branch, Frontier Wolf, The Lantern Bearers* and *Dawn Wind*) where service to the Eagle of a regiment is the supreme obligation. This loyalty is no cold matter of expediency and duty to the young men who serve in the legions, but a strong binding force, a symbol of the strength of the disparate races that make up the Roman army. The Eagle lost in the Caledonian hills when the Ninth Legion disappeared, and recovered and hidden by the son of the commander, comes to light again by chance in a pillar of the hypocaust in a villa belonging to the Aquila family. Flavius, descendant of that vanished commander, thinks about the past as he mounts the battered bronze bird on to a new spear-shaft:

> The thing was strangely potent under his hands. What things it must have seen – bitter and dark and glorious things – this maimed bird of gilded bronze that was the life and the honour of a lost Legion. And now, he thought, it must feel that the old days were back. Again there came to him as he worked that sense of kinship with the young soldier who had made a home in this downland valley, the young soldier who surely had brought the lost Eagle of a lost Legion home to its own people, so that Eagle and farm were linked, and it was fitting that the ancient standard should go out from here to its last fight.[43]

The last fight is to defeat the rebel and murderer Allectus and establish the rule of the Emperor Constantius in the province of Britain. Flavius's descendant, Alexios Aquila, preparing to evacuate a fort north of the Wall threatened by a massed tribal rising, makes his own dispositions for preserving the symbol of the Frontier Wolves, a command less orthodox in composition and behaviour than the earlier forces of Rome in Britain but still powerfully held by this symbol of military unity:

> He had taken down the Ordo dragon and laid it on the table, and was hammering the snarling fantastic head flat, with the heavy iron-shod butt of its own spear-shaft . . . He gave the thing a final blow, and flung the spear-shaft aside. The fierce head that had used to rear up in beauty, drinking the wind when the troops went by at the gallop, was a grotesquely flattened mask of bronze and silver wires, as he looked down at it. But it was the Ordo dragon still. He took it up and began to bind the bright wind-sleeve like a silken scarf about his waist, starting at the tail-tip and tucking the flattened head into its own folds last of all.[44]

The power of Rome symbolised by the images of eagle and dragon transcends the mixed races and beliefs that make up the legions but it does not obliterate the basic differences between one individual soldier and another. Unity and difference go together. The young centurion Marcus, discussing the patterns on a shield-boss with his slave and close companion Esca, son of a chief of the British Brigantes and enslaved by the fortunes of war, is made to realise by this youth of his own age that his country's conquests may destroy more than physical entities. Esca points out how Roman decorative patterns have become standard for Celtic craftsmen:

'You are the builders of coursed stone walls, the makers of straight roads and ordered justice and disciplined troops. We know that, we know it all too well. We know that your justice is more sure than ours, and when we rise against you, we see our hosts break against the discipline of your troops, as the sea breaks against a rock. And we do not understand, because all these things are of the ordered pattern, and only the free curves of the shield-boss are real to us. We do not understand. And when the time comes that we begin to understand your world, too often we lose the understanding of our own.'[45]

Many generations later Marcus's descendant Alexios sets himself to understand the beliefs of the Votadini, uncertain allies of the Romans stationed in the outpost fort of the Wall; when he buries men from his mixed troop he may use the words of the Christian or the Mithraic observance or the rituals of one or other of the Celtic or Germanic tribes contributing to the Ordo.

This is more than mere military expediency. The overriding theme of these stories of Roman Britain, continuing through the ensuing centuries to the twelfth century in *Dawn Wind* and *The Shield Ring*, is the idea of reconcilement, the picture of an island people created from warring elements, and united over the years by intermarriage and the gradual interrelating of cultures. The sequence of books which starts with the enterprise in which young Marcus Aquila sets out to find the truth of his father's disappearance ends with the growing up of a Viking boy in the Lake District whose link with Rome had come through his father's Welsh forebears. Celtic Britons, Romans, Saxons, Norsemen and Normans fight in turns for supremacy in Britain and each wave of invasion is absorbed into an island nation. The Aquila father and son and their descendants are linked in the stories by a ring of flawed emerald shaped like a dolphin which is preserved in the family (though with many accidental losses and recoveries): the family survives but it survives by taking into itself individuals not of Roman stock.

The enemy of today becomes the ally of the future and this is Rosemary Sutcliff's answer to that question 'Who is the enemy?' which is forced upon the writer tackling the problem of war. The sense of continuity transcends the pattern of invasion and conquest. When Aquila, a young Decurion, deserts the legion when it is recalled to Rome because he feels a stronger tie with the province of Britain, he is enslaved by Jutish invaders; in their country he reads the Odyssey to Bruni, renowned warrior now weak in old age, to whom he has been presented as a gift by Bruni's swaggering grandson. The past lives – in this and in many other episodes we are made aware of this, as we are made aware of the patterns held in the future. The light kindled in the town at Rutupiae by the deserter Aquila speaks of one man's faith that life will go on in Britain though the legions have been finally withdrawn. Aquila's faith is temporarily justified by the stand made by Ambrosius and his Romanised kinsman Artos against the Saxon invaders. Many years later an old Welshman sees another kind of light for the future:

> 'Owain, has it ever seemed to you that a strange thing is happening between the British and the Saxon kind? It is three generations since Artos died, and the years between have been lost and dark and very bloody, so that if one looks backward it is as though one peered through night and storm, to catch the last brave glimmer of a lantern very far behind . . . Yet I remember how we spoke once, you and I, of the Truce of the Spear; I believe that there are other kinds of truce, more binding, and some that may change and grow and strengthen . . .'[46]

British Owain, thrall to a Saxon family for many years, has taken over and defended the household after his master's death: it is this gleam of light which the old man welcomes for the future of the island.

Change is constructive in the context of the slow amalgamation of antagonistic races in Britain. Destructive change as it affects places provides one of the ways in which Rosemary Sutcliff examines the dark side of war, the inglorious opposite to the virtues of loyalty and comradeship in arms. The individual eye operates here, as everywhere in the books. Aquila, torn between his duty to his legion and the pull of the Roman province where he has been born and brought up, is very sensitive to the state of the coastal fort of Rutupiae now being abandoned to the barbarians. Description, as always in Rosemary Sutcliff's stories, is organic and personal; this is not the author's overview of the fortress of the great Pharos but the view of a disturbed, desperate young soldier:

> The vast plinth, long as an eighty-oared galley and three times the height of a man, rose like an island in the empty space, and from it the great central tower sprang up, crested with its iron beacon brazier against the sky. A few shreds of marble facings, a few cracked marble columns upholding the roof of the covered ways for the fuel-carts, remained of the proud days, the days when it had stood shining in wrought bronze and worked marble here at the gateway to Britain, for a triumphal memorial to Rome's conquest of the province. But they had used most of the broken marble for rubble when they built the great walls to keep the Saxons out. The

tower rose up bare and starkly grey as a rock, with the seagulls rising and falling about it, the evening light on their wings. The light was beginning to fade; soon the beacon would be lit, and the night after it would be lit, and the night after that, and then there would be no more Rutupiae Light.[47]

In an equally tense mood the boy Owain, orphaned in a Saxon raid, approaches Viroconium, once a thriving Roman city and now abandoned by its few inhabitants and sacked by the enemy. Here change can be perceived as it were in strata:

> Viroconium had been half empty when he came that way before. It had been falling into decay for a hundred years, becoming slowly sleepier and more unkempt, the grass and the little dusty shepherd's purse creeping further out from the sides of the streets. But there had still been life in Viroconium when Kyndylan's war-host had gathered in the spring; voices and footsteps in the streets, and children playing on doorsteps, and smells of cooking towards evening. Now, the city was dead. The streets were silent, and the houses stood up gaunt and gutted, with blind eyes and blackened roof-beams fallen in.[48]

Owain is still a boy and there is a touch of juvenile delight in housekeeping as he and the waif Regina, banded together against loneliness and fear, set about finding food, fire and shelter; but there is nothing trivial in their plight or their brave resourcefulness against danger and death. When Rosemary Sutcliff uses young heroes, or leads children towards manhood when they will take up a hero's role, she never allows a suggestion of historical charade to dilute the strong emotional content of her stories. Her children are recognisably young but their actions presage their future. They are on trial, apprentices to maturity, and in them courage is no less apparent than the courage of the young legionaries who are her more frequent heroes; merely, it is shown on a different level of experience and action.

There are many reasons why Rosemary Sutcliff's novels could be called, in the widest sense, educational, but as far as young readers are concerned, there is more value in the honest, firm emotional ebb and flow in them than in the interpretation of particular periods of history in which Britain became an island nation. Most of all they can learn from her celebration of certain moods and stages of development in young manhood – a reckless risking of physical forces and a rejoicing in physical prowess; an ardent sexual comradeship in arms; the pride of service to an accepted cause; the half-realised tug of one's native land; a flexibility due to curiosity about other places and other experiences; family ties and affections; the mixture of nervous fury and apprehension in battle; the blow to pride in thralldom; the unexpected tenderness of a relationship with a woman; the bleak despair of enforced loss; the perplexed pain of conflicting loyalties. All this and much more, to open the minds and spirits of the young to worlds larger and more challenging than their own and yet worlds of emotion to which in their own way they too may have to travel. And in presenting her tales of warriors long ago, balancing the nobility and the sordidness of war, she is reaching back to legends – of Beowulf, of Arthur, of Charlemagne – and so, ultimately, to those myths of conduct and creation where story begins.

15. Censorship and the Theft of Words

The power and passion of the continuous comment exercised on fiction suggests an educational or a didactic aim in the case of books for adults and children alike. Pressure on adult writers comes from critics and advertisers, on writers for children from a wider range of caring guardians. The expectations are different. Because it is generally agreed that children can be at risk from inexperience in their response to the written word, it is assumed that writers must accept a grave responsibility for what they write. It should not therefore be accepted, as it commonly is, that writers must convey to their readers the views held by a consensus of opinion in their particular culture and period and that they must be expected to be judged by the degree to which they fulfil this duty.

Children are not, of course, the only victims of didacticism nor is the sociological trend in literary criticism confined to books for the young. Northrop Frye complained that many literary critics 'attach what for them are the real values of literature to something outside literature which literature reflects' and comments that his 'proposal to take literature itself as the area of critical investigation, without granting anything else priority to it, causes Freudian and Marxist anxieties to go up like barrage balloons'[1] and Richard Church deplored 'all the proselytisers and doctrinaires who seize the novel-form with zealous hands, and wrench it to purposes other than that of poetry, the ever-flowering tree of truth, and of understanding'.[2]

The novel must necessarily reflect the bias of its author and therefore of its period, and the adventure story is as vulnerable as any other form of fiction to social change and social opinion, even when it is distanced from contemporary life by a past or a future setting. One writer who has come to accept its use for propaganda, Hammond Innes, said in an interview:

> I never go back because I am a forward looking person . . . I have spent all my life seeing this country going downhill and looking forward to seeing it go uphill. That's why we have to become merchant adventurers again. I was convinced of this when I was working as a journalist in the 1930s. I was convinced then that we had been simply living off the fat our forefathers left. And by God we were.[3]

378

He has moved steadily from the general exposition of heroism and endurance in novels like *The Mary Deare* to a conscious pursuit of a theme – greed and exploitation in elephant poaching in *The Big Footprints*, man's innate aggressiveness in *Levkas Man* – in response to what seems to be a growing demand for or submission to didacticism in the novel of action.

This didacticism offers, so far as it goes, constructive lessons: proposing an undesirable situation, the writer urges that it should be corrected. Since children are in theory more amenable to authority and, again in theory, less able to discriminate for themselves between good and evil, their books are subject not only to adjurations and prescriptions but also to prohibitions. As an Australian author, Lilith Norman, has pertinently remarked, 'The way we want children to grow depends on the clarity and honesty of our vision; but that is always distorted by the contact lenses of our own time and conditioning, and by our own taboos.'[4]

One at least of these taboos is common to adult and junior adventure stories. The resistance to the death of the hero is the consequence of the convention that such stories should have a happy ending. When in fact a hero does die, this does not constitute a breaking of the taboo: complying with a tradition handed down from the earliest action stories – that is, heroic epic or legend – the hero dies in the fullness of his active virtue, and so, paradoxically, the need for a 'happy' ending is satisfied. On the contrary, we do feel a taboo has been broken when a young hero dies, the taboo of the present century against death in junior fiction (or, at least, the death of 'good' characters) which marks a break with Victorian literary tradition. In adventure stories circumstances are most likely to shadow the death of a hero or heroine with a sense of failure or degradation rather than with a sense of triumph. Many readers have a feeling of false conclusion, of unwarranted grotesqueness, in Robert Cormier's *The Chocolate War*, and this, I believe, is not only a literary reaction but also a primitive, instinctive one.

The need for that amalgam of intent, action and mood which we call 'heroism' is strongest in our response to junior stories, whether we read them as adults or as children. I could quote as evidence for this a novel of adventure by Jean MacGibbon, *Liz*, published in 1966 and still exceptional in the way the taboo against death is faced and negated. The drowning of Alan, one of the four central young characters, does not stem from a resolve to break what had become almost a rule of fiction-writing in the junior sphere. It is a death brought about by a mixture of chance and intention, the result of a girl's hurt anger and natural aggression, of a boy's pride in ignoring physical weakness, a very human and natural mixture of good and bad impulses steered to disaster by coincidence. The author saw the story pointing in this direction and had the courage to follow her instincts rather than complying with a custom more compelling at the time when she wrote than it would be now.

Taboos exist to protect people as well as the entities or ideas which they shield or seek to perpetuate and the taboo against death in junior adventure stories seems to be designed to protect the young reader from the distress that a more realistic approach might cause. If this is so, it may well be one area of the adventure story where change is inevitable. Somewhere the frontier between adventure stories and problem novels, of novels or protest, is being shifted because of writers like Robert Cormier.

If I am right in predicting a change in this direction, it will be a natural, not a willed change. It will come about as part of the tendency of novels to reflect the pattern of the society in which they are written – that is, the views generally accepted in that society and the rebellions against those views necessary for social evolution. Just as naturally, I hope, the taboo against sex in junior adventure fiction will give way to a proper discrimination by writers, who will take their own way in accordance with the needs of a particular plot or theme. Again, if such a change comes about naturally and not as a result of a determination to be fashionably permissive, it will be reflected in a more candid and perceptive mode of drawing characters within the scope of the adventure-story format.

The existence of taboos which authors are all too often willing to accept does in fact act repressively not only on the theme and action of a story but, most of all, on its characters. But taboos cannot be forced out of existence: they have to disappear naturally and gradually as the temper of the times renders them unnecessary. To change an attitude by force and pressure is worse than useless. This may be seen most obviously in the current anti-sexist propaganda which bedevils the course of literary criticism, exercises unwarranted constraint on the necessary freedom of writers and causes a mistaken censorship of much notable fiction of past years.

Propaganda is a different thing from the evolution of attitudes. The weapons of feminism (and it is in the form of feminism that anti-sexist views are most often expressed) may be strident and exaggerated in adult novels as in junior counterparts, or they may be handled easily and with a certain cynical bow to fashion.

The light-hearted manner of an article on the latest 'girl' to help television's Dr Who in his struggle for the right does not hide the topical truth of the evidence that 'Today's *Dr Who* girl' is quite a different species from her pioneer counterpart:

> In the beginning she was a shy, frightened, wide-eyed teenager. She has moved through the stages of being a dolly bird scientist, bright journalist and extra-terrestrial animal woman to arrive at last in the new series at the supreme position of Time Lady – and Doctor's equal. She has also got gradually livelier, and her liberation has taken twelve years to achieve.[5]

Carole Ann Ford, who played the Doctor's first assistant, said 'the only talent needed then was to be a good screamer' and professed to be jealous of the 'modern girls . . . Those lovely, sexy, independent parts'.[5] Adult propaganda, aimed at readers with at least some mental resilience, can afford to adopt many tones, from the jocular to the bullying, from the time-serving to the properly serious. The compulsion to influence children through their reading is altogether more rigid and more dogmatic.

We can, all the same, suppose that a certain resistance has always existed even in the young caught in the educational net. A century or so ago the blurbs advertising books for girls were full of such phrases as 'pure and healthy in tone and teaching', 'bright, sensible, and with a right tone of thought and feeling' and 'inculcates in an unostentatious way lessons of thoughtfulness and kindness', while a typical advertisement for a boy's story (a piece quoted from a review) described:

> A capital story telling the deeds of . . . a midshipman on board His Majesty's cutter *Kestrel*, on the look-out for smugglers, Jacobite fugitives, and outlaws. We have love-making, perilous ventures, and neck-or-nothing escapes, and as much fighting as one could wish for.

It is easy to see why girls habitually read boys' stories as well as, and often in preference to, their own. Equally we may be sure that when girls read *Little Women* or *Holiday House* or *The Mill on the Floss* or indeed any of the gift books grouped in a list suitable for their sex with the nauseating title of 'The Lily Series', they would not have been greatly influenced by the publisher's claim that 'the popular appreciation of its purity of tone, and high standard of literary merit, has shown no signs of decrease'. Another piece of advertising copy presenting Ethel Turner as 'Miss Alcott's true successor' and praising in her books 'the same absence of primness and the same love of adventure' would have been far more to their taste, a taste which I imagine in many cases sisters borrowed from their brothers. W. Towrie Cutt, remembering his own boyhood favourites (among them books by Ballantyne, Kingston and Fenimore Cooper) augmented the fairly small library available to him in Orkney by a few girls' books:

> . . . *Oh, Christina* (if that was the title) amused me; it was about a girl who was always doing the wrong thing and shocking her guardians. I have a vague memory of reading about a very proper girl who was always putting younger children and her elders right. That very sensible girl did not interest me, though I did not find her objectionable.[6]

In short, the feminist movement is dominated by an insistence on equality which takes the form of demanding a place for women in every province controlled by men. It is an equality going only in one direction and this direction is taken by anti-sexist propaganda, more often than not. Long before the campaigns of our own time, girls were demanding 'equality' with boys by acting like them, in real life as in fiction. Daphne du Maurier remembers resenting the fact that boys in the Bible stories 'did all the brave things' while:

> . . . I had to make do with pretending, tuck my dress into my knickers, find a stick and wave it like a sword. Angela did not mind being a girl. In our make-up games she took the part of a girl, and would throw open the window of the Wendy house in the garden calling 'Save me! save me!' Then bravely I would slash at the bushes, our enemies, and run to her rescue.[7]

In junior fiction, Enid Blyton's Georgina, who disturbed the balance of the Famous Five (two girls, two boys and a dog) by insisting on being called George and behaving as far as possible like a boy, is the crudest representative of a huge class of tomboy heroines.

The understandable sense of injustice felt by girls reading junior fiction will never be rectified by force or by severe admonitions to publishers and writers. Token scenes in stories of boys doing the housework and girls servicing cars will never work unless the situation is backed by convincing characters. As far as children's stories are concerned (and this is not the place to take the argument into other fields), the need is not for equality but for parity – that is, for scenes which derive naturally from the individuality of girls and boys working within the story. Parity is developing in our society and books need to reflect this development as it comes rather than forcing the issue. The efforts to impose sanctions or to correct one taboo by inventing another are designated neatly in an article by the Australian critic Walter McVitty, who was puzzled to find inconsistencies in a purpose-built series of 'anti-sexist' tales for children. He concludes with gentlemanly irony:

> . . . no prize has ever been awarded to a book with an Australian Rules footballer as a hero, and Catholics are curiously absent from Carnegie and Newbery lists. In the whole field of children's literature, with nearly 6,000 new titles in the English language alone each year, the non-portrayal of teachers (or librarians for that matter) in positive roles worthy of emulation and identification is alarming in its implications. These examples of prejudiced values on the part of authors and publishers (some receiving government subsidies) should not go unnoticed. Any lobby group could find suitable examples of neglect.[8]

While self-perpetuating committees are busily investigating 'suitable examples of neglect', authors like Philippa Pearce, Emma Smith and Geoffrey Trease are redressing the balance in their own way, by attending to the balance of individuals in a story without a limiting calculation of gender.

Censorship is a natural consequence of the attempt to enforce certain attitudes in children's books. In recent years we have seen many nursery classics like *Little Black Sambo* and certain of the Dr Dolittle stories banned in the interest of racial harmony, implying a doubt whether children have the wit to discriminate between past and present or between fantasy and reality. Determination on the part of parents and other guardians of childhood can, where good will exists, see to it that children acquire through wide reading a sense of period and of social change and need not be protected by being restricted to books expressing the recognised attitudes of their own time.

There is a more insidious, often invisible kind of censorship which is more difficult to locate and to combat – the gradual theft of words. An increasingly rigid demarcation of the sphere of children's books from those for adults, combined with a necessary attention to a wider readership after the Second World War, has induced in critics and the guardians of childhood a nervous desire that children should understand what they read and (here is the danger) without undue strain. Phrases like 'élitist' and 'minority read' suggest a disapproval of stories whose quality depends on style as well as on content. In the interests of universal literacy and enjoyment, the whole aesthetic experience of reading a piece of fiction is in danger of being undermined. Yet it is part of the education of a child to learn, to be helped to respond to a story in the same way as to a piece of music or a painting; if it is not suggested that a Mozart piano concerto or a Rembrandt portrait should be filleted, altered, recreated to suit a young learner, nor should it be possible to entertain the idea of rewriting a story, or deliberately underwriting it, to suit a child on whose gradually developed responses will depend his whole existence as a lifelong reader.

There are two ways in which censorship may be exercised – by the alteration of books already written or by pressure (of fashion as well as of direct demand) towards 'easiness'. The prevailing theory that books should be readily understood by *all* children has affected the adventure story all the more readily because of the influence of television. Enjoying the pace and dramatic energy of a television tale of action, children will not automatically realise that they must compensate, when they read similar stories, for the fact that they are not actually seeing characters or settings. Unless they can be helped to exercise the muscles of imagination, whole areas of the adventure story will not exist for them unless that story provides them with proper equivalents, in verbal description and the development of character, which they can extend through their own inferences and experience.

I do not suggest that we should return to the lengthy descriptive settings which, even in a different kind of domestic culture, children probably skipped in the works of, for instance, Scott and Marryat. A bareness and barrenness in narrative, a conscious avoidance of anything more than statement and chat, found in so many adventure stories offered to the young of the television age, may surely be considered to be a theft of words. Some years ago a critic discussed the search for bald realism in novels and commented:

> A novel is an arrangement, a pattern, designed so as to have a certain effect upon the reader and evoke a certain response from him: it resembles a semi-abstract painting, of the kind that includes representational elements, far more closely than it resembles a photograph.[9]

Too many of the adventure stories offered to children today concentrate on a photographic background while allowing too little time and space for the kind of organic detail, or (to follow the quotation) the 'semi-abstract' clues and shapes which exist to establish atmosphere, to substantiate the undercurrent of feeling and meaning which offer the greatest satisfaction to the responsive reader. Reading needs time. It is a slow processs and, notwithstanding the difficulties, readers need to find that time, that good will, to take in the manner, the overtones, the full flavour of an adventure story.

A story apparently concerned with the outward forms and effects of action may, in fact, be sustained by less explicit but essential elements. In one novel now almost a century old, for example, description is more than mere scene-setting. In Rolf Boldrewood's *Robbery under Arms* the brisk, robust sequence of chases and escapes as bushrangers, headed by the legendary Captain Starlight, elude the forces of law and order in 'the Bush and the Goldfields of Australia', would be both more sordid and less genuinely exciting if it were not for the pervasive effect of intermittent, direct description of places and people, and of people in relation to places. Nor would the obvious moral of the book – crime never pays – which the narrator, James Marston, reiterates as he contemplates his criminal past in a prison cell, have its due effect without the recurrence of a particular place in this book as a metaphor as well as an actual location.

The Hollow, supposedly haunted and consequently shunned by the settlers of New South Wales, is a valley enclosed in precipitous rocks and bush which has from time to time been used as a cache for stolen cattle and horses; it becomes a refuge for Jim Marston and his brother Dick and their thieving father when the law comes dangerously close to them. It is also, in a deeper sense, a Garden of Eden, a distant vision of good and peace which casts its aura over Jim and makes his moment of self-doubt and his death-bed repentance believable (as they must necessarily come to be, for the reader, in a traditional adventure story where the narrator, a criminal, can be felt to be potentially 'good').

The author gives space to his descriptions of the Hollow because they are organic descriptions: they relate to, and reflect upon, the emotions of the characters. Jim's first view of the place is clouded by the fears of a social outcast:

> Three o'clock in the morning – the stars in the sky, and it so clear that we could see Nulla Mountain rising up against it a big black lump, without sign of tree or bush, underneath the valley, one sea of mist, and we just agoing to drop into it; on the other side of the Hollow, the clear hill we called the Sugar-loaf. Everything seemed dead, silent, and solitary and a rummer start than all, here were we – three desperate men, driven to make ourselves a home in this lonesome, God-forsaken place! I wasn't very fanciful by that time, but if the devil had risen up to make a fourth amongst us I shouldn't have been surprised. The place, the time and the men seemed regularly cut out for him and his mob. . . . [10]

385

but next day, waking at sunrise, he takes a different view:

> Opposite where we were the valley was narrow. I could see the sandstone precipices that walled us in, a sort of yellowish, white colour, all lighted up with the rays of the morning sun, looking like gold towers against the heavy green forest timber at the foot of them. Birds were calling and whistling, and there was a little spring that fell drip, drip over a rough rock basin all covered with ferns. A little mob of horses had fed pretty close up to the camp, and would walk up to look curious-like, and then trot off with their heads and tails up. It was a pretty enough sight that met my eyes on waking. It made me feel a sort of false happiness for a time, to think we had such a place to camp in on the quiet, and call our own, in a manner of speaking.[11]

The father's practical praise of the Hollow as 'not a bad earth for the old dog-fox and his cubs when the hounds have run him close'[11] does not negate the more emotional attitude his son has expressed. The place remains, for Jim Marston, a distant goal and far more than a place of escape from the law, and it adds an extra dimension to the book for the reader who can see more than externalised description in it. The adventure story needs this kind of organic use of background. The snowscapes in Emma Smith's *No Way of Telling* contribute to the reverberance, as well as the reality, of that excellent story (see p. 254). Peter Dickinson's use of underground tunnels in *Annerton Pit* (see p. 327) and of a building site in *The Gift*, amounts to the placing of a metaphor within the narrative, extended from the close attention to 'representational elements' which the books also demand.

No illustration can ever substitute for this more than pictorial type of verbal description. Short cuts sacrifice richness of narrative to a mistaken goal of speed and brevity or an equally misguided desire for 'simplicity', which leads to this kind of uninspired, end-stopped scene-setting:

> The Isle of Gloom certainly lived up to its name. It was a most desolate place, as far as the children could see. It seemed to be made of jagged rocks that rose into high hills in the middle of the island. A few stunted trees grew here and there, and grass showed green in some places. The rocks were a curious red colour on the seaward side of the island, but black everywhere else.[12]

Even the mildly intriguing difference of colour noted in the last sentence proves to be irrelevant to the story, while the inhospitable nature of the island as a whole has little, if any, effect on the four children who easily penetrate its mysteries. Beside the pedestrian, perfunctory attempt to rouse associations of danger with darkness so frequent in Enid Blyton's stories we can place, for comparison, the adventures in which Leon Garfield uses darkness and light as constant, enriching metaphors.

The opening chapter of *Smith* (Garfield's third novel, published in 1967 and still perhaps his best in many ways) opens a tale of dark mystery and dark deeds with an attention to atmosphere easy and unobtrusive but compelling to the reader on several levels. There is, first, the outward setting, the streets of a London two centuries ago with dark, narrow alleys and entries, windows bricked in to avoid tax, surrounded by the murk and gathering darkness of a December day. Avoiding set description, Garfield works through adjectives and phrases and with additional details adding to the rich counterpoint of his tale – the starlings rising from St Paul's and the solitary, dusty raven flying out of the court where a man is murdered; the brown clothes of the killers; the houses round Curtis Court, where 'the flat, pale and unhealthy moon-faces of the clerks and scriveners' are 'glimpsed in their dark caves through dusty windows, silent and intent'[13] and where one particular face peers which proves to be that of the ultimate villain in this tale of greed, cunning and deception.

A boy of twelve has witnessed the murder: just before the old man collapses, he has picked his pocket: his prize is a document which is worthless (and dark) to him, because he cannot read. From the metaphorical darkness of the document, the actual and symbolic centre of the intricate mystery, we are led to a second actual and metaphorical darkness as Smith, fleeing from the two men, set on by the unseen watcher to get the paper from the terrified boy, meets head on at the opening of an alley a tall, stout gentleman who proves to be blind. And as the relationship develops between the dirty street boy and Mr Mansfield, the blind magistrate, the idea of emotional darkness gradually interpenetrates the story, through the magistrate's enforced move from accepted justice to genuine, natural compassion and through Smith's change from simple curiosity and acquisitiveness to an equally genuine sympathy for and loyalty to the blind man.

All through the book the contrast of darkness and light, of deception and enlightenment, is expressed in small touches of description – the shadowy rooms of Newgate and the ghastly darkness of the flues through which Smith tries to escape, the snowy wastes of the common over which a coach creeps on its slow, dark way, the black angel on a tombstone where the actors in the mystery converge in a violent climax. Now and then, description of a more traditional, open kind adds a specific, pictorial shock – for example, in a kind of introductory fugal statement to a new stage in Smith's dangerous fortunes in which snow is an important factor:

> The worn old streets were gone; the blackened roof-tiles were gone; the mournful chimneys and the dirty posts wore high white hats – and the houses themselves seemed to float, muffled, in a sea of white. Never, in all its life, had the Town looked so clean; it shamed the very sky, which was of a dirty, yellowish grey.
>
> The business of the Town was slow and tedious; carriages and chairs crawled along where they supposed the streets to be like huge, tottery snails, bearing snow houses on their backs and leaving wet black trails to mark their passing. Even the nimble pie-men capered silently, sometimes slipped and lost their smoking trays so that half a hundred hot pies burned into the snow and pitted it like a black pox.[14]

Eighteenth-century, for Garfield, has always been a metaphor as much as – even more than – an historical period and setting. In a later book, *John Diamond*, the dual darkness of soot and fog, facts indeed in the city at the time when this story too is set, are extended into sonorous, particular images to reflect and intensify the dangerous, cruel, perplexing scenes leading the young hero from stage to stage of his search for his past, his parentage and his identity. Dickensian, perhaps (and this comparison is by now almost too firmly attached to Garfield) but also in the tradition of the classic adventure story, from Stevenson down to Buchan. Stanley Weyman's consistent use of candlelight and shadow to lead the reader into an atmosphere that will affect his reception of the actual events of the story; the brilliant juxtaposition of two opposite windows, one dark and one glaring with lamplight, which sets the tone of Quiller-Couch's fine novel of action and emotion, *The Shining Spur*; the opening scene on the beach in Buchan's *Prester John* which stirs curiosity and apprehension together with its simple ingredients of darkness and light infinitely varied; these and many other scenes in classic tales are proof enough that their length, the density of their writing, has been sacrificed in all but a few novels in our own time to the mistaken goals of speed, simplicity and succinctness.

This use of metaphor has died hard. Hammond Innes, in an early stage of writing for the young as 'Ralph Hammond', invoked tradition in the plain, direct, concrete style which suits our time but still has something of the old, substantial way of narrative in it. In *The Isle of Strangers*, published more than thirty years ago and first serialised in the junior magazine *Elizabethan*, he introduced his villain, an oil-prospecting villain scarred by the Second World War, in terms of a metaphor no less potent because the source of light is neither the moon nor the shadow-throwing beam of a candle but seemingly unromantic electricity:

> Out of the darkness a shadow emerged. It had the shape and form of a man, but it came towards me quite silently like something stalking its prey.
>
> My hand groped in the pocket of my coat and grasped my torch. I pulled it out and with trembling fingers switched it on. A stranger leapt into vision at one end of the beam. He was short and dark and sallow, and the right side of his jaw was swollen.
>
> I knew instinctively who he was. This was the stranger my uncle had spoken about. This was the *utlending*. Stark terror gripped me as he walked towards me, silently like a cat, his eyes dark coals in the light, his thin mouth twisted in a smile that showed the gleam of gold teeth.[15]

Here are run-of-the-mill adjectives with none of the panache or the unexpected visualisations of Garfield but with the same object, to employ the overtones as well as the immediate meaning of words to create a particular effect. Through words that *suggest*, through extended and implied metaphors (of light and darkness, of sound and silence, of flood and drought, and so on) an atmosphere, a totality is created in a book which can convey something to the reader beyond the immediate 'story' and an essential part of it. The changes in that element which can be called in general terms 'style', changes dictated partly by theories of universal education, partly by the influence of television on the expectations of fiction, have provided children with entertainment but, in the general run of adventures at least, have robbed them of the more complex way in which words can work. To achieve that suspension of disbelief by which fiction lifts an ordinary event into a more exciting and more deeply educative sphere, words must act subliminally on the reader. Metaphor in description is perhaps the most valuable way in which words play on the reader's emotions and experience to give stories depth and substance. Vernon Lee argued that words, the writer's raw material, were:

> . . . *signals* which call up the various items – visual, audible, tactile, emotional, and of a hundred different other sorts – which have been deposited by chance in the mind of the reader.[16]

Current fashion in narrative fiction (in much best-selling adult fiction as well as in the juvenile sector) has led to a weakening of those 'signals' which amounts to the theft of a reader's right to the best that fiction can offer in the rich and reverberant use of words.

*

The rights of reading children are assailed also, all too often, by the way those novels we call classics are offered to them. *Treasure Island* seems a suitable example to use here, since it has always been widely read and has probably inspired more sequels, parodies and imitations than any other story for the young. Why do we call it a classic? Is it because it has held its place (for whatever reasons) for a full century or because it is more than a simple tale of pirates and treasure? Stevenson himself might have been surprised at the amount of critical attention and intellectual analysis lavished on a tale he wrote to entertain a stepson of thirteen. In an article written in response to a literary comment which Henry James had made on the book (a comment which Stevenson in fact enjoyed) he wrote:

> . . . in this elementary novel of adventure, the characters need to be presented with but one class of qualities – the warlike and formidable. So as they appear insidious in deceit and fatal in combat, they have served their end. Danger is the matter with which this class of novel deals; fear, the passion with which it idly trifles; and the characters are portrayed only so far as they realize the sense of danger and provoke the sympathy of fear. To add more traits, to be too clever, to start the hare of moral or intellectual interest while we are running the fox of material interest, is not to enrich but to stultify your tale. The stupid reader will only be offended, and the clever reader lose the scent. . . .[17]

and he comments that the novel of adventure appeals to 'certain almost sensual and quite illogical tendencies in men . . .'[18] In this shrewd definition Stevenson seems to acknowledge the persuasive power of bloody encounters and narrow escapes and also the ancient, non-legal and non-moral law of finders keepers, a necessary attitude in the adventure story as against the problem-novel.

Yet he did move beyond both these points of direction, without falsifying them. As Jim Hawkins is drawn into the adventure on his own account we sense through him a growing unease about the justification of the whole enterprise, expressed in the closing words of the story (which, after all, is largely told in his words) when he says roundly that the survivors of the *Hispaniola* used their shares of the treasure 'wisely or foolishly, according to our nature'[19] and that 'Oxen and wain-ropes would not bring me back again to that accursed island'.[20]

This is not to suggest that Stevenson overloaded his book with serious meanings. Few tales read as easily or with such a spontaneous pace as the tale which began in the sketching of a map, in cheerful competition with the young Lloyd Osbourne, and proceeded in a spirit of gay complicity with that first listener (not to mention Stevenson's father, who claimed the task of enumerating the contents of Billy Bones's sea-chest). Not even a break of some weeks between the writing of the first fifteen and the remaining chapters could interfere with the youthful vigour and fun of the enterprise. Stevenson extended the scope of his tale simply because he was not writing only for that stepson or for potential young readers like him but also for himself. Harvey Darton believed that *Treasure Island* and *King Solomon's Mines* were a stimulus to the boys' book as a genre:

> They made it grow up into greater maturity, but in doing so gave it also the chance of growing clean out of boyhood. To put it contrariwise, they increased the youthward frontier of the novelist's kingdom.[21]

Maturity of this kind *within* the accepted convention and limits of stories for the young is a distinguishing mark of the accepted classics.

How much of this maturity is due to the characters? Edwin Muir, comparing the novel of action with the novel of character, asserted that the response of the characters to the action in a story is incidental and exists to help the plot. Of *Treasure Island* he writes that:

> . . . Trelawney must be unable to keep a secret, otherwise the pirates would never know he was sailing to find the treasure. Silver, in the same way, must be a diplomatist, otherwise the crew would not reach the island without being suspected; and the pirates must conveniently quarrel, or the few faithful hands would never win in the end. Had Silver and his followers killed all the loyal ship's company, secured the treasure, sailed away, been captured, taken to England and executed, *Treasure Island* would not have been a novel of action, but something else, probably of far greater value.[22]

Later, describing the novel of action as 'a fantasy of desire rather than a picture of life', he concludes, with some contradiction, that it is 'never of much literary consequence except when, as in Scott and Stevenson, it is also in some measure a novel of character'.[23]

The whole validity and excellence of the adventure story seems to be challenged in that last phrase, 'of far greater value'. Presumably the critic was suggesting that Stevenson might have scrutinised and probed Long John Silver as he did the Master of Ballantrae, recognisably of the same species. Something of the disaster that this would have been can be seen if we read Denis Judd's *The Adventures of Long John Silver* and its sequel, *Return to Treasure Island*, with this comment in mind; in these novels a *curriculum vitae* is provided for that ambiguous one-legged sea-cook. His experiences as slave-trader and slave, plantation owner and pirate, are described at great length in order to show how his basic goodness of heart and sense of moral values were gradually eroded by circumstances.

But the suppressed sympathies and crises of conscience in Judd's Silver have nothing to do with Stevenson's villain-hero; nor is the crudely villainous Barbecue in Leonard Wibberley's *Flint's Island* any nearer, though this 'sequel', written to satisfy a long wish to know the fate of the unlifted treasure, runs on logically enough from Stevenson. Silver's function in *Treasure Island* is to be a mystery. He lives in the memory for what we do not know about him and what Stevenson wisely chose not to tell us. In the adventure story as a whole the characters are held in a special kind of suspension, which is upset if we are gratuitously told too much about their past or given too searching an analysis of their characters. (The same idea of immediate, self-contained completeness in the drama was discussed many years ago in an essay by L. C. Knights on critical method with the significant title, 'How many children had Lady Macbeth?')

This is not the same as saying that character is less important than action. The special tensions, surprises and structural shapes of a good adventure story depend partly on their completeness. There should be no bled-off edges. Imagine how *Lord of the Flies* would read if the choice of those air-passengers, their backgrounds and their embarkation, had been described in detail. By its very nature an adventure story needs to start somewhere in the middle: part of the pleasure for the reader is being let into secrets little by little but never totally, and boringly, satisfied with 'the whole truth'.

With Long John Silver, Stevenson took this narrative convention as far as it could go. There is no accident in the way we see the sea-cook in profile, as it were, as others see him and as Silver obviously intends that they shall see him. There is the Squire's first meeting with him on the dock in Bristol, quoted earlier, with the old sailor who kept a public house but wanted 'a good berth as cook to get to sea again. He had hobbled down there that morning, he said, to get a smell of the salt'[24]. There is Jim Hawkins's first view of him at the Spy-Glass Inn:

> His left leg was cut off close by the hip, and under the left shoulder he carried a crutch, which he managed with wonderful dexterity, hopping about upon it like a bird. He was very tall and strong, with a face as big as a ham – plain and pale, but intelligent and smiling. Indeed, he seemed in the most cheerful spirits, whistling as he

moved about among the tables, with a merry word or a slap on the shoulders for the more favoured of his guests.[25]

Too clever for him, as Jim confesses, Silver's behaviour lulls the suspicions that come to the boy when he finds Black Dog at the inn, and even after he has overheard, from the apple-barrel, enough to convict the ship's cook completely, Silver still has it in him to draw from the boy a certain admiration and even liking. The man's courage, his astuteness and his quick manoeuvres impress the lad who, as prisoner with the pirates, has time to assess the situation and to contemplate:

> . . . the remarkable game that I saw Silver now engaged upon – keeping the mutineers together with one hand, and grasping, with the other, after every means, possible and impossible, to make his peace and save his miserable life. He himself slept peacefully, and snored aloud, yet my heart was sore for him, wicked as he was, to think on the dark perils that environed, and the shameful gibbet that awaited him.[26]

At no time in the book does Stevenson allow any summarising of Silver's character, either authorial or from the chosen narrator. Apart from anything else, the man has to remain an enigma so that the effect of the adventure on Jim Hawkins can be believable. Had Silver been more precisely defined, either as a villain or as the warped character Denis Judd has made him, he would not have been the main factor in the lad's move out of boyhood. Jim Hawkins grows up because he looks squarely at Silver's ambiguities, accepting human inconsistency for the first time in his life. Within the conventions of his story, without ostentation, Stevenson makes it clear that his young hero is changed by events just as surely as, by his impetuous, youthful conceit of himself and his initially romantic view of the enterprise, he changes those events. This is surely the 'something of far greater value' that Edwin Muir suggested Stevenson had missed in his adventure story.

The vitality of a classic may be judged partly by the number of conjectural sequels, imitations and parodies which it inspires. Denis Judd's two novels were written for adults and made their appeal to nostalgic memory as well as to a literary appreciation of their ingenuity in prolonging Stevenson's fiction. This appeal may be most effective with those who, having only a rather vague but pleasurable recollection of *Treasure Island*, read Denis Judd's books as historical tales in their own right. We may disregard the hyperbole of the advertisement on the cover of Corgi's paperback reprint of *The Adventures of Long John Silver*, which tells us this is 'At last – the spellbinding prelude to Robert Louis Stevenson's immortal classic . . .' and note instead the cautionary Author's Note, which explains:

> This book does not seek to emulate Robert Louis Stevenson, and certainly not to mock him. The events described and the adventure related are merely designed to answer some of the riddles and unanswered questions in *Treasure Island* itself. The book is, above all, supposed to be fun.[27]

Even with the utmost good will towards one more pirate-treasure tale we shall have to admit that the fun in the first of these two post-Stevenson tales is somewhat muffled by an elaborate historical and social background, a logical but laborious following-up of the hints with which Stevenson told us as much as we needed to know about the minor characters, and a dialogue that veers between gadzookery and neutral idiom, with an unsuitable, frenetic Cockney put into Silver's mouth. There is far more fun, and genuine ingenuity, in the second book, *Return to Treasure Island*, where Silver is plausibly involved in the Boston Teaparty and with General Washington and where he casually drops a phrase to the effect that his erstwhile pirate chief, Captain England, expects his crew to do its duty – a phrase which the seasick midshipman, Horatio Nelson, victim of piratical attack, remembers and turns to his own use later. Such witty impudence is enough to justify this particular tribute to Stevenson.

Another such tribute can be found in Robert Leeson's *Silver's Revenge*, which speculates on the sea-cook's career after the events on Kidd's Island in a spirit of burlesque, in a kind of Marxist frolic. There is nicely judged parody in the structure of the tale, told in the first person by orphan Tom Carter, who is taken on as ship's boy in a ship chartered by the optimistic and financially oppressed Squire, fifteen years after the *Hispaniola* adventure. Tom's part in the voyage to lift the bar-silver from the island follows that of Jim Hawkins but with a wryly comic reversal of attitudes. The conspiracy which Tom overhears from the apple-barrel is between Silver (now a respectable entrepreneur, Mr Argent, with a false leg running on ball-bearings) and the impetuous Squire himself, and the alternations of mastery in the stockade and around the island end in an attempt by Mr Argent's band of rebels to set up a kind of Shelleyean democracy of which the inventor Somerscale, Argent's associate, remarks sourly, 'It seems to me your society, founded upon irrationality, setting its face against progress and the march of history, is bound to fail.'[28] The sardonic edge to the story is emphatic in the non-ending, in the picture of the various groups of treasure-seekers, corrupt in motive and socially quarrelsome, trying to work out a future either on the island or on a curiously designed escape vessel.

Following an old tradition, Robert Leeson gives his romping tale an exact provenance. 'I'm stowing this story in a rum cask,' Tom Carter writes on 6 September 17—, 'and floating it off on the north-east current which they say washes the shores of Old England.' But the book ends with an editorial note – 'Sea water must have got into the rum cask, for parts of the manuscript are indecipherable – R. L.'.[29] This witty, ingenious tale reflects certain social attitudes of our time. In particular, Mr Argent's version of the *Hispaniola* venture, a neat reversal of Jim Hawkins's partisan view, offers an implied condemnation of the Squire's claim to the treasure and a comment on the convention on which treasure-hunt stories depend. Without trying to explain Silver, Robert Leeson has looked at *Treasure Island* from the standpoint of another century.

This is neither rewriting nor imitation, but an interpretation that reflects a change of attitudes. The same may be said of Emma Tennant's fantasy, *The Search for Treasure Island*. The immediate purpose of her story is an intriguing juxtaposition of past and present. Again the narrator is a boy in that watershed between heedless youth and approaching maturity. In bed with a cold, young Sam, for whom *Treasure Island* has always been a key book, is snatched away by an intruding Jim Hawkins; half afraid and half joyously excited, he finds himself on the *Hispaniola* with the Squire and Doctor Livesey but still retaining his knowledge of his own time:

> It was odd, in this mix-up of time I was living, to see the great jets overhead, carrying passengers to and from America. And I saw Concorde once, high above us, but when I pointed it out to Jim he glanced up at the sky and gave an angry shrug. 'We can't see these things, Sam,' he said. 'It's not fair if you show off about them. I can't even *imagine* what they're like!' And he sighed.[30]

It is easy enough for Sam to adapt to this dream-world, knowing the book as he does, but he does need Jim's explanation of the presence of Admiral Guinea, who has stepped out of Stevenson's dramatisation of *Treasure Island*, with that earlier 'lost' treasure map which is to point the venturers to a different island in the Galapagos and a different treasure. Beyond the entertaining variations played on the original theme (Silver's gang of pirates has been regrouped by the Admiral's Amazonian daughter Arethusa, on a submarine identified by the *Hispaniola*'s crew as a dolphin – a startling confusion of time and space), the story has its main direction in the ambiguity of the treasure-hunt. What is the treasure the antipathetic parties are seeking? Is it the bar-silver or is it a natural species, plant or animal, unknown to man? Can the aim of any of the seekers be described as moral? Afloat on Ben Gunn's coracle, escaping from the disputes that break the silence of Kidd's Island, Sam outstrips the rest through his knowledge of the Panama Canal and finds the 'treasure', a shell which affords him a wide and alarming vision of evolution past and to come.

But this is not in fact the climax of the book, though it does add one more modern comment on the non-morality of the traditional treasure-hunt. In her open-ended conclusion Emma Tennant seems to be assenting to Stevenson's conception of Silver as a villain-hero or hero-villain. As Sam takes his first look through the peephole in the shell:

> Long John Silver stood before me. His round, smooth face beamed into mine. He leant on a crutch with one arm and, with the other, he propped himself against the tree. 'Well, boy!' he said. And he pointed up to the sky. 'You've come for the treasure. So look – and it's yours!'
> I lifted my face upward. I gasped. And all I remember, as the sky turned black, is the sound of Silver's laughter and my own head hitting the ground with a bang as loud and terrible as Arethusa's exploding submarine.[31]

Sam returns to his own time more or less unscathed by an adventure rather more serious than he had ever hoped for. The point of this post-Stevenson tale is not a *rite de passage* but an oblique look at the treasure-theme and at the enigma of Silver. The last sentence of the book makes this clear enough:

> But I wouldn't mind looking into the future one more time – to see them arrive at Coco Island and find Long John Silver there.[32]

For of course there is no explanation of how the bland sea-cook found his way there.

The ultimate test to apply to the many 'versions' of *Treasure Island* may be taken to be the way each writer interprets the character of Long John Silver. Is the temptation to analyse this ambiguous individual resisted or not? Resisted it certainly was by R. F. Delderfield, although in fact he wrote *The Adventures of Ben Gunn* in reply to questions from his son and daughter after he had read Stevenson's story to them no less than three times. As the eighty-year-old Ben Gunn tells his story to Jim Hawkins, now (in 1805) squire of a Devonshire village, he fills out the characters of Pew, Israel Hands, Black Dog, as well as adding explanatory details of the to-and-fro on the island, but the maroon's view of Silver is essentially the view Stevenson offered to his readers:

> You see, John was neither black, white, or piebald, and no-one, not even a man like Flint, ever found a way to come safely alongside him. Sometimes you'd reckon he was rank bad, through and through, from stem to stern, crow's nest to keel, but no sooner had you made up your mind to this than he'd clap you on the shoulder and set you wondering if you was sadly misjudging the best shipmate you'd ever run across.
>
> You could never trust him, of course; sooner or later, the minute it suited him, he'd always leave you in shoal water, but no matter how many times this happened you could never profit by it, for inside the hour he would have talked you into believing he'd done you a good service. He could do that after leading you slap up to the gallows-foot, and have you blessing him with your dying breath so to speak.
>
> . . . he wasn't a man at all but rather a cross between a devil, a savage, a good mess-mate and a lady's maid.[33]

Delderfield's intention, as he said in a Preface to his book, was not to write a sequel to *Treasure Island* nor (he hoped) a bad imitation of it, but 'more of a supplement, and one, I feel, of which Stevenson might have approved, at least in principle'. Like Stevenson, he was writing for young readers but, at least in the first instance, for children rather than for the thirteen-year-old Lloyd Osbourne, a boy with the maturity of an only child much with adults. Delderfield's children of nine and eleven asked practical questions about how Ben Gunn found the treasure, how Pew lost his eyes and Silver his leg, as well as enquiring what had made Silver a bad man. This last question, as we have seen, Delderfield did not try to answer. But his approach to the writing of another pirate-and-treasure yarn raises the broad question, at what age should a child read *Treasure Island*? It is a question crucial to the appreciation of a book which some may feel has been made a classic by adults rather than becoming one by a consensus of the opinion of children.

Perhaps in the past it did not matter if a boy or girl read the book, at eight or nine or even ten, simply as an openly active narrative (albeit a violent one) of exciting action, for there was a good chance that this young reader would come to the book again a year or two later and respond to it in a different way, finding more of its richness. But we can no longer take rereading for granted; there are too many books, and too many other activities for any but obsessive readers to be sure of enjoying this most

enduring of pleasures. J. C. Furnas, examining Stevenson's reputation, which he considered had been damaged by the wrong kind
of fame attached to *Treasure Island*, argued in exclamatory terms
against coming to the book too soon:

> Ah, pirates my dears, ah, the Spanish Main, ah, pieces of eight and
> shiver my timbers! The cultivated aunt wishing her small nephew
> normally but hygienically pirate-minded furnished him with Jim
> Hawkins's story. Few items of warranted literary standing can
> compete so well with dime novels or comic books. So *Treasure
> Island* appeared on children's shelves long before they could savour
> it – it was written, after all, for the early teens, not the kindergarten
> – and was left off high-school reading-lists . . . because it was a
> 'child's book'. Here are remarkable anomalies: woolly animals and
> Silver panting aloud as he knifes the honest hand. The patter of
> little feet and Israel Hands trailing across the deck with the great
> wound in his thigh and the blood-sticky dirk in his yellow teeth.
> Patty cake and the stiff-as-a-crucifix deadness of O'Brien lying
> 'across the knees of the man who had killed him, and the quick
> fishes steering to and fro over both'. The films usually completed
> the sabotage by casting Jim as a child of nine or ten instead of as a
> boy in his teens conceivably capable of snatching up a cutlass in the
> mêlée at the blockhouse.[34]

Allowing for excusable hyperbole, there is truth here, especially
in the comment on dramatic versions of the story. The absurdities
of Captain Hook do not interfere with the enigmatic, bland
figure of Stevenson's Silver but not even an actor of the calibre of
Alfred Burke could suggest, in the visual medium of a recent
television film, anything but a stage pirate, an eighteenth-century
con man. *Treasure Island* has been and will continue to be given
too soon to the young at the period in their lives when parents
and teachers feel they should become acquainted with 'the classics':
an apparently congenial plot, the certainty of moral value
(though the value which the guardians of childhood find in the
book is not necessarily what Stevenson intended to supply), a
concrete and lucid narrative style, all commend the book as a safe
and suitable one with which a child may begin his literary
journey. Here once more the feeling that books for the young
must be in some way improving robs many of their right to find
the classics for themselves, and at the time when they can most
fully and urgently respond to them, preferably without thinking
of them as classics at all.

A more serious theft, and one which it is hard for the young to
resist when they are still apprentice readers, is the rewriting and

abridgment of the classics. As a logical extension of the intellectual snobbery which suggests powerfully to the guardians of childhood that there are certain books that should be read and be
known to have been read, many classics have been simplified in
the expectation that to read a version of a book is to read the
book itself. Such versions have been made sometimes to save
children from having to make an effort to read a type of prose
outside their normal experience, sometimes to escape supposedly
extraneous matter (description, philosophising, soliloquy which
in fact constitutes an essential of this or that classic) and to reduce
the book to a more customary length for today. This attention to
an invisible but powerful hierarchy of letters is not altogether
cynical, of course; many educationists genuinely want to give
children a reading experience which they might otherwise miss.
Good will does not alter the fact that when children read an
abridged or rewritten version of *Treasure Island* they are not
in fact reading Stevenson's book. A few may possibly turn to
Stevenson from curiosity later: most will go through life thinking
they have read *Treasure Island*.

The motives behind the Ladybird series of 'Children's Classics'
are likely to be a mixture of commercial astuteness and a sincere
wish to help the young to the 'education' of reading the classics.
Readers of limited ability may find it easy enough to follow the
plot in Joyce Faraday's recast *Treasure Island* but in many ways
abbreviation has defeated its own ends. Unless young readers
(ten or so, probably) already have strong built-in associations of
pirates and treasure (and pirates have retreated as comic-book
characters recently, displaced by space-heroes and bionic humans)
they may well wonder what all the fuss is about as the filleted
narrative gallops through the first nine or ten chapters of Stevenson's
tale in about six hundred words.

Not only is there no time for any atmosphere of suspense to be
created or for any expansion of the word 'treasure' which hardly
works the necessary spell on its own, but there is no space for any
differentiation of character and therefore no real motives for any
of the action. It is not made clear that there was a previous
connection between the sea-cook engaged by the Squire and the
'tough men' helpfully picked out by him for the voyage; and
because of this, and because no description is given of Silver
other than that he has lost a leg and walks with a crutch, the brief
comment that 'He was well-liked by all and the men looked on
him as a leader'[35] is both flat and unclear, as flat as the words that
Jim Hawkins uses to describe his reaction when he overhears from
the apple-barrel Silver and Hands discussing mutiny – 'I could not

believe my ears'.[36] The graceless prose offers no inkling of a boy's feelings in such a crisis; no reader is likely to be moved to identify with such a wooden hero. Style, the prick of words, has been stolen in the name of simplicity. And more than just the exchange of banal for selected words is in question.

The necessary surprise, tension and pace of an adventure story depends on the reader being allowed enough *time* to assimilate the story and to respond to it fully. One example will illustrate the need for more than abrupt statement. This is how Joyce Faraday renders the crucial scene (crucial because it marks an important stage in Jim's enlightenment as well as being an implied warning of danger for the reader's benefit) when the boy watches Silver murdering one of the honest ship's hands:

> I felt faint, and the whole world swam before me in a whirling mist. When I pulled myself together, Silver, crutch under his arm, was wiping his knife on a tuft of grass.[37]

Stevenson makes us see and feel with the boy:

> I do not know what it rightly is to faint, but I do know that for the next little while the whole world swam away from before me in a whirling mist; Silver and the birds, and the tall Spy-glass hill-top, going round and round and topsy-turvy before my eyes, and all manner of bells ringing and distant voices shouting in my ears.
> When I came again to myself, the monster had pulled himself together, his crutch under his arm, his hat upon his head. Just before him Tom lay motionless upon the sward; but the murderer minded him not a whit, cleansing his blood-stained knife the while upon a wisp of grass.[38]

The truncated version misses not only the interaction of character and action but the pace and tension which account for much of the magic, the conjuring-trick illusion of the adventure story.

The motives behind the version of *Treasure Island* issued as one of a new series of adaptations in 1977, published in Pan's Piccolo Adventure Library, were carefully argued by the General Editor of the series, Edward Blishen, and must be taken seriously. Describing himself as a 'convert to the adaptation for young readers of books they might otherwise never encounter', Blishen is firm in his belief that it is possible to produce versions in the spirit of the originals and to retain some part of the original text, the method being a combination of abridgment and rewriting. The justification offered is that 'Inside every long and difficult book lies a shorter, easier book, waiting to be liberated' and the aim is to ensure that 'no young reader will fall asleep over his reading because the language, or the nature of the narrative prevents the essential activity of the story from getting through'.[39]

The word 'activity' is significant. It is used also to commend the crude, grotesque drawings provided by Tom Barling, who was also the adapter – drawings advertised as bold and vigorous, which show the pirates as comic-cuts characters and depict the young hero either as a ferocious youth of eighteen or so or something like a chimpanzee. As far as the action of the story goes, the brief has been fulfilled and the story is here, with recognisable characters and a modicum of description to preserve the atmosphere of a treasure-hunt. As for simplification, it may be questioned whether *Treasure Island* could ever be described as 'long and difficult' with 'a shorter, easier book waiting to be liberated'. Liberation, in this case at least, reveals clearly enough that it was not Stevenson's vocabulary that was 'difficult': the rewriting has robbed children not of words so much as of rhythms and varied sentence-constructions which, however absent from the clipped prose-style in favour today, are not essentially 'difficult' for any young reader willing to accept them; they offer a flavour and a density of detail which are essential to the book.

In *Treasure Island* we listen to the individual voice of the author-cum-narrator as he *expands* simple circumstances as part of the technique of narrative. The difference between plain, bald statement and judicious expansion, calculated to add emotional colour, hints of character, atmospheric tone, may be seen in comparing two passages describing the strange captain lodging at the inn. Stevenson gave young Jim this view of Billy Bones:

> All the time he lived with us the captain made no change whatever in his dress but to buy some stockings from a hawker. One of the cocks of his hat having fallen down, he let it hang from that day forth, though it was a great annoyance when it blew. I remember the appearance of his coat, which he patched himself upstairs in his room, and which, before the end, was nothing but patches. He never wrote or received a letter, and he never spoke with any but the neighbours, and with these, for the most part, only when drunk on rum. The great sea-chest none of us had ever seen open. . . .[40]

and those who read the adaptation will get no more than:

> The captain never bought new clothes, mending his coat himself until it was nothing but patches. He never wrote or received letters, only speaking to our neighbours when he was full of rum. None of us ever saw his great sea-chest open.[41]

Apart from the uninteresting, flat sound of the prose in Tom Barling's version, the jettisoning of so much detail means that we have lost the sense of the passage of time, as well as of the strangeness of the captain's behaviour, necessary to cast forward shadows and lead up to the coming of his enemies: the slow winding into the main story line is one of the structural excellencies of the book.

There are occasional lapses into vulgarity in this adaptation (like Jim's cliché-phrase that the overhearing of Silver's conspiracy 'froze me to the spot'); the Squire's letter from Bristol is quoted almost unaltered but the significant phrase with which Stevenson suggests Silver's role-playing, that 'he said' he had hobbled down to the quay to get a smell of the salt, has been omitted; the Squire's comment that Captain Smollett was 'unmanly, unsailorly, and downright unEnglish'[42] in disturbing the aim and plan of the *Hispaniola*'s voyage, has been, oddly, changed to 'unmannerly, unsailorly and unEnglish',[43] which is hardly relevant.

These are minor blemishes compared with the way the emotional and structural substance has been boiled off the bones of the story. One of the most important examples comes at the moment when the Squire's party first enters the treasure-cave. This is a vital moment in the adventure as it affects Jim Hawkins, and Stevenson uses it with brilliant simplicity:

> It was a large, airy place, with a little spring and a pool of clear water, overhung with ferns. The floor was sand. Before a big fire lay Captain Smollett; and in a far corner, only duskily flickered over by the blaze, I beheld great heaps of coin and quadrilaterals built of bars of gold. That was Flint's treasure that we had come so far to seek, and that had cost already the lives of seventeen men from the *Hispaniola*. How many it had cost in the amassing, what blood and sorrow, what good ships scuttled on the deep, what brave men walking the plank blindfold, what shot of cannon, what shame and lies and cruelty, perhaps no man alive could tell. Yet there were still three upon that island – Silver, and old Morgan, and Ben Gunn – who had each taken his share in these crimes, as each had hoped in vain to share in the reward.[44]

The version introducing children to this classic offers little in the name of simplicity:

> We all entered the cave where Captain Smollett lay by the fire. All around were heaps of coins and piles of gold bars: Flint's treasure, for which we had come so far, and that had cost the lives of seventeen of the *Hispaniola*'s crew. How much blood had been spilled in its collection we could only guess at.[45]

Rhetoric has, it seems, become a dirty word.

A story is not just a story. Each piece of fiction, whatever its quality, is an individual, unique construct, an artefact, a piece of craftsmanship. It does not admit of an alternative, any more than a piece of music or a painting admits of a version of any kind. The aim to give children books they might otherwise miss is not to be achieved by providing them with retold or abridged versions, for the book itself has gone. J. C. Furnas defined the literary value of *Treasure Island* in a way that separates its most obvious appeal from its intrinsic merit:

> I know of no more striking example of an artist's taking a cheap, artificial set of commercialized values – which is fair enough to the Victorian 'boys' story' – and doing work of everlasting quality by changing nothing, transmuting everything, as if Jane Austen had ennobled soap-opera.[46]

The attempt to liberate a simpler book from Stevenson's, in the name of education, has merely given the young a conscientious but inferior treasure-island soap-opera.

16. Predictions

In any literary banquet, adventure stories will be placed below the salt and will in consequence find themselves next to children's books, relegated as lower forms of literature. If leagues and hierarchies be necessary, children's books as a whole and the adult genre of the adventure story could claim an upward move if only for the reason that each has consistently preserved that essential element of fiction, the story, where it has often been pushed aside in the interests of novelty of structure, psychological analysis or verbal experiment.

The relegation of children's fiction has followed inevitably from the difference in readership, in age and experience; the 'difference' of youth has come to be accepted almost as being 'inferior'. The separation of children's books from those written for adults, an obvious practical convenience for those engaged in producing, sorting and promoting books, has done a disservice to all but the most enterprising young readers. Conscientious assumptions about what children could be expected to understand, in terms of style and subject-matter, have led to an unnecessary dilution of emotional and literary experience.

One of the solutions to this juvenilising, a solution which the young found for themselves, is an invasion of the adult bookshelves. Sometimes, indeed, this has been unwittingly encouraged by their elders, as J. S. Bratton commented. Writing of the kind of books given to boys a century ago – Marryat's *Poor Jack*, for example, the novels of Scott and Fenimore Cooper – he points out:

> These were often the books remembered by fathers from their own boyhood, or recognised vaguely as classics, rather than carefully chosen as suitable; probably few purchasers bothered to re-read them, or reflect that they had been thought childhood reading in a period which had far less choice in such matters, and moreover a less fastidious discrimination of what might be too coarse or rough for young eyes. Consequently boys were cheerfully allowed to form literary tastes on novels which derived from the eighteenth-century tradition of Fielding and Smollett, and on romances which dealt largely and freely in adventure social and sexual as well as heroic.[1]

404

From such books, he argues, boys were shown the qualities of self-reliance and self-confidence, and of national pride, which were considered desirable for their education.

At the same time, the substantial narrative style and mature subject matter of this type of fiction was accompanied by an emotional tone as close to young experience as it was to adults looking for entertainment in their reading. J. S. Bratton observes of Mayne Reid's novels:

> . . . prize and Reward purchasers were often confused enough by the similarities of titles and style to give his adult romances to the young, who found in them much the same mixture, but held together by a story of full-blooded passions instead of the ancient didactic formulae of question and answer. This chance error may have added to his popularity with young readers, for they were probably able to share most of Captain Mayne Reid's dreams, which are all very like the fantasies of male adolescence.[2]

These 'fantasies of male adolescence' form an integral part of the adult adventure story. Richard Church made a similar point in stressing the boyishness of Scott's novels, the 'unsophisticated gift of enjoyment, of seeing people and things from outside, as a spectacle lit by surprise and even rapture.'[3]

In fact the adventure story as a genre provides the most convenient bridge when the young are ready to cross over from their own literary territory to the world of adult fiction. Differences in style and emotional content are often minimal because of the buoyancy and active energy common to adventure stories for all ages. The structural demands of pace, surprise and tension need not be altered. The type of prose best suited to tales of action can be undiluted. Writers who serve both adult and young readers – Hammond Innes, Lionel Davidson and Peter Dickinson are obvious examples – do not have to alter the plain, nervous, direct prose natural to them and appropriate to the genre. The difference between, for example, Peter Dickinson's *Pride of Heroes*, an adult thriller, and his story for the early teens, *The Gift*, does not lie in vocabulary or syntax, nor in the approach to character, but in the degree of inference demanded of the reader in each case. The best writers for the young, in our time and in the past, have respected their readers enough to invite their response to a varied social scene and a substantial story. T. H. White's jocular prescription for a novel has a good deal of sense behind its hyperbole:

My next novel must be picaresque. A pursuit perhaps, with Russian spies, a great-great-grandson of William Wordsworth, aeroplanes, and a drunk wildfowler lying in a puddle with two bottles of whisky. Also a Harem out for a walk, in a crocodile; and the suggestion of a local anaesthetic for boys who have got to be beaten at school.[4]

The junior adventure story as we know it today could do with a far wider range of subjects and characters than is commonly achieved and a far more substantial documentation. The credibility of characters essential to any piece of fiction, and no less necessary in adventure stories because there is less room for deep probing of motive and reaction, needs to be increased by a bolder balance of adult with young. Peter Dickinson's *The Gift* may be cited here, a book in which the interaction of personality and action depends on equal attention to a boy's uncomfortable extrasensory perception and an adult's weakness of purpose. An investigation into 'Violence, Horror and Sensationalism in Stories for Children' and the typical reading of boys and girls of ten and eleven in London schools led to the conclusion that 'they are, by this age, ready for more realistic presentation of adults and of children's relationships with them, at least for part of the tales'.[5]

As I have suggested, the typical themes of adventure-story are readily interchangeable between books for young people and for adults. Certain plots will be changed but not abandoned entirely. Instead of rescuing distressed damsels in romantic circumstances (if this happens in any sense in junior stories, it will be within the inverted commas of 'fun'), the young may set out to rescue a condemned building, a threatened playground, an endangered animal species or habitat. The impulse behind the adventure will differ in degree but not in kind.

It should be possible, and it seems to me entirely desirable, for adult and junior adventure stories to grow more closely together. Besides being ready for more emotional depth than they are usually accorded in their stories, young people deserve a more substantial allowance of what one might call political and economic truth. Take, for example, a popular subject for historical adventure, the navvies and the building of the railways in England in the last century. Isolationism is the rule here, as elsewhere. The central character, a boy (usually) in the early or mid-teens, is involved with adults to a carefully limited degree. Sabotage is an obvious danger in which a boy's talents for lurking and overhearing may be plausibly employed: the economic motives for sabotage are as a rule stated so simply as to be subordinate, where a little more background fact would have added purpose and substance and, to the reader, a certain enlargement of perspective. Issues such as payment by token and the menace of the tally-shops and the pattern of village life as it was affected by the proximity of what amounted to an alien race – these are seldom allowed in historical tales on this subject for the young. The limitation not only encourages the supposedly necessary dilution of material but because home backgrounds are sketched rather than developed, it encourages an emphasis on male characters which benefits nobody in the end. An injection of more mature material and a more mature approach to the themes of adventure could well be accepted by the young and, indeed, seems no more than their right.

But can we assume that there is still a future for the traditional type of adventure story? Many constraints operate against it in the present day. Modern communications have made the world so familiar, in superficial terms, that unknown, unexplored lands can no longer be found as settings for adventure and, as a result, the familiar map has often been exchanged for the cartography of space. Children's adventures have lost such useful narrative devices as quarantine, while automation has taken much of the colour out of the investigations of detectives and spy-masters.

Communications, as they become yearly more complex, have left the adventure story less room to manoeuvre. A good deal more is at issue here than plot and subject material. We are dealing with a kind of fiction governed by conventions of structure and approach which was able to operate with a certain artificiality, a selectiveness of material possible because it was addressed to a particular range of readership. The continual shifts of class and attitude since the Second World War and the influence of the media have meant that the literary frontiers of adventure-story have been and are being blurred and altered. A genre which has always reflected the social life and preoccupations of its time as incidental is now called upon to give social comment a more prominent place in the totality of the story. This is as noticeable in the more recent thrillers of Dick Francis, the police-novels of Ed McBain and John le Carré's spy-stories as it is in the reinterpretation of legend by writers like Anthony Burgess and Robert Nye: and children's adventure stories by Robert Leeson, Peter Dickinson and many others can be seen to be turning the genre into something more like the 'Novel of Protest'. Categorising also looks absurd when the adventure story reflects the universal fear of global annihilation through the fantasies of science- and space-fiction. Given such terrifying material, can the story-telling, entertainment-offering impulse of the adventure story survive?

Two apparently contradictory needs have to be, and have always been, satisfied by adventure stories – curiosity and concern. The first is an animal instinct, the second a manufactured product of the Puritan work ethic. Curiosity demands excitement in reading, the enlightenment of new settings and new ideas, the tug and stimulus of a good story: concern with the problems of fictional characters is activated by the writer's attitudes. Both depend, ultimately, on a combination of literary skill and emotional commitment.

The adventure story by tradition deals with serious matters – with dangers overcome, evil countered by good, the single-minded devotion and determination of heroes. Whatever pressures of social unrest are exercised on this fictional genre, its basic tone is one of optimism. Good triumphs over evil. Man's capacity for courage, endurance, resource, compassion is vindicated. The small enterprises, mistakes, exercises of everyday life are relieved in stories whose compulsive words speak of larger issues, greater conflicts, unimagined people and places, virtues still current and still desirable in the most threatened world. Nobility is not usually reckoned to be a natural concomitant of everyday life; this is no reason why the nobility of heroes in adventure-story must be assumed to be artificial or why it should not be thought salutary and enlarging for readers to contemplate it as an emotional force.

The adventure story directs its special verbal magic to the imagination first and only after that to the mind and the heart. The reader's curiosity must be first aroused by an invitation to a world with more extremes of colour, more mystery and more persuasive power than any he will inhabit or visit in reality; equally, the invitation may be to an entirely unsuspected view of the environment he thinks he knows well. Exhilaration and a sense of wonder, conveyed through an author's own particular manipulation of words, help us to adapt to the heady oxygen of imagination. The elements of narrative – dialogue and description, pace and tension, the dynamics of behaviour and feeling – satisfy our need for surprising and unexpected insights into people and places. Curiosity is aroused and, eventually, satisfied.

Like any other literary form, the adventure story has the capacity to change and still to endure because of its basic qualities. Change there must be – less dependence on Establishment assumptions, a greater acerbity, more disputation, more shading of good into evil and evil into good, new ways with that most flexible tool, prose. But in the balance of curiosity and concern, of enjoyment and enlightenment, the hero and the adventure will surely survive.

References

The page references to quotations relate to the accessible editions I have had at my disposal; the dates of these editions occur within brackets, and the date of first publication, when it differs, is given outside the brackets.

1. Escape or Enlargement
1) Paul Zweig: *The Adventurer* (London: Dent, 1974, Preface vii).
2) London *Daily Chronicle*, 24 April 1897, quoted in J. C. Furnas: *Voyage to Windward* (London: Faber, 1952, p. 380).
3) Ford Madox Ford: *The English Novel* (London: Constable, 1930, pp. 99–100).
4) Colin Watson: *Snobbery with Violence* (London: Eyre and Spottiswoode, 1971, p. 98).
5) Quentin Oates: 'Critics Crowner' in *The Bookseller* (London: Whitaker, 5 June 1982, p. 2136).
6) Michael Innes: *Stop Press* (London: Gollancz, 1939, p. 10).
7) J. I. M. Stewart: *Young Patullo* (London: Gollancz, 1975, p. 135).
8) J. I. M. Stewart: *Full Term* (London: Gollancz, 1978, p. 279).
9) Kornei Chukovsky: *The Silver Crest* (London: Oxford University Press, 1977, p. 45).
10) Michael Joseph: *The Complete Writing for Profit* (London: Hutchinson, 1930, p. 718).
11) John Sutherland: *Bestsellers. Popular Fiction of the 1970s* (London: Routledge and Kegan Paul, 1981, p. 235).
12) John Carwelti: *Adventure, Mystery and Romance* (Chicago: University of Chicago Press, 1976, p. 13).
13) Anthony Burgess: *The Novel Now* (London: Faber, 1967, p. 206).
14) F. J. Harvey Darton: *Children's Books in England* (Cambridge and London: Cambridge University Press, 3rd ed. rev. Brian Alderson, 1982, p. 294) 1932.
15) Graham Greene: 'The Lost Childhood' in *Collected Essays* (London: The Bodley Head, 1969, p. 14).
16) ibid., p. 15.

2. The Romanticising of Fact
1) Joseph Conrad: *The Rover* (London: T. Fisher Unwin, 1926, p. 14) 1923.
2) Joseph Conrad: *Heart of Darkness* (London: Penguin Modern Classics, 1973, p. 79) 1902.
3) Joseph Conrad: *Youth* (London: Pan Classics, 1976, p. 177) 1902.
4) Joseph Conrad: *The Shadow-Line* (London: Dent, 1923, p. 4) 1917.

References

5) Joseph Conrad: Author's Note to *Within the Tides* (London: Dent, 1923, Preface vii–viii) 1915.

6) Joseph Conrad: *Typhoon* (London: Heinemann, 1907, p. 6) 1903.

7) Joseph Conrad: *Lord Jim* (Edinburgh: William Blackwood, 1939, pp. 5–6) 1900.

8) ibid., p. 83.

9) ibid., pp. 215–16.

10) ibid., pp. 148–9.

11) ibid., p. 395.

12) Joseph Conrad: *The Nigger of the 'Narcissus'* (London: Pan Classics, 1976, p. 33) 1897.

13) ibid., pp. 34–5.

14) John Masefield: *Victorious Troy* (London: Heinemann, 1935, p. 208).

15) John Masefield: *The Bird of Dawning* (London: Heinemann, 1933, p. 168).

16) John Masefield: *Victorious Troy*, op. cit., pp. 188–9.

17) Richard Armstrong: *Chosen for Children* (London: Library Association, 1957, pp. 52–3).

18) Richard Armstrong: *Sea Change* (Leicester: Brockhampton Press Knight, 1969, p. 9) 1948.

19) ibid., p. 39.

20) ibid., p. 191.

21) ibid., p. 113.

22) Richard Armstrong: *The Lame Duck* (London: Dent, 1959, pp. 185–6).

23) Richard Armstrong: *The Albatross* (London: Dent, 1970, p. 143).

24) Patrick O'Brian: *Post Captain* (London: Collins, 1972, p. 196).

25) Captain Marryat: *Frank Mildmay* (London: Dent, 1929, pp. A–B) 1829.

26) Captain Marryat: *The King's Own* (London: Cassell, 1884, pp. 8–9) 1830.

27) ibid., pp. 323–4.

28) Oliver Warner: *Captain Marryat: a Rediscovery* (London: Constable, 1953, p. 146).

29) Captain Marryat: *Newton Forster* (London: Dent, 1896, p. 4) 1832.

30) Captain Marryat: *Mr Midshipman Easy* (London: Macmillan, 1896, p. 204) 1836.

31) Virginia Woolf: 'The Captain's Death Bed' in *The Captain's Death Bed and Other Essays* (London: The Hogarth Press, 1950, p. 44).

32) ibid., pp. 42–3.

33) Captain Marryat: *Percival Keene* (London: George Routledge, 1895, pp. 289–90) 1842.

34) Patrick O'Brian: *The Ionian Mission* (London: Collins, Fontana, 1982, pp. 69–70) 1981.

35) ibid., p. 11.

36) ibid., p. 45.

37) ibid., p. 46.
38) C. S. Forester: *The Hornblower Companion* (London: Michael Joseph, 1964, p. 32).
39) C. S. Forester: *The Happy Return* (London: Michael Joseph, 1937, p. 21).
40) C. S. Forester: *The Commodore* (London: Michael Joseph, 1945, p. 171).
41) C. S. Forester: *Lord Hornblower* (London: Michael Joseph, 1948, p. 6).
42) C. S. Forester: *The Happy Return*, op. cit., p. 203.
43) C. Northcote Parkinson: *The Life and Times of Horatio Hornblower* (London: Penguin Books, 1973, p. 145) 1970.
44) W. H. G. Kingston: *The Three Midshipmen* (London: Hutchinson, 1907, pp. 129–30) 1862.
45) Edward Salmon: 'Juvenile Literature as it is' (1888), quoted in Rev. Maurice Rooke-Kingsford: *The Life, Work and Influence of William Henry Giles Kingston* (Toronto: Ryerson Press, 1947, p. 196).
46) ibid., p. 185.
47) ibid., p. 173.
48) W. H. G. Kingston: *The Three Midshipmen*, op. cit., pp. 67–8.
49) ibid., p. 354.
50) W. H. G. Kingston: *The Three Lieutenants* (London: Oxford University Press, 1917, p. 384) 1875.
51) W. H. G. Kingston: *The Three Commanders* (London: Griffith, Farran, Browne & Co., 1891, p. 146) 1876.
52) Showell Styles: *Midshipman Quinn* (London: Hamlyn, Beaver, 1976, p. 12) 1956.
53) Showell Styles: *Quinn of the Fury* (London: Faber, 1958, p. 9).
54) Showell Styles: *Midshipman Quinn Wins Through* (London: Faber, 1961, p. 23).
55) Captain Marryat: *Percival Keene*, op. cit., p. 187.
56) Jan Needle: *A Fine Boy for Killing* (London: André Deutsch, 1979, pp. 190–1).
57) ibid., p. 149.

3. Honour and the Unattainable Ideal

1) Joseph Conrad and Ford Madox Hueffer (Ford): *Romance* (London: Smith, Elder & Co., 1903, p. 25).
2) ibid., p. 133.
3) ibid., p. 310.
4) ibid., pp. 462–3.
5) H. Rider Haggard and Andrew Lang: *The World's Desire* (London: Longman, Green & Co., 1913, p. 247) 1890.
6) H. Rider Haggard: *Wisdom's Daughter* (London: Hutchinson, 1923, p. 240) 1923.
7) H. Rider Haggard: *She* (London: Hodder and Stoughton, 1961, p. 187) 1887.
8) ibid., p. 237.

413

9) H. Rider Haggard: *Ayesha. The Return of She* (London: Ward Lock, 1905, p. 7).
10) ibid., pp. 363–4.
11) H. Rider Haggard: *She and Allan* (London: Hutchinson, Arrow, 1960, p. 134) 1921.
12) John Masefield: *Captain Margaret* (London: Nelson, 1908, p. 25) 1907.
13) ibid., p. 45.
14) ibid., pp. 263–4.
15) John Masefield: *Odtaa* (London: Heinemann, 1926, p. 337).
16) John Masefield: *Sard Harker* (London: Heinemann, 1924, pp. 66–7).
17) Anthony Trollope: *The Prime Minister* (London: Edmund Ward, 1938, p. 120) 1876.
18) Paul Girouard: *The Return to Camelot* (New Haven and London: Yale University Press, 1981, p. 290).
19) Lord David Cecil: *The Fine Art of Reading and Other Literary Studies* (London: Constable, 1957, p. 141).
20) Isabelle Jan: *On Children's Literature*, trans. and ed. Catherine Storr (London: Allen Lane, 1969, p. 116).

4. Ruritania

1) Anthony Hope: *Memories and Notes* (London: Hutchinson, 1927, pp. 119–20).
2) Dorothy L. Sayers: *Have His Carcase* (London: Gollancz, 1932, pp. 234–5).
3) Paul Girouard: *The Return to Camelot*, (New Haven and London: Yale University Press, 1981, p. 265.
4) Anthony Hope: *Memories and Notes*, op. cit., pp. 120–1.
5) ibid., p. 252.
6) Anthony Hope: *The Prisoner of Zenda* (London: Dent, 1950, p. 9) 1894.
7) ibid., p. 10.
8) ibid., p. 27.
9) ibid., p. 179.
10) ibid., p. 189.
11) Anthony Hope: *Rupert of Hentzau* (London: Arrowsmith, 1938, p. 319) 1898.
12) George A. Birmingham: *King Tommy* (London: Hodder and Stoughton, 1923, p. 12).
13) ibid., p. 251.
14) ibid., p. 313.
15) Richard Usborne: *Clubland Heroes* (London: Barrie and Jenkins, 1974, p. 44).
16) Dornford Yates: *Blind Corner* (London: Hodder and Stoughton, 1927, pp. 133–4).
17) Dornford Yates: *Perishable Goods* (London: Ward Lock, 1928, pp. 114–15).
18) ibid., p. 170.

19) John Buchan: *Huntingtower* (London: Nelson, 1922, Dedication).
20) ibid., pp. 225–6.
21) John Buchan: *Castle Gay* (London: Nelson, 1925, p. 37).
22) John Buchan: *The House of the Four Winds* (London: Hodder and Stoughton, 1935, pp. 37–8).
23) ibid., p. 281.
24) ibid., pp. 106–7.
25) Frances Hodgson Burnett: *The Lost Prince* (London: Hodder and Stoughton, 1915, p. 127).
26) ibid., p. 57.
27) ibid., p. 64.
28) ibid., p. 118.
29) ibid., pp. 85–6.
30) Ann Thwaite: *Waiting for the Party* (London: Secker and Warburg, 1974, p. 232).
31) Violet Needham: *The Bell of the Four Evangelists* (London: Collins, 1947, p. 193).
32) Hilary Wright: 'Violet Needham: the Last of the Victorians' in *The Junior Bookshelf* (Huddersfield: Woodfield and Stanley, vol. 47, no. 5., October 1983, p. 192).
33) ibid., p. 193.
34) Violet Needham: *The Emerald Crown* (London: Collins, 1940, p. 115).
35) ibid., p. 116.
36) ibid., pp. 244–5.
37) Violet Needham: *The Black Riders* (London: Collins, 1939, p. 10).
38) Violet Needham: *The Stormy Petrel* (London: Collins, 1942, p. 15).
39) Noel Streatfeild: *The House in Cornwall* (London: Dent, 1940, p. 103).

5. The Jacobite Rebellions

1) Sir Walter Scott: *Rob Roy* (Edinburgh: A. and C. Black, coll. ed. 1871, pp. 296–7) 1818.
2) Sir Walter Scott: *Redgauntlet* (Edinburgh: A. and C. Black, coll. ed. 1871, pp. 9–10) 1824.
3) ibid., pp. 26–7.
4) Robert Louis Stevenson: *Kidnapped* (London: Dent, 1962, p. 116) 1886.
5) M. R. Ridley: Introduction to *Kidnapped* and *Catriona* (London: Dent, 1962, Preface viii).
6) Robert Louis Stevenson: *Kidnapped*, op. cit., p. 38.
7) ibid., p. 59.
8) ibid., pp. 107–8.
9) ibid., p. 146.
10) Andrew Balfour: *To Arms!* (London: Nelson, 1918, p. 256) 1898.
11) ibid., p. 257.
12) ibid., pp. 257–8.
13) John Buchan: *Midwinter* (London: Nelson, 1925, p. 263) 1922.

14) ibid., pp. 262–3.
15) ibid., pp. 169–70.
16) Roger Lancelyn Green: *A. E. W. Mason* (London: Max Parrish, 1952, pp. 83–4).
17) A. E. W. Mason: *Clementina* (London: Nelson, 1907, p. 280) 1901.
18) D. K. Broster:*The Flight of the Heron* (London: Heinemann, 1925, pp. 74–5).
19) ibid., p. 125.
20) Olivia Fitzroy: *The Hunted Head* (London: Jonathan Cape, 1956, pp. 175–6).
21) Mollie Hunter: *The Lothian Run* (London: Hamish Hamilton, 1971, p. 93).
22) Iona McGregor: *An Edinburgh Reel* (London: Faber, 1968, p. 11).
23) Barbara Leonie Picard: *The Young Pretenders* (London: Edmund Ward, 1966, p. 5).
24) ibid., p. 18.
25) ibid., p. 42.
26) ibid., p. 152.
27) ibid., p. 133.
28) ibid., p. 237.
29) ibid., p. 265.

6. The Querying of Morality

1) Nicholas Freeling and P. M. Hubbard: 'The conventions of crime fiction' in *The Times Literary Supplement* (London: 19 June 1969, p. 666).
2) Interview of John Le Carré by Bolivar le Franc in *Books and Bookmen* (Croydon: Brevet Publishing Co., March 1969, p. 10).
3) Robin Denniston: 'Problems facing the publisher of Spy Books' in *The Bookseller* (London: Whitaker, 6 May 1972, p. 2161).
4) Erskine Childers: *The Riddle of the Sands* (London: Dent, 1970, Preface xiii) 1900.
5) ibid., p. 209.
6) ibid., p. 65.
7) ibid., pp. 247–8.
8) ibid., p. 270.
9) John Le Carré: *Tinker Tailor Soldier Spy* (London: Hodder and Stoughton, 1972, p. 312).
10) ibid., p. 102.
11) ibid., p. 138.
12) ibid., p. 297.
13) ibid., p. 299.
14) Ian Fleming: *Casino Royale* (London: Pan Books, p. i), 1953.
15) John Le Carré: *Call for the Dead* (London: Penguin Books, 1964, p. 8) 1961.
16) ibid., p. 145.
17) John Le Carré: *The Spy Who Came in from the Cold* (London: Pan, 1964, p. 100) 1963.

18) John Le Carré: *A Murder of Quality* (London: Penguin Books, 1964, p. 83) 1962.
19) Graham Greene: *The Confidential Agent* (London: Heinemann, 1939, p. 77).
20) ibid., p. 67.
21) Arthur Hopcraft: 'Who is Smiley, what is he?' in *Observer Magazine* (London: Observer Newspapers, 16 September 1979, p. 100).
22) Margaret Kennedy: *The Outlaws on Parnassus* (London: The Cresset Press, 1958, pp. 170–1).
23) Antonia Forest: *The Marlows and the Traitor* (London: Faber, 1953, p. 107).
24) ibid., pp. 163–4.
25) ibid., p. 153.
26) Percy F. Westerman: *The Riddle of the Air* (London: Blackie, 1916, pp. 9–10).
27) M. Pardoe: *Four Plus Bunkle* (London: Routledge and Kegan Paul, 1939, p. 46).
28) M. Pardoe: *Bunkle and Belinda* (London: Routledge and Kegan Paul, 1948, p. 153).
29) M. Pardoe: *Bunkle Baffles Them* (London: Routledge and Kegan Paul, 1949, p. 228).
30) John Pudney: *Tuesday Adventure* (London: Evans, 1953, p. 136).
31) John Pudney: *Spring Adventure* (London: Evans, 1961, p. 73).
32) K. M. Peyton: *Thunder in the Sky* (London: Oxford University Press, 1966, p. 14).
33) Robert Westall: *Fathom Five* (London: Macmillan, 1979, p. 30).
34) ibid., p. 244.
35) Peter Dickinson: *The Seventh Raven* (London: Gollancz, 1981, pp. 95–6).
36) Robert Cormier: *After the First Death* (London: Gollancz, 1979, p. 143) 1970.

7. Cops and Robbers
1) Bernard Ashley: *A Kind of Wild Justice* (London: Oxford University Press, 1978, p. 14).
2) Noreen Shelley: *Faces in a Looking-Glass* (London: Oxford University Press, 1974, p. 79).
3) Nina Bawden: *The White Horse Gang* (London: Gollancz, 1966, p. 86).
4) Nina Bawden: *Squib* (London: Gollancz, 1971, p. 98).
5) ibid., p. 10.
6) Nina Bawden: 'Emotional Realism in Books for Young People'; typescript of paper read at I.B.B.Y. Congress, Wurtzburg, 23–25 October 1978.
7) ibid.
8) Stephen Chance: *Septimus and the Danedyke Mystery* (London: The Bodley Head, 1971, p. 11).

9) Leslie McFarlane: *Ghost of the Hardy Boys* (London: Methuen/ Two Continents, 1976, p. 60).

10) ibid., p. 62.

11) ibid., p. 145.

12) ibid., p. 63.

13) ibid., p. 202.

14) Robert Still: 'The Hardy Boys, the Ghost and the Old Books' in *Weekend Magazine* (New York, 15 December 1973, p. 15).

15) Patricia Craig and Mary Cadogan: *The Lady Investigates* (London: Gollancz, 1981, pp. 155–6).

16) C. Day Lewis: *The Otterbury Incident* (London: Putnam, 1948, p. 145).

17) ibid., p. 147.

18) Erich Kästner: *Emil and the Detectives* (London: Jonathan Cape, 1931, p. 96) 1929.

19) ibid., p. 13.

20) E. W. Hildick: in *Junior Radio Times* (London: January 1960, sheet 2).

21) E. W. Hildick: *The Boy at the Window* (London: Chatto and Windus, 1960, p. 9).

22) ibid., p. 86.

23) E. W. Hildick: *The Nose Knows* (Leicester: Brockhampton Press, 1974, pp. 13–14).

8. The Hero

1) Nathalie Sarraute: 'The Age of Suspicion' in Robert Scholes (ed.): *Approaches to the Novel* (San Francisco: Chandler Pub. Co., 1961, p. 215).

2) Ivan Southall: 'Real Adventure belongs to us', May Hill Arbuthnot Lecture, 10 May 1974, in *Top of the News* (Chicago: American Library Association, June 1974, p. 393).

3) Jerry Palmer: *Thrillers* (London: Edward Arnold, 1978, p. 20).

4) Stanley Weyman: *The House of the Wolf* (London: Nelson, 1907, pp. 14–15) 1890.

5) ibid., p. 317.

6) ibid., pp. 218–19.

7) ibid., p. 377.

8) Stanley Weyman: *Under the Red Robe* (London: Penguin, Peacock, 1962, p. 167) 1894.

9) ibid., p. 180.

10) Roger Lancelyn Green: *A. E. W. Mason* (London: Max Parrish, 1952, p. 89).

11) A. E. W. Mason: *The Four Feathers* (London: Nelson, 1907, p. 5) 1902.

12) ibid., p. 8.

13) ibid., p. 56.

14) ibid., p. 236.

15) John Buchan: *The Half-Hearted* (London: Hodder and Stoughton, 1900, p. 166).

References

16) ibid., p. 312.
17) ibid., p. 290.
18) ibid., p. 315.
19) Janet Adam Smith: *John Buchan* (London: Hart-Davis, 1965, p. 468).
20) John Buchan: *Sick Heart River* (London: Hodder and Stoughton, 1941, p. 218).
21) John Buchan: *Greenmantle* in The Adventures of Richard Hannay (London: Hodder and Stoughton, 1930, p. 151) 1916.
22) John Buchan: *The Thirty-Nine Steps* in The Adventures of Richard Hannay, op. cit., p. 5, 1915.
23) ibid., p. 18.
24) ibid., p. 19.
25) Janet Adam Smith: *John Buchan*, op. cit., pp. 266–7.
26) John Buchan: *Huntingtower* (London: Penguin Books, 1956, p. 17) 1922.
27) ibid., p. 20.
28) John Buchan: *Castle Gay* (London: Penguin Books, 1956, pp. 14–15) 1925.
29) ibid., pp. 155–6.
30) ibid., p. 265.
31) ibid., p. 266.
32) John Buchan: *The House of the Four Winds* (London: Hodder and Stoughton, 1935, pp. 299–300).
33) ibid., pp. 315–16.
34) ibid., p. 318.
35) H. Rider Haggard: *She and Allan* (London: Hutchinson, Arrow, 1960, p. 14) 1921.
36) H. Rider Haggard: *The Days of My Life* (London: Longman, Green and Co., 1926, vol. 2, pp. 85–6).
37) ibid., vol. I, pp. 216–17.
38) H. Rider Haggard: *Finished* (London: Ward Lock, 1920, p. 13) 1917.
39) ibid., p. 17.
40) ibid., p. 19.
41) H. Rider Haggard: *King Solomon's Mines* (London and Glasgow: Blackie, 1961, p. 61n) 1885.
42) H. Rider Haggard: *Child of Storm* (London: Cassell, 1916, p. 2) 1913.
43) H. Rider Haggard: *Marie* (London: Cassell, 1915, p. 36) 1912.
44) H. Rider Haggard: *Finished*, op. cit., p. 235.
45) ibid., pp. 33–4.
46) H. Rider Haggard: *Maiwa's Revenge* (London: Hodder and Stoughton, 1920, p. 59) 1888.
47) H. Rider Haggard: *The Ivory Child* (London: Cassell and Co. 1919, p. 140) 1916.
48) H. Rider Haggard: *The Days of My Life*, op. cit., vol. I, pp. 66–7.
49) ibid., p. 220.
50) ibid., p. 74.

51) ibid., p. 75.
52) H. Rider Haggard: *Allan Quatermain* (London: Macdonald, 1949, p. 25) 1887.
53) ibid., p. 29.
54) H. Rider Haggard: *The Days of My Life*, op. cit., vol. II p. 274.
55) H. Rider Haggard: *Nada the Lily* (London: Dent, 1933, p. 207) 1907.
56) H. Rider Haggard: *The Days of My Life*, op. cit., vol. I, pp. 103–104.
57) ibid., p. 105.
58) Fred Ingles: *The Essential Discipline* (London: Methuen, 1968, p. 1).
59) Arthur Catherall: *Ten Fathoms Deep* (London: Dent, 1954, p. 91).
60) Arthur Catherall: *Jackals of the Sea* (London: Dent, 1955, p. 88).
61) Stanley Weyman: *The Story of Francis Cludde* (London: Cassell, 1894, pp. 427–8) 1891.
62) Rudyard Kipling: 'Mowgli's Brothers' in *The Jungle Book* (London: Reprint Society, 1955, p. 13) 1894.
63) ibid., p. 20.
64) ibid., 'Tiger! Tiger!', p. 52.
65) ibid., p. 65.
66) ibid., 'Mowgli's Song' in *The Second Jungle Book*, (London: Reprint Society, 1955, p. 315) 1895.
67) ibid., 'The Spring Running', p. 315.
68) Rudyard Kipling: *Kim* (London: Macmillan, 1901, p. 4).
69) ibid., p. 16.
70) ibid., pp. 403–4.
71) Patricia Wrightson: letter to M.F., 31 May 1977.
72) J. M. Marks: 'The Problem of Identification' in *Bookmark* (Edinburgh: Moray House College of Education, no. 5, Autumn 1979, pp. 40–1).
73) J. M. Marks: *Jason* (London: Oxford University Press, 1975, p. 58) 1972.
74) ibid., p. 151.

9. Making Room for the Heroine

1) G. A. Henty: *A Soldier's Daughter* (London and Glasgow: Blackie, 1906, p. 8).
2) ibid., p. 103.
3) ibid., p. 110.
4) From a set of reviews.
5) Bessie Marchant: *The Unknown Island* (London and Glasgow: Blackie, 1916, p. 256).
6) John Ezard: 'Classroom role guide reissued' in *The Guardian* (London, 3 November 1978).
7) Geoffrey Trease: *The Hills of Varna* (Leicester: Brockhampton Press, Knight, 1967, p. 67) 1948.
8) Geoffrey Trease: *The Crown of Violet* (London: Penguin, Puffin, 1968, p. 141) 1952.

9) A. D. Langholm: *The Clover Club and the House of Mystery* (London: Methuen, 1980, pp. 52–4).

10) Malcolm Saville: *Mystery at Witchend* (London: Collins, Armada, 1971, p. 52) 1943.

11) ibid., p. 59.

12) Malcolm Saville: *The Man with Three Fingers* (London: Collins, Armada, 1969, p. 10) 1966.

13) Malcolm Saville: *Not Scarlet but Gold* (London: Collins, Armada, 1962, p. 6).

14) Malcolm Saville: *Home to Witchend* (London: Collins, Armada Original, 1978, p. 10).

15) Malcolm Saville: *The Elusive Grasshopper* (London: Collins, Armada, 1972, p. 181) 1951.

16) Janet Morgan: 'Deadlier than the Male' in *The Guardian* (London, 2 August 1982, p. 10).

10. The Villain

1) A. E. W. Mason: *No Other Tiger* (London: Hodder and Stoughton, 1927, p. 26).

2) Jerry Palmer: *Thrillers* (London: Edward Arnold, 1978, p. 23).

3) Dornford Yates: *Storm Music* (London: Ward Lock, 1934, p. 17).

4) Sir Arthur Conan Doyle: *The Valley of Fear* (London: John Murray/Jonathan Cape, 1974, p. 18) 1914/15.

5) John Buchan: *Mr Standfast* in The Adventures of Richard Hannay (London: Hodder and Stoughton, 1930, p. 777) 1919.

6) John Buchan: *The Thirty-Nine Steps* in The Adventures of Richard Hannay (op. cit. p. 128) 1915.

7) John Buchan: *Huntingtower* (London: Penguin Books, 1956, p. 157) 1922.

8) S. R. Crockett: *The Red Axe* (London: Smith, Elder and Co., 1898, p. 74).

9) ibid., pp. 123–4.

10) Robert Louis Stevenson: *Treasure Island* (London: Nonesuch Press, 1963, p. 61) 1883.

11) ibid., pp. 65–6.

12) ibid., pp. 253–4.

13) John Buchan: *Prester John* (London: Nelson, 1910, p. 104).

14) Emma Smith: *No Way of Telling* (London: Collins, Armada Lions, 1973, p. 21) 1972.

15) ibid., p. 51.

16) ibid., p. 55.

17) ibid., pp. 114–15.

18) ibid., p. 187.

19) Emma Smith: *Out of Hand* (London: Macmillan, 1963, p. 95).

20) ibid., p. 135.

21) ibid., p. 263.

22) John Rowe Townsend: *Gumble's Yard* (London: Hutchinson, 1961, pp. 15–16).

23) ibid., p. 133.
24) John Rowe Townsend: *The Intruder* (London: Oxford University Press, 1970, p. 4) 1969.
25) ibid., pp. 183–4.

11. Learning the Land
 1) John Buchan: *A Prince of the Captivity* (London: Hodder and Stoughton, 1933, p. 94).
 2) Paul Zweig: *The Adventurer* (London: Dent, 1974, p. 227).
 3) James Fenimore Cooper: *The Pioneers* (London: Dent, 1929, p. 428) 1823.
 4) James Fenimore Cooper: *The Deerslayer* (London: Nelson, 1905, p. 5) 1841.
 5) James Fenimore Cooper: *The Last of the Mohicans* (New York: New American Library, 1962, p. 138) 1826.
 6) James Fenimore Cooper: *The Deerslayer*, op. cit., p. 57.
 7) James Fenimore Cooper: *The Pioneers*, op. cit., p. 190.
 8) Mark Twain: *The Adventures of Tom Sawyer* (London: Penguin, Puffin, 1950, Preface) 1876.
 9) ibid., pp. 92–3.
10) ibid., p. 221.
11) Anne Bowman: *The Kangaroo Hunters or Adventures in the Bush* (London: G. Routledge and Co., 1859, pp. 162–3).
12) ibid., pp. 210–11.
13) Joan Phipson: *The Way Home* (London: Macmillan, 1973, p. 124).
14) Richard Jefferies: *Bevis* (London: Jonathan Cape, 1932, p. 356) 1882.
15) ibid., pp. 33–4.
16) ibid., p. 121.
17) ibid., p. 395.
18) 'B.B.': *Brendon Chase* (London: Ernest Benn, 1944, p. 5).
19) ibid., p. 68.
20) ibid., p. 71.
21) Mary Treadgold: *We Couldn't Leave Dinah* (London: Jonathan Cape, 1941, p. 88).
22) Arthur Ransome: *Swallowdale* (London: Penguin, Puffin, 1968, p. 280) 1931.
23) Arthur Ransome: *Swallows and Amazons* (London: Penguin, Puffin, 1962, p. 183) 1930.
24) Arthur Ransome: Letter to Miss Ferris, 18 March 1937, quoted in Hugh Brogan: *The Life of Arthur Ransome* (London: Jonathan Cape, 1984, p. 349).
25) Arthur Ransome: *Swallowdale*, op. cit., p. 340.
26) ibid., p. 264.
27) Roland Pertwee: *The Islanders* (London: Oxford University Press, 1950, pp. 16–17).
28) ibid., pp. 40–1.

References

12. Desert Islands

1) H. de Vere Stacpoole: *Bird Cay* (London: Wells, Gardner, Darton, 1913, pp. 6–7).
2) Daniel Defoe: *The Life and Strange Surprising Adventures of Robinson Crusoe of Yorks., Mariner* (London: Penguin Books, 1938, vol. I, p. 142) 1719.
3) ibid., p. 103.
4) Walter de la Mare: *Desert Islands* (London: Faber, 1930, p. 70).
5) ibid., p. 55.
6) Daniel Defoe: *Robinson Crusoe*, op. cit., vol. 2, pp. 347–8.
7) Michel Tournier: *Friday or The Other Island*, trans. Norman Denny (London: Collins, 1969, p. 6) 1967.
8) ibid., p. 162.
9) ibid., pp. 215–16.
10) Michel Tournier: *Friday and Robinson. Life on Speranza Island*, trans. Ralph Manheim (London: Aldus Books, 1972, pp. 84–5) 1971.
11) Johann R. Wyss: *The Swiss Family Robinson*, ed. W. H. G. Kingston (London: Macdonald, 1949, p. 53), first English ed. 1814.
12) ibid., p. 370.
13) ibid., p. 9.
14) Captain Marryat: *Masterman Ready or The Wreck of the 'Pacific'* (London: Routledge, 1885, Preface v–vi) 1841.
15) ibid., p. 2.
16) ibid., p. 3.
17) Barbara Hardy: 'Robinson Crusoe' in *Children's Literature in Education* (New York: A. P. S. Publications, 1977, vol. 8, no. 1, whole no. 24, p. 7).
18) ibid., p. 7.
19) ibid., p. 10.
20) R. M. Ballantyne: *The Coral Island* in The Ballantyne Omnibus for Boys (London: Collins, 1932, p. 21) 1858.
21) ibid., p. 11.
22) ibid., p. 13.
23) ibid., p. 282.
24) ibid., p. 108.
25) William Golding: *Lord of the Flies* (London: Faber, 1954, p. 29).
26) ibid., p. 248.
27) Jules Verne: The Mysterious Island. Part 1. *Dropped from the Clouds*, trans. W. H. G. Kingston (London: Sampson Low, Marston, Low, and Searle, 1875, p. 169).
28) ibid., p. 145.
29) ibid., pp. 64–5.
30) Jules Verne: The Mysterious Island. Part 2. *Abandoned* (London: Sampson Low, 1876, p. 258).
31) ibid., p. 119.
32) ibid., pp. 150–1.
33) Jules Verne: The Mysterious Island. Part 3. *The Secret of the Island* (London: Sampson Low, 1876, p. 222).

34) ibid., p. 299.
35) T. C. Bridges: 'How to Write Serial Fiction' in Michael Joseph: *The Complete Writing for Profit* (London: Hutchinson, 1930, p. 799).
36) Herbert Strang: *Palm Tree Island* (London: Oxford University Press, 1934, p. 180) 1910.
37) ibid., p. 115.
38) ibid., pp. 115–16.
39) ibid., p. 417.
40) Ivan Southall: *To the Wild Sky* (London: Penguin Books, 1971, p. 32) 1967.
41) ibid., p. 9.
42) ibid., p. 215.
43) Ivan Southall: *A City Out of Sight* (Australia and London: Angus and Robertson, 1984, 1985, Author's Note.)

13. Techniques of Description
 1) Farley Mowat: *Lost in the Barrens* (London: Pan, Piccolo, 1979, pp. 183–4) 1956.
 2) John Masefield: *The Taking of the Gry* (London: Heinemann, 1934, p. 109).
 3) ibid., p. 112.
 4) ibid., pp. 171–2.
 5) William Mayne: *The Member for the Marsh* (London: Oxford University Press, 1956, p. 67).
 6) ibid., p. 87.
 7) ibid., p. 11.
 8) William Mayne: *A Parcel of Trees* (London: Hamish Hamilton, 1964, p. 158) 1963.
 9) Peter Dickinson: *Annerton Pit* (London: Penguin, Puffin, 1979, p. 165) 1977.
10) *The Guardian*, 18 May 1983.
11) John Masefield: *Live and Kicking Ned* (London: Heinemann, 1939, p. 222).
12) ibid., p. 253.
13) ibid., p. 299.
14) ibid., p. 342.
15) ibid., pp. 232–3.
16) André Norton: *Catseye* (London: Gollancz, 1962, pp. 116–17) 1961.
17) André Norton: *The X Factor* (London: Gollancz, 1967, pp. 73–4) 1965.
18) Mary Lascelles: *The Story-teller Retrieves the Past* (Oxford: The Clarendon Press, 1980, p. 160).
19) Jeffery Farnol: *The Broad Highway* (London: Sampson Low, Marston and Co., 1952, p. 266) 1910.
20) ibid., p. 6.
21) M. E. Atkinson: *Horseshoes and Handlebars* (London: The Bodley Head/Children's Book Club, 1958, pp. 60–1).
22) Anne Barrett: *The Journey of Johnny Rew* (London: Collins, 1954, pp. 118–19).

References

14. Who is the Enemy?

1) Patrick O'Brian: *The Road to Samarcand* (London: Hart-Davis, 1954, p. 38).
2) Peter Dickinson: *Tulku* (London: Gollancz, 1979, pp. 78–9).
3) ibid., p. 250.
4) F. J. Harvey Darton: *Children's Books in England* (Cambridge and London: Cambridge University Press, 3rd ed., rev. Brian Alderson, 1982. Appendix 4, p. 340) 1932.
5) G. A. Henty in *The Boys' Own Paper*, December 1902, quoted in Guy Arnold: *Held Fast for England* (London: André Deutsch, 1980, p. 63).
6) Geoffrey Trease: *Tales Out of School* (London: Heinemann, rev. ed. 1964, p. 80) 1949.
7) Captain W. E. Johns: *Biggles, Pioneer Air Fighter* (London: Collins, Armada, 1982, p. 10) 1932. First published under this title 1954: originally *The Camels are Coming* (London: John Hamilton, 1932).
8) 'R. van Eeghen' in *The Captain*, May 1908, quoted in Guy Arnold: *Held Fast for England*, op. cit., p. 22.
9) Guy Arnold: *Held Fast for England*, op. cit., p. 80.
10) ibid., p. 93.
11) G. A. Henty: *A Jacobite Exile* (London and Glasgow: Blackie, 1894, pp. 283–4).
12) G. A. Henty: *Maori and Settler* (London and Glasgow: Blackie, 1897, p. 193).
13) Martin Green: *Dreams of Adventure, Deeds of Empire* (London: Routledge and Kegan Paul, 1980, p. 3).
14) G. A. Henty: *For Name and Fame* (London and Glasgow: Blackie, 1886, pp. 35–6).
15) W. E. Johns as 'William Earle': 'The White Fokker' (London: *Popular Flying*, 1932, Foreword).
16) W. E. Johns: *Biggles Learns to Fly* (Leicester: Brockhampton Press, 1955, rev. ed. 1955, pp. 13–14) 1935.
17) ibid., Author's Note, p. 9.
18) ibid., pp. 38–9.
19) ibid., p. 141.
20) W. E. Johns: *Biggles Flies East* (London: Oxford University Press, 1935, p. 253).
21) ibid., Foreword, pp. 6–7.
22) ibid., p. 115.
23) W. E. Johns: *Biggles, Pioneer Air Fighter*, op. cit. p. 55.
24) W. E. Johns: *Biggles Goes to War* (London: Oxford University Press, 1938, p. 30).
25) W. E. Johns: *Biggles Flies East*, op. cit., p. 36.
26) W. E. Johns: *Biggles and Co.* (London: Collins, Armada, 1962, pp. 134–5) 1936.
27) ibid., p. 136.
28) W. E. Johns: *Biggles Buries the Hatchet* (Leicester: Brockhampton, 1958, p. 20).

29) W. E. Johns: *Biggles Looks Back* (London: Hodder and Stoughton, 1965, p. 190).
30) John Harris: *The Fledglings* (London: Penguin, Puffin, 1980, pp. 99–100) 1971.
31) John Harris: *The Professionals* (London: Penguin, Puffin, 1977, p. 7) 1973.
32) ibid., p. 125.
33) John Harris: *The Victors* (London: Penguin, Puffin, 1980, p. 92) 1975.
34) T. R. Barnes: 'Captain Johns and the adult world' in *Young Writers Young Readers*, ed. Boris Ford (London: Hutchinson, 1960, p. 116).
35) ibid., p. 118.
36) W. E. Johns: *Biggles and the Leopards of Zinn* (Leicester: Brockhampton, 1960, pp. 9–10).
37) ibid., pp. 182–3.
38) Robert Westall: *The Machine-Gunners* (London: Macmillan, 1975, p. 88).
39) ibid., p. 89.
40) ibid., p. 91.
41) ibid., p. 133.
42) Fred Ingles: *The Promise of Happiness* (Cambridge and London: Cambridge University Press, 1981, p. 51).
43) Rosemary Sutcliff: *The Silver Branch* (London: Oxford University Press, 1957, p. 163).
44) Rosemary Sutcliff: *Frontier Wolf* (London: Oxford University Press, 1980, p. 124).
45) Rosemary Sutcliff: *The Eagle of the Ninth* (London: Oxford University Press, 1970, p. 75) 1954.
46) Rosemary Sutcliff: *Dawn Wind* (London: Oxford University Press, 1961, p. 203).
47) Rosemary Sutcliff: *The Lantern Bearers* (London: Oxford University Press, 1972, p. 15) 1959.
48) Rosemary Sutcliff: *Dawn Wind*, op. cit., pp. 28–9.

15. Censorship and the Theft of Words

1) Northrop Frye: *The Secular Scripture. A Study of the Structure of Romance* (Cambridge, Mass., and London: Harvard University Press, 1976, pp. 24–5).
2) Richard Church: *The Growth of the English Novel* (London: Methuen, 1951, p. 213).
3) Hammond Innes in an interview with Barry Free (London: *Observer* Magazine, 6 March 1977, p. 11).
4) Lilith Norman: 'Writing for Children Today' in *Orana* (Oatley, NSW: November 1982, vol. 18, no. 4, p. 125).
5) Liz Hodgkinson: 'Who's Girls' in *Radio Times* (London: BBC Publications, 2–8 September 1978, pp. 5–6).
6) W. Towrie Cutt: *Faraway World. An Orkney Boyhood* (London: André Deutsch, 1977, p. 108).

References

7) Daphne du Maurier: *Growing Pains. The Shaping of a Writer* (London: Gollancz, 1977, p. 26).
8) Walter McVitty: 'Slugs and Snails and Puppy Dogs' Tails' in *Reading Time* (Canberra: Children's Book Council of Australia, no. 61, October 1976, p. 8).
9) Christopher Derrick: *Readers' Report on the Writing of Novels* (London: Gollancz, 1969, p. 136).
10) Rolf Boldrewood: *Robbery under Arms* (London: Macmillan, 1922, p. 160) 1888.
11) ibid., p. 161.
12) Enid Blyton: *The Island of Adventure* (London: Macmillan, 1983, p. 91) 1944.
13) Leon Garfield: *Smith* (London: Constable Young Books, 1967, p. 10).
14) ibid., p. 105.
15) 'Ralph Hammond': *The Isle of Strangers* (London: Collins, 1951, pp. 38–9).
16) Vernon Lee: *The Handling of Words* (London: John Lane the Bodley Head, 1923, p. 43).
17) Robert Louis Stevenson: 'A Humble Remonstrance' (1884), reprinted in *Memories and Portraits* (1887), quoted in Miriam Allott: *Novelists on the Novel* (London: Routledge and Kegan Paul, 1965 (1959), pp. 82–3).
18) ibid., p. 82.
19) Robert Louis Stevenson: *Treasure Island* (London: Penguin, Puffin, 1977, p. 223) 1883.
20) ibid., p. 224.
21) F. J. Harvey Darton: *Children's Books in England* (Cambridge and London: Cambridge University Press, 3rd ed., rev. Brian Alderson, 1982, p. 300) 1932.
22) Edwin Muir: *The Structure of the Novel* (London: The Hogarth Press, 1928, pp. 20–1).
23) ibid., p. 23.
24) Robert Louis Stevenson: *Treasure Island*, op. cit., p. 44.
25) ibid., p. 48.
26) ibid., p. 189.
27) Denis Judd: *The Adventures of Long John Silver* (London: Corgi Books, 1978, Author's Note) 1977.
28) Robert Leeson: *Silver's Revenge* (London: Collins, 1978, p. 185).
29) ibid., p. 176.
30) Emma Tennant: *The Search for Treasure Island* (London: Penguin, Puffin, 1981, p. 40).
31) ibid., p. 100.
32) ibid., p. 103.
33) R. F. Delderfield: *The Adventures of Ben Gunn* (London: Hodder and Stoughton, 1956, pp. 57–8).
34) J. C. Furnas: Appendix A, 'The Dialectics of a Reputation' in *Voyage to Windward* (London: Faber, 1952, p. 378).

35) Joyce Faraday (reteller): *Treasure Island* (Loughborough: Ladybird, Children's Classics, 1979, p. 10).
36) ibid., p. 11.
37) ibid., p. 14.
38) Robert Louis Stevenson: *Treasure Island*, op. cit., p. 89.
39) Advertising leaflet (London: Pan, Piccolo Adventure Library, 1977).
40) Robert Louis Stevenson: *Treasure Island*, op. cit., p. 5.
41) Tom Barling (reteller): *Treasure Island* (London: Pan, Piccolo Adventure Library, 1977, p. 11).
42) Robert Louis Stevenson: *Treasure Island*, op. cit., p. 58.
43) Tom Barling: *Treasure Island*, op. cit., p. 53.
44) Robert Louis Stevenson: *Treasure Island*, op. cit., p. 53.
45) Tom Barling: *Treasure Island*, op. cit., pp. 153–4.
46) J. C. Furnas: *Voyage to Windward*, op. cit., p. 182.

16. Predictions

1) J. S. Bratton: *The Impact of Victorian Children's Fiction* (London: Croom Helm, 1981, pp. 105–6).
2) ibid., p. 138.
3) Richard Church: *The Growth of the English Novel* (London: Methuen, 1951, p. 135).
4) T. H. White: *England Have My Bones* (London: Macdonald, Heritage, 1981, p. 208) 1936.
5) P. M. Pickard: *I Could a Tale Unfold* (London: Tavistock Publications, 1961, p. 136).

Index

Numbers in parentheses indicate entries in the references.

431

Index

Index

Index